THE ATLANTIC CROSSING GUIDE
Third Edition

RCC Pilotage Foundation

First and second editions edited by
PHILIP ALLEN

Revised and updated by
ANNE HAMMICK

ADLARD COLES NAUTICAL
London

INTERNATIONAL MARINE
Camden, Maine

Published by Adlard Coles Nautical
an imprint of A & C Black (Publishers) Ltd
35 Bedford Row, London WC1R 4JH

Copyright © RCC Pilotage Foundation 1983, 1988, 1992

First edition published in Great Britain by
Adlard Coles 1983
Reprinted with amendments 1984, 1985
Second edition 1988
Revised reprint 1989
Third edition published by Adlard Coles Nautical, 1992
Reprinted with amendments 1994
Reprinted 1996

ISBN 0-7136-3599-1

Published in USA by International Marine
an imprint of TAB Books, a division of McGraw-Hill Inc.
PO Box 220
Camden, ME 04843

ISBN 0-87742-371-7

A CIP catalogue record for this book is available in UK from
the British Library and in USA from the Library of Congress.

Typeset in Garamond, by Create Publishing Services Ltd, Bath
Printed and bound in Great Britain by The Bath Press, Bath

Caution
Every effort has been made to ensure the accuracy of this book. It contains selected information and thus is not
definitive and does not include all known information on the subject in hand; this is particularly relevant to the
plans which should not be used for navigation. The Pilotage Foundation believes that its selection is a useful aid to
prudent navigation but the safety of a vessel depends ultimately on the judgement of the navigator who should
assess all available information, published or unpublished.

Charts and diagrams
Where indicated, plans and diagrams were based with permission on British Admiralty Charts and Publications and
where foreign information was used, permission was sought from the Hydrographic Services of France, Spain,
Portugal, the USA and Canada.

THE RCC PILOTAGE FOUNDATION

In 1976 an American member of the Royal Cruising Club, Dr Fred Ellis, indicated that he wished to make a gift to the Club in memory of his father, the late Robert E Ellis; of his friends Peter Pye and John Ives; and as a mark of esteem for Roger Pinckney. An independent charity known as the RCC Pilotage Foundation was formed and Dr Ellis added his house to his already generous gift of money to form the Foundation's permanent endowment. The Foundation's charitable object is 'to advance the education of the public in the science and practice of navigation'. This it does by publishing and revising pilot books and charts and by promoting the development and maintenance of pilotage, navigation and other aids to safety at sea.

The first entirely new work undertaken by the Foundation was the production of *The Atlantic Crossing Guide*, edited by Philip Allen and published in 1984. The usefulness of such a guide was earlier pointed out by another member of the Club, Colin McMullen, who made available his extensive knowledge of the subject, and Philip Allen went on to do a magnificent job, most ably supported by his wife and fellow sailor, Plat, assembling a mass of information both personal to himself and obtained from a range of contacts with wide experience of the Atlantic and of ocean cruising in general. Since then techniques, gear, navigational aids, hazards, port facilities and a host of other factors have changed so greatly as to make a complete revision of the work necessary. This has been undertaken by Anne Hammick, who has eight Atlantic crossings by nearly as many routes already in her log and who is excellently qualified to do the job.

O H Robinson
Director, RCC Pilotage Foundation

PHILIP ALLEN – an appreciation

Phil Allen was a man of talent and, though shy and hampered by a stammer, his charm immediately made itself felt. The talents most easily perceived by a stranger were his skill with water colours and in gardening, if only because his house was full of the one and surrounded by the other. Sooner or later it might emerge that he was also a joiner, a technical draughtsman and a good seaman. Yet it would still be possible to miss the fact that he both designed and helped build his last yacht, *Tallulah*.

After retiring from a successful business career, Philip was able to take *Tallulah* to the Atlantic which he did most happily with his wife Plat, whom he met whilst studying art shortly after leaving school. *Tallulah* was one of the early yachts to cruise in the West Indies. When the Foundation started work on *The Atlantic Crossing Guide* money was short, and an editor had to be found who would give the very considerable amount of time required for no rewards other than the satisfaction of doing the job and being of service to cruising people. Philip's character and experience clearly made him the candidate for the job.

Though not a professional writer he had a shrewd idea of the work involved and only took on the task after considerable hesitation. In a roundabout way his stammer helped him hone his skill in writing. He devoted himself to the book. As an artist he was utterly ruthless in demanding the very highest standards from himself and from others. Based on his extensive experience of the Atlantic and through exhaustive correspondence, he produced a manuscript which others might have delivered to the publishers with relief as their final word. Not so Philip; being the self-effacing man he was, he insisted on circulating it chapter by chapter to his critical friends. And then, to incorporate all their suggestions, he started all over again.

The success of the original edition lay in Philip's insistence on perfection. Now that the time has come for it to be updated, Philip, who sadly died in 1990 aged 79, would have been the first to welcome Anne Hammick as his successor.

W H Batten
Chairman, RCC Pilotage Foundation

Other books sponsored by the RCC Pilotage Foundation

Lesser Antilles (Imray Laurie Norie & Wilson)
ISBN 0 85288 153 3

Atlantic Islands (Imray Laurie Norie & Wilson)
ISBN 0 85288 267 X

Atlantic Spain and Portugal (Imray Laurie Norie & Wilson)
ISBN 0 85288 298 X

Channel Islands Pilot (Adlard Coles Nautical)
ISBN 0 7136 5771 5

North Biscay Pilot (Imray Laurie Norie & Wilson)
ISBN 0 85288 245 9

North Brittany Pilot (Imray Laurie Norie & Wilson)
ISBN 0 85288 162 2

RCC Faeroe, Iceland, Greenland (Imray Laurie Norie & Wilson)
ISBN 0 85288 268 8

North Africa (Imray Laurie Norie & Wilson)
ISBN 0 85288 155 X

The Baltic Sea (Imray Laurie Norie & Wilson)
ISBN 0 85288 175 4

Other books by Annie Hammick

Atlantic Islands (Part author), (Imray Laurie Norie & Wilson)
ISBN 0 85288 267 X

Ocean Cruising on a Budget (Adlard Coles Nautical; International Marine Publishing)
ISBN 0 7136 4069 3

Other titles of interest

Atlantic Pilot Atlas, James Clarke (Adlard Coles Nautical; International Marine Publishing)
ISBN 0 7136 3640 8

World Cruising Handbook, Jimmy and Doina Cornell (Adlard Coles Nautical; International Marine Publishing)
ISBN 0 7136 4419 2

World Cruising Routes, Jimmy Cornell (Adlard Coles Nautical; International Marine Publishing)
ISBN 0 7136 4070 7

CONTENTS

DIAGRAMS AND CHARTS

PHOTOGRAPHS

Part III – Port Information

INTRODUCTION TO THE FIRST EDITION

I can think of few things more exciting (or at times more worrying) than preparing for the first ocean voyage, knowing as we do that anything forgotten, overlooked, omitted, or badly done may prove to be a matter of some consequence, and that, perhaps for the first time in our lives, we will be dependent entirely on our own resources for everything; when we get to sea there will be little chance of assistance, even if it occurs to us to seek it, should some disaster befall. As the months slip quickly by and the weeks then shrink to days, it seems as though those long lists of requirements which we have prepared with such care, have ticked off, added to, revised and redrafted again and again, will never be completed by the set sailing date. And the questions we ask ourselves (and others): Will the eggs really keep if smeared with Vaseline? Does the roll of new charts, clean and smelling enticingly of good paper and printer's ink, cover our requirements, with harbour plans of likely ports of arrival such as Crosshaven, Falmouth, Cherbourg in the east; or Barbados, mangrove hedged English Harbour, Newport and St John's in the west? Is there a spanner aboard to fit that awkward little nut on the bilge pump, or to service the roller reefing gear and alternator? Have we sufficient sail needles and twine, shackles, screws, rope, Primus prickers? And, above all, are we carrying enough water (suppose it does not rain) and food so as to be independent of the land for at least twice as long as we expect the passage to take? Do we have all we need for navigation, and the ability to use it with confidence when, for weeks on end, our only trustworthy guides will be the sun, moon and stars?

Then there is the broad overall plan to consider: which way to go, where to put in, how long will it take, and what will the weather be like? In earlier days, and I am thinking back more than twenty-five years to my first Atlantic crossing, information about these important matters certainly was available, but we had to search for it. For a start we read as many as possible of the accounts written by earlier small boat voyagers, a fascinating occupation which in the rush of today is often omitted, for not only did it reveal much of the character of each seaman/author, but told us which places he had found most suitable and enjoyable, which to avoid, and in general what kind of conditions he experienced. The big volume *Ocean Passages for the World*, first printed in 1923, was available with its lists of routes which experience had shown to be most beneficial to sailing vessels, and its pocket at the back bulging with route, current and rather sketchy wind diagrams. Most important of all there was that remarkable dogged collation of weather information provided by hundreds of thousands of ships ... the US *Pilot Charts*, one for each month of the year for the North Atlantic.

To select the most advantageous route twenty-five years ago indeed took time and patience; but now, with the publication of this book, planning for an Atlantic crossing in either direction will be much quicker and simpler than it was in the day of Nutting, Long and Robinson, Mulhauser, O'Brien and Worth, for thanks to Philip Allen and his fellow members of the Royal Cruising Club, assisted by many others, including members of the Cruising Club of America, it will no longer be essential to do so much time-consuming research. In this one volume will be found most of the required information simply presented and enriched with a wealth of individual knowledge and experience, together with much good advice on preparing the vessel, on stores, navigation and radio. It has a certain something, difficult to define: a love, I think, of small vessels and the people who sail them, an aura of confidence, and – this is the essence of the deep water community – a desire to assist.

How very much easier it would have been for Susan, my wife, and I and others of our day if such a comprehensive book had been available when we were preparing, a little apprehensively, to set out on our first Atlantic crossing.

Eric Hiscock

PREFACE TO THE THIRD EDITION

There is a strong element of responsibility in writing any book on which other people may depend. Being entrusted with updating a well-known work which already contains the pooled knowledge and experience of some of cruising's most respected figures only adds to the feeling.

It seemed to me that there were two possible approaches: either to simply revise the Second Edition, altering a word here and there and updating the Port Information but basically leaving the original work as it stood; or to undertake a major reconstruction and re-organisation, building on the fabric of both previous editions but with major additions and alterations. Having started with the intention of doing the former, I soon found myself edged into the latter course for a whole variety of reasons.

In ocean sailing as in all other fields, the march of progress can and does change not only the way most people do things but, more radically, the way in which they think and plan. This has undoubtedly happened during the decade since the Atlantic Crossing Guide first appeared. Perhaps the most obvious changes are the increasing reliance on navigational electronics (and electronics generally), the coming-of-age of roller-furling headsails, and the general improvement in facilities and communications to be found in the more popular cruising areas. The net result is a perceived lessening in the demands on those aboard – mental, physical and emotional – which may be partly why ever more yachts are being sailed by small and relatively inexperienced (though often highly competent) crews. This alone led to many changes.

Being reluctant to rely entirely on my own judgement I asked a number of fellow yachtsmen to read and comment on the Second Edition. All were active sailing people who had cruised the Atlantic circuit in their own boats, mostly within the last couple of years. Their verdicts were surprisingly unanimous, and gave me the confidence to apply major surgery in some areas. Thus while **Part I – Preparations** has retained its original form, the chapters have been reorganised both in order and content. **Part II – Passages and Landfalls** has seen the greatest changes, being an amalgamation of the previous Part II – Ocean Passages and Part III – The Island Groups, to emerge in a somewhat different format. A new section on the South Atlantic is also included for the first time. **Part III – Port Information** has probably changed least (apart from the fact that it was previously Part IV), though a few harbours have been dropped while several new ones are introduced. As in previous editions, the aim is to include those currently most useful to ocean cruisers. I hope that readers will find the result an even more convenient and up-to-date book to use.

There is no possible way in which every topic can be covered in detail without rivalling the *Encyclopaedia Britannica*, and a comprehensive bibliography of specialist works is included for further reference. It must rest with the individual to decide which can be left at home and which should form a part of the yacht's permanent library.

Finally may I wish all those considering putting the information within these covers into practice as much enjoyment, as many good friendships, and as few dramas and emergencies, during the course of their ocean cruising as have come my way in the sixteen years since my own first Atlantic crossing.

Anne Hammick
May 1992

ACKNOWLEDGEMENTS FOR THE THIRD EDITION

In addition to those people acknowledged in the prefaces to the first two editions, many of whose contributions still stand, I would particularly like to thank the following for their assistance in compiling this edition: Andrew Bray (port information), George Chell (port information), Hugh and Angela Farrant (port information), Peter Flutter (comments on second edition), Liz Hammick (comments on second edition), John Hines (radio), George B Holmes (port information), Graham and Avril Johnson (port information), Mike and Francoise King (comments on second edition), Tom Lemm (comments on second edition), Morgan and Mandy Macdonald (UK/US glossary), M & P Miller Maritime Booksellers (research materials), Janet Murphy (encouragement and patience), Ian Nicolson (port information), Geoff Pack (electronics and UK/US glossary), Oz Robinson (encouragement and assistance throughout), Mark Scott (comments on second edition and port information), Charles Watson (comments on second edition) and finally my mother (meticulous proof reading and sensible suggestions).

Photographs, diagrams and charts

There are many more photographs than in either of the previous editions, and these are credited individually. The vast majority are new, though a very few have deliberately been retained for what might almost be termed sentimental reasons – notably those by Philip Allen and Eric Hiscock. For the use of other pictures I would like to thank: Ann Fraser, Mike & Libby Grubb, Liz Hammick, Trevor Leek, Oz Robinson, Mark Scott, Tony & Jill Vasey, Charles Watson, Sepha Wood, Falmouth Harbour Commissioners, Gibraltar Tourist Office and Marina de Vilamoura.

Again, some previously used diagrams and charts have been retained, but a great many – and nearly all those concerning passage planning – have been newly drawn for this edition by Jennifer Johnson.

PART I – PREPARATIONS

1   THE PHILOSOPHY OF OCEAN CRUISING

Probably the most essential quality in the ocean cruising skipper and his or her vessel is self-sufficiency. To some extent this may be said of anyone who ventures beyond the harbour mouth, but the coastal cruise will normally be planned around convenient harbours where water, fuel, provisions and, if necessary, emergency repairs are available. Regular and accurate weather forecasts are also an accepted benefit of cruising within the home waters of most countries. Awareness of the need to become self-sufficient begins when, with growing experience, one ventures further afield only to run short of some necessity in a place where it is simply not available.

Self-sufficiency implies many things. First, that the yacht herself should be sound and seaworthy; second, that her crew should be capable of sailing her, maintaining her and effecting all normal repairs both in port and at sea; and third, that careful forward-planning should have ensured that she is so equipped and provisioned as to avoid running short of any essential item where a replacement cannot be found.

The sound and seaworthy ocean cruiser must be more than just a strongly built hull that does not leak, with an efficient rig and good gear. In addition to seaworthiness in the accepted sense, sufficient not only to avoid catastrophe but also to inspire those aboard with a reasonable degree of confidence in her abilities, she needs to have a further quality, that of seakindliness allied to an interior in which it is possible for her crew to live in reasonable comfort for extended periods of time. Whereas the average yacht spends most of her time at moorings or in a marina, the ocean cruising yacht will sometimes spend weeks on end at sea, and those aboard cannot exist on snacks and the odd hot drink for that length of time. Neither can they be expected to catnap in insecure seaberths. The most limited resource aboard the ocean cruising yacht is the energy of her crew, and without regular food and sufficient sleep this cannot be maintained.

Self-sufficiency is of course a relative term, and a small community such as the crew of a yacht cannot survive for ever without calling on outside help. The newcomer to ocean cruising usually tends to overstock in the anxiety not to run short in far-off places. With growing experience it becomes apparent that some things can be replaced easily, others with difficulty, and a few only at home. One learns too, that a place that is good for one thing may be unexpectedly bad for others, that water does not always come conveniently piped, that when something which will be needed later is available it had better be bought while the going's good.

A yacht capable of crossing oceans is a complicated and diverse piece of equipment, and it is obvious that those aboard must possess the skills to keep at least the more important aspects functioning. The idea that 'I'm the skipper, he's the engineer, she's the cook' is long dead aboard cruising yachts, and every ocean skipper must of necessity become a jack-of-all-trades, aided when appropriate by a manufacturer's handbook or well illustrated manual. Rope, canvas, blocks, shackles and many more items of chandlery which once were universal currency, interchangeable between yachts and fishing boats, are no longer always so and it is unreasonable to expect that an isolated fishing village will be able to supply much that will suit the modern yacht. Wear and tear is likely to reach its peak as the cruise progresses – bear this in mind when laying in spares and repair equipment.

To live aboard a well found boat and cruise in her over long distances is to experience a sense of independence and freedom that is almost beyond description. The petty annoyances of the land fall away, you live by the look of the sky, the feel of the wind and the run of the sea. As time goes on, both you and your craft become increasingly conditioned to deal with any eventuality, and that sense of affection and empathy felt by nearly all long distance sailors towards their vessels begins to make itself felt. Putting to sea, while still a busy time full of anticipation, loses its overtones of anxiety and the prospect of an ocean passage no longer looms quite as large as it once did. However to reach this happy state you must observe the rules, which are simple but exacting: careful planning, good seamanship and vigilance.

There is no ideal type of ocean cruiser. Comparatively few yachts have been designed specifically for ocean passagemaking, and the majority of people who make long voyages do so in boats which, while they may have been bought with long distance cruising in mind, were not necessarily designed for the task. Equally, if you have owned your yacht for a long time and cruised her in home waters it is likely that (unless she is totally unsuitable) you will trust her and will wish to use her for an Atlantic cruise. A vessel built for coastal sailing may, however, need some modifications before she can be considered fit for ocean work.

Kirsty is a heavy displacement cruising yacht in the traditional mould. Apart from the bonuses of charm and character, one of the advantages of an older vessel is that repairs can more often be carried out without the need for hi-tech assistance. Their main drawback tends to be slowness in light winds.

The hull

Of whatever material it is constructed, the hull must be sound. This implies that a steel hull has not become dangerously corroded, that fibreglass has not succumbed to serious osmosis, and that wood has no worm, rot or sick seams. Do not take any of these for granted, but get hold of the best surveyor you can, tell him your plans, and ask him to look critically at your boat in order to find out what needs to be done prior to making an ocean voyage. If sailing a wooden hulled yacht built of softwoods, be aware of the possibility of attack by the various boring-

worms that thrive in tropical waters and take professional advice about combating the threat.

Skin fittings

Assuming a sound hull, the next thing to investigate is the condition of all skin fittings. Every hole in the hull must be protected by a seacock, and this should preferably be a bronze lever type seacock rather than a gate valve. Gate valves, which are operated by turning a small wheel, depend for their action upon two opposing screws one within the other, and in tropical seas the thinner of the two threads is apt to suffer from electrolytic action and may fracture unexpectedly. Seacocks of the lever operated type, where two tapered cones rotate one inside the other, rarely fail, are simple to maintain and will always operate if kept greased.

Double hose or jubilee clips of good quality stainless steel should be used to secure hose to skin fitting, and softwood bungs in a range of sizes to fit all through hull apertures kept handy. Ideally each fitting should have its own plug attached on a lanyard, ready for immediate use in an emergency.

The stern gland

The stern gland is one of the most frequent sources of leakage, partly because access is often poor and adjustment difficult. If it is of the type which requires packing this should be replaced before departure to ensure plenty of scope for further adjustment, but if on inspection the propeller shaft shows signs of wear no adjustment of the gland will stop a leak. Even marine quality bronze bolts (such are used on the glands of stern tubes and seacocks) can degenerate under the action of salt water, especially if the stern tube or shaft is made of a metal well separated on the galvanic table. These bolts should be examined, replaced if defective and a stock of spares held. If a greaser needs to be turned regularly while the boat is motoring it must be installed in an accessible position and be large enough to limit messy refilling to an occasional chore.

Decks and hatches

Having satisfied yourself that water is unlikely to enter the hull from below, have a look at the state of things on deck and ask yourself a number of questions. Unless you are satisfied with all the answers the defects must be put right.

First of all, is the cockpit too big? The possibility of it being filled to the top of the coamings is a real one. Are the drains adequate in size, and likely to empty it before another wave comes aboard? Are locker lids stout, with strong hinges and clasps that can be secured shut in bad weather? Is the permanent barrier between cockpit and companionway high enough, and the washboards strong enough? A bridgedeck between cockpit and companionway is a great source of structural strength, but even if there is no bridgedeck the companionway should be watertight at least up to cockpit seat level and not, as is

Few modern designs take the bridgedeck concept as seriously as the Rival 38, where entry is via an ordinary hatch. 'Granny bars' steady the climb, while the enormous spray cover gives welcome protection from the elements. *Photo: Anne Hammick*

sometimes the case, open down to the cockpit sole. Washboards that drop into slots must be capable of being secured or released from both the cockpit and below, with lanyards so that they cannot be lost. There should be at least one strong exterior attachment point for harness lines within reach of the companionway.

Are all hatches watertight, and so well secured that there is no possibility of a hatchcover being ripped off by a powerful sea? Even if not actively dangerous a leaking hatch can make life on an ocean passage miserable, render bunks untenable and ruin possessions. Frequently it is not the hatch itself which leaks so much as its fitting on the deck, in which case removal and rebedding may do the trick.

In a wooden yacht which has spent her life in a cool damp climate there will be the risk that her deck and coachroof will open up under the tropical sun. Consider putting her in a warm dry shed for a few weeks and having the whole of her upperworks restopped and covered with fibreglass, and thus be done with deck leaks for ever. If this seems too draconian, make it a rule to dampen her deck and coachroof with salt water morning and evening, and never neglect to set up the awning in harbour.

Bilge pumps
Inevitably a little water will sometimes find its way below, and at least two efficient, high-capacity bilge pumps are essential. One should be operated from the cockpit (without the need to keep a locker open) and the other from below, and both must be hand-operated. By all means have an electric bilge pump if you wish, but it should be additional to, not instead of, the others. Spare parts for all pumps are essential.

The rig

Masts and spars
Both keel and deck stepped masts have their own advantages and drawbacks, and both have been well proven at sea. A keel stepped mast has at least some inbuilt support, and should it break will probably do so high enough to furnish at least the beginnings of a jury rig. However it is difficult to prevent leaks where it passes through deck or coachroof, and an older aluminium mast may suffer from corrosion at its heel. A mast stepped on deck is utterly dependent on the rigging for its support, and any failure there is likely to lead to disaster. While both types require considerable reinforcement below to prevent the hull distorting, usually a main bulkhead, a deck stepped mast should also have a kingpost to transfer its loading to the hull.

Aluminium spars should be checked for corrosion around every fitting, particularly those of stainless steel. It is quite possible for the aluminium to degrade unnoticed, until either the fitting pulls out under strain or the spar simply tears and folds. If mast steps are fitted, a lanyard should be run from each step out to the nearest shroud to prevent halyards snagging.

Standing rigging
It should not be necessary to stress the importance of ensuring that all standing rigging is above reproach.

Nevertheless, many stock designs which of necessity are built to sell in a price-conscious market have rigging that is barely adequate. If you decide to have all your standing rigging replaced by a larger size remember that the size and state of the rigging screws (bottlescrews or turnbuckles) and other attachments is just as important as that of the wire itself. Stainless rigging has a lifespan of about ten years, though terminals and rigging screws may often be re-used.

Examine the points of attachment of all standing and running rigging – chain plates (including those for forestay and backstays), sheet tracks and eyebolts. Satisfy yourself that they are strong enough in themselves, and that their anchorage to the hull or deck, and the way in which the loads are spread, is adequate also. Check that all shrouds are fitted with double toggles, to ensure that no unfair wringing strains are transferred to their attachment points.

Go up the mast and check the upper ends, where all shrouds should be attached via double tangs and heavy clevis pins. The growing habit of terminating shrouds in a hook which engages in a plate on the mast itself, while aerodynamically efficient for round-the-buoys racing may not be equal to the strains imposed by ocean cruising.

Any terminal which has ever sustained damage must be immediately suspect – even if returned into almost perfect shape it will have barely visible hairline cracks which will weaken it seriously. Short of testing to destruction it is difficult to check the state of older stainless steel fittings.

Your surveyor may or may not be an expert on this subject. Consult a man who is, and take his advice.

Running rigging
If your halyards depend on wire to rope splices, give serious consideration to replacing them with pre-stretched polyester. Not only are possibly troublesome splices eliminated, but so are jagged 'fish hooks' to injure fingers and clothes. At the same time check all sheaves for wear, and replace if necessary. Since going to the masthead in mid-ocean is not everybody's idea of fun it is also sensible to have a spare halyard for each sail – most often an over-strength topping lift or spinnaker halyard. If these use blocks at the masthead rather than running through a sheave the block must also be of suitable proportions, and in the case of a spinnaker halyard, which may double as a standby jib halyard or possibly hoist one of a pair of running sails, it is necessary to ensure that it will not chafe against the forestay.

Below decks
Comfort as well as safety demands that attention be paid to the situation down below.

Ventilation
If a yacht from cooler climes is to be taken to the tropics the problems of ventilation should be studied with great

Cruising yachts come in all shapes and sizes. These represent four different rigs (ketch, cutter, schooner and sloop), four construction materials (GRP, wood, steel and ferro) and a size range of 40 ft down to only 22 ft. All these yachts later crossed the Atlantic without mishap. *Photo: Anne Hammick*

A yacht which would be pleasantly cool in a hot climate. Windscoops could be used to increase airflow if necessary. *Seadas* is a 37 ft Endurance, built in GRP. *Photo: Mike Grubb*

care. The ideal is to have a good-sized hatch in each cabin, preferably of the type which can be opened both from on deck and below and with reversible hinges allowing it to be opened either forward or aft. A smaller hatch or opening port in the heads will also be appreciated. Opinion on opening ports in the living quarters is mixed amongst long-term ocean cruisers – they sometimes leak and could be a potential source of weakness in heavy weather; equally they can provide a welcome draught if secured beam-on to the wind. Heavy nylon frames are to be preferred over aluminium, which may corrode and distort, leading inevitably to leaks.

Dorade type ventilators should have two holes in the top of the box, one over the watertrap and the other immediately over the deck inlet. In port the vent can be put directly over the inlet with a cover on the other opening. The reverse position is used at sea. There should also be an emergency cover for the deck inlet in case the box is smashed.

Comfort below is greatly improved by proper insulation, which may also prove beneficial on the return to colder areas. In a steel or glassfibre boat the whole of the area under the deck and coachroof should, if accessible, be covered with one of the proprietary forms of expanded polyurethane, the thicker the better. This should not be done in a wooden boat where it might promote rot, but in any case timber provides relatively good insulation.

The galley
No crew will be at their best unless properly fed, making the galley one of the most important areas below. The general layout will probably not lend itself to major alterations, but even so certain improvements can be made. Whereas the average boat's galley is mostly used in port, the ocean cruiser's must continue to work efficiently at sea. The stove itself must be able to swing freely on its gimbals to at least 35 degrees in either direction, while a high surrounding rail and efficient pot-clamps are essential. So is a protective 'crash bar' in front, both to protect the cook from possible injury and to decrease the likelihood of gas taps being turned on or off by accident. Some people also like a strap to lean against while cooking, in which case one should be provided.

Even if bulk food stores are stowed elsewhere, the many items used regularly must be handy to the galley. This means safe stowage for a variety of containers – often bins or shelves with high fronts are more secure than lockers, which may dump their entire contents when the door is opened – and somewhere to put implements or open containers while in use. If space is available deep troughs can be constructed, though in a smaller yacht the sink will probably have to suffice. Remember also that you will not always be over on one tack. Rhythmic rolling is far more difficult to contend with than heeling and a frequent source of spills and frayed nerves in the galley.

An important feature of the galley layout, and one which can sometimes be improved with a little thought, is that of ensuring that the cook can work without interfering with (or being hampered by) those who need to get past. If the cabin sole is varnished some form of nonslip surfacing should be employed in the galley area. The final necessity is provision for rubbish – preferably two bags, one for biodegradable rubbish which can be disposed of at sea, and one for plastic and items to be taken ashore.

Cooking fuel

Perhaps the most basic decision to be made about the galley is the choice of fuel for cooking. Alcohol (methylated spirits in the UK), which has long been popular in the USA, is not advisable as the primary means of cooking aboard a yacht visiting Europe or the Lesser Antilles where, if available at all, it is usually expensive. The choice lies therefore between LPG (liquefied petroleum gas) and paraffin (kerosene). The former is relatively cheap and widely available, but has the disadvantages of production in different forms and pressures in a variety of non-interchangeable bottles, plus the potential danger of explosion if handled carelessly. Kerosene replaces the danger of explosion by that of fire (notably if priming is skimped), and in some areas may be difficult to obtain or of poor quality. Alcohol, methylated spirits or a small heat torch must also be carried for priming.

As mentioned, LPG comes in more than one variety. Broadly speaking, propane is supplied for boats in North America, Bermuda, the Caribbean (other than the French islands) and Scandinavia, while butane is more usual throughout the rest of Europe and the offshore islands. The primary difference is one of pressure, propane being stored at considerable higher pressure than butane and needing a different regulator. Propane cylinders incorporate a pressure release valve whereas most butane cylinders do not. Although in many places butane cylinders will be filled with propane without comment or objection this is a *highly dangerous* practice – do not assume that just because the supplier agrees to do so it is safe. Although propane cylinders can safely be filled with butane, which may then be run through a propane regulator without risk of explosion, this is not ideal and for long-term use a butane regulator should be fitted.

Both Calor Gas (propane or butane) and Camping Gaz (butane only) are available in the UK, in bottles that are hired and exchanged, while in France only Camping Gaz is available, again exchanged. Throughout the rest of Europe Camping Gaz bottles can usually be exchanged without problem while other types generally need to be refilled. In a few places this is all but impossible and in others may mean taking them to the factory itself, rendered more difficult by the fact that many taxi drivers refuse to carry LPG bottles. Horta is currently the only place in the Azores where gas bottles may be refilled, though Camping Gaz can be exchanged on all the islands.

Throughout the Lesser Antilles all bottles will be refilled rather than exchanged, and propane will be used. The only exception to this is in the French islands, where Camping Gaz bottles (butane) will be exchanged but it is not usually possible to get others filled. In the USA and Bermuda only propane is available, and cylinders not fitted with safety-valves will be refused.

It will therefore be necessary for a yacht embarking on an Atlantic cruise to carry equipment suited to both types of gas, and the following steps should be taken:

1 Check that stoves and any other gas operated appliances (eg water or cabin heaters) can be used with both butane and propane. Check also the state of all piping and connectors and renew if necessary.

The cosy interior of a 31 ft Rustler. The oil lamp and paraffin heater would come into their own if the cruise were to include more northerly waters. *Photo: Anne Hammick*

2 If a British yacht fitted with Calor Gas, exchange butane cylinders for propane before departure, at the same time replacing the regulator. If lockers were built to take Camping Gaz bottles this may be more difficult, owing to the larger size of Calor bottles. One or more Camping Gaz bottle(s) for use in areas where this is more readily obtainable may also prove useful.

3 Obtain from Calor Gas Ltd a variety of adaptors and connectors, including a Camping Gaz/Calor Gas adaptor to enable Camping Gaz bottles to be attached to a Calor butane regulator. In addition to use aboard, these may be handy when cylinders are being refilled.

4 If an American or Canadian yacht, it will be possible to get propane in the UK, Scandinavia and some other parts of mainland Europe, either by getting the yacht's own cylinders refilled or by temporary hire of Calor Gas bottles. In the Portuguese and Spanish islands only butane will be available, and if planning more than a brief visit a butane regulator should be fitted. It may prove simpler to fit a separate Camping Gaz (butane) system.

A great deal of useful information on both types of gas is contained in the leaflet *LPG (Bottled Gas) for 'Blue Water' Yachtsmen*, published by Calor Gas Ltd and available free from showrooms or direct from the manufacturers.

However democratic the skipper wishes to be in running his ship, gas is potentially so dangerous that basic safety procedures must be laid down and then observed so routinely that they become habit. The ideal is to turn the gas off at the bottle as soon as it is no longer required. If, as is usually the case, this means going out into the cockpit and opening a locker, a shut-off valve should be fitted where the piping enters the cabin (far enough from the stove to be accessible in the event of fire) for those occasions when the gas would otherwise inevitably be left on. Even so it should be turned off at the bottle at the end of every meal, particularly when the yacht is at sea. Newer gas stoves and other gas appliances are likely to be fitted with some form of flame failure device; it may be possible to add this to older equipment. However this will not prevent leaks from defective piping.

Stove spares are amongst the many that will need to be carried aboard. If burners or grill rust out, as they well may do, replacements will be almost impossible to find. Many long distance cruisers also carry a single burner Primus stove, tucked away in a locker with a can of kerosene, a pint of alcohol and a pricker. Supplies of gas can run short in West Indian islands, and even in tropical climates a diet of uncooked food pales quickly.

Refrigeration

Although not essential, some method of keeping food and drink cool in the tropics should be high on the agenda, the choice being between self-contained refrigeration and an insulated ice-box. The former will require some method of generating power other than the yacht's engine; the latter is dependent on ice from ashore, and therefore of little use on longer passages. Even if a fridge or ice-box is already fitted, in a yacht built for northern climates it will almost certainly need extra insulation (a minimum of 4 in (10 cm) in the tropics) and should also have a drain.

Water tankage

In many boats it will be necessary to increase fresh water capacity before undertaking an ocean voyage. About 2.5 litres (just over half an imperial gallon or nearly three-quarters of a US gallon) per person per day should be sufficient in cooler areas, but is barely enough in the tropics and allows little for personal washing or laundry. Allowance must also be made for a longer than anticipated passage time, and therefore minimum capacity for the Canaries/Barbados passage aboard a 35-footer with a crew of three might be:

2.5 litres × 3 people × 24 days = 180 litres
+ 50% reserve = 270 litres
(about 60 imperial gallons or 75 US gallons)

It should be stressed that this is the absolute *minimum* consistent with safety, and 400 litres (100 gallons) or more would be preferable. At least 45 litres (10 gallons) of this should be carried in plastic containers, reasonably accessible in case of emergency and with enough air inside to ensure they will float. For preference the rest should be spread over more than one tank, with a closeable linking valve to prevent a leak or contamination in one tank spelling disaster. The suction pipe for withdrawal of water should go through the top of the tank, to avoid total loss of water in case of a fracture at the joint, and if a secondary take-off (perhaps to the heads) reaches only part way down it will provide warning of the tank running dry.

A good method of metering water consumption is to have a service tank, so that usage may be measured by recording each refill from the main tank. This service tank may be of whatever size is most convenient and need call for no elaborate plumbing – in a small yacht, a 5 or 10-litre plastic container with flexible piping might prove suitable. If a pressurised system is fitted, considerable self-control must be exercised by those aboard if consumption is to be kept down. It may be best to turn the pressure off while at sea and rely on hand pumps (which must in any case be fitted as back-up) – having to work for it deters most people from being careless with fresh water.

The plastic containers mentioned above in which reserve water should be carried will also be invaluable in those places where it is not possible to fill the tanks by hose. It may sometimes be necessary to carry water several hundred yards before transporting it out in the dinghy, and for this reason 5 or 10-litre cans (1 or 2 gallons) will be preferable to the unwieldy 22–litre (5 gallon) variety. They are also easier to stow, and should one can split only a small part of the reserve will be lost. Where a tap but no hose is to be found, one of the flat, reel-up hoses with a variety of connections will be invaluable.

Berths

Along with regular food, adequate and relaxing sleep will do much to keep those aboard not only functioning but reasonably cheerful through the worst conditions. It is essential that there are as many good sea berths as there are people aboard – hot bunking may be acceptable aboard a racing yacht, but over the course of a cruise each person deserves their own bunk together with adjacent lockers. This may prove difficult in a small boat where the fore-peak will probably be untenable except when going downwind, and though some skippers prefer not to have bodies sleeping on the saloon settees, as sea berths these are likely to be amongst the most comfortable. Quarter berths, plus pilot berths in the saloon, are the alternatives. All berths must be fitted with leecloths or removable wooden leeboards which can be slotted into position, and these must be amply strong both in themselves and in their attachment points.

Stowage

The ocean cruising boat will need more space devoted to stowage than will her coasting counterpart. Much of this will be devoted to food stores, but extra sails, clothes, spares, tools and all kinds of other paraphernalia must also be accommodated. The modern stock boat with more berths than are good for her should have one or more of them pressed into use for stowage, and suitably partitioned or adapted in whatever way seems best.

Lockers – whatever they are to hold – should be lined so that water cannot spoil their contents. This is easy to do in a wooden hull where battens or hardboard can be fixed over the timbers but may be less easy with steel or fibreglass. Never allow a locker shelf, or the cabin sole, to be fitted flush with the hull. If this is done, any water trickling down will collect on the shelf, soaking the contents and probably causing rot in the longer term.

The engine and electrical system

Although it is quite possible to cruise the Atlantic without an engine if other provision is made for charging, as anchorages become more crowded so manoeuvring under sail alone has become increasingly nerve-wracking. A few harbours and most marinas are impossible to enter without motive power, and the newcomer to shallow coral waters will probably wish to gain confidence under engine before attempting to sail between the isolated heads. It is also difficult to set an anchor reliably unless one can back it in, though in waters both warm and shallow enough for diving this is less of a problem.

Thus on most Atlantic cruises an engine is needed less for propulsion at sea than for battery charging and harbour work. In any case, few auxiliary yachts carry enough fuel to give them much range under power, though it can nevertheless be useful occasionally to motor for one hundred miles or so, perhaps to get the yacht out of a calm or speed the last lap to her destination.

It hardly needs saying that the engine should be thoroughly serviced before departure and comprehensive spares carried. If it requires any specialised tools these should be bought also. Diesel mechanics are to be found almost everywhere, and even if more used to fishing boats or tractor engines, will be able to carry out work on a yacht's diesel provided the correct spares and tools are provided. The chances of buying these abroad should they be needed are slim.

The engine should have its own starting battery, kept fully charged, with one or more batteries for domestic usage according to the demands that will be made on it. The circuit should be designed so that it is possible to charge or run on any desired combination of batteries, while avoiding the charge levels between engine and domestic batteries equalising – usually achieved either by manual switches or blocking diodes. A battery state indicator is also useful, and should again be installed in such a way that it can meter either overall output or the state of each battery individually.

Fairly new on the British market are the battery sensing devices such as the TWC Regulator, which monitors the battery status at the terminals and controls the alternator output so allowing quicker and more efficient charging. No battery will survive long if left in an uncharged state, so after a period of prolonged or heavy duty make a point of recharging it as soon as possible. When excessive loads are being imposed (such as prolonged use of an anchor windlass) the engine should be run while the load is being applied. Alternative means of charging are considered in Chapter 3.

Corrosion

Any water cooled engine is liable to be affected by galvanic or electrolytic action. A salt water cooled installation should have sacrificial zincs somewhere in the water-jacket and these will need regular inspection and replacement. Even when fresh-water cooling is used, the heat exchanger is exposed to the corrosive action of hot salt water and an anode may be needed for its protection. The water-cooled exhaust and silencer are also potential weak spots and may need replacing after a few years' use. Get them checked professionally before leaving and

replaced if at all suspect. At least one external hull anode must be fitted, linked by heavy cables to the engine and propeller shaft. Fit a new one when the boat is antifouled before departure and be sure to carry at least one replacement.

Routine maintenance

Keeping up with routine maintenance is essential to the smooth running of the long distance cruising yacht. Part of it will be cosmetic – brightwork in particular quickly falls victim to the tropical sun if allowed to deteriorate – but more is related to her safety at sea. Regular inspection on the 'stitch in time' basis will often avoid more serious damage. Checking sails for worn stitching; sails and running rigging for chafe; shackles and other metal fittings for rust, corrosion or abrasion; a softwood hull for worm attack; timber generally for the beginnings of rot – all may avert failure at a critical moment. They will also prolong the life of the yacht's gear and markedly reduce the frequency with which it must be replaced.

One advantage of the ever increasing number of charter yachts based in the Caribbean is the dramatic improvement in facilities, including slipways and travel lifts, over the past two decades. However most are in constant use and it may be necessary to book weeks or months in advance. If you have a full set of plans for the boat it can do no harm to carry them with you, though photographs to show sling positions, hull shape and length of keel may be of more practical use. The majority of yachts on one-year Atlantic circuits do not actually need hauling whilst away, but it is reassuring to know that the possibility exists.

In tropical waters much routine work on the hull can, if necessary, be done with the boat afloat. With snorkel and facemask it is easy to keep the hull clean and inspect the rudder fittings, propeller and anode regularly. Seacocks can be removed for greasing by the insertion of softwood plugs from the outside, though this will not be possible for the engine cooling water inlet which should be protected by a strainer. Modern antifoulings should be good for at least twelve months if several coats are applied (remember also to bring your boot-topping up several inches before departure to allow for the fact that, when fully laden for an ocean voyage, she will be much lower on her lines).

Before going to sea, run through a checklist and mark each item off as you inspect it. Always go over the rigging meticulously. Ensure that rigging screws are properly secured, that every shackle is wired, and all masthead sheaves are running freely. Check the engine is in good shape – the belt of an alternator may look perfect but, unless it is new, it may have a weak place and give out suddenly. Dry batteries for torches and other equipment should be renewed and wet batteries topped up and fully charged. Navigation lights should be checked individually, a task often best done several nights before departure.

The spares and tools most likely to be required will naturally vary from boat to boat, but some suggestions will be found in Chapter 3.

3 EQUIPMENT FOR OCEAN AND WARM CLIMATE CRUISING

Much of the equipment discussed in this chapter may already be on board, particularly if the yacht has already cruised extensively in home waters, but its importance is such that it deserves further mention.

Ground tackle

For many people, one of the greatest differences between cruising in home waters and cruising long distance will be anchoring – not only its frequency but also the element of choice. On hearing a gale warning in the UK most people immediately think in terms of finding a secure mooring or sheltered marina berth (not least because these now occupy so many of the best former anchorages). On an ocean cruise there will be many occasions when there is no alternative to riding out bad weather at anchor, sometimes in indifferent holding or poor shelter and possibly with rocks or coral heads astern. At these times the safety of both vessel and crew will be totally dependent on the weight and quality of her ground tackle and the skill with which it is deployed.

Anchors

Most cruising yachts use a CQR, Danforth or Bruce as their main (bower) anchor. All three have imitators which may not be manufactured to the same exacting standards, so be sure to buy the real thing. The CQR is probably the favourite general use anchor and can often be stowed permanently on the bow roller; the Danforth, though superior in very soft ground, is notoriously difficult to handle. The Bruce, the only one-piece anchor in common use, claims to overcome both these problems but may have difficulty in digging into very hard bottoms.

Every cruising yacht should carry at least three such anchors, preferably of different types, and though the rough guideline of one pound per foot overall (1.5 kg per metre) may be adequate for two of these, at least one (not necessarily the main bower) should be substantially heavier. In some areas, such as the Spanish coast which many yachts visit during an Atlantic cruise, a traditional Fisherman anchor will also be useful for rock or kelp. A light 'lunch-hook' kedge will be of less use, though a grapnel-type dinghy anchor is very handy for exploring or diving expeditions.

Anchor cable or rode

As with the different patterns of anchor, so both chain and rope have their advantages – and their adherents.

Rope is cheap to buy, light to stow and useful for other purposes, but may chafe through on unseen rock or coral and requires considerable scope if the anchor is to lie at a proper angle – at least 7:1 for real security. This, coupled with the fact that anchor lines only a few feet beneath the surface are easily snagged by passing yachts or dinghies, has become a very serious disadvantage in the crowded anchorages typical of many of the Atlantic's best cruising grounds.

Chain on the other hand is expensive, heavy to carry and pretty well useless for anything else. However it increases holding power to such an extent, both through its own weight and by forcing the anchor to lie flat and dig in, that scope of 3:1 is sufficient in light conditions while increasing scope remains a powerful weapon if the wind increases. This alone would be enough to make it the unhesitating choice of at least 90 per cent of experienced cruising yachtsmen. Additionally, except in very blowy conditions, it will drop almost sheer from the bow, and thus be next to impossible for others to snag. It is virtually impervious to chafe and is far easier to handle and stow, particularly if a windlass is fitted. Self-stowing will be improved if the chain falls straight down from the chain gypsy into a deep locker, without any pipe or chute to make it heap up.

There are few anchorages along the normal Atlantic route with depths much in excess of 15 m (50 ft), and

A good cruising foredeck incorporating double bow roller, manual windlass, on-deck anchor stowage and no less than three cleats. A solid pulpit, double guardrails and non-skid deck covering are all important from the safety aspect.
Photo: Anne Hammick

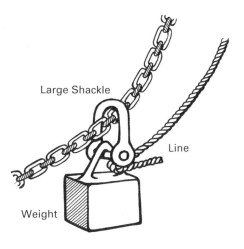

Fig 1 The 'Chum' helps to prevent snubbing the anchor-rode in a hard blow. Suitable for use with chain cable, but would chafe a nylon line.

provided chain is to be used then 60 m (200 ft) should be sufficient. Carrying more than one chain rode would be difficult, and in any case there is a great deal to be said for having at least one mixed rode – 15 m (50 ft) of chain plus 75 m (250 ft) of heavy three-strand or multiplat nylon – for those occasions when a second or third anchor must be taken out by dinghy, a task almost impossible with chain. It is no bad thing in these circumstances if the anchor is somewhat heavier than the main bower to compensate. This line will also be invaluable in those steeply shelving Caribbean anchorages where one drops a bower anchor and takes a stern line ashore – or more probably enlists the aid of a local boatman – and should therefore not be permanently attached to the chain.

It is seldom a steady pull which breaks out an anchor. Far more often snatching and jerking are to blame and a boat which rides steadily, or can be made to do so, will apply a more even strain than one which is constantly sheering or pitching heavily. A 'Chum' anchor weight (Figure 1) is one way of achieving this. Another is the use of a short length of line fitted with one of the various rubber 'dog bones', which has the additional advantage of not transmitting noise as the chain shifts around on the seabed.

Automatic steering

Unless intending to cruise with at least four aboard, some form of automatic steering will be essential, and even with a large crew it will make life considerably easier.

Mechanical systems
A windvane self-steering gear is the traditional choice of the cruising skipper. A course is maintained relative to the apparent wind, independent of any power supply, and the more powerful models are capable of steering a yacht through gale or storm conditions – even running under bare poles. However some makes have trouble down-wind, particularly in light airs, while others become confused if the yacht is going fast and creating a disturbed wash. None work under power. It takes some time to learn both to get the best out of a mechanical self-steering system and to trust it in difficult conditions, and for this reason it should be fitted well before departure.

Windvane steering systems are both heavy and expensive, and if buying new there is less choice available than formerly, but this remains one of the relatively few pieces of equipment which can reasonably be considered essential to the serious cruising yacht.

Electronic autopilots
An autopilot differs from a windvane system in that it is both electronic and dependent on the ship's batteries for power – two factors which result in relatively frequent problems. Steering a compass course can sometimes result in problems under sail, but most makes come with the option of a small windvane and some can be plugged into the vessel's masthead wind instruments. An autopilot is extremely useful under engine and in lighter conditions, though nearly all have limitations when it comes to coping in bad weather or large quartering seas.

It is unwise to consider an electronic autopilot as an alternative to a mechanical self-steering gear. The ideal is to carry both and a great many yachts do so, but a mechanical system should only be dispensed with if it is clearly accepted that the crew may have to hand steer the boat for long periods if necessary.

No self-steering mechanism has the 'sixth sense' a good helmsman has. They can react, but they cannot anticipate – on the other hand neither do they tire. Before engaging any kind of robot it is important to sail the boat and get the feel of her and to know that she is happy. Only when she is well balanced and easy on the helm is it fair to ask a machine to take it over.

Sails

If ordering new sails give careful thought to their weight and design. It is a fallacy to think that cruising sails need to be heavier than racing sails, and unless those already aboard are showing signs of wear and tear there may be no need for new sails in any case. If the boat has done much racing she may well have more sails than will be needed on an ocean cruise, when she might carry the following:

Mainsail
Two or three headsails (whether or not roller furling is fitted)
Storm jib
Trysail
Mizzen and mizzen staysail if a ketch or yawl
Spinnaker or cruising 'chute if already aboard

A major enemy of synthetic fibre sails is sunlight, and their casualty rate will be high unless great care is taken to protect them. Covers for main or mizzen are essential, roller-furling headsails must have heavy protective strips up the leech and bags must be provided for any sails which may have to stay on deck. All coverings should be of a thick, dark material (nylon is not suitable) that will really stop the sun's rays from reaching the sails. Sails should be triple-stitched with thread of contrasting colour so that broken threads can more easily be spotted, and careful attention paid at all times to avoiding chafe.

Mainsails

Few yachts in this day and age carry mainsails cut specifically for cruising. However, if it will be required for nothing else there is much to be said for a vertical-cut mainsail without roach or battens, which is not only less likely to split but can be taped along its leech to give it even more strength in its most vulnerable part. A less extreme alternative is to have a conventional horizontal-cut sail, but again dispense with both roach and battens – generally the point at which damage to the sail first occurs. It is also possible to do away with a headboard by the use of an extra-large thimble. A strong leech line should emerge from its sleeve at a point above that to which the sail will be reefed for force 6 (25 knots).

Trysails

Opinion about the need for a trysail is divided and many long-distance cruising skippers do not carry one, preferring to rely instead on a very deep third reef on the mainsail. On those occasions when it might be used under storm conditions it will in any case be almost impossible to hoist and set unless a second, separate, mast track is provided. A major advantage of the trysail is that it is set loose-footed, and if the decision not to carry one is made then consideration must be given instead to setting the (probably reefed) mainsail in the event of a broken boom.

Headsails

Choice and handling of headsails is one aspect of ocean cruising which has changed markedly over the last decade or so, with the vast majority of cruising yachts carrying at least one furling headsail. Many highly experienced skippers, including circumnavigators, now swear by them, and there appears to be little doubt that if a reputable gear is chosen and correctly fitted the likelihood of problems is relatively low. However the sail will be vulnerable to the elements even when not in use, and it is most important that an effective UV protection strip is sewn up the leech. Lightweight nylon will not be sufficient and may need to be reinforced by material similar to that used for the mainsail cover.

If using a roller headsail it may become necessary to deal with a blown-out sail or jammed gear at sea, something best practised for the first time on a windless evening in harbour. Specialised tools may also be required. At least one reserve headsail of No 2 genoa or working jib size should also be carried aboard, both in case of lengthy repairs and for setting up a downwind rig.

Whatever other headsails are aboard it is essential to carry a really small, heavy storm jib, set on a wire luff and fitted with shackles to pass around the stay at head and foot for extra security. If using roller-furling, either a permanent or temporary inner forestay will be needed on which to hoist it. This forestay will need proper support, either from running backstays or additional lower shrouds swept well aft, and the deck fitting must of course be substantial.

Downwind rig

The origins of twin running sails were bound up with the demand that they should steer the boat on a downwind course. Since the introduction of self-steering they no longer have to do this, and purpose-built, high-cut 'twins' are now very uncommon.

An easily handled downwind rig aboard a Contessa 32, using two poled-out genoas set in a foil with twin luff grooves. *Photo: Ann Fraser*

Favoured alternatives vary, both according to the preferences of the skipper and the characteristics of the yacht in question. Humphrey Barton, who crossed the Atlantic more than twenty times, recommended using the mainsail and a boomed-out genoa. Others whose experience includes much offshore racing habitually use mainsail and spinnaker. My own preference is to minimise wear and chafe on the mainsail – and also the possibility of an accidental gybe – by keeping it stowed and instead using two of the headsails already aboard, one held out by a spinnaker pole and the other sheeted via a block on the end of the main boom, itself held rigid by topping-lift and preventer or fore-guy (described in detail in *Ocean Cruising on a Budget*).

Whatever you decide, one or more spars will be needed for booming out headsails. A spinnaker pole and its normal gear may serve if you already have it, otherwise a stout scaffold pole of light alloy with a gooseneck fitting at one end and eyes to which sheet blocks and guys can be shackled will provide a spar at reasonable cost. If two headsails are to be poled out without using the main boom two separate tracks will be needed on the foreside of the mast, each with its own halyard. Each pole should also be provided with its own topping-lift and guy, though a fore-guy or downhaul can probably be dispensed with. For full control in squally conditions the sheet should always be

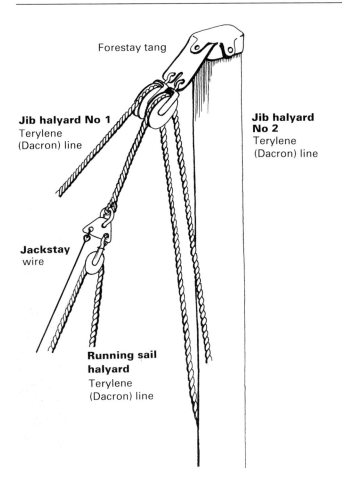

Forestay tang

Jib halyard No 1
Terylene
(Dacron) line

**Jib halyard
No 2**
Terylene
(Dacron) line

Jackstay
wire

**Running sail
halyard**
Terylene
(Dacron) line

Fig 2 Rigging a removable jackstay and halyard for a second headsail.

led through a snatch-block at the pole end, *never* attached to the pole itself. If using a roller furling sail, this has the additional benefit of allowing sail area to be altered without touching the pole.

If roller furling is in use it is possible to obtain gear with two luff grooves to take twin headsails, and several owners have reported success at varying sail area by the simple expedient of furling the two sails together. The alternative, whether with furling or conventional headsails, is a second forestay. Twin forestays placed close together are to be avoided – their close proximity can cause a snarl up and it is better if the second forestay is brought down to a point several feet aft of the main forestay. Except on a true cutter-rigged yacht, this inner forestay will need to be removable for windward work, and may either be fixed at or near the masthead and the foot brought aft when not required, or hoisted on a spare jib halyard when needed. For the latter a triangular plate is sent up, to which are attached both a wire jackstay and a single block through which a halyard is rove (see Figure 2). One of the headsails is hanked to the jackstay and hoisted on the halyard. When not needed the whole contraption can be lowered and stowed below.

Rhythmic downwind rolling can be a major problem, but in most cases it is possible to dampen it to some extent. The most common approach is to set a reefed mainsail or trysail sheeted flat, or possibly a small headsail set approximately where the trysail would be. However it must be

accepted that a certain amount of rolling is inevitable when going downwind in large seas, and thought be given to preparing 'working' areas such as the galley and chart table to cope with it. At worst, some compensation may be derived from consideration of how much nastier the motion would be if going to windward.

Power generation

A great many cruising yachts rely solely on their main engine for the generation of electricity, particularly those whose power requirements are low. However if the regular use of refrigeration is intended, or to a lesser extent that of electronic navigation systems or an amateur radio transmitter, then additional means of power generation will be required.

The first choice of the British cruising yachtsman is usually a wind-driven generator, that of Americans more likely to be solar panels (also favoured by British racing yachts). Possibly this reflects conditions at home as much as utility while actually cruising.

Until a few years ago permanently mounted wind-driven generators were generally limited to ketches and yawls, with sloops more often hoisting the entire contraption into the rigging in harbour and then retrieving it before going to sea. Some models also have a towing option and generate power from the yacht's movement via a log-type rotator. Recently it has become accepted practice to mount the 'windmill' on a pedestal at the stern, making sure it will not interfere with the windvane or decapitate crew working aft. Some wind generators have the drawback of being distinctly noisy, and may increase the natural tendency of the boat to vibrate in windy conditions.

Output varies from little more than a trickle charge on some models to 5 amps or more on others, depending also on wind strength. The more powerful ones will require a voltage regulator to avoid the risk of overcharging. There will be few times and places during a typical December-to-April cruise in the Lesser Antilles when there will not be breeze enough for a wind generator, though during the crossing itself wind over the deck may sometimes be very light. The breeze drops for long periods in the Caribbean summer, and if planning to stay in the area for that season solar panels might be a better choice.

Solar panels have outgrown their early reputation for unreliability, and have the twin advantages of being unobtrusive and silent. Like wind generators their mounting has changed over the last few years, with an increasing number of owners forsaking deck or coachroof in favour of the stern, either on the pushpit itself or via a raised framework. Although solar panels are claimed to work in shade as well as full sun this ensures maximum light plus minimum chance of damage. Output depends to a large extent on area, and again a voltage regulator will probably be needed in areas of strong sunlight.

Shore mains equipment
If intending to plug into mains power in a foreign country it will be necessary to check that equipment is compatible with the supply in both voltage and frequency. In Europe and its offshore islands mains power (where available) is always 220 V 50 Hz; in America, Bermuda and the Caribbean 110 V 60 Hz is standard, though 220 V 60 Hz may

Saecwen is a 34 ft Buchanan Saxon; built in 1961 she has four Atlantic passages under her keel. As a wooden yacht it was important that her teak decks be protected from drying out in the sun, hence the batlike proportions of her awning. *Photo: Charles Watson*

occasionally be found. There may also be a difficulty over plug sizes – UK domestic plugs are a different size to those used throughout the rest of Europe, and in any case most yacht harbours and marinas require waterproof connections. Local advice will need to be sought.

Awnings and forced ventilation

Harbour awnings
If your Atlantic passage will take you to the tropics an awning will be essential, and ideally this should cover an area reaching from near the mast right back to the stern. Although a cockpit-only awning is better than nothing, shade over coachroof and decks will keep the inside of the boat noticeably cooler. Stretchers are needed to spread the awning athwartships – either at fore and aft ends or in the middle – and many people favour a central ring to attach to a halyard. Side curtains provide protection against both rain and sun, and it should be possible either to brail these up or remove them altogether when not required. The final necessity is for numerous tie-downs to keep the awning under control in the strong winds which often blow through Caribbean anchorages. Geoff Pack's *Ocean Cruising Countdown* includes a particularly clear and useful description.

A secondary use for an awning is to collect rainwater in areas where shore water is expensive, suspect, or both. Plastic pipes can be attached using small plastic through-hull fittings, and should ideally be long enough to reach the tank filler. It may be best to set up the awning and experiment with a hose to discover the natural 'low points' where the pipes should be placed.

Awnings should be made from a fairly heavy, limp, rot proof, synthetic material – the acrylic used for many spray hoods is ideal. Light nylon is not satisfactory – sunlight rots it and much ultraviolet light will in any case pass straight through. Because of its light weight it will rattle in any breeze. The final requirement of an awning is to be simple. The less effort that is required both to rig and stow it, the more it will be used.

Sailing awnings, or 'biminis'
Rigid awnings for use at sea, known as 'bimini tops' in the United States, are seldom seen on British cruising yachts, and if none but permanent crew will be aboard may not be necessary. However if family or friends will be flying in to escape a northern winter, and particularly if young children will be aboard, some form of shade while the boat is at sea will be much appreciated. It must obviously be removable in heavy weather, and preferably use some form of folding frame which is not too cumbersome to stow.

Forced ventilation
The simplest method of forced ventilation when in harbour is by means of windscoops – lightweight nylon triangles, shaped rather like miniature spinnakers, set above each hatch to direct the breeze below. As already

Inflatable dinghies, like other cruising gear, benefit from regular maintenance. *Photo: Jill Vasey*

mentioned, if intending to be in the Lesser Antilles during the usual cruising season there will nearly always be enough breeze for a windscoop to be effective.

In less breezy areas or during the Caribbean summer one or more electric fans will make life more pleasant, particularly in the galley. Power consumption may limit running time, however, and this should be checked on purchase. Small solar-powered ventilators are available which will get round this problem, but while useful in the heads or for a boat left closed up and unattended they cannot be expected to cool the interior significantly. If an extractor fan or blower may ever have to deal with explosive gases it must be fitted with a flame-proof cowling to ensure that sparks from a commutator cannot ignite any dangerous fumes.

Mosquito netting

There are very few places in the Lesser Antilles where mosquito nets will be required, particularly aboard a boat which anchors off, and few cruising yachts bother to carry them. However if your cruise will take in West Africa, continue into the South Pacific and Indonesia, or take you to Maine or the Canadian coasts, nets will certainly be needed. A light wooden frame can be made to fit the washboard area, with nets for hatches set on elastic or Velcro. Most opening ports are supplied with removable mosquito mesh. Anti-mosquito coils are obtainable in the West Indies, but many people find they irritate the eyes and throat, and they should not be left burning while the crew are asleep. The best defence against mosquitos is to anchor well out of range and encourage a good draught.

Dinghies and outboards

Choice of dinghy obviously lies between rigid and inflatable, and many owners will already have strong feelings on the subject. Some will not even consider a 'rubber-dubber', while others insist on being able to stow their dinghy in a cockpit locker. Much depends on the size of yacht and the number and agility of those aboard. Each type has its strengths and weaknesses, and if there are to be three or more in the permanent crew serious thought should be given to carrying one of each.

Rigid tenders are generally easier to row, with care might last as long as the yacht and are a less likely target for theft. However hoisting and stowage on deck must be both secure and simple, particularly as recovery aboard every night may be necessary in a few harbours. Deck stowage during an ocean passage can never be 100 per cent secure, and might possibly lead to damage or even the loss of the dinghy in really bad conditions.

Small inflatables have the obvious advantage of being light to lift aboard and presenting less bulk when stowed, whether this is on deck or in a cockpit locker. A few skippers even carry theirs below, in the forepeak or a quarter berth. Although the more expensive inflatables are reasonably robust, care will be needed if one is to survive well. It must never be over-inflated during the cool of the day, and not dragged over sharp rocks or coral or left alongside in areas subject to heavy surge. There is much to be said for an inflatable fitted with rigid stern and possibly floorboards, not least because it is usually possible to carry a more powerful outboard. For those who enjoy snorkelling, an inflatable is much easier to climb in-to from the water than a rigid dinghy.

Choice of dinghy will to some extent dictate whether or not an outboard will be necessary, and if so what size. Again this is a purely personal choice, though it should be remembered that in some Caribbean anchorages there may be a considerable distance to be covered to the shore. Outboards are in common use by fishermen almost every-where that yachts cruise, so stand more chance of being repaired should they fail than is the case with much yacht equipment. Even so, it is unwise to rely too heavily on an outboard and workmanlike oars – not token paddles – should *always* be carried.

Dinghies are an obvious target for theft, and not just in the tropics. A long, padlockable wire to attach the dinghy to the yacht's pushpit or a bollard ashore should be carried – a combination lock may be found more con-venient than having to carry keys. Painting the parent craft's name prominently on the tender is an obvious pre-caution (and generally an insurance requirement), while further distinctive markings will make her less tempting to a potential thief and easier to locate amongst a crowd, particularly in the case of the ubiquitous Avon. If an out-board is used it should always be firmly padlocked in place, as should the fuel can if separate.

Spares and replacements

It has been said that, for the perfectionist, the only solu-tion to the spares problem is to tow a replica of the boat astern. The man who has always done his own fitting out will have a better idea of what to take than one who has relied entirely on a boatyard, and the problem can be further simplified if a policy of simplification and stan-dardisation is adopted. Many boats have, for example, six

Improvisation is a by-word amongst ocean cruisers. With no sailmaker available in St Helena to repair a torn spinnaker, the local seamstresses were happy to do the job.
Photo: Liz Hammick

or eight different sizes of shackles in various locations – with a little thought these might be reduced to three. The same reasoning can be applied to everything from running rigging to bilge pumps. That way spares will be interchan-geable, with cannibalisation a possible last resort.

All things mechanical are certain to need servicing, and possibly replacing, during the course of a long cruise. Pumps will need new valves and gaskets; engines will need new oil seals, filters and injectors; alternators will need new brushes and belts. Hard working winches will need to be stripped down for cleaning and oiling from time to time, and in this case spares should include not only inter-nal parts but also several extra handles – a costly winch whose only handle has gone overboard is just so much misplaced ballast.

Diesel injector pumps are costly, but cannot be repaired except by experts so if embarking on a long cruise it might be wise to carry a spare. Carry also a complete set of those funny shaped moulded rubber hoses which fit to various parts of the engine. If they fail there is no substitute. Do not imagine that if you have bought an engine maker's recommended package of spares and replacements it will necessarily include everything you need. Think back, if you can, about those things which have failed in the past and try to provide for possible recurrence.

Most ocean cruising yachtsmen do much of their routine work themselves, both for convenience and cost. Workshop or users' manuals will be found useful in servicing less familiar equipment and may also be request-ed by a professional – an electronics engineer will prob-ably wish to consult a circuit diagram, for instance. Facil-ities for getting reliable work done throughout the Lesser Antilles have improved dramatically over the last decade, and though the same cannot be said of the islands of the eastern Atlantic there are few places where it is not possible to find a diesel mechanic or electrician. If you carry the necessary spare it will generally be possible to get it fitted, but trying to buy it locally may be quite a different story.

Synthetic sheets and halyards will last for years if not subjected to chafe but a few hours of careless use may destroy the strength of an important line. A replacement coil should be carried for each diameter in use. To suggest carrying enough stainless steel wire to replace any part of the rigging *en route* would perhaps be a counsel of perfec-tion. Ideally there should be a coil of wire equal to the heaviest weight in use and longer than the longest stay in the rig, with which to completely replace a damaged shroud, but in the shorter term a couple of one metre lengths will enable one to effect a temporary splice or reinforcement for the damaged area. A plentiful supply of bulldog grips (wire rope clamps) must be carried, stowed together with a spanner of the correct size with which to tighten the nuts. A couple of extra rigging screws and Norseman or other terminals should also be aboard.

Sail repairs will be routine when ocean sailing, even if the sails are brand new at the start of the voyage. Palm, needles, sail hooks, beeswax, twine, and sailcloth in the weight and texture of each sail will be needed. Needles are best stored in a tin containing plenty of grease.

When deciding what to take and what not to take, make two lists. One should be of those things which you can reasonably expect to be able to replace away from home, the other of items which may not be obtainable. Ordinary paint, for instance, can be bought in most towns throughout the world whereas specialised kinds such as antifouling will not be available except in yachting centres. (It is also true that products intended for the use of the local population are likely to be more reasonably priced than specialised imports for the marine market, and not just in more distant parts of the world.)

Having made these lists and bought all the items you think you will need, stowage must be carefully arranged and recorded. It is not enough to know that an essential spare is aboard 'somewhere' – the more urgently it may be needed the more accessible it must be. A few minutes could mean the difference between catching a problem before it can escalate, or being faced with a whole chain of damage and disaster.

The toolbox

Tools must be appropriate to the jobs they will be expected to do, and may need to be bought specially – particular spanners to fit individual nuts are a case in point. Almost without exception good quality tools are easier to use than inferior ones and will last a lifetime with reasonable care.

The loss of an important tool could prove serious, and neither tools nor pieces of dismantled equipment should ever be left lying about on deck where they could go overboard. If working aloft or leaning outboard – such as to adjust a self-steering gear – wrist lanyards will be helpful.

Tools are often needed in an emergency and should therefore be readily accessible and in known locations. Few yachts under the 40 ft mark boast a complete workbench, but well sited and organised tool stowage is nevertheless essential. In smaller yachts this might best consist of several closed boxes, each devoted to tools of a different type – mechanical, electrical, woodwork, etc. Immediate access to the right tool is as important to the running of the ship and the safety of those aboard her as is carrying the vital spare it will be used to fit.

4 OCEAN NAVIGATION

Ocean navigation by the sun and stars has never lost its reputation as a black art, a skill well beyond the abilities of ordinary mortals. This, along with a natural desire for greater accuracy in difficult conditions, has led to such a dramatic increase in the use of electronic navigation systems (see Chapter 5) that the ocean-going yacht equipped only with a sextant has become the exception rather than the rule. Even so, until electronics attain 100 per cent reliability – probably about the same time that pigs fly – the means to navigate by traditional methods must *always* be carried, and one person at least must know how to use them.

The chart table

In navigation, as in any other craft, the right tools will help in producing the best results, and principal among these is the chart table.

The most practical chart table in heavy weather is one facing either fore or aft, and for many years the dimensions of those aboard British yachts have been dictated by the size of a standard Admiralty chart. Currently this is 28 in deep by 42 in wide (71 cm × 107 cm), though aboard smaller yachts a chart table 28 in deep by at least 21 in (53 cm) wide will allow most American or Admiralty charts to be used folded. However Admiralty charts are set to increase in size – in line with European standards – to about 33 in × 47 in (84 cm × 119 cm), or 33 in × 23.5 in (84 cm × 59.5 cm) if used folded. If building or modifying a chart table it would obviously be sensible to allow for this.

There must be provision to stow folded charts flat, since few things are as disruptive as a chart perpetually trying to roll itself up while in use. A depth of 2 in (5 cm) will take a hundred charts folded once.

Nearly as important is a secure and comfortable seat where the occupant can sit safely wedged with all necessary equipment within easy reach, and unless one person does all the navigation (a potentially risky practice) this should not entail evicting another person from their bunk.

It should not be thought that the chart table will be wasted space when the yacht is in harbour. Some area other than the saloon table is invaluable for letter writing and other paperwork, and a good chart table will double as a desk – or even a temporary bar.

Navigation tools

As well as the basic pencils, erasers, dividers and parallel rule or patent plotting device, many of the other tools necessary for ocean navigation will be familiar from coastal or offshore work – a reliable clock or watch; compass and distance log, plus a log book in which to note regular readings; charts, pilot books and ancillary publications. Only the sextant and its attendant tables will be strange.

The log book

The fashion for having separate navigator's log and deck log has largely disappeared, but this does not imply that keeping an accurate and up-to-date record has become any less important. The log is also a legal document and possible evidence in the event of a collision or insurance claim. Whether you use a purpose-designed ship's log or a ruled exercise book is immaterial, but in either case allow enough room to devote a separate page to each full day at sea.

It is always the responsibility of the person on watch to write up the log; in larger crews where formal watches are not kept during the day the task may be willingly undertaken by a younger or less active crew member. Two hourly is the usual interval, with changes of course or other relevant facts noted as they occur. Position fixes, whether derived from celestial or electronic input, should be recorded in the log without fail. Always treat a reliable fix as though it might be your last for some time – as indeed it might – and even if not planning to plot it at once, allow yourself the means to do so later if you change your mind.

The essentials for regular recording are:

1 Exact time
2 Course steered (it is not always the same as the one designated)
3 Log reading
4 Wind strength and direction
5 Barometric pressure

It is a good habit to fill in every column each time any change is entered, even if at the time it appears unnecessary. Many a navigator has been left guessing by a fix or new course carefully noted down, unaccompanied by time or log reading. Other useful, interesting or memorable events can also be mentioned, and the odd remark about dolphins or a triumph of cordon bleu cookery will not detract from the log's basic purpose as the record from which the dead reckoning is updated.

Accurate time

It is relatively simple to calculate one's longitude relative to that of any celestial body, but in order to find the longitude of the body itself it is essential to know the exact time. This was impossible at sea until the invention of the chronometer in the late eighteenth century, replaced by the quartz movement in the last two decades.

The small size and low price of modern quartz clocks means that there is no excuse for not carrying at least three. One should be permanently mounted on a bulkhead away from likely harm or damp, another might be wrapped in polythene and kept in the sextant box, another in clips above the chart table. All should be individually powered by dry cell batteries. Although a sophisticated radio set or satellite navigator will have a built in clock, your source of time must not depend on the ship's main electrical supply, or be at risk if the radio or other equipment fails. Some people use a wrist-watch to time sights, others (particularly those with less than perfect sight) prefer a clock, but in either event there will be much less likelihood of error if it has a digital rather than an analogue face (when it is all too easy to misread both minute and second hands). Inaccuracy in timing will produce the biggest error in terms of position near the Equator, where four seconds of time equal nearly a mile of longitude.

Thus even with the extreme accuracy of quartz movements, often to within a few seconds per month, it is prudent to check all the clocks against both each other and an outside source (most commonly a radio 'time tick') at regular intervals. The practice of calibrating a timepiece before departure and drawing a graph to show regular error has become largely redundant, but even so their purchase should not be left until the last moment – a weekly check over six weeks or so will demonstrate if any is out of line.

Once on the move radio time checks can be received from several sources, including hourly time signals on the BBC World Service (GMT), and continuous 'time ticks' from WWV at Fort Collins, Colorado (UTC, effectively the same as GMT), and CHU, in Ottawa, Canada (Eastern Standard Time, or GMT–5). Details of other possible sources are given in the *Admiralty List of Radio Signals Volume 5*.

Checking the compass

Even having left home with a compass checked and if necessary corrected for deviation, it is not impossible for new error to be introduced while at sea – a lightning strike is the most obvious cause. As this will affect all compasses on board (a newly-installed steering compass is most easily checked against a hand bearing compass and/or objects ashore), it will then be necessary to compare against bearings of known, external indicators. If the yacht has bulkhead compasses it will be necessary to fabricate some kind of pelorus by which a bearing can be taken relative to the boat's heading. A swivelling protractor or even a compass rose cut from a chart might do duty in an emergency, with a central shadow-pin for use with the sun.

There are three methods of checking the deviation of the compass when out of sight of land. The rough and ready one is to take a bearing of the Pole Star (easier in lower latitudes where Polaris lies nearer the horizon), which will give a rough indication and is accurate enough to confirm a suspected error or to set one's mind at rest. A second, readily available to all who use a sextant, is to take a bearing of the sun with the pelorus as a sight, and compare the result with the azimuth (true bearing) produced by calculation.

The other method is by amplitude (true bearing of the sun at sunrise or sunset) as described by Eric Hiscock in *Cruising Under Sail*. This is undoubtedly more accurate, but has the limitation that only one bearing can be taken on each occasion, and the deviation discovered will apply only while the yacht remains on much the same course as when the amplitude was taken. Neither is there any guarantee of a clear sky in the morning or evening, particularly in the aftermath of bad weather.

It matters little whether the compass course is recorded as it is read, as a magnetic bearing (corrected for deviation, if any), or as a true bearing (corrected for both deviation and variation). What is important is that whichever is chosen should become the standard, and if for any reason a different form is used it should be very clearly marked as such.

Barometers and thermometers

Whether or not to carry a barograph depends on personal opinion and cost, but in any case a normal aneroid barometer will be needed. It should be calibrated before departure and pressure recorded regularly whilst at sea. In some areas of the Atlantic a thermometer will be useful for checking water as well as air temperature, particularly on the fringes of the Gulf Stream.

Dead reckoning

Careful ocean navigation relies as much on accurate dead reckoning (DR) as does coastal or offshore work, perhaps more so. Whether position fixing is by traditional or modern methods, dead reckoning serves to cross-check for possible error and, if a sextant is used, is in any case an integral part of plotting the final position. While it is fun to transfer daily progress to a small scale chart (1:10 000 000 is about right), detailed DR demands a far larger scale.

Several specialised plotting sheets are available for ocean use: the re-usable type such as *Baker's Position Line Chart*, the smaller *Plotting Sheets and Sight Forms for Yachtsmen* available in pads from Imray Laurie Norie & Wilson Ltd, and the *Universal Plotting Sheet*, also in pad form, published in the USA by the Defense Mapping Agency. All feature a graduated latitude scale, plus a diagram from which the appropriate distance between parallels of longitude can be measured for whatever latitude is required. The latest known position is plotted as near as possible to one edge of the sheet, leaving space enough for the day's run by DR to be added to the plot, as well as position lines and fixes as they occur.

A few yachtsmen still prefer the BA Mercator projection plotting sheets. However these have the dual disadvantages of being printed in series for a given latitude, and being so large as to be unwieldy on the average yacht chart table.

For both dead reckoning and plotted positions to be accurate, it is important that the watchkeeper records the course which he or she believes the yacht has actually averaged, even if this differs from the one they had hoped to steer. It should be accepted that there will be occasions on which it will be impossible to steer the course set, and that to attempt to cover this up will only compound the error.

Charts, pilots and other publications

Charts

There is no basic difference between the charts required for an Atlantic cruise and those needed for home waters, except perhaps their quantity. Do not rely on buying charts along the way – sometimes they may be available (usually at vastly inflated prices) but the chances are they will not – certainly do not expect to find Caribbean charts for sale in Madeira or the Canaries. Well before departure buy and study a copy of NP 131, the world-wide edition of the *Catalogue of Admiralty Charts*, or its US equivalent the *Defense Mapping Agency Catalog of Maps, Charts and Related Products – Part 2*, of which Volumes 1 to 3 and Volume 10 will be relevant to an Atlantic cruise. The Armchair Sailor Bookstore in Newport, Rhode Island, produces a useful *Atlantic Crossing Checklist* of relevant charts and other publications kept in stock, including the above.

Deciding which charts to order can be difficult, particularly if they cannot be inspected prior to purchase. Having established what route you propose to take, the entire voyage must be covered by small scale passage charts, with larger scales for landfalls and inshore work. Very large scale harbour plans are generally unnecessary to the yachtsman, since these areas are likely to be used by shipping and therefore well buoyed and lit. Charts relevant to areas in Parts II and III of this book are listed in the text.

Pilot books and yachtsmen's guides
Ideally pilots or guides should also be bought before departure, not least so that they are on hand for the first landfall in a new region. However it can often be difficult to find those for Caribbean or American areas on the east side of the Atlantic, and vice versa. Yachtsmen's guides written by private authors vary drastically in their up-to-dateness and accuracy, and it may be worth enquiring amongst people who know the area well for recommendations both as to the best guide available and how far it should be trusted. The *Sailing Directions* produced by the British Admiralty and the US Defense Mapping Agency are highly accurate and updated by regular supplements, but are slanted towards larger vessels to an extent which means that many small harbours suitable for yachts will not be included. Pilot books and guides relevant to areas in Parts II and III of this book are listed in the text.

Annual publications
Opinion differs amongst experienced yachtsmen as to how many annual publications need be carried aboard the yacht equipped with a good set of current charts. Tide tables and tidal stream atlases are obviously a necessity for areas (usually continental margins) in which tidal influences are great, but are less necessary for the Atlantic and Caribbean islands. Either local almanacs or the *Admiralty Tide Tables Vol 2* should be carried. Both the *Admiralty List of Lights and Fog Signals – Vols D and J* and the *Admiralty List of Radio Signals* should also be considered, the choice amongst the dozen volumes of the latter being appropriate to the radios carried. Tide tables expire on 31 December, so if (as is the case with most British yachts) you will be returning the following year, some form of replacement will need to be arranged. This need be no more than a single sheet, as tidal streams, differences for secondary ports, etc, can all be taken from the expired edition. Suitable almanacs for celestial navigation are considered on page 21.

Notices to Mariners
Charts, pilot books, light lists and lists of radio signals have a longer life than almanacs, but do not last for ever.

Up-dating is by means of weekly *Notices to Mariners*, which in Britain may be obtained free of charge at Customs Houses or can be ordered on a regular basis through any official BA Chart Agent. In the USA, *Notices to Mariners* are available from the Defense Mapping Agency Hydrographic/Topographic Center, Washington DC 20315, also free of charge.

The ideal, if away for any length of time, would be to persuade a friend at home to check the accumulated issues from time to time, clipping any relevant *Notices* to forward out. (The format of *Notices to Mariners* is such that this is neither a lengthy nor particularly technical task.) In practice few yachtsmen actually bother to do this, and if away for a year or less most accept that minor changes will occur.

However recently a chart or pilot book has been corrected, always allow for possible discrepancy between the theory and the fact. Navigational aids are carefully maintained in Europe and on the North American coast, but this is not always the case further afield. Additionally there will always be some delay between any change taking place and details appearing in *Notices to Mariners*. If in the least doubt, stay offshore until improving light or weather conditions provide reassurance.

Gnomonic charts and Great Circle sailing

The shortest distance between two points on the surface of a sphere is a Great Circle, ie, one whose plane cuts the centre of the sphere. A straight line (rhumb line) drawn on a Mercator chart is not a Great Circle course unless it lies true north or south, or along the Equator. The simplest method of calculating a Great Circle course geometrically is to use a Gnomonic chart. BA 5095 covers the North Atlantic and BA 5096 the South Atlantic, with WOAZC 17 and WOAZC 24 the equivalents from the US Defense Mapping Agency. A straight line can be ruled between any two positions on a Gnomonic chart, and the points where it intersects with lines of latitude and longitude are then transferred to a Mercator chart. Rhumb lines connecting these points will then approximate to a Great Circle course, which will appear as a curve. Alternatively, most electronic navigation systems and many navigational calculators can compute a Great Circle course, giving a number of waypoints which can then be plotted on a Mercator chart.

In low latitudes the difference between a Great Circle and the rhumb line is so small as to be negligible, and in other areas the benefits gained from favourable winds or currents may outweigh the advantages of taking the shortest course. Equally there is little to be gained over short distances. On an Atlantic cruise, the time when sailing a Great Circle may prove most worthwhile is on the long, higher latitude passage from west to east or vice versa, when a considerable distance may be saved (see Chapter 22).

Navigation by sextant

Dispelling a few myths
The point has already been made that navigation by traditional means has gained a totally undeserved reputation as a black art. Without attempting a potted instruction course, a few paragraphs of explanation may help

The sextant in use. An approximate reading has been set by swinging the index arm with final adjustments made on the micrometer drum. Note the lanyard, hanging near the author's right wrist. *Photo: Liz Hammick*

overcome the mystery. Subjects in capitals receive further discussion later in the text.

The SEXTANT is used to measure the apparent height above the horizon of whatever it is aimed at, most often the sun, which requires a skill not unlike that needed to take a crisp photograph. A few corrections are then made to the result, none requiring more than simple addition or subtraction. Knowledge of the exact time the sight was taken, plus a current NAUTICAL ALMANAC, makes establishing the Geographic Position or GP of the sun (the place on earth where it would be directly overhead) for the moment the sight was taken the work of a few minutes.

Using the convenient fact that any object, be it the sun, a tree or your own mast, appears to grow higher as one approaches, the next stage is to use the angle measured by the sextant to work out how far one is from this GP and in approximately what direction. SIGHT REDUCTION TABLES provide the simplest method of doing this, but since it would plainly be impossible to produce tables relating every single place on earth to every other place, the usual method is to pick a spot reasonably near your dead reckoning position, but rounded off to the nearest parallel of latitude and chosen to be a whole number of degrees of longitude from the GP. This is your Assumed Position (AP), and the difference in longitude between it and the GP is known as the Local Hour Angle (LHA). Find the page in the sight reduction tables for the latitude of your chosen AP, and then the point where the column representing the sun's latitude (or Declination) crosses the column representing the LHA, and you come up with a second angle – what your sextant would read if you really were at your Assumed Position. The difference between this angle and the one actually measured by the sextant tells you how far you are from your AP, and therefore from the GP itself.

As so often there is one snag. The resulting measurement may be accurate to within less than a mile in terms of distance, but the bearing is no more than an indication, so that effectively one ends up with a vast circle around the GP. Such a small segment of this circle fits onto a plotting sheet that it can be drawn as a straight line, the Position Line (PL) or Line of Position (LOP), which will obviously lie at right angles to the direction of the sun. From thereon it is treated not unlike a running fix, except that rather than sailing past the object to obtain a different bearing you wait for some hours until the bearing (and therefore the angle of the PL) has altered of its own accord. The original PL is advanced across the plotting sheet by dead reckoning and crossed with the new PL, and hey presto – a fix. By using two or more different objects – sun and moon, moon and planets, several stars, etc, two PLs can be calculated for approximately the same time and an immediate position obtained.

This may seem a longwinded way of going about things

and fortunately there is a daily short cut – the meridian passage or noon sight. This is a sight taken at local noon, when the sun reaches its highest point in the sky. The sextant reading is corrected as before, and the result subtracted from 90°. Finally the *Nautical Almanac* is checked to establish the maximum Declination (latitude) of the sun's GP on that day. Either add or subtract these two numbers (depending whether you and the sun are on the same or opposite sides of the Equator), and the answer is your own latitude – effectively another Position Line.

The best way to learn celestial navigation is probably to be taught at sea by someone who really understands the process (a great many perfectly competent navigators actually do it by rote). The alternatives are evening classes, a correspondence course, or a book such as Mary Blewitt's *Celestial Navigation for Yachtsmen*, Conrad Dixon's *Basic Astro Navigation* or John P Budlong's *Sky and Sextant*. Eric Hiscock's *Cruising Under Sail* – a classic which should be carried aboard every cruising yacht – also covers the subject in detail. Captain O M Watts' *The Sextant Simplified* explains the choice, use and adjustment of the instrument itself.

Not only is navigation by sextant essential knowledge for all ocean sailors, whether other systems are carried or not, but it can also be the source of a surprising amount of satisfaction and genuine enjoyment. Watching the land come up exactly as predicted after weeks of regular sun sights is a thrill not fully shared by those whose navigation consists of pressing buttons.

Almanacs, tables, sight forms and navigational calculators

Reference has already been made to the *Nautical Almanac* and *Sight Reduction Tables*, and their part in working out a sextant sight. The former is an annual publication, NP 314 in the UK, unnumbered in the US (the two are virtually identical). Although other almanacs, including *Reed's*, do give the necessary information it is in a very condensed form and much less easy to use. Almanacs expire at the end of each year, and though it is possible to apply a correction to the previous year's edition this may well lead to error. They are published in the autumn, and a replacement should be arranged in advance if your cruise is likely to span two calendar years.

There is also a choice of Sight Reduction Tables. Most yachtsmen prefer the *Sight Reduction Tables for Air Navigation*, AP 3270 in the UK or HO 249 in the US. These come in three volumes, of which only Volumes 2 and 3 are necessary for navigation by the sun. NP 401, the *Sight Reduction Tables for Marine Navigation*, occupy six volumes. They are fractionally more precise, but since no sextant angle taken from a yacht at sea is likely to be accurate to within less than a mile this extra detail is largely redundant. All these tables last for ever.

Many navigators like to use a sight reduction form on which to work out their sights, rather than a blank sheet, and it is certainly helpful to the beginner to be reminded of the necessary steps and their correct order. There are probably as many ways of laying out a sight reduction form as there are navigators, and for the many who learn their navigation ashore it is worth adopting (or evolving) one or other and then making enough photocopies to last until working out a sight has become second nature.

Another possibility is to use a navigational calculator.

These range from the basic programmable model loaded with a card to replace the sight reduction tables, through to highly sophisticated machines which carry a perpetual almanac in the memory and only need to be entered with time, sextant angle and AP to produce an answer. Their advantage in terms of time and effort saved are obvious, but should an error occur it may be less easy to track down. Even if backups are carried, the necessary books must also be aboard, as it is not beyond the bounds of possibility to sustain a lightning strike which could wipe all the memories clean.

Using the sextant

Since it is quite possible to attend evening classes and collect a certificate in celestial navigation without ever having handled a sextant, a few remarks concerning its construction and use may not be out of place.

A sextant consists of a roughly triangular frame, with a movable index arm mounted at the apex and a scale in degrees (the arc) along the base. A telescope and two mirrors, each equipped with several shades, form the optics. When taking a sight, the index arm is swung so that mirrors move in relation to each other until the image they reflect touches the horizon. The reading on the arc equals the angle of whatever has been observed above the horizon. (Although a sextant automatically calls up thoughts of celestial navigation, it can also be used to measure the apparent height of a known object such as a lighthouse for calculating distance off, or on its side to measure the angle between, for instance, two headlands.)

One necessity that no sextant comes with is a lanyard. This should have a loop large enough to drop comfortably over the user's head (remembering that many people wear a hat in the tropics), and be long enough so that the sextant can be placed on a flat surface or preferably back in its box before the lanyard is removed. Something around 30 in (76 cm) is about right. The sextant should always be laid down handle-side downwards, and picked up by its frame and *never* by the index arm, mirrors or telescope. Even so, over the course of time the instrument may drift out of alignment. Small screws are provided for its adjustment, a topic covered in most of the books previously mentioned, but the temptation to fiddle with these too frequently should be resisted lest they work loose.

It is best to practise taking sights on land before attempting the feat on a moving yacht, and though standing on a beach with a clear horizon obviously is the ideal, bringing the sun down to a convenient roofline will suffice. The greatest problem faced by the inexperienced is in finding a relatively small object in a large sky, and having found it to keep it in the field of view. However with a little practice it is possible to guess the angle above the horizon with remarkable accuracy, so allowing the arm to be pre-set. (It is sometimes advocated that the index arm should be set to zero and the telescope aimed directly at whatever is being sighted, but though useful for moon or stars this method can be dangerous if the sun is being used, as a momentary glimpse through an unshaded ×4 magnification telescope might well cause permanent damage to the eye.)

When taking sights at sea, wait until the boat is on a crest and then try to bring the sun down so that its lower edge (or limb) just touches the horizon. While you are turning the micrometer screw swing the sextant gently from side to side like a pendulum, so that the sun 'kisses' the horizon at the bottom of its swing. It will probably take several attempts before you do this to your satisfaction. At first it is as well to record, work out and plot several sights on each occasion, discarding those which are obviously false. This builds confidence, since three lines of position almost coincident are unlikely to be wrong. Others suggest averaging the results and plotting only this, but the chance of error in the mathematics is increased and the time is generally better spent in working two or three sights through from scratch. A third method is to plot the angles and time lapses on graph paper, which will immediately show up an errant sight. In fact, with growing experience one becomes aware of which sight out of a series is likely to be the most reliable.

Most yacht navigators try to get a morning sight followed by a meridian altitude or noon sight, and then put their sextant away for the rest of the day. However, on a cloudy day, when you have to grab any chance of getting a sight, do not wait around in the hope that the sky may be clear when the meridian altitude is due. Take any chance of snatching a sight that presents itself, record the details, and later choose the one which you consider likely to have been the most accurate. Ideally the angle between two PLs should be at least 60°, but this is not always possible. Even one PL over the course of a day is a great deal better than nothing.

Moon, planet and star sights

So far the sun has been mentioned as the preferred body for celestial navigation, being the easiest both to observe and to calculate, and many yachtsmen rely on nothing else. However it has also been pointed out that by bringing other heavenly bodies into play it is possible to get a position immediately, which may occasionally be invaluable. It also adds considerably to the interest of the subject, and anyone who becomes hooked on the fascinating job of taking and working out sights at sea will sooner or later wish to do more than just observe the sun, day after day.

When aiming to widen one's repertoire, daylight observations of the moon are the next thing to attempt and may often be crossed with a sun sight taken at the same time. The workings are basically the same as those for the sun, with a few extra corrections. Any sight taken after dark presents additional difficulties – the horizon may be indistinct (and is easily confused with a wave crest which will give a totally erroneous result), and if using planets or stars there is always the possibility of observing the wrong body in the first place. This is one occasion when the practice of setting the sextant to zero, aiming the telescope directly at the observed body, and then slowly swinging the sextant down and the index arm up until the horizon appears can be most effective. Another possibility is to invert the instrument before carrying out the above. Every navigator develops their own preferred way of doing things.

The moon and brighter planets merit their own columns in the *Nautical Almanac*, while stars are listed in relation to an imaginary meridian in the sky known as the First Point of Aries. Those stars most used by navigators are listed in Volume 1 of the *Sight Reduction Tables for Air Navigation*, the *Selected Stars*, in such a way that their approximate altitudes and azimuths (bearings) can be predicted and the sextant pre-set. Since the stars are

moving fractionally in relation to each other, Volume 1, the *Selected Stars*, requires replacement about every ten years or so.

While stars and planets can be observed with accuracy from the bridge of a ship, the results obtained from the heaving deck of a small boat may be less reliable. If at first they do not agree with the position derived from sun sights it is almost certain to be the planet or star sights which are wrong. Do not ignore such a discrepancy: re-check both sets of workings, and if you can find no apparent fault with either have confidence in the sun sights rather than in a possibly shaky star sight.

Recording the sight

Until using the sextant becomes familiar it is as well to ask another person to time and record sights, if at all possible. When working alone some people advocate the use of a stop-watch while others simply glance immediately at a clock or wrist-watch. Those who have to take glasses off to use a sextant and replace them to read a clock may find it useful to start counting slowly as the sight is taken, check the clock on reaching ten seconds and subtract this from the result. It has already been remarked that a digital clock is considerably easier to read, with less likelihood of error, than an analogue and it is good practice to write the result down in reverse order – first the seconds, then the minutes to the left of them and finally the hours. The time should always be recorded first, before the sextant reading or other details. Some people like to keep their navigation clocks on GMT, others on local time, and provided the correct difference is applied there is little to choose between the two.

It is as well to have a notebook devoted to nothing but recording sights, with columns for each entry. In addition to the exact time and sextant reading, each sight (or series of sights if they only span a few minutes) should be accompanied by a note of the date, the object observed, a log reading and the course steered. A final column for the navigator's opinion as to the likely accuracy of that particular sight would not come amiss.

Choosing a sextant

To produce good results a sextant does not have to be elaborate, but it does have to be well made, mechanically sound and without backlash. It should also have a micrometer drum to read minutes of arc rather than a vernier. A telescope giving ×4 magnification is convenient aboard a yacht, and the larger the diameter of its optics the less the sextant will be limited by poor light. Large mirrors also make operation easier. If bought secondhand it should either come from a reputable firm or should have been tested and, if necessary, adjusted and approved by them. Built in lighting on the arm and micrometer drum is useful if one plans to take sights at night, but by no means necessary. Sextants so equipped will usually have a hollow handle fitted to take ordinary torch batteries.

Until the early nineteenth century sextants were often made of wood, but since then brass or aluminium have been the standard materials. More recently plastic sextants have appeared on the market, and though it is quite possible to take accurate sights with them more care is needed. They tend to distort if allowed to get warm in sunshine, making it doubly important to check for index error every time the sextant is used. They are also very light and as such can be difficult to hold steady – though admittedly many brass sextants err the other way. A plastic sextant makes a fine backup, but does not exude the same air of fine workmanship which is one of the joys of using a traditional instrument.

Landfalls

It is when closing the land that accurate navigation becomes of primary importance, since the possible results of any error are likely to be so much graver than would be the case when surrounded by several hundred miles of ocean. Any electronic aid which has not been in use during the passage should be checked a couple of days before it is needed, to allow time for rechargeable internal batteries to be charged up or dry cells to be replaced. Should a machine refuse to work, this will at best allow an opportunity for repairs or even time to construct a substitute – or at worst give the navigator a chance to consider how best to do without.

If the landfall is in an area subject to strong tidal streams the appropriate tidal atlas should be marked with hourly notations and details of ranges and times worked out. The IALA B buoyage system used throughout most of the Caribbean and in American waters (summed up by the mnemonic 'red right returning') differs from IALA A ('some red port was left') as used in Europe and its offshore islands, and on the African coast. Make certain you know which system will be encountered and are familiar with it.

Continental coasts are often subject to fog or mist, and visibility may be worst just when you need to be able to find your way in strange waters. However if no more sophisticated aids are available then a DF receiver combined with careful dead reckoning will have to suffice, with the echo-sounder coming into use on reaching soundings. Do not overlook the possibility of combining DF bearings with lines of position derived from the sun or other bodies. Users of satellite based navigation systems should beware of over-reliance on the accuracy of charted co-ordinates. While they may well read off a position accurate to within 100 metres – less than 0.05 miles – many islands and other charted features are still given in the positions established by sextant in the nineteenth century. Only as new editions are published will this source of error be corrected.

If there is *anything at all* about the landfall which makes you doubtful – if the area is unfamiliar, you are arriving after dark, the weather or visibility are poor, lights or objects on the land do not appear to tally with the chart, or you are simply very tired – consider heaving-to or standing off. Far more yachts come to grief making landfalls than ever sink at sea, and even a relatively minor grounding may result in the loss of the yacht in an area where no assistance is available to get her off.

Finally, keep all forms of liquid celebration until the yacht is safely in harbour, whether or not the ship is normally 'dry' when at sea. The temptation to relax this rule in anticipation of a successful voyage can be immense, but this is also the time when the entire crew needs to be at their most alert, both mentally and physically.

Radio and electronics are highly specialised subjects which cannot be covered in anything like comprehensive detail here. A number of excellent books exist on different aspects – VHF, radar, electronic navigation systems, etc – all intended to guide the less technical owner through the stages from initial choice and installation (where this is not a professional job), to operation and basic trouble-shooting.

At the same time it must be stressed that sophisticated radio and electronic equipment is by no means essential to ocean cruising, and until quite recently was considered the exception rather than the rule. Much of it is expensive, and for those whose funds are limited it should be one of the first areas in which to economise.

Some indication of costs has been attempted, even though this can be misleading in a book which may be studied some years after publication. Those given are approximations, current at the time of writing (1992).

Radio

The purposes for which the oceangoing yachtsman may need radio are:

1 Reception of time signals, weather bulletins, direction finding, news, entertainment
2 Two-way communications with other vessels or the shore
3 Distress transmissions

If a radio transceiver is fitted it is a formal requirement that a permanent listening watch be kept on the distress channels, and also that a radio log be maintained. How practical either of these rulings are aboard small yachts is open to question, but certainly some record of transmissions should be kept if only in the ship's log.

Receivers

It is worth investing in a good quality receiver with a frequency range from 150 kHz to 30 kHz – several in the Sony range have proved themselves at sea over months or years. It should be able to receive both ordinary public broadcasts, such as those transmitted by national and commercial radio stations, and single sideband emissions, used where frequency crowding and power consumption have to be minimised – for instance long range communications. It should be capable of running off dry batteries (either permanently or on a dual system) in case of failure in the ship's supply, with several sets of spare batteries always carried.

Such a receiver is probably the most useful single piece of radio equipment on an ocean voyage, and with the addition of a suitable antenna may double as a direction finding receiver or even become part of a Weatherfax system. It is likely to cost a minimum of £150, though it would be easy to spend more.

Two-way communications (transceivers)

These fall into three groups according to working frequencies:

Very High Frequency (VHF) 30 to 300 MHz	Short range communications, effectively limited to line of sight between aerials
High Frequency (HF) 3 to 30 MHz	Long range communications, including those amateur bands most relevant to yachtsmen
Medium Frequency (MF) (0.3 to 3 MHz (300 to 3000 kHz)	Medium range communications (about 500 miles) including some of the commercial marine radio telephone channels

Very High Frequency (VHF)

Already familiar to coastal and offshore yachtsmen, a VHF installation is rapidly becoming more than a convenience. In addition to communication with other vessels at sea, an increasing number of port authorities and marinas expect to be called before a yacht enters – most monitor channels 16, 37 or 80, sometimes backed by their own working channel. A less obvious occasion when VHF is not only reassuring but a definite safety aid is during bad weather at anchor, when those aboard may be the last to realise that their own boat is dragging or about to be fouled by another already on the move.

Some of the frequencies allocated to numbered channels vary between Europe and the USA (though 16 is common to both) and this must be taken into account when purchasing a set (see Appendix E). There is a wide choice available at very competitive prices: robustness, the number of channels available and power consumption are all factors to consider. A masthead aerial will maximise range for ordinary use, but a compact emergency back-up should also be carried in case of dismasting. An alternative would be a hand-held VHF housed in a waterproof wallet, which may also come in useful for dinghy work, towing or rescue.

In Britain VHF sets must be licensed and the person in charge hold a certificate of competence, though someone else may operate the set under their supervision. Only approved sets can be licensed, though in practice this covers nearly all makes on the market today. In Britain both installation licences and operator's certificates are administered by the Ship Radio Licensing Section, Room 613, Radiocommunications Agency, Waterloo Bridge House, London SE1 8UA. Operators' courses are organised by the RYA and many sailing schools, adult education centres, etc. The syllabus is usually covered in a matter of hours, and concentrates largely on the operation of the set with particular reference to emergency transmissions. VHF sets begin at well under £200.

High Frequency (HF)

Divided into commercial marine HF working at around 2MHz (technically into the MF wavebands), and amateur or 'ham'. Transmitters aboard yachts are known as Maritime Mobile stations and operate largely in the 14 MHz bands or around 21 MHz or 7 MHz, though other multiples or divisions of the 14 MHz wavelength may also be used.

Marine HF uses channels to which the radio is pre-tuned (as does VHF) since, bearing in mind the distances over which a signal may carry, precision in the selection of frequency is essential to avoid interference with other stations. Sets built for professional use are expensive and may have special features such as automatic monitoring of distress frequencies – the international maritime distress frequency of 2182 kHz falls within the HF band. The Restricted Certificate for operators takes on average two days to attain if a VHF licence is already held.

Amateur radio transceivers are fast growing in popularity amongst ocean yachtsmen. Not only are they extremely useful in passing on position or weather reports and port information, but amateur radio has several times served as the only link in an emergency. Numerous regular nets operate, usually co-ordinated by a shorebased operator. Times and frequencies may change from time to time, but those of potential interest currently include:

GMT	Freq (MHz)	Net and Area
0800	14.303	UK Maritime Mobile Net
1030	3.808	Caribbean Weather Net
1130	21.325	South Atlantic Round Table
1230	7.240	Caribbean Maritime Mobile Net
1300	21.400	Transatlantic Net (North Atlantic and Caribbean)
1700	14.313	International Maritime Mobile Net
1800	14.303	UK Maritime Mobile Net
2230	3.815	Caribbean Weather Net
2330	21.325	South Atlantic Round Table

Unlike a commercial HF set, ham radio allows the operator to tune to any frequency within the band, similar to turning the dial of a conventional radio receiver. However the level of skill required means that the syllabus for the operator's examination must include considerable technical detail. The course (usually evening classes though it can be done by correspondence) takes at least six months, with British national examinations held in May and December. Allowing for delay in receiving results (those for May come through around the end of July), a minimum of a year will be needed if starting from scratch. Although most ham operators work in plain speech (usually English), to gain the full licence it is also necessary to pass an examination in sending and receiving Morse code at twelve words per minute.

At the same time that the theory is being studied for the operator's licence it is well worth reading up on the practical aspects, which may well make the theory more intelligible and will certainly be invaluable when assembling the installation. There are many components in the system, and all must be compatible if they are to work together efficiently. Second-hand equipment is regularly advertised in the specialist magazines and £350 should purchase the basics, though new prices start at around £700 and spiral upwards. It must be remembered that, unlike most onboard electronics, ham radio is not basically marine orientated and many sets are designed to work off mains rather than 12 V.

The aerial – which must be designed and constructed to work on the band(s) to be used – is almost as important as the receiver, and not always easy to accommodate aboard a yacht. If renewing rigging for an ocean cruise this is the time to consider building an aerial into the system. Another consideration is that a typical transceiver may draw up to 18 amps when transmitting, so thought must be given to both battery capacity and minimising cable runs which could lead to power loss.

For information about individual licences or their issue contact the Radio Licensing Centre, SSL, PO Box 885, Bristol BS99 5LG. Enquiries about the Radio Amateur's Exam should be sent to the City and Guilds of London Institute, 46 Britannia Street, London WC1X 9RG, while those about the Amateur Radio Morse Test should go to the Radio Society of Great Britain, Lambda House, Cranborne Road, Potters Bar, Herts EN6 3JE. For other enquiries contact the Amateur Radio Licensing Section, Radiocommunications Agency, Room 613, Waterloo Bridge House, Waterloo Road, London SE1 8UA. In America contact the American Radio Relay League, Newington CT 06111 for advice on all aspects of amateur radio communication. Note that, unlike VHF, the transmitter itself does not require a licence and the call sign is allocated to the operator rather than to the installation.

Some HF sets designed for commercial operation can receive the amateur bands. While it would be possible to modify these for ham transmission, they would be very inconvenient to operate and it is not recommended. Equally, some amateur sets will receive on the commercial frequencies and can also be modified to transmit on them, but as these sets cannot be type approved such a transmission would be illegal except in the case of genuine distress.

There is scope for linking an appropriate receiver or ham radio to other equipment such as a Weatherfax decoder, or to a computer/printer loaded with the appropriate software. The same combination might also be able to receive text or even (depending on transmission facilities at the shore station) scanned images such as charts.

Medium Frequency (MF)

This is most often used for medium-range ship-to-shore or, by prior arrangement, ship-to-ship communications. It is of less interest to the ocean-going yachtsman whose requirements are more likely to be for either short range VHF or long-range HF communications.

Distress transmissions

Everyone aboard, whether licensed or not, should know how to send a distress message or Mayday on every transmitting radio the boat carries. The standard format is given in radio manuals, nautical almanacs, etc, and it is worth making a copy for permanent display – the best memory can fail in times of stress. On VHF, use channel 16 world-wide. Many boats not equipped with HF or ham radio carry a small transceiver and portable aerial operating on 2182 kHz solely for emergency use.

Emergency position indication radio beacons (EPIRBs)

These fall into two categories. The first is essentially an air distress beacon, having great range to over-flying aircraft whose crews monitor the appropriate channels – 121.5 MHz for civil and 243 MHz for military aircraft. The former is also tracked by satellite, but in order to relay the information the satellite must be in line of sight with both the transmitter and the ground station, which can lead to long delays. Onward transmissions from aircraft or satellite alert SAR organisations, whose aircraft are equipped to home in directly on the beacon. These EPIRBs are generally both compact and relatively cheap – about £120.

The second type works on 406 MHz and is the system which has recently become mandatory for many long distance races. Monitoring is by the international SARSAT network which provides continuous satellite coverage, and beacons are designed to identify the individual craft. Their two disadvantages are being bulky (though this may improve) and, at around £1000, expensive.

The authorities urge that both types of EPIRB, once activated, should be left on continuously while batteries last as otherwise searchers are likely to lose contact.

Electronics

Many on-board electronics rely on radio reception in one form or another, but from the user's point of view radio may reasonably be regarded as covering normal types of communication, most often verbal, while electronics covers echo-sounders and logs as well as radar, weather map reception and navigational warnings, plus sophisticated electronic navigation systems.

Echo-sounders

This humble piece of electronics remains one of the most useful aboard. The average ocean-going yacht spends a high percentage of its time within soundings, very often in unfamiliar waters, and a reliable echo-sounder is a must. In the event of failure it should be possible to improvise a leadline (flag halyard and winch handle?), if only to estimate scope when anchoring. From £115 upwards.

Logs

Some form of log is essential for accurate dead reckoning, though many long distance sailors still favour the purely mechanical towed variety over the electronic. The latter is more likely to have a speed readout and possibly a trip mechanism (and will co-exist with a fishing line), while the former has the dual advantages of being independent of any power supply and easily cleared if fouled by weed. Both start at around £120 in their most basic forms.

Radar

Radar is relatively costly and may be thirsty in its power requirements (typically between 3.0 and 5.0 amps, though the latest LCD sets draw considerably less than this). Though still uncommon aboard ocean cruising yachts it is a highly desirable aid to passage-making, not only for collision avoidance in poor visibility but for navigation (especially landfalls) and squall-spotting during the tradewind Atlantic crossing. Modern sets are compact, with radomes weighing as little as 12 lb (5.5 kg). Prices generally start around £1200, though a few sets are available at under £1000.

Weatherfax

Once the preserve of large racing yachts, it was only a matter of time before Weatherfax, by which synoptic charts can be received and printed in considerable detail, found its way aboard cruising boats. A complete installation is still relatively expensive – about £1000 – but prices are falling and if an appropriate receiver and computer/printer combination are already carried this will considerably reduce the overall cost. Inexpensive adaptation kits and computer software are available in both the United Kingdom and the United States.

Navtex

Navtex monitors continuously on 518 kHz, receiving navigational warnings, gale warnings and weather forecasts and distress information. Although technically offering coverage for the entire Atlantic, the quality of information received is likely to be lower once away from European or North American shores. Navtex sets start around £200.

Position fixing systems

The three main electronic navigational systems currently in use are DF, land based Hyperbolic, and Satellite based.

DF

DF is less used than formerly, and some marine transmitting stations are being discontinued as vessels rely increasingly on other means. However all major airports are equipped with aero-beacons, and DF can be a valuable aid when making landfalls on oceanic islands or in areas of poor visibility. It should remain a useful back-up for the foreseeable future. From £150 but likely to become difficult to buy.

Land based hyperbolic systems

The practical systems now encompass Loran and Decca. Traditionally Loran C has been the system used almost exclusively in the US, with coverage extending the length of the eastern seaboard as far south as the Florida Keys, while Decca is received over much of Europe. Neither cover the Atlantic island groups – the Madeiras, Canaries, Cape Verdes or Azores.

There is still confusion over the future of Decca, though in Britain the decision has been made to retain it into the next century. However other European countries favour its replacement by Loran C, which should eventually offer continental coverage from Norway to the eastern Mediterranean. There are no plans to extend Loran C into the eastern Caribbean, and though Bermuda is covered reception does not extend further south at sea.

When buying a Loran set make certain that it has good filters (to eliminate Decca and other interference). If relying on Decca when making landfall in European waters it is essential to check by an independent fix that it is locked into the correct zone. Both Loran and Decca currently start at around £350.

Satellite based systems

These fall into two categories: Global Positioning System (GPS) and TRANSIT.

GPS became fully operational in 1993 and is already very widely used aboard ocean sailing yachts. It offers its masters in the US Department of Defense continuous, reliable fixes of an accuracy reputedly within a matter of feet, though this has deliberately been desensitised to around 100 ft for civilian use. It is clearly the optimum system and almost every skipper's first choice.

TRANSIT (commonly referred to as satnav) is the older of the two systems, and though initially plagued by unreliability and long delays between fixes has assisted thousands of yachtsmen on their first ocean crossing. It is reasonably accurate and not affected by atmospheric conditions, but the disadvantage of having to wait for a satellite passage remains. With GPS now in place, TRANSIT will gradually be allowed to downgrade, though it is likely to remain usable for several years yet. Handheld GPS sets currently start at well below £500, with permanent installations somewhat more expensive.

Postscript

It hardly needs saying that radios and electronics must be kept dry. This is particularly true of cheaper models – the innards may be of equal quality but often the casing is not. Even so they may be upset by violent movement, vibration, interference, electrical storms, low battery output or simply Act of God.

No Atlantic cruise should be allowed to flounder to a halt because of electronic failure. Consider the alternatives and, for the more important items, make sure you not only carry the traditional equivalent but know how to use it. Remember that Joshua Slocum didn't even have a second hand on his alarm clock.

6 THE CREW

More long-term cruises come apart because of crew problems than for any other single cause, which may be the reason why so many of those engaged in cruises of more than a year's duration are either couples or singlehanders. Those crews who come 'ready made', having been chosen for qualities other than those necessary aboard a small yacht at sea, present no problems in the matter of selection. However if this is not the case it will be worth taking as much trouble to find the right people as it is to find a suitable boat. With a happy ship's company consisting of people who know how to live afloat and who enjoy each other's company, a long voyage can be an experience which all will remember with deep and lasting satisfaction. A similar voyage blighted by friction or open argument amongst those aboard will be hell.

Recruitment

There are two aspects to this: firstly, lining up suitable crew before starting a cruise and secondly, finding replacements en route, possibly for longer passages only. There is a risk in attempting to do the former too far in advance, as promises are often made by people who are full of enthusiasm until you try to pin them down to a firm sailing date. Others may genuinely intend to come, but be prevented by changes in circumstances beyond their control. Before approaching anybody it is best to have the cruise planned in broad outline, with a firm though flexible sailing date in view. Initial misunderstandings are to be avoided at all costs, and points to discuss should include:

1 Starting date and possible duration
2 Who pays any travelling expenses to or from the points of embarkation and disembarkation
3 What contribution, if any, the crew is to make towards his or her keep
4 What contribution, if any, the crew is to make towards the boat's running costs
5 What liability, if any, the owner will accept in the event of accident or injury

The owner of any vessel is liable, by international law, to repatriate any crewman who leaves, for whatever reason, wherever the vessel may be. In the vast majority of cases the person in question is leaving by pre-arrangement and already holds an airline ticket, or in some cases may be transferring to another yacht. However in the case of virtually unknown crew picked up on the dockside it could be a wise precaution to insist on their depositing with the skipper the cost of a flight from the furthest point of the cruise back to their country of origin, to be returned on leaving the yacht.

All prospective crew will obviously need valid passports, with visas where necessary, and it is important that these should not expire during the duration of the cruise.

Selecting crew

Actually deciding whom to invite is of necessity a personal matter on which little advice can be given. Provided that the owner-skipper is competent in all aspects of seamanship and navigation he will be entirely free in his choice, whether it be a young novice crew or experienced older sailors. He (or she) should therefore concentrate on finding, if he can, people with whom he will get along and who will get along with each other, taking account of character and temperament rather than technical knowledge or skill. Even so, one of the crew will have to be second in command and whoever this is must, because of experience or age – preferably both – be acceptable to the others without question. The only reliable test as to whether people can sail together in harmony is to go for a short trial cruise.

Replacements en route

Crew changes during the course of a cruise may be pre-arranged, or may be somewhat haphazard and rely on finding a suitable person when and where they are needed. The former should be simple enough – many people cannot take the time off work for an entire cruise, but may be eager to join for a limited period. A firm cruising schedule will allow flights to be booked well in advance, though it must be accepted on both sides that other things may intervene. Completely rigid schedules are not practical, particularly allowing for the vagaries of local airlines, and may in any case ruin a relaxed cruise by robbing it of flexibility. Rather than push the pace to reach a particular rendezvous, in the West Indies it may be better for crew to 'island hop' by Leeward Islands Air Transport (LIAT) to join or leave a yacht lying at another island.

Picking up casual crew presents other problems. The seaports of the world all have, from time to time, itinerants who go from boat to boat, trying to thumb a passage to some other place. There may well be good crew among them, but a fair percentage will not be. The really good ones more often find paid work on charter yachts and do not have to rely on casual berths. Screen quayside applicants carefully, always ask for references from previous skippers and whenever possible take them up.

Training

Forging a group of individuals into a team capable of coping in difficult conditions will inevitably take time, and in any case it is impossible to simulate ocean sailing conditions except by making an ocean passage. Assuming that all potential crew have basic sailing skills, all that really remains is to give each person the chance to get to know the boat they will be sailing. The sensible skipper will encourage feed-back, and even if he has sailed the boat for years may find that a different viewpoint based on different experience may enable him to improve layout, routines or equipment. At the same time it is the skipper's prerogative to say 'I prefer this particular job done like so'. If any of the crew are not prepared to accept this they would do better to look for another boat.

Every ship has her own routine – 'different ships, different long splices' – and this should be established as early as possible. Some standardisation is essential to safety: which line goes to which cleat, exactly how to belay a sheet or halyard, where each item of gear is kept (and the importance of always keeping it in the same place). These are not just owner's fads – they could mean the difference between life and death on a dark night.

Ground rules regarding standards of tidiness and cleanliness are seldom voiced openly, but nevertheless there may be times when one person's belongings infringing the limited space of another, or a galley habitually left for others to clear up after the turn of the watch, will lead to argument and recrimination. These and similar small matters have to be nipped in the bud if harmony is to prevail.

It would be ridiculous to suggest that the skipper should make a formal daily round in a small boat, but at the same time that the boat herself is being checked for chafe or other problems in the making – something which should take place at least once a day – the skipper is in a good position to keep an unobtrusive eye open for other brewing problems. Praise is equally important, and few things are as dispiriting to the hardworking crew as to have their efforts go unremarked.

Division of responsibilities

The small size of the average ocean cruiser's crew demands that each member should have some special skill – or preferably several – and for both efficiency and to encourage a sense of involvement a clear division of responsibilities is essential. Assuming that the skipper expects to be in charge of navigation (though only the foolhardy will neglect to train a back-up), the only other department which tends often to be an individual responsibility is the galley. Even if the actual cooking is shared on a rota basis, the catering and storing up can only be overseen by one person. Regular food is fundamental to the efficiency and well-being of the whole ship's company, yet there is no more difficult task than cooking, day in day out, at sea in a small yacht. If one person is able and willing to do all the cooking, the rest should count themselves lucky. Certainly any such person should be suitably rewarded – perhaps by exemption from the 0000–0400 'graveyard' watch.

Friction aboard

A happy ship's company is so well worth attaining that no effort should be spared in the attempt. The skipper has to deal not only with the relationship between himself and each of his crew, but must also try to prevent disputes arising between crew members – should these occur he will often be called on to arbitrate, an unenviable task in which it is seldom possible to satisfy all parties. In a happy ship we tend to accept the situation gratefully, without question, and only when the reverse happens do we conduct an inquest. The wise man enquires into the reason for success as well as failure.

Crew problems may arise in port as often as at sea, perhaps more so. The common challenge of actively sailing a small yacht will often paper over minor cracks, but when this is removed they may reappear. It also tends to be in port that differences in personal habits become more marked – preferred times of rising, eating and turning in, sociability towards fellow yachtsmen, consideration over the use of a dinghy on which others also depend. Regular routine maintenance will also need to be carried out, and it must be made abundantly clear at the outset that visitors or passengers are one thing, but regular crew will be expected to do their share. One compromise is for the morning to belong to the ship with the afternoon for relaxation.

The skipper

The position of the skipper is to a large extent dependent on the formation of his crew – a family crew is obviously not going to regard the skipper in the same light as a crew composed of semi-strangers, who will in turn have a different attitude than would friends who have sailed together for thirty years. However except in the case of those rare couples who genuinely sail as co-skippers, one person will be boss. They must be prepared to shoulder the responsibility not only for the safety of the boat and all those aboard, but within reasonable limits for the happiness of those aboard also.

The old idea of doing an 'apprenticeship' as crew before aspiring to skipper one's own yacht across an ocean no longer prevails, and a great many first-time skippers may have no more experience of ocean passage-making than their crews. Any person who did not feel some nervousness at the prospect would not only be less than human but also dangerously over-confident, but judgement will be needed as to how much it is sensible to confide in the crew. Calmness and confidence are essential, as is cheerfulness, but if this is overdone there is always the chance of a backlash. Nothing is worse than muted mutterings along the lines of 'what's that maniac grinning about now? I'm beginning to wonder if he has any idea at all what's going on' etc.

It is for the skipper to set the tenor of life aboard, and he can do this more by his reactions to events, and to people, than by any other means. The problem of incompatibility in a small ship's company is often the result of inexperience – living at close quarters is an art which does not come easily to all. For every cruise that has been spoiled by one selfish individual there have been many others so rewarding that their recollection binds us to those with whom we sailed for the rest of our lives. For this to happen a lot of things must go right. But if the skipper doesn't get his bit right, the rest can do little to help.

Whether or not the task of cooking on passage is to be shared among the crew, calculating and buying food stores is best done by one person. It is important that they not only take into account the length of time the boat is expected to be away, but also have some idea of the stowage space available, what can be bought en route, the limitations of the galley equipment and particularly the stove itself, and not least the individual likes and dislikes of those on board.

Storing before departure

There is a major difference between storing up at home for an Atlantic cruise, the first leg of which may perhaps be only a few days across the Bay of Biscay or down to Bermuda, and storing for a specific passage, such as the Atlantic crossing. Before leaving home is the time to lay in those items which are likely to be overly expensive or simply unavailable elsewhere: tea and coffee, dried yeast, canned meats and favourite branded products would fall into this category. So would 'national' foods, whether it's a British liking for Branston pickle and tinned steak and

kidney pie or an American addiction to peanut butter and jelly. Calculate probable consumption by all means, but within reason buy as much as you will be able to stow. However, avoid over-buying on staples or foods of foreign origin which can be found almost everywhere – flour, pasta, rice, canned fish, canned fruit and vegetables and fresh eggs. A couple of weeks' supply of all of these will be ample for any boat leaving northern Europe – perhaps a little more if the first passage is to be a long one.

Storing for a single passage

Calculating stores for a specific passage is more complicated. The first step is to establish how many meals will be expected each day, and the type of food to be eaten at each – cooked breakfast or cereal? Meat and two veg at lunch or just a snack? Puddings or fresh fruit? If possible the whole crew should be consulted. Eating habits will almost certainly change at sea, and a generous allowance of nibbles such as biscuits (both sweet and savoury), chocolate bars and sweets will never go amiss. Having estimated what might be consumed on any given day it

Just some of the stores for an Atlantic passage stacked in the main cabin of a Rival 41. A smaller yacht could face major stowage problems. *Photo: Tony Vasey*

There's no doubt that varnishing prolongs the life of food cans, particularly if they are to be kept in a damp bilge. It's also an excellent way of using up old lumpy varnish. *Photo: Anne Hammick*

should not be difficult to expand this to cover the entire passage, allowing an extra fifty per cent for unforeseen delays. Some people like to do a dummy run in home waters, laying in and then living off stores for a one-week cruise to check if anything has been forgotten. Much depends on the experience of the person in charge of catering – few people used to running and feeding a household will need this kind of reassurance.

Provisioning in different areas

Storing up for a long passage is best done at a port of some size for the obvious reason that it is likely to have the best resources. The ports listed in Part III are capable of meeting most needs unless stated otherwise. Even so it may be useful to have a broad indication as to what each area is likely to offer.

All the staples mentioned above are readily available throughout Europe and the Atlantic islands. The Iberian peninsula is noted for the quality of its fruit and is an excellent place to stock up on Mediterranean produce such as pasta and olive oil. Canned fish and seafood of all kinds are another speciality. Porto Santo has little available, but both Madeira and the Canaries are excellent in terms of both supermarkets and local produce, making stocking up for a long passage a positive pleasure. The same cannot be said of the Cape Verde Islands, which are both very dry and very poor. If calling in here before the trade-wind passage, arrive with the yacht already stored up.

In the Lesser Antilles themselves both the quality and

variety of imported foods have improved markedly over the last fifteen years, and a judicious mixture of modern supermarkets, smaller stores and the generally excellent local markets should provide almost every need except perhaps those listed at the beginning of this chapter. A handy rule of thumb regarding locally grown food in an area where sunshine can virtually be taken for granted is that rainfall becomes critical, and rainfall depends to a large extent on height. Those islands which the chart shows as mountainous (Grenada, St Vincent, St Lucia, Martinique, Dominica, etc) produce excellent fruit and vegetables, those which are generally low (Antigua, St Maarten, the British Virgin Islands, etc) generally do not. In addition to fine local produce, the French islands are noted for the range and quality of imported foods such as cheese and paté.

The quality of food available along the eastern seaboard of the United States and Canada is well known, though owing to the wide use of freezers it may be difficult to find canned meats and other perishables. There is a greater likelihood of fruit and vegetables having been chilled (which will affect their keeping qualities) than in less sophisticated areas, but a little asking around may well lead one to a farm shop or growers' co-operative. British yachtsmen are frequently stunned by the trouble to which their American hosts will go to assist them – to have a virtual stranger insist on transporting you from boat to supermarket and back again, or even to lend you a car, is almost routine.

Although supermarkets in Bermuda are well-stocked, since nearly all food must be imported it is probably the most expensive place to store-up on the entire Atlantic circuit. The boat without a freezer will again be at a disadvantage, and it is also extremely difficult to find fresh produce which has not been chilled. All in all it is best to avoid being forced into a major re-stock in Bermuda.

The Azorean islands vary, with by far the best provisioning at Horta in Faial, Angra do Heroismo in Terceira and Ponta Delgada in São Miguel, towns which also have good markets. Basics such as bread, fish and some fruit and vegetables are available on all the islands, but imported foods may not be.

Non-perishables

Aboard the smaller yacht every cubic inch of space under settees and bunks must be adapted for the storage of food and other essentials. The purist, and certainly the owner of a very small yacht, will go to great lengths to keep weights as low as possible, but if tins are to be kept in the bilge they should have the contents marked in indelible pen, their labels removed and then be varnished.

The galley itself should include a ready-use locker for coffee, tea, sugar, salt, etc, and many cooks also like to keep a day or two's supply of food handy in order to avoid scrabbling in the bilges or forepeak lockers after dark or in heavy weather. If, as is usually the case, bulk stores are spread around the boat then some kind of system will be needed. By far the most efficient, and quite essential if more than one person is doing the cooking, is to have a notebook showing where each item will be found and, in the case of tins and packets, how many are on board. A pencil stub tied to the notebook, reinforced by dire threats from the chief caterer, should ensure that each individual item is crossed off as it is used.

Some non-perishables will of course be bought in bulk, and it may be possible to negotiate a small discount on cans bought by the case. However always test unknown brands before buying in quantity. Equally to be avoided is the 'giant economy pack'. It may not fit your boat's lockers and once opened, unless its contents can be used quickly, will probably go bad. Dry stores may of course be bought in bulk and decanted into smaller air-tight containers for use as required. This is also true of margarine, available in large square containers from which a table tub can be refilled. Margarine seems to keep for ever and to retain a semi-solid state even without refrigeration, whereas butter, even in tins, is best avoided unless the boat has refrigeration.

Along with edible non-perishables it may be convenient to include those 'housekeeping' items without which the cruise will not be a happy one. In the galley: kitchen towel, detergent (dish soap) and surface cleaners. Elsewhere washing powder, bleach or the equivalent, and toilet rolls. Though the last can be bought everywhere, the standard in some countries leaves a lot to be desired.

Fresh stores and storage

The length of time that fresh stores will keep depends both on their quality and the care with which they are stored. Sound potatoes and onions will last for a month-long voyage even in tropical latitudes provided they are picked over regularly and any suspect ones removed. Fresh eggs will also last for a month without treatment, but not if they have been chilled at any time. Twice weekly turning will prevent the shells from drying out and the yolks from settling.

Fruit is less predictable. Green tomatoes will ripen gradually in a warm atmosphere, but do not need daylight. Nearly all citrus fruit will keep for weeks if not months, providing a useful source of vitamin C. A hand of green bananas will be inedible for several days but will then all ripen at once. Nevertheless, half a hand is well worth putting aboard if obtainable at your departure port and even over-ripe bananas make a delicious pudding cooked in rum. If faced with unfamiliar local produce in West Indian markets, the local ladies will generally be delighted to advise, and it may also be worth buying a book on Caribbean cookery.

Fishing

While it would be most unwise to depend on catching fish for food, they can nevertheless provide welcome variety. If fish are needed for survival, the extremes available are plankton dredged up by trawling with a fine-mesh fabric, and catching sharks with heavy tackle, hauling them aboard and (with both danger and difficulty) slaughtering them, and eating the liver.

The average yachtsman will be more likely to think in terms of a towed hook and lure, possibly attached to a rod. The line will need to be both strong and easy to grip, and heavyweight gloves may be useful. If towing a line for long periods it is common practice to run a few turns anticlockwise around a winch before making up the inboard end. Any pull on the hook will cause the winch to spin, alerting the crew immediately. Ideas on suitable lures vary – the polished spoon can work well, others prefer to camouflage the hook among strips of coloured polythene cut from carrier bags. Special lures can also be bought to attract squid. If a large fish has been landed and is thrashing around, a little neat spirit poured into the gills will pacify it immediately.

Many cruising areas are nature preserves where fishing is either restricted or totally banned. Spear fishing is forbidden in the Tobago Cays, parts of Antigua, the Virgin Islands and Bermuda among other places, although local people are allowed to fish by traditional methods, usually traps or pots. The local cruising guide should give the details.

Towing a lure offshore is generally acceptable, but owing to the prevalence of ciguera poisoning in the northern Antilles the fishing line should be stowed on reaching Antigua – about 17°N. Ciguera only affects predatory fish, which build up dangerous concentrations of the poison in their bodies through years of feeding on the smaller reef fish. Predatory fish include kingfish, tuna, dorado, dolphin fish and barracuda, all of which are otherwise excellent eating. The first three are of the familiar tuna shape, the dolphin fish (no relation of the mammal) somewhat tall and narrow with iridescent blue colouring, and the barracuda a long, evil-looking beast with a powerful jaw and large teeth. The barracuda is the only one of the above likely to be met when snorkelling, when it can be unnerving though seldom actually dangerous.

In the tropics there may be the bonus of flying fish landing on deck during the night, and displaying a light will tend to attract them. Even so there are unlikely to be enough to provide a substantial breakfast except perhaps for the singlehander.

A fine dolphin fish. The major problem for a crew without refrigeration would be in consuming such a monster while still fresh. (The dolphin fish, incidentally, is no relation of the dolphin or porpoise.) *Photo: Jill Vasey*

Liquid refreshment

The subject of drinking water and tankage has already been covered in Chapter 2. Choice and quantity of non-alcoholic beverages will of course depend on the tastes of the crew, but whereas carbonated drinks are generally available it may be difficult to find a dilutable fruit squash away from home.

Whether to lay in bonded stores before departure will depend both on the habits of those aboard and the intended route of the cruise – only the most discerning palate will insist on stocking up with French wine before spending several weeks cruising Spain and Portugal. For the yacht without refrigeration there is also the question of which drinks to forgo because they will not be pleasant unless chilled. Not all departure ports have bonded stores stockists nearby, and British yachts leaving from Falmouth may find the cost of having stores delivered from Plymouth makes it uneconomic, unless a considerable quantity is required. In addition a large, sealable locker will be needed. A further consideration is that bonded stores bought in an EC country cannot be broached until the yacht has departed EC waters or duty will become payable.

Many yachtsmen prefer to experiment with the local brew as the cruise progresses. Iberia produces wine, port, sherry and brandy (all for sale in the Canaries); 'Madeira' comes in a range from very dry indeed to rich and creamy – free tastings allow plenty of chance for selection; in the Caribbean of course rum is the staple, with many yachtsmen considering Mount Gay Eclipse from Barbados to be the best in the world. The French islands (Martinique, Guadeloupe, St Barts and St Martin) are good places to stock up with wine or brandy. The latter two are duty free ports where beer is also an excellent buy. Bermuda appears to sell everything, at a price, while the Azores offer Portuguese brands in addition to their own locally made wines. Only the dedicated whisky drinker really needs to think in terms of duty free stores.

In addition to responsibility for the boat, her equipment and her crew, the master of any small vessel must deal with her day-to-day affairs, from coping with officialdom to changing the clocks and organising watch systems. The following are a mixed bag of reminders and suggestions.

Watchkeeping systems

A happy voyage depends to a great extent on establishing a daily routine which not only ensures that all necessary work is done but with which those aboard can co-exist for weeks at a stretch. This also applies to singlehanders, who must work out for themselves whatever compromise between sleep and watchkeeping they feel they can live with. Nevertheless, be there one person aboard the small cruiser or sixteen on a maxi racing machine, the energy and resilience of those aboard is a finite resource which must never be squandered.

Though the watch system must take account not only of the sailing of the yacht but also of daily chores such as navigation, cooking and ongoing maintenance, its prime objective must always be to ensure the safe conduct of the ship. Ideally this entails having enough manpower on deck to deal with whatever needs to be done without calling those below, but as few cruising yachts will have more than one person on watch at a time this may not always be feasible. In a storm when perhaps it may be necessary to run before large seas, or in conditions of extreme cold, one hour on deck steering by hand may be as long as even a strong, fit person can stand. In such conditions the yacht with a crew of three or less will be highly dependent on a powerful self-steering gear, and it is essential that it should be equal to the task.

Many watchkeeping systems have been evolved for small boats and those which follow are no more than suggestions:

Watch systems for two people
1 A straightforward system of three- or four-hour watches with extended periods to provide a two-hour overlap twice a day at mealtimes. Convenient where one person does all the cooking and the other all the navigation, as each person is on watch during the same period each day – Figure 3(a).
2 The above, but not considering overlap periods as part of a watch. This allows the times each person is on watch to alternate between one day and the next, providing some variety aboard those boats where both navigation and cooking are shared equally – Figure 3(b).

(Both the above systems are described more fully in *Ocean Cruising on a Budget*, which was written primarily for smaller yachts with crews of two or three.)

Watch systems for three people
1 An adaptation of either (1) or (2) above, with watches carried on day and night – Figures 3(c) and 3(d).

2 Formal watches during the hours of darkness only. It will still be necessary for someone to keep at lookout at all times, but this may be on a volunteer rather than a duty basis – Figure 3(e).

Watch systems for four or more people
1 Again a straight three- or four-hour system, either permanently or just in darkness (nearly twelve hours on a trade wind crossing). Assuming that only one person is normally on watch at any time this will effectively mean the crew spending most of the night in their bunks, so sleep during the day is unlikely to be more serious than the odd nap – Figure 3(f).
2 If one person is doing all the cooking for a larger crew they deserve a suitable reward, possibly exemption from the unpopular 0000–0400 'graveyard' watch or even exemption from watches entirely. This is also feasible if cooking is alternated, a full night's sleep being awarded to the day's cook – Figure 3(g).

As a general rule, the more people there are aboard the easier it will be to organise a system which fulfils not only the purposes outlined above but also allows time for relaxation, hobbies and some feeling of community amongst the crew – a regular 'happy hour' before supper is often popular. With a very small crew it is possible barely to exchange a word with the other person/people for days at a stretch, other than for a few minutes on handing over the watch and a brief period at mealtimes.

With any crew of more than two it will be important to keep chat at the change of watch as quiet and as brief as possible, particularly at night. Many skippers sleep with half an ear open, and to be regularly disturbed while off watch is plainly going to do nothing for either temper or alertness in the long-term. It must also be clearly designated who is 'on call' should assistance be needed on deck. On some yachts this will always be the skipper, on others the person due on watch next. Though it must depend ultimately on the capabilities and experience of the crew, the skipper should beware of inviting so much broken sleep as to have no reserves of energy, both physical and mental, should a real emergency arise. Bad weather or a sudden crisis can disrupt the watch system – and therefore sleep patterns – without warning.

Ship's time

While the navigational clock will normally be kept on GMT it is best to alter the saloon clock periodically during the course of an east/west (or west/east) crossing, if only to avoid a major alteration on reaching land. Many skippers also prefer not to allow the noon sight to interrupt lunch!

Try to ensure that, if the time change is made during the night, the additional or subtracted hour does not always occur when the same person is on watch.

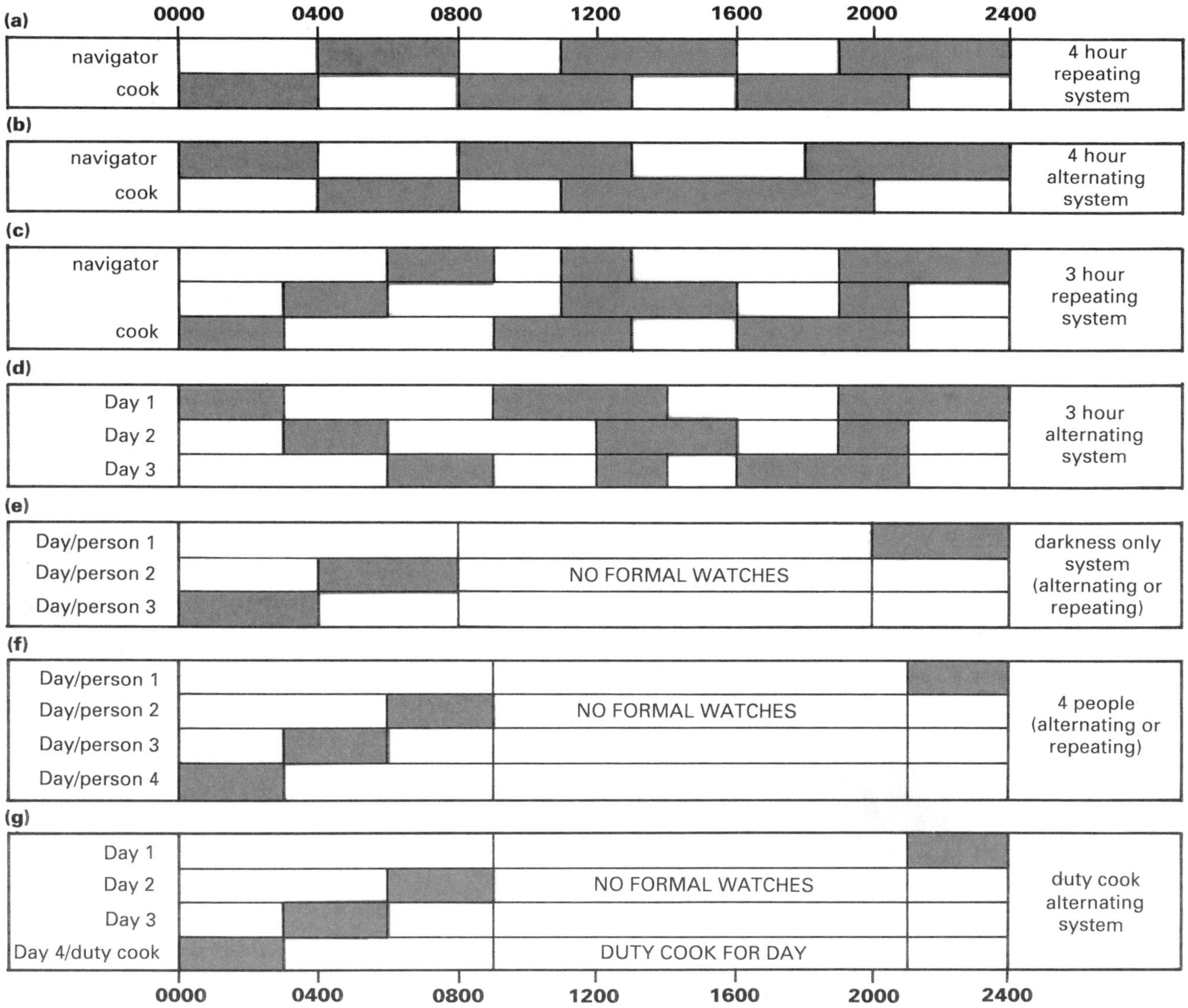

(a) 0000 0400 0800 1200 1600 2000 2400

navigator
cook

4 hour repeating system

(b)

navigator
cook

4 hour alternating system

(c)

navigator
cook

3 hour repeating system

(d)

Day 1
Day 2
Day 3

3 hour alternating system

(e)

Day/person 1
Day/person 2
Day/person 3

NO FORMAL WATCHES

darkness only system (alternating or repeating)

(f)

Day/person 1
Day/person 2
Day/person 3
Day/person 4

NO FORMAL WATCHES

4 people (alternating or repeating)

(g)

Day 1
Day 2
Day 3
Day 4/duty cook

NO FORMAL WATCHES

DUTY COOK FOR DAY

duty cook alternating system

0000 0400 0800 1200 1600 2000 2400

Fig 3(a)–(g) Watchkeeping systems for crews of two or more people.

Paperwork

Documentation

Requirements vary from country to country and it makes sense to carry anything one might possibly be called upon to produce. Several sets of photocopies may also come in useful, with a further set left ashore. The first part of this list comprises those documents which will be inspected routinely, the second part those requested only occasionally.

1 Valid passports for everyone on board, with visas as required. If the crew are multi-national it must be remembered that some may need visas for a given country while others do not. Neither passports nor visas should expire during the course of the cruise, though it may be possible to renew the latter *en route*.

2 Crew list, with formal Crew Manifest if paid crew are carried. Normally everyone aboard should be listed as crew rather than passengers, as some countries levy high fees for charter yachts or other passenger-carrying vessels.

3 Certificate of Registry, or Small Ships documentation. American yachts may need to renew documentation annually, which can be a problem when away from home. Full British registration is valid indefinitely, SSR for ten years. A few harbour authorities insist on holding passports and/or registration documents pending departure, and though this is unpleasant it may be unavoidable.

4 Evidence of VAT status – either the tax has been paid or the vessel is exempt, most often on grounds of age (yachts launched before 1.1.85). The correct document is the Single Administrative Document or SAD, in practice Copy 8 of the multi-part Form C88 which is used throughout the EC in connection with the movement of goods. A full Certificate of Registry gives the date when the vessel was first registered and should be acceptable as evidence of age (the SSR certificate does not do this), but there has been at least one case of a Portuguese customs official refusing to recognize anything other than the SAD and attempting to levy VAT on a yacht built and registered, some forty years ago.

5 Clearance papers from the previous port of call. In certain countries, notably Spain and the Canaries, these can be difficult to obtain.

6 Stores list, which should differentiate between opened and unopened items. In practice very few countries are interested in stores other than alcohol.

7 Cruising Permit (issued to visiting yachts in the USA, Canada and some Caribbean islands) if applicable.
8 VHF and other radio licences/operator's certificates as applicable.
9 Insurance papers – a few marinas will not allow uninsured boats to berth.
10 Bill of Sale including VAT documentation.
11 World Health Organisation Yellow Card, plus Bills of Health or Pratiques acquired en route. Few countries now demand a Bill of Health, but this should be checked and possibly re-checked from time to time. A sudden epidemic could alter the rules overnight.
12 Charter documents, if applicable.
13 Ensign Warrant, if applicable.

Preparations for arrival

The last few hours of an ocean voyage may be amongst the most demanding of the entire passage for the skipper/navigator, and the practical aspects of making a landfall are covered in Chapter 4. However while the crew can often fall into their bunks as soon as the anchor is down or the yacht secured, few officials allow the skipper to catch up on sleep before dealing with the formalities. For this reason it is worth making a few preparations in advance.

Check through the entry procedures for the country to which you are going, not least to ensure that the port for which you are headed is an official port of entry. If they monitor VHF, check what frequency is in use and whether or not calling is mandatory. Once secured, does customs and immigration come to you, does the skipper go ashore alone, or do the entire crew need to present themselves?

Collect all the documents listed above, and make out a crew list with full names, dates and places of birth and passport numbers. Some people advocate carrying photocopied crew lists, but though this can obviously do no harm it will not take account of any changes of crew. Some countries demand different types of information, and many insist that the details should be written on their own printed forms. Make a list of dutiable stores, especially wines and spirits, and ensure it is correct. If you have medical drugs aboard there should be an accompanying certificate from a doctor, naming the patient and stating the quantity of each drug. Place everything that might be needed in a sealed bag, along with some currency and a phrase book if applicable, ready to take ashore. The more weary the skipper, the greater the chance of something being forgotten and the more irritating the chore of returning for it.

Finally replace the national ensign if it has not been worn at sea, and have both the quarantine flag and a courtesy flag ready to hoist on entering territorial waters. Undivided attention can then be devoted to the landfall itself.

The ship's stamp and modern equivalents

It used to be fashionable to have a ship's stamp – often a small drawing of the boat together with name, home port and perhaps registered number or radio call sign – with which to adorn customs documentation. However times have changed, and officials in nearly all countries are now educated professionals who will be unimpressed if you mess up their paperwork. Keep a rubber stamp for books

Hoisting the Grenadian courtesy ensign and Q flag at the end of a passage up from the South Atlantic. *Photo: Mark Scott*

and letterheads.

A more appropriate modern equivalent might be smart business cards with the boat's picture, or small adhesive address stickers. It is also possible to get adhesive-backed prints made, bearing a coloured photo of the boat and/or her crew together with brief written details. These look well in visitors' books and may even make suitable small gifts for local people.

Books and miscellaneous paperwork

Those publications directly connected with navigation are listed in Chapter 4. In addition separate bibliographies devoted to various topics will be found among the Appendices. While it is not suggested that every single volume should be carried, there are some which can claim to form the nucleus of every yacht's bookshelf. For lighter reading most yachts carry stacks of paperbacks, especially on long passages, exchanging them either with other yachts or in one of the book-swaps established in most of the larger harbours. Letter writing is another favourite occupation with some people, so lay in some airmail pads and envelopes (preferably with self-sealing flaps which won't stick until you intend them to). Plenty of notebooks, both lined and plain, take up little space, and a pad of tracing paper may also be found useful. Plenty of pencils, pens, coloured felt-tips, erasers and adhesive tape complete the stationery locker.

Money

There is much to be said for obtaining a limited amount (perhaps around £60 or $100) of the currency of each country it is intended to visit before leaving home. Dues will frequently need to be paid on arrival, and though this can often be done in US dollars the exchange rate may sometimes be exorbitant. There is no doubt that dollars are the most widely accepted single currency around the Atlantic margins, and in many places not only officials but taxi drivers, restaurants and bars will accept them without question. It is wise to carry a reserve cash fund in US currency.

Travellers' cheques and credit cards are the simplest means of obtaining funds as they are needed. Barclaycard/Visa, Access/MasterCard and American Express are the most widely accepted, and Barclays International is particularly well represented in the Lesser Antilles. In the Azores and the Cape Verdes only banks on the larger islands are likely to have credit card machines (Visa only), and a passport is likely to be required for identification. It will of course be necessary to authorise either your bank or a trusted individual at home to pay the bills on time.

Should a very large sum be needed it may be worth arranging a telegraphic transfer from your home bank, and this will be a great deal easier to organise if you have arranged for someone to hold power of attorney for you in your absence. Consult your bank.

Insurance

Marine
Whether or not to insure is a personal decision, but if one stops to think of the kind of third party claim which might have to be met in the event of an accident involving others some protection seems highly desirable. However it is becoming increasingly difficult for yachts sailed by two or even three people to get insurance cover, and the desirability of having insurance may have to be balanced against the undesirability of being forced to carry extra crew. If you do opt for insurance, be prepared to accept a large excess (deductible), probably in the region of £1000 ($1700) during the crossing itself and around half this whilst cruising the island groups, though it should be possible to negotiate reduced excesses on the dinghy and other individually listed items. Few companies will let one make the longer passages uninsured and then renew cover for coast or island hopping without insisting on a full survey on arrival, thus effectively ruling out this option.

Medical
If you carry medical insurance it may or may not cover you while cruising, and this should be checked and the policy amended if necessary. Private medical fees are high in the West Indies and the USA compared with Europe, though many West Indian islands have perfectly acceptable free health schemes based on the British National Health model. Europeans should complete a form E111 (available from post offices) which entitles one to free or reduced-cost treatment in EC countries on a reciprocal basis.

The law

Most yachtsmen will encounter the law only in the guise of customs and immigration, the latter being a particularly

In some areas, a visit from customs and immigration may mean welcoming six or eight thirsty officials aboard – and their launches never carry fenders! *Photo: Sepha Wood*

sensitive subject in some areas. While there undoubtedly is the odd occasion on which a blameless yacht receives a hard time for no apparent reason, there are, unfortunately, a very small minority of yachtsmen who tend to spoil the pitch for the rest of us. Equally, there appear to be a small number of customs or immigration officials who are not above lining their pockets by levying unofficial 'fines' for supposed infringements of the rules. Do not anticipate this as routine though – most fees for cruising permits or overtime are perfectly genuine. Ask for a receipt if in doubt.

Try putting yourself in the shoes of an official whose task it is to check your credentials when you arrive in his country. He knows that vessels purporting to be yachts occasionally smuggle drugs and illegal immigrants. He also knows that yachts sometimes leave without paying. He has seen innumerable yachts arrive, some of them manned by crews who have looked and behaved like vagabonds, and some with skippers who have treated him less than courteously. His whole training is based upon the need to spot potential trouble, and to the extent that you give him cause for suspicion – whether by behaviour or appearance – you start out on the wrong foot. Simply being polite and reasonably tidy may prove nothing, but at least it gives no reason to suspect that you may either be a crook or be totally impoverished. The cruising yachtsman is in a potentially vulnerable situation whenever he is in a foreign port, and only a fool would deliberately court suspicion.

The authorities in most countries are concerned first with drugs and potential immigrants, and second with dutiable merchandise. Nearly every boat must carry some drugs (if only medicines), some human beings (who might jump ship or want to find work), and some dutiable stores. Many cruising grounds, including much of the Caribbean, have high local unemployment and any attempt to seek work ashore will be viewed very seriously. Almost certainly the immigration documents signed by the skipper will include one stating that no paid employment will be entered into, and should any one of the crew break this undertaking the skipper will also be held responsible.

Always be meticulous in declaring all medicinal drugs and dutiable imports, and make sure that each member of the crew does likewise. It is rare for a yacht to be searched other than on her return home and in many Caribbean islands the skipper visits officials ashore rather than vice versa, but there is always the exception. The obligation of declaring everything correctly always lies with the captain – a lapse of memory or the accidental writing of a wrong number is no defence, nor is it any excuse to say that the paper you signed was in a foreign language.

Finally, few transitory yachtsmen would be so unwise as to get mixed up in local politics, however remotely, but even voicing an opinion may be unwise. In areas which until comparatively recently were governed by colonial powers, perceived interference by expatriates can provoke strong feelings.

Clothing

An Atlantic cruise calls for a variety of clothing. Some of the northern routes are in near-arctic temperatures, though for the majority of cruising people the whole object of the exercise is to reach the tropics.

If starting from a northern area waterproof clothing will probably be in daily use at sea. Once you get into the tropics it may be put away for several months, but will be needed again on approaching home waters. Good quality oilskins (foul weather gear) are essential, as is a rinse in fresh water and careful storage when not in regular use – don't just cram oilskins into a locker and forget them.

In the tropics clothes will be light and few in number, but they will need frequent washing so take plenty of changes. It is a pleasant habit to keep a set of clean clothes tucked away for arrival – the first chance of a freshwater shower may well predate the chance of getting laundry done. It is also obvious that a reasonably clean and tidy crew will make a better impression on customs or immigration officials than one in the last stages of dishevelment.

Although almost anything will pass on the beach, it is possible to cause offence in many areas by not conforming to local standards of dress in public places such as restaurants or shops. Except in the most informal bars men will be expected to wear a short-sleeved shirt, while women in overly skimpy blouses or shorts may attract undue attention. In any case, looser clothing or a cotton skirt may well be cooler. A very few places will expect men to wear a collar and tie and possibly a jacket when dining ashore, though if such clothing is not carried one can always seek out a less formal establishment.

Shoes are also important. Although many people prefer bare feet on deck it is both slovenly and dangerous to walk ashore without shoes – broken glass, sea urchins and fallen fruit of the manchineel tree (common on Caribbean beaches) can all cause painful injuries. Some form of footwear is considered a part of normal dress in nearly all areas and many restaurants will not serve barefooted customers. Plastic 'jelly shoes', rubber flip-flops or lightweight sandals are both practical and cool.

Stowage of clothes

It is only fair to allow each person aboard some private stowage space, much of which is likely to be devoted to their clothes – no one should be expected to live for weeks out of their luggage. In larger lockers not provided with shelving, generous use of polythene bags, preferably of the self-seal variety, will provide protection from damp and some semblance of order. Ideally the only shared locker should be for oilskins, though in many yachts this will also have to double as a hanging locker for whatever tidy clothes are carried. Protect the latter with plastic sacks or those purpose-made zipped clothing bags.

Pests

These fall into three categories: waterborne, airborne and land-based.

Of the waterborne pests, owners of wooden yachts will rightly be concerned about teredo worm and gribble, though some protection can be derived from regular antifouling. Almost every yacht collects a crop of goose barnacles towards the end of a tradewind crossing, but these do no real harm and are easily removed at the end of the passage.

Airborne pests include flies, mosquitoes and occasionally wasps. The best protection is to anchor well off and ensure good ventilation at all times – see Chapter 3. Experience suggests that the vast majority of mosquito bites are sustained whilst ashore, particularly around dusk.

Anchoring off will again give protection against many land-based pests, other than those unwittingly brought aboard in food or boxes. In some areas, including the Caribbean, rats may make their way on board a yacht with lines ashore and once established can be very difficult to get rid of. They seem to like chewing on plastic, and as well as the obvious targets in the galley may damage electrical insulation or water pipes, including those attached to open seacocks. Rat guards for mooring lines can either be bought locally or improvised from large funnels threaded on the rope, buckets with holes drilled in their bases or even large plates – anything which provides an agile rat with a real obstacle.

Weevils are difficult to avoid, since they are generally brought aboard in the food in which they are later found. However they are much less prevalent than used to be the case and it is now unusual to find infested flour, rice or pasta. In the mid 1970s one expected to sieve, wash or shake as a matter of routine. Cockroaches are the most unpleasant of the insect pests if they are allowed to gain a firm hold. Preventives include avoidance of lying alongside, careful examination of all foods brought aboard, especially fruit and vegetables, and a complete ban on cardboard cartons which frequently harbour eggs. Scrupulous cleanliness, and frequent use of one of the sprays available is probably the best protection.

Crossing an ocean aboard a seaworthy yacht carries no more inherent risk than coastal sailing – in many ways less, since the chance of grounding is removed and that of collision much less than in crowded inshore waters. However, equally, the option to run for shelter at the onset of bad weather is removed and should something serious go wrong the chances of attracting immediate assistance are very much reduced. On an ocean voyage you are on your own. It is not the purpose of this book to teach basic seamanship, and before contemplating an Atlantic passage the skipper should be satisfied that he and his crew are equal to most eventualities and that he knows how his boat should be handled, and how she will react, in all foreseeable circumstances.

The chance of meeting bad weather is always present, and must be faced as a fact of life. Fire, collision, man overboard and, to a large extent, gear failure are avoidable and must be prevented if possible, but will have to be dealt with should they occur. The possibility of illness or injury cannot be ignored, and both skipper and crew should be aware of any ailment to which one of them might be prone. However a well-prepared boat in the hands of a competent and resourceful crew has no more reason to encounter problems while crossing the Atlantic than while crossing the English Channel. In particular, anyone who has learned to sail in unforgiving northern waters subject to strong tides, heavy traffic and frequently bad visibility should be well equipped to deal with whatever the open ocean can throw at them.

The deck: design features

Moving about the deck of a small boat at sea has been likened to trying to walk on a wet sloping roof in an earthquake. It is surprising how few of us fall off. Preventive measures should begin with the yacht designer. While high topsides may prevent some water coming aboard, excessive height (often in the interests of interior accommodation) can increase the danger to those working on deck when it is rough. We all know that the higher you go up the mast when at sea, the worse the motion. The same thinking should apply when deciding on the height of a boat's deck above the waterline – the lower it can be, consistent with keeping it out of the water, the safer it will

The Rival 41 is a yacht designed with serious cruising in mind – wide sidedecks, solid toerail and stanchions, plenty of handholds and so-called 'granny-bars' either side of the mast. The dinghy would probably be deflated and stowed below on longer passages. *Photo: Tony Vasey*

be as a working platform. The camber of the deck of a good ocean cruiser should be a compromise: excessive camber may make the weather deck more or less level when the vessel is heeled, but the lee deck will be untenable. It should be possible to move all around the deck even in the worst conditions.

A solid toerail is essential, though deep bulwarks combined with low freeboard, such as grandfather's boat had, were a mixed blessing, often scooping up water and holding it there. Lifelines also provide some protection, but it is doubtful whether even the strongest could save a heavy person thrown right across the deck. Stanchion sockets must be securely attached – bolted to a wooden or fibreglass hull or welded to a metal one. If plastic covered stainless steel wire is used it should be renewed before the start of the cruise since any defect will be hidden by the plastic coating. Pre-stretched polyester line, very little thicker than the covered wire, can be equally strong and any defect will be obvious. Wire lifelines should always be secured by lashings rather than small turnbuckles – they are less subject to the ill effects of distortion and can swiftly be cut should the need arise.

If dodgers (weather cloths) are fitted there must be a gap of at least 4–6 in (10–15 cm) between them and the deck. Otherwise, should a big sea come aboard they are likely to carry away, possibly taking lifelines and stanchions with them. Many skippers favour brailing up dodgers at the onset of bad weather. Similarly, a sprayhood may be best lowered, in which case lashings will be needed to prevent it flipping backwards.

Pulpits must be strong beyond all question. A man working at the stemhead must both feel and be completely safe. It should be possible to move all over the deck from one handhold to another without ever having to let go with both hands – grabrails along the entire length of the coachroof on each side are very desirable. Waist-high stainless steel rails either side of the mast are still seen relatively infrequently, but give valuable support to a person working at its foot.

Finally, give some thought to the deck and coachroof surfacings, which must provide as good a grip when wet as when dry, for bare feet as for seaboots. GRP decks often have a diamond pattern moulded in, but with an older yacht this may have become worn and ineffective and some form of commercial non-skid deck covering may be required.

Heavy weather

It is a fact that most people cross the Atlantic, especially by the more southerly routes, without ever experiencing truly severe weather. Gales with winds of 35 to 45 knots may occur relatively frequently north of about 40°, but storms with gusts reaching 60 knots are much less common – unless one chooses to cross out of season or sail the very high latitudes. Even so, the possibility of a deep depression or early season hurricane is always present and only a fool would set off on an ocean crossing unprepared for the eventuality.

The best tactics to employ in the face of severe weather must depend to a large extent on the yacht herself and on the number, strength and skill of those aboard. Few people are deliberately going to seek out a gale before departure in order to test out their theories, and in any case ocean seas are very different from those met with in confined waters (and not always worse). However, experimenting with heaving-to, lying a-hull and running under bare poles, with or without warps, even in force 6 to 7 (25 to 30 knots) will give a good idea of how the boat will behave in stronger winds.

Unless the crew will be a large one there is no point in adopting a strategy which calls for someone on the tiller at all times – in a small boat in really severe weather the safest place for the crew is below, with the boat under self steering or lying with her helm lashed. There are many excellent books on the subject of coping with bad weather at sea, notably *Heavy Weather Sailing* by K Adlard Coles, revised by Peter Bruce, and *This is Rough Weather Cruising* by Erroll Bruce. Learn the lessons they teach.

While it is impossible to prevent solid water coming aboard any yacht, steps must be taken to ensure that it will disappear again as quickly as possible, and that only a small amount will find its way below. A cockpit filled with seawater can seriously affect a boat's trim and stability, making her much more susceptible to the next wave, and should the cockpit be overlarge it may be worth thinking of filling part of it in. Generous drains are of course the first priority, and if fitted with strainers these must be cleared regularly. In practice, the violent movement generated by seas likely to come aboard will often throw much of the water out the same way it came in.

The importance of a solid bridgedeck and strong washboards has already been touched on in Chapter 2, along with the need to be able to secure locker lids. Doghouse and coachroof windows are an obvious source of weakness aboard some yachts, and should be provided with plywood covers for use either as protective screens or as a temporary repair in the event of breakage. GRP yachts with small, aluminium-framed windows of toughened glass are less likely to be at risk, though perspex slabs secured only by bolts or, even worse, set in rubber frames are another matter. The former frequently leak, the latter are potentially lethal and *must* be replaced before departure.

The 1979 Fastnet gale drew stark attention to the hazards of a knock-down, and particularly to those posed to the crew by heavy, unsecured fittings flying about below. Few yachts these days carry inside ballast, but if you have no option make sure that it is immovable. See that batteries are so fixed that, even if the boat is rolled right over, they cannot move. Check that the gimbals supporting the stove are of the closed variety, preferably backed up by bolts. Make sure that lockers containing heavy tools, cutlery or glassware cannot empty their contents if capsized. You will not achieve complete success and, if it should happen, you will certainly wonder how on earth some of the items managed to get where they did, but do your best – loose gear can cause serious trouble even in a partial knock-down.

Many knock-downs actually occur after the worst of the weather has passed, when the seas are still big but the wind has begun to moderate. This is particularly true if a front has gone through and the wind direction changed significantly. If the boat is undercanvassed and sluggish she will be more at the mercy of rogue waves than if she has the power to answer the helm quickly. Increasing sail early runs counter to the natural inclination of a tired crew to take life a little bit easy for a while and ensure the worst really *is* over, but it is a point worth remembering.

Truly horrible weather seen from the foredeck of a 28 ft Twister. Even with lee decks under a mass of solid water, she kept going with windvane self-steering, proving that seaworthiness has little to do with size. *Photo: Trevor Leek*

An ocean gale is an awe-inspiring spectacle but some of us can remember much worse moments in more confined waters. Try to have your gale in deep water, with plenty of sea-room and as far as possible from a lee shore. This is not quite as silly as it sounds. Although we cannot choose what weather we shall have for our landfall, we can choose when to start the voyage. If you leave with a forecast of three or four days' good weather and use it to put a few hundred miles between you and the land, preferably clearing any continental shelf there may be in those parts, you will have done your best. Both boat and crew will have had a chance to settle down, and from then onwards you'll take it in your stride.

Lightning

One facet of bad weather which worries many people, more for the damage it causes than any immediate threat, is being struck by lightning. Although comparatively rare it does occur from time to time in all the seas of the world and little can be done to prevent it. A minority of yachts have lightning conductors fitted, usually in the form of heavy copper strapping from the masthead straight down through deck and kingpost to the keel, terminating in a large grounding plate. However there is some question as to how effective any conductor could be, particularly on a aluminium-masted yacht whose decks might well be running with water at the time.

The effects of a lightning strike were described graphically by Philip Allen in an earlier edition of this book:

And what happens if your boat is struck by lightning? There is a real risk of this and, unless you have experienced it, you may not be aware of what it can do to the vessel's electrical installations. I speak from personal experience. I was aboard with my family when it happened and, although none of us was harmed, nor was the yacht marked outwardly, the

electrical and electronic equipment was all destroyed beyond repair. The main fuse-box was reduced to shattered fragments and little blobs of copper and brass, so that all wiring and light fittings had to be replaced; and the radio set, which was battery-operated with a loop antenna and totally unconnected to any of the ship's wiring, was reduced to scrap. The compass had an error of 45° induced.

Very few accounts of lightning strikes at sea mention injury to the crew (though a helmsman holding a metal wheel would be well advised to wear gloves) or damage to the yacht herself, other than to her electrical equipment and electronics. However in the majority of cases these are effectively written off, making the navigator's ability to find his way by old-fashioned methods doubly important – even a programmable calculator would probably be ruined. There is also the possibility of fire. A strange effect reported aboard one yacht was that every light bulb in the vessel glowed for ten seconds or so – and then blew within the next couple of days. As the skipper ruefully remarked, you expect to carry a few spare bulbs, but not enough to replace every single one aboard.

Gear failure

Prevention is better than cure. Routine inspection for chafe should be made every day, and careful checks made before, during, and after each passage to ensure that both

The seriousness of gear failure often depends as much on 'when and where' as on 'what'. This boom folded (due to corrosion at the kicking strap attachment) only hours before arrival in Madeira, where it was repaired without difficulty. Had it failed in the first few days of an Atlantic crossing it would have been much more serious. *Photo: Anne Hammick*

standing and running rigging are in good order. All seacocks and pumps should be worked periodically and all machinery given regular tests to make certain that it will function when needed. See Chapter 2.

Emergency steering

Any wheel-steered yacht *must* carry an emergency tiller for use should the linkage to the wheel fail. If the boat is tiller steered it is up to the skipper to decide whether there is any real prospect of it breaking, or whether the attachment to the rudder is the potential weak link. Other forms of steering – a sweep over the stern, towing buckets or warps, or simply balancing under sails – should be experimented with.

Collision

Ninety-five per cent of collision avoidance depends on three things:

1 A good lookout
2 Efficient navigation lights
3 An effective radar reflector

The other five per cent is down to sheer luck. Yachts do occasionally hit semi-submerged debris which the most conscientious lookout could not hope to spot, and in gale or storm conditions visibility is often severely restricted, radar almost useless due to wave clutter, and scope for taking avoiding action in any case limited. However hitting debris is not necessarily very serious, particularly to a relatively slow-moving cruising boat, and many ocean cruisers have received a loud and unexpected thump way out of soundings without any real harm to the hull beyond a few scratches or chipped gelcoat.

Collision with a ship would be another matter, and there is little doubt that from time to time yachts are indeed lost in this way. The risk factor may be about equal to that of having a car coming the other way across the motorway central barrier – we all know the possibility exists, but it does not stop us using the motorways. Keeping a good lookout is the best defence, with white flares ready to hand and judicious use of the VHF. It is surprising how many ships will give way to a yacht in the open ocean, but it would plainly be foolish to rely on this – in any case one usually sees few vessels during the centre portion of an Atlantic crossing. The continental margins are much busier, possibly entailing formal shipping lanes (see Chapter 10), which adds to the potential problems inherent in any landfall.

Although the risk of being run down is ever present and vigilance should never be relaxed, electronic aids may take part of the burden. Many singlehanders swear by radar detectors, generally fitted with omni-directional alarms, which would be useful aboard any yacht in poor visibility in the absence of active radar. Reflectors of the octahedral type should be hoisted in the catch-rain position, but the majority of experienced cruising skippers prefer the cylindrical Firdell or Gillie Firth reflectors, often permanently mounted on a mast bracket.

Oil rigs

There appear to be fewer exploratory oil rigs stationed in the western approaches to the UK than was the case in the early 1980s, but the occasional fixed rig may still be encountered. They may also be found off the coasts of Nova Scotia and Cape Cod (see Chapter 19), or may occasionally be met under tow. Fixed rigs should be shown on up-to-date charts while newly-installed ones are listed in *Notices to Mariners*.

In fact it would be extremely difficult to collide with an oil rig unless no watch at all was being kept. They present a confusing sight at night – a mass of lights visible from far off in clear weather, either alone or in groups, with the chief hazard being the many unlit buoys marking the end of mooring cables. Rigs on the move are attended by several tugs whose long tow-lines may be submerged and therefore invisible.

Night or day, fixed or moving, give all oil rigs a wide berth. International regulations require vessels to keep more than 500 m (1640 ft) away from rigs except to save life, if in distress or through stress of weather, though at least a mile would be wise. It seems sensible for a yacht to identify itself to those aboard, and should an up-to-date position be required any static oil rig will be an excellent and totally reliable source.

Whales

There have been a number of well-publicised accounts of yachts having close encounters with whales, and most ocean cruisers see whales at some stage. However in very few cases does a collision or any direct contact take place. Attacks by whales almost invariably take place in the vicinity of whaling fleets – now confined to the Pacific Ocean and hopefully soon to be a thing of the past even there. Otherwise the danger is of running into a whale dozing on the surface, usually at night, and as with floating debris the faster the yacht is going the greater the likelihood of serious damage. A 40 ft lightweight racing catamaran was lost on the return leg of the 1991 Azores and Back Race after hitting a whale, but it is likely she was doing at least 12 knots at the time. A cruising boat travelling at five or six knots might well have survived.

If a whale approaches the boat of its own accord, keep calm. They have a great deal in common with dolphins, including curiosity, and are only likely to react violently if startled. If there are whales in the vicinity and you suspect they may not be aware of your presence, start the engine but keep the revolutions low. If a whale seems to be taking too great an interest in your boat, one recent suggestion is to pump a cupful of toilet cleaner or other concentrated chemical out via the heads. Finally, don't forget to reach for the camera.

Fire

Serious fires aboard cruising yachts are very uncommon, particularly with the decreasing number of paraffin (kerosene) stoves and petrol (gas) engines in use. Less tolerance towards smoking may also be reflected.

Galley fires

The most common cause of flare-ups in the galley is attempting to relight a paraffin pressure stove without repriming. Fuel spillage, either of paraffin/kerosene or of methylated spirits/stove alcohol, is another possible cause and, though neither of these fuels is volatile, wood or fabric soaked in either of them will burn vigorously. It is not enough just to mop up any spillage – the area should be washed with detergent to emulsify paraffin or to dilute and render alcohol harmless. Carelessness with bottled gas is more likely to cause an explosion than a fire. Careful installation and maintenance, plus always turning off at the bottle when not in use, is the best way to guard against this risk (see Chapter 2). Galley fires have also been started by the ignition of hot fat or cooking oil – deep frying should never be risked at sea.

Engine fires

It is hard to see how a modern diesel engine could catch fire unless started by some other means. Aboard a large yacht with electrical panels sited in the engine room this might occur, but since the average yacht's engine lives alone in a boxed-in compartment well away from the switchboard this potential danger has been removed.

A fire in the engine compartment, depending on its nature, may flare up if the engine hatch is opened. The ideal way to combat this is with a permanently installed extinguisher with nozzles at all danger-points, either automatic or operable manually by remote control. Since the operator will not be near the fire, CO_2 may be used safely. An alternative is a hole in the front of the engine casing through which a hand-held extinguisher may be pointed.

Electrical fires

The chance of an electrical fire must be greatest on the older boat, where additional loads have been added into the system without wiring being upgraded. Overloading may result in overheating, and poor connections in dangerous sparks, either at the switchboard or elsewhere. Starter motors, alternators and electric anchor windlasses consume or generate very high loads and call for wiring and circuitry of the highest standard. Fuses of the correct size must always be used – keep a list of fuse ratings, and beware replacing a blown fuse with one of a higher capacity. Keep an eye on wiring generally, as even light cables can generate considerable heat.

Smoking

Smoking can be a fire hazard as well as unpleasant, and is banned below decks on most yachts. If smoking is allowed in the cockpit, care must be taken that a lighted end does not fall into an open locker or get flipped into the dinghy (a particularly common failing amongst non-sailing guests). Smoking in one's bunk *must* be forbidden.

Lightning

Perhaps surprisingly, lightning strikes seldom result in fires. However if there is thunder in the vicinity it would make sense to have an extinguisher to hand.

Firefighting equipment

CO_2 – very effective in confined spaces because it denies the fire oxygen. Dangerous, for the same reason, to the operator unless remote control is possible.
Dry powder – effective and safe below decks. Powder creates a lot of mess – but so does a fire. This type of extinguisher needs shaking regularly if the contents are not to settle and solidify. In the UK distinguished by a blue label or cannister.
Halon (BCF) – smothers the fire with foam to suffocate it. It will not damage electrical wiring or connections and is easier to clean up than dry powder, but gives off danger-ous fumes in confined areas. In the UK it has a green label or cannister.
Liquid chemicals – liable to produce toxic fumes, so generally unacceptable except in the very unlikely event of a fire actually on deck.
Water – readily available in large quantities, and could be used on a smouldering fire started by a match or cigarette end. Never use on electrical, fat or fuel-based fires.
Fire blanket – effective for smothering a small fire and particularly appropriate in the galley. It must be accessible *without* having to reach over the stove itself.

Siting of extinguishers

This is important. There must be extinguishers on both sides of any point at which a fire may start so that, wherever you or your crew are, it will be possible for you to approach the fire with the right equipment in your hands. Boats are usually well ventilated, a condition conducive to the rapid spread of fire. To contain the blaze it may be necessary to fight the fire while below deck with hatches closed, limiting the possible use of CO_2 or gas extinguishers. Yachts over a minimum size and registered sail training vessels may be subject to national maritime law regarding extinguishers and their siting.

Lifesaving equipment

Liferaft

If you already own a conventional liferaft it will need servicing by an approved centre before departure. Ask to remain and watch as it is inflated (preferably in company with your crew) but do not be tempted to pull the cord at home. Not only is the canister or valise likely to be badly damaged but the valve will probably freeze as the pressurised CO_2 expands (if used at sea the water dissipates the chill). At the testing centre the sealing gasket is first removed and the raft then inflated by air pump.

An increasing number of cruising yachtsmen are replacing their conventional liferafts with sailing tenders such as the 'Tinker' range from JM Henshaw (Marine) Ltd, which are available with CO_2 bottles and an inflatable canopy if required. Among the dedicated rafts various options are again available, including different types of container, single or double floors and more or less comprehensive emergency packs. The ocean-going yacht will obviously require the full pack, but even so an emergency 'grab bag' should be assembled and kept accessible. Suitable contents might include extra food and water, foil survival blankets, flares and possibly a hand-held VHF set. Some skippers also like to include ship's papers and passports for the duration of each passage.

Lifebuoys

At least two fluorescent lifebuoys, both equipped with automatic lights and one attached to a danbuoy, should be within reach of the helmsman ready for throwing overboard. The danbuoy pole will need a brightly coloured flag on top and a counterweight to keep it upright. The whole assembly must be carefully stowed so that danbuoy, lifebuoy, light and connecting line can be jettisoned instantly without fouling.

Danbuoy, lifebuoys, harnesses and lifejackets all benefit from having reflective tape stuck on them for location in

Running downwind in large seas under poled-out headsails – conditions in which crew on deck *must* wear harnesses. The yacht may appear relatively steady, but it would be a lengthy job to turn her round. *Photo: Mike Grubb*

the dark. Some materials do not hold their reflective quality indefinitely, so make sure that those in use at the start of the voyage are in good order.

Flares

It makes sense to carry plenty of flares, particularly of the parachute type – it is said that the first draws attention, the second confirms it wasn't an illusion and the third provides the opportunity to take a bearing. An ocean cruising yacht should carry at least a dozen, plus orange smoke flares and possibly dye markers.

Personal safety gear

Harnesses

Losing a person overboard is one of every skipper's worst nightmares, and ground rules may have to be laid down as to when harnesses are worn. Whether a harness is mandatory whenever one person is on watch alone, only at night, only if leaving the cockpit or only in bad weather must be agreed by all, but the skipper gets the last word. Having been agreed on, it *must* be observed. Wearing a harness without getting snarled up takes a little getting used to, and an inexperienced crew would be wise to practise working in a harness before needing to do so in anger.

Most harnesses are manufactured to nationally approved standards, and each person should be responsible for adjusting and stowing their own. The safety line is as important as the harness itself. It should be about 2 m (6 ft) long, with a clip at each end and preferably in the middle also. This should be seized on to the line

rather than knotted or spliced in and must be used in addition to, and not instead of, the main clip. In cooler climates there is much to be said for the harness being built into an oilskin jacket, but during a tradewind passage or in the Caribbean one may sometimes need to wear a harness without wanting the additional warmth and weight such a jacket provides.

A harness is no stronger than its point of attachment. Several through-bolted eyes will be needed in the cockpit, one for the helmsman and another within reach from inside the companionway, together with webbing jackstays running along the sidedecks.

Lifejackets

Very few adults routinely wear lifejackets, but every cruising yacht should carry enough for the maximum number who may ever sail aboard. A good lifejacket should support a heavy person with their head out of the water, even if unconscious, and be equipped with a whistle and possibly an automatic light which will activate when immersed.

Regulations in some countries require lifejackets to be carried in the dinghy when going ashore (leaving the problem of what to do with them once landed), and non-swimming guests should always be given the opportunity to put one on.

Personal flares packs

Several types of miniature flares, small enough to fit in the pocket, are available and could prove invaluable at night or in high seas.

Man overboard

Every boat should have its own drill to recover a person in the water, and this must reflect both the boat's handling characteristics and the capabilities and physical strength of the crew left aboard. Too many of the drills commonly taught assume a crew of at least four and very often concentrate of doing the recovery under sail. This results in a fine exercise in seamanship, but the fact remains that those people who have actually had to recover a person from the water in bad weather have almost without exception chosen to do so under power, whether or not the mainsail was still hoisted.

Aboard larger yachts there is much to be said for each person carrying a whistle, with which to rouse the watch below for man overboard or any other emergency. However on the average yacht with her crew of three or four at most – and more likely two – formal drills are less appropriate. Even the oft-repeated rule that one person should concentrate solely on watching the person in the water must be disregarded. It therefore becomes doubly important to get the danbuoy assembly over immediately and then stay nearby, or if the boat cannot immediately turn (perhaps because she is under downwind rig) to establish an accurate reciprocal course on which to backtrack.

Opinion is divided as to the best way to achieve the former with the sails still hoisted, but either heaving-to or sheeting everything in hard and lashing the tiller to leeward to make the boat go round in small tack/gybe circles can be performed by one person (who is themselves likely to be suffering from shock). It is worth finding out how your boat performs both these manoeuvres in a variety of wind and sea states. If one can remain close to the person in the water, and they are not injured, there is a good chance of them being able to reach the boat rather than vice versa.

If the yacht is running under spinnaker or twin jibs, at least some sail handling will have to be done before she can turn and this is another good reason for not attaching jibs directly to pole ends (see Chapter 3). It takes a great deal less time to hand a jib leaving the pole in place than to recover both, and roller jibs can obviously be got rid of much more quickly than conventional hanked sails. Provided a relatively straight course has been steered – if she has been under self-steering it should not have been disturbed – now is the time to get the engine on *after recovering any trailing lines*, including the log. The practice of throwing handy floating objects such as cockpit cushions to provide a 'return trail' also makes good sense.

Recovery and lifting gear

Having got back to the victim the first essential is to attach them to the boat by any method available, and if they are unable to help themselves by this stage the dilemma arises as to whether another person should go overboard to assist. There is no hard-and-fast answer to this – I know of one case in which both victim and rescuer were lost, another in which it might well have saved a man. It cannot even be considered unless the crew left aboard will be strong enough to recover both.

One advantage the yacht on an ocean passage may well have over her home-waters counterpart is to be traversing warmer seas – the person in the water is less likely to be suffering from hypothermia and is therefore much more likely to be able to take an active part in their own rescue. They may also be wearing lighter clothing to become heavy and waterlogged.

It is worth experimenting to discover the position in which your boat will lie most nearly stationary in the water under both bare poles and a range of sail combinations. Because nearly all conventional recovery drills are intended to be carried out under sail they assume a head-to-wind position, but if under power alone (perhaps having dropped or rolled up twin headsails) many boats will blow their bows off as soon as they are no longer making way. If a boat is intent on lying tail-to-wind it is probably best to let her do so.

Recovery is nearly always easiest on the lee side, generally amidships. A fit person who is not too exhausted may be able to climb a boarding ladder with assistance from above, or a large crew physically to pull someone from the water, but more likely some form of lifting gear will be required. Again this depends on the yacht, her crew and her resources. Some recommend a part-inflated rubber dinghy – or the liferaft – others a sail rigged as a scoop (probably easier in theory than in practice). If a harness or makeshift sling can be tied around the victim then lifting and swinging inboard on a halyard or via a purchase on the boom-end might be easiest, and can be practised from the dinghy.

The bottom line to all man overboard situations is that they should not be allowed to occur in the first place. A properly planned cockpit and deck incorporating non-skid surfacing and plenty of handholds, together with firm rules on when harnesses are to be worn, are the best way of keeping the crew on board where they belong.

The singlehander

One might expect singlehanders to devote considerable thought to the problem of getting back aboard should the worst occur, but strangely this seems seldom to be the case. Most accept that if they should go overboard unharnessed while the boat is moving fast under automatic steering, that will be it. A very few tow a knotted or looped line, others have arranged lanyards with which to release a boarding ladder or can climb up their self-steering gear, and many are punctilious about wearing a harness – or at least claim to be.

Possibly the fact of not having others to worry about makes their generally fatalistic attitude more understandable. There is no doubt that sailing singlehanded entails a greater element of risk than sailing with crew, and going overboard is only one aspect of it. Give it some thought.

Illness and injury

Neither injury nor serious illness is frequently heard of aboard cruising boats. By far the commonest illness, which can affect most people at some time or other, is seasickness. Fortunately, this is usually a passing phase only and after a couple of days most people recover and become immune for the rest of the voyage. Of the various remedies on the market, Stugeron seems to be the most effective of the pills and Transderm (an adhesive patch worn behind the ear) has also had excellent reports, but though available over the counter in the States must be obtained on prescription in the UK.

Medical and dental check-ups before departure are an

obvious precaution, and while a chronic condition should not necessarily prevent anyone from crossing oceans it is only fair for the rest of the crew to know the details. A good supply of medication or drugs will obviously be needed, and these should be accompanied by a doctor's certificate to show to customs officials. Many years ago there was a fashion for ocean sailors to have their appendix removed, but unless it has already given trouble this seems over cautious. It is worth remembering that during the typical Atlantic cruise a yacht will only be out of touch for a very small part of the time.

Accidents are much more likely to happen ashore than in the familiar environment on board, particularly if sensible precautions are taken against burns and scalds while cooking in heavy weather and against accidental gybes (when the mainsheet and carriage can cause nearly as much damage as the boom itself). However the risk is there, and everybody should have a knowledge of first aid. In addition it is worth carrying a book on the subject (see Appendix A).

The first aid kit

A medicine chest should not just be bought over the counter in a yacht chandlery. Either consult your doctor or a first aid manual and lay in the basic medicines to deal with a whole spectrum of minor complaints from constipation to dysentery, from stomach ache to sunburn. Powerful painkillers and broad spectrum antibiotics are also essential. Do not forget a clinical thermometer, a sling, assorted elasticated bandages (strains are amongst the most common of minor injuries), thumb and finger stalls and plenty of sticking plasters. There should also be a hot-water bottle aboard.

Blood transfusions

With the increasing spread of the HIV virus (AIDS) in some parts of the world, the possible need for a blood transfusion – or even the stitching of a relatively minor injury – is a growing worry. The best way of approaching the latter problem is to carry a pack of sterile equipment including needles and syringes, available in the UK from Masta (tel: 071–631 4408) or IPS (tel: 061–928 3672) or from some larger chemists.

Blood transfusions pose more of a problem. It is not possible to carry an emergency supply of blood or plasma aboard because of the controlled storage conditions necessary, though if speed is not of the essence British subjects abroad can usually be supplied with blood from the UK. Another possibility might be for one member of the crew – or indeed a volunteer from another yacht – to donate blood for the immediate use of the victim. In all events, having blood groups checked before departure is an obvious precaution. Local Blood Transfusion Centres will be able to offer more detailed advice.

Security

Although the subject of security when sailing foreign waters is often brought up by those who have not done so, it is not generally amongst the primary concerns of those who have spent much time in foreign parts. Stories of crews being injured or even murdered aboard their yachts

receive a great deal of publicity, not least because (unlike muggings on city streets) they are so rare – about one every four or five years. As there must be at least 5000 yachts in the Lesser Antilles this makes the chances of attack something like one to 25,000. All the island governments rely heavily on tourism for income, and are well aware that one unpleasant incident could cost them dearly. They also know that one account will get passed on by word of mouth, gaining embellishments until it becomes three or four separate incidents.

Some theft occurs pretty well everywhere, at home as well as abroad, and in both cases there are two kinds of thief. The serious one will steal valuables for which there is always a ready sale, the petty thief picks up any trifle left within reach. The first will steal outboard engines and rubber dinghies, and has even been known to unscrew winches from yachts left unattended on moorings. The second will take the oars or rowlocks from a dinghy on the beach, or a coil of rope left on deck and within easy reach. Neither are likely to resort to physical violence unless extremely frightened. Sensible precautions include never leaving the boat unlocked, marking the dinghy indelibly and unmistakably, and in some areas chaining up both dinghy and outboard when ashore and, overnight, to the stern of the yacht.

Piracy at sea is also another favourite topic for discussion before departure. The fact remains that in Atlantic waters piracy is almost totally confined to those areas in which drug smuggling is rife, notably off the coast of Colombia and in a few areas of the Bahamas. There have been no cases in the Lesser Antilles for decades. By all means spend uneventful watches dreaming up defence systems – parachute flares fired bazooka-style are one favourite – but on a normal cruise the chances of ever having to put such a scheme into action are virtually nil.

Firearms

One gets the impression that fewer and fewer yachts are carrying guns, but since most countries demand their declaration and removal ashore for safekeeping it may simply be that those who do chose to carry them do not talk about it. It is obviously a personal decision, but as a means of defence there is a great deal to be said against firearms (carrying a gun because you like to keep your eye in by potting at floating cans is something entirely different).

Producing a gun will almost certainly make any situation more dangerous, if only by frightening the attacker, and unless you are *certain* that someone coming alongside after dark is up to no good you run the risk of shooting a fisherman, a local teenager (perhaps with petty theft in mind) or even another yachtsman. Should this occur, and particularly if the victim is a local person, justice would not be weighted in your favour. A bright floodlight with which to illuminate the deck, operable from below, is almost as good a deterrent and can safely be turned on at the least hint of alarm. Some people also like the idea of being able to lock themselves in.

If the decision is made to carry firearms of any kind, it would be sensible to contact the authorities of all the countries one is planning to visit, well before departure, to ask for copies of their current regulations.

PART II – PASSAGES AND LANDFALLS

10 THE NORTH ATLANTIC – BACKGROUND

Routes, seasons and timing

Among the many things which go to make a successful ocean cruise, two are essential. One is to be in the right place at the right time, the other to move in the right direction. It is an over simplification, but a useful one, to think of the North Atlantic as a giant roundabout always turning clockwise. The ocean currents revolve in a clockwise direction and the weather systems (though not always the local winds) do too. Both have their centre west

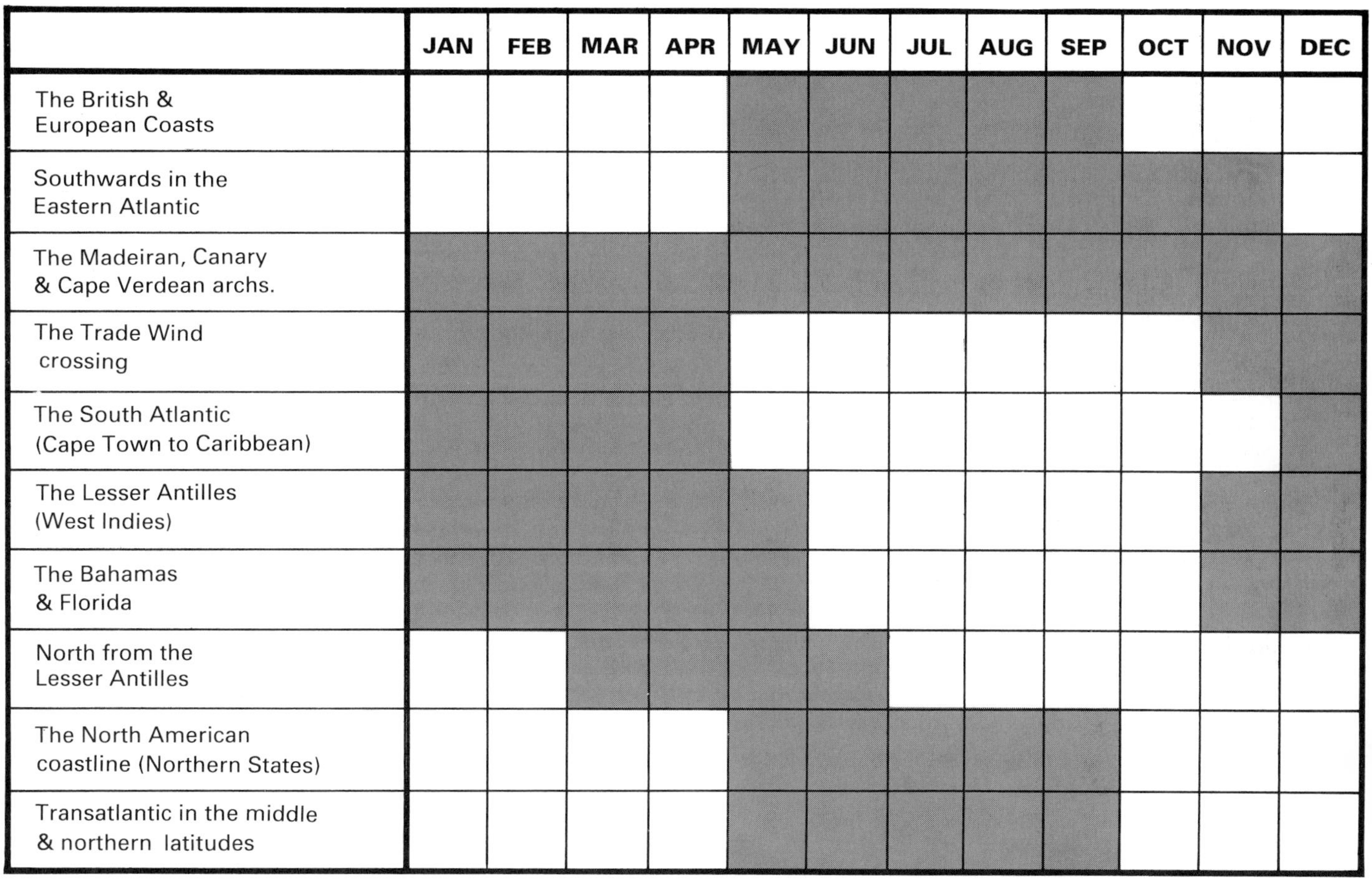

	JAN	FEB	MAR	APR	MAY	JUN	JUL	AUG	SEP	OCT	NOV	DEC
The British & European Coasts					■	■	■	■	■			
Southwards in the Eastern Atlantic					■	■	■	■	■	■	■	
The Madeiran, Canary & Cape Verdean archs.	■	■	■	■	■	■	■	■	■	■	■	■
The Trade Wind crossing	■	■	■	■							■	■
The South Atlantic (Cape Town to Caribbean)	■	■	■	■								■
The Lesser Antilles (West Indies)	■	■	■	■							■	■
The Bahamas & Florida	■	■	■	■								■
North from the Lesser Antilles			■	■								
The North American coastline (Northern States)					■	■	■	■	■	■		
Transatlantic in the middle & northern latitudes					■	■	■	■	■	■		

Fig 4 Where to be and when. Shaded areas indicate best times for cruising or passage-making.

of the Azores. Keeping within the limits of a favourable wind system and receiving assistance from helpful currents may involve you in extra miles, but the sailing will be far more pleasant and you may well reach your destination quicker than by a more direct route.

No matter where you begin your Atlantic cruise, hop on to the roundabout and let it help you on your way. From America or Canada, head east during the summer; from northern Europe, head south in summer or early autumn; from Madeira or the Canary Islands, wait until November or December and make for the trade wind zone (perhaps with a stop in the Cape Verde Islands) before heading west. From the West Indies, go north or north-west in the late spring. Figure 4 shows, in simplified form, the best times and seasons for each cruising area or ocean passage. Detailed information will be found in the chapter relevant to each.

Winds and weather

Winds and weather in the North Atlantic are dominated by the permanent high pressure in mid-ocean and by the relatively low pressures surrounding it. Winds therefore tend to blow clockwise and slightly outward around the Azores High. This is true for the eastern side of the ocean to about 45°N, and for the trade wind latitudes north of about 10°N and on towards the Bahamas and Florida. There are modifications elsewhere, for the land mass of North America, together with the warm Gulf Stream and its confluence with the cold Labrador Current, results in unstable conditions in that region. These give rise to the typical weather patterns of the British Isles – a succession of lows which form over the North Atlantic and are then propelled east or north-east towards Europe. Each of these depressions creates its own wind system in its immediate locality – anticlockwise around the low. In spite of this, the whole area from west to east, in the forties and fifties of latitude, is known as 'the Westerlies', indicating that the wind blows from that quarter more often than not. Gales are frequent in this area at all seasons, though generally less severe in summer. Details of weather forecast transmissions will be found at the end of this chapter.

Hurricanes

Tropical revolving storms, or hurricanes, are usually confined to the months of June to mid-November. As the old rhyme has it:

> June, too soon
> July, stand by
> August, come she must
> September, remember
> October, all over

Actually this is not entirely accurate, as Figure 5 shows.

Hurricanes currently average just under twelve per year, by no means all of which touch land, though it is speculated that incidence may increase if even minimal global warming takes place. They often begin life in the vicinity of the Cape Verde Islands, move westward across the Atlantic towards the Lesser Antilles, and then follow totally unpredictable courses. The entire Caribbean, the

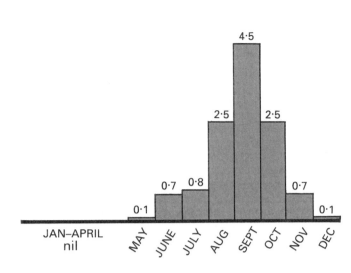

Fig 5 Hurricane months in the Caribbean.

Bahamas, Bermuda and the eastern seaboard of America lie in the hurricane belt, though they are much less frequent in the southern islands and along the coast of South America. The US Coast Guard provides a monitoring and forecasting service of which yachtsmen can take advantage.

In a typical one-year Atlantic cruise there is no need to be in the hurricane zone during the dangerous season. However an increasing number of cruising yachts are spending the summer in the area – when the best advice is probably to stay well south – and others may be caught soon after arrival by a late season hurricane. It is even possible to feel the muted effects of one, in terms of swell and perhaps an increase in the wind, up to two thousand miles away. If remaining in the area during the season when a hurricane might be encountered, keep one ear to the radio and remain within reach of a good 'hurricane hole'. These are listed in all the local cruising guides, but the really good ones are few in number and will fill up rapidly.

Fog

When a south or south-west wind takes warm moist air over the cold Labrador Current, fog becomes widespread on the coast of Maine and in the region of the Grand Banks. It is most prevalent in spring and summer, and can be expected on about ten days out of each month. The whole of the coastal areas on the eastern side of the North Atlantic, from Norway southward, are subject to fog.

British and European yachtsmen who tend to associate fog with light winds or calms should be aware that this is often not the case in the western Atlantic, where fog may be accompanied by steady winds of 25 knots or more.

Ice

Icebergs are spawned by the breaking up of pack ice in the Arctic and 'calving' of glaciers, and are then carried south

Ordnance Bay, the inner anchorage of English Harbour, Antigua, is a landlocked 'hurricane hole' in which boats have ridden out the worst of storms. *Photo: Eric Hiscock*

by wind and currents. They are almost totally confined to an area north of 40°N and west of 40°W, though stray bergs have very occasionally been found well south or east of this, and reach their greatest extent between March and September. The International Ice Patrol locates the position of bergs and gives radio reports.

Ocean currents

There is a close but complex relationship between prevailing winds and ocean currents. That currents will be set up wherever the surface water is continually blown in one direction is fairly obvious, but that this should in turn give rise to coastal currents may be less so. Basically, the head of moving water must go somewhere on reaching the continental margins, and is generally deflected towards the 'intake' area of the next major wind-driven current.

Thus the north-east trade wind gives rises to the North Equatorial Current, flowing east to west across the Atlantic between about 10° and 25°N. This creates a head of water in the Gulf of Mexico and the Caribbean Sea, which emerges through the Strait of Florida and, named the Gulf Stream, flows in a north-easterly direction until it meets the Labrador Current flowing south around Newfoundland and Nova Scotia. This causes the Labrador Current to divide, one part forcing a passage down between the Gulf Stream and the American coast and the other turning eastward and combining with the Gulf Stream to form the North Atlantic Current.

The North Atlantic Current, urged on by the prevailing westerly winds, eventually meets the obstruction of the British Isles and the continent of Europe. Again it divides, one stream going north of Scotland and the other being deflected south-east and then south to form the Azores

Snugged up into the mangroves in Ordnance Bay when a late season hurricane threatened in 1984, with a cat's cradle of lines to hold *Wrestler* secure. In the event there was little wind and the mosquitoes feasted. *Photo: Anne Hammick*

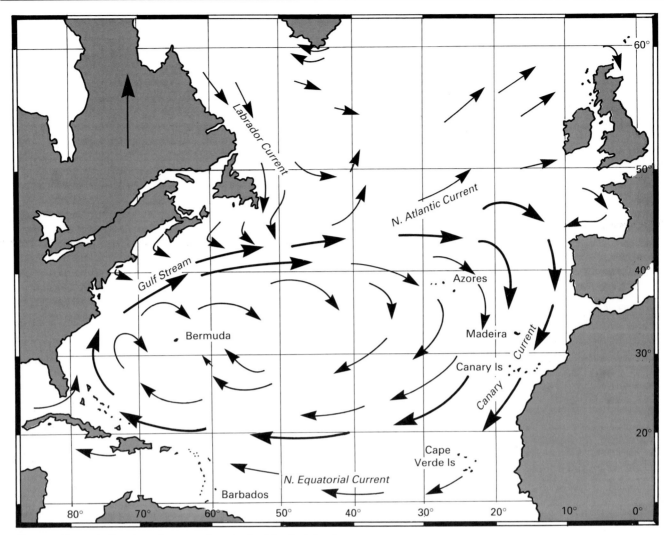

Chart 1 General direction of current flow in the North Atlantic.

Current, the Portuguese Current and finally the Canaries Current. This in turn feeds the embryo North Equatorial Current to complete the giant circle.

There are of course local features, such as the currents flowing into the English Channel, the Bay of Biscay and the Mediterranean, but these have little importance beyond their own margins.

When a current flows past a continental coastline its course tends to be more or less orderly, but if it encounters islands in its path, or is free to wander in mid-ocean, its track may split in two or become very ragged at the edges. In some places there are well-documented changes of course, due to land masses, and there are areas in which eddies or counter-currents occur predictably. The study of these can be important because parallel courses only a few miles apart may be in waters moving in opposite directions. When this happens the choice of the right route could make a difference of thirty miles to the day's run.

There is no means of measuring in mid-ocean what a current is doing – you can measure only what it has done. It is therefore important to learn all one can from recorded information in order to benefit from a favourable current whenever possible and to know how much to allow in the dead reckoning.

The Gulf Stream is carefully monitored by the US Coast Guard, and their 1600 and 2200 GMT weather forecasts from NMN in Portsmouth, Virginia (see end of this chapter) give the co-ordinates of the West or Cold Wall (the line of demarcation between the Gulf Stream and the Labrador Current flowing along the US coast) the speed and position of the middle of the Gulf Stream at various latitudes and the position of major established eddies. That this costly service is considered to be necessary emphasises that it cannot be predicted – it has to be observed and reported.

Sources of information

Until very recently there was no route planning information compiled specifically for yachts, and when the classic *Ocean Passages for the World* talked about sailing vessels it meant square-riggers. The same is true of both the British and American *Sailing Directions*, though this is not to say that these publications do not contain much information relevant to all vessels, sail or power.

Detailed information regarding prevailing winds and currents, percentage frequency of gales and calms, wave and swell heights, hurricane tracks, icebergs and fog is presented on the Admiralty *Routeing Charts* (BA Chart

5124, monthly numbers 1–12) and the US *Pilot Charts* (DMA Pilot Chart 16, quarterly, three months in each). These charts, which are more or less identical in form, are compiled using reports from merchant vessels, naval units and weather ships collected over a long period. While they can only show the average, they give an excellent basis for timing and route planning.

Much the same information, presented visually on monthly charts with explanatory text, but in a more handy size and format for the yacht with a small chart table, is to be found in the *Atlantic Pilot Atlas* compiled by James Clarke. This covers the North Atlantic and Caribbean in considerable detail and the South Atlantic and Mediterranean in more condensed form.

The opposite approach is taken by Jimmy Cornell in *World Cruising Routes*. Rather than presenting seasonal information for the entire area he takes the same approach used in this book and its earlier editions – that of discussing each area individually, together with the various passages between them. There is much to be said for consulting at least one representative of each approach.

Charts

Charts will need to be bought over a period of time. Basic ocean passage charts (see Chart 2) will be found useful for reference in the early stages of planning and again later for plotting daily positions at sea. As each section of the intended route is studied the relevant coastal passage

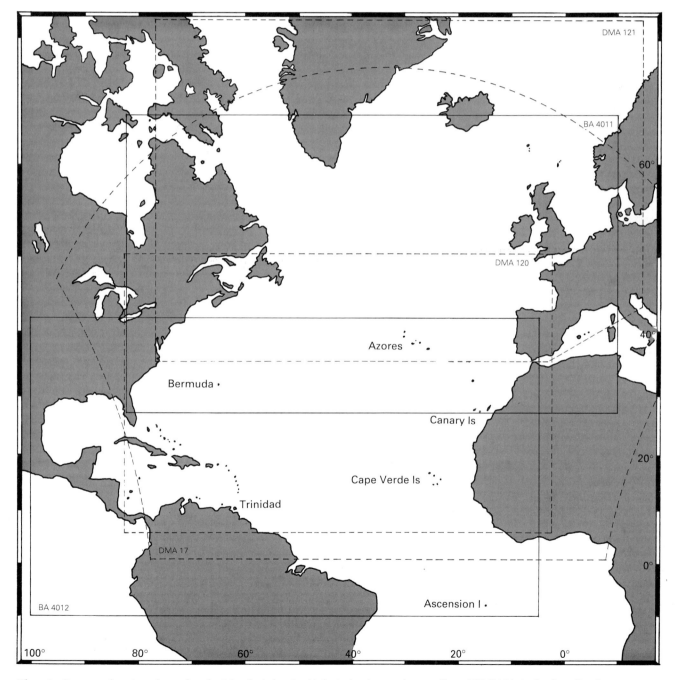

Chart 2 Passage planning charts for the North Atlantic. (Admiralty in continuous lines, US DMA in broken lines).

planning charts will be found useful –lists are included in each chapter. These small scale charts carry little detail, and it will not matter if they are months or a few years out of date by the time the cruise commences.

No attempt has been made to provide a comprehensive list of all charts available for each area. Far too many are published, and in any case needs will vary according to the route chosen. First plan your itinerary – where you intend to stop, where you will make coastal passages and where you will be well offshore – then consult a current chart list and order from an official agent. Allow plenty of time for the order to be filled, but do not collect them until shortly before departure. This is particularly important in the UK where charts should be corrected up to the date of sale, less so in the United States where uncorrected latest editions will normally be supplied.

Ocean passage charts

Coverage	Admiralty	US
Northern N Atlantic	4011 (1:10,000,000)	121 (1:5,870,000)
Southern N Atlantic	4012 (1:10,000,000)	120 (1:6,331,100)
Gnomonic (Great Circle)	5095 (1:13,500,000)	17 (Variable scale)

Pilots, guides and sailing directions

Pilots and guides fall into two distinct types – official publications intended primarily for the use of shipping, and those written purely with the yachtsman in mind.

Chief amongst the former are the *Sailing Directions* published by the British Admiralty, the US Defense Mapping Agency and the Canadian Hydrographic Service. The boundaries of each volume are clearly delineated, and a complete list and accompanying area charts forms Appendix C.

The Atlantic margins are particularly rich in cruising guides and yachtsmen's pilots, and a comprehensive list of these is included as Appendix B. However it should be remembered that privately researched guides vary dramatically in their content and accuracy, and may also continue to be sold long after becoming out-of-date.

Both official and unofficial pilots applicable to each area are listed in the relevant chapter.

Weather forecast transmissions

Ocean weather forecast areas tend to be large and may frequently be relevant to several different passages. Times and frequencies may be altered; if no broadcasts are received, consult the *Admiralty List of Radio Signals*.

Eastern Atlantic Ocean
Radio France Internationale: 36–hour forecasts, including gale warnings, synopses and area forecasts, broadcast in French at about 0555, 1130 and 1850 GMT though times are flexible to fit programme schedules. Frequencies 6175, 15300, 15365, 17620, and 21645 kHz. Normally broken

into four regions, each of which may be further subdivided. Forecasts for areas south of 35°N may be included during some parts of the year. Regions:

A: 45°N / 55°N – 22°30′ W / 35°W
B: 45°N / 55°N – 10°W / 22°30′ W
C: 35°N / 45°N – 22°30′ W / 35°W
D: 35°N / 45°N – 10°W / 22°30′ W

European coastal waters to 15°W
British Broadcasting Corporation: shipping forecasts daily on 198 kHz/1515 m at 0048, 0555, 1355 and 1750 local time (effectively GMT in winter and GMT+1 or British Summer Time from mid-March until early October). Includes a synopsis of North Atlantic weather patterns, area forecasts and weather reports from coastal stations. The 0033 forecast extends to 35°N 'Trafalgar', others terminate at 41°N 'Finisterre'.
Forecasts for inshore waters: daily on 198 kHz/1515 m at 0038, following the shipping forecast. Also on 1215 kHz/ 247 m at 0655. Nearly all British weather forecasts give wind speeds in terms of the Beaufort Scale.

All those countries with Atlantic coastlines broadcast weather forecasts for their own national waters, generally in their own language. In addition there are many regional forecasts on local radio stations. Current details will be found in *Reed's Nautical Almanac*.

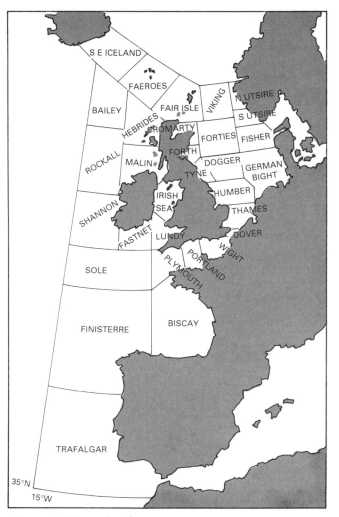

Chart 3 BBC weather forecast areas.

Southern North Atlantic

Radio France Internationale: forecasts for areas south of 35°N may be included at the times and frequencies already listed during some parts of the year.

Caribbean Sea – Lesser Antilles – Bahamas

Curacao (PJC): Caribbean Sea, North Atlantic south of 25°N and west of 45°W. On 8725.1 kHz at 1305 GMT.
US Coast Guard (NMR): from San Juan, Puerto Rico, covering Caribbean Sea, Puerto Rico and Virgin Islands. On VHF channel 22 and 2670 MHz at 0305, 1210, 1505 and 2210 GMT.
Nassau, Bahamas (C6N): Bahamas and adjacent waters. On VHF channel 27 and 2522 kHz on the odd hours (0100, 0300, etc) GMT.
Radio Antilles: used to transmit weather forecasts for the Caribbean area on 930 kHz at 0810 and 1820 local time. Unfortunately it has been off the air since its Montserrat transmitter was damaged by Hurricane *Hugo* in 1989, but may return.

Almost every island in the Caribbean has at least one radio station, most of which put out weather reports of varying accuracy. All will carry frequent and repeated hurricane warnings should one be in the vicinity.

US coastal waters

Continuous forecasts on US VHF channels WX 1–4 (162.40, 162.475, 162.55 and 163.275 MHz) for inshore waters to about 25 miles offshore.

Florida (WOM): AT&T broadcast weather forecasts at 1300 and 2300 in the 4, 8, 13, 17 and 22 MHz bands. Frequencies are:

SHIP'S RX	SHIP'S TX
4363	4071
8722	8198
13092	12245
17242	16360
22738	22042

New Jersey (WOO): AT&T broadcast weather forecasts at 1200 and 2200 in the 4 and 8 MHz bands. Frequencies are:

SHIP'S RX	SHIP'S TX
4387	4095
8749	8225

Canadian coastal waters

Continuous forecasts on US VHF channels WX5–6

(161.650 and 161.775 MHz). These are the receive frequencies on European duplex channels 21 and 83.

Most American and Canadian local radio stations broadcast weather forecasts for their own areas. Current details will be found in the US edition of *Reed's Nautical Almanac*.

Western Atlantic Ocean and Gulf Stream

US Coast Guard (NMN): from Portsmouth, Virginia, covering the West Central N Atlantic, South West N Atlantic, Gulf of Mexico, Caribbean Sea and New England waters. Boundary co-ordinates are listed at each transmission. US Coast Guard HF SSB frequencies are:

SHIP'S RX	SHIP'S TX
4426	4234
6501	6200
8764	8240
13089	12242
17314	16432

Listen in the following bands at the appropriate times for area forecasts:

GMT	Band					Area
0400	4 MHz	6 MHz	8 MHz	–	–	Offshore
0530	4 MHz	6 MHz	8 MHz	–	–	High seas
1000	4 MHz	6 MHz	8 MHz	–	–	Offshore
1130	–	6 MHz	8 MHz	13 MHz	–	High seas
1600	–	6 MHz	8 MHz	13 MHz	–	Offshore/ Gulf Stream
1730	–	–	8 MHz	13 MHz	17 MHz	High seas
2200	–	6 MHz	8 MHz	13 MHz	–	Offshore/ Gulf Stream
2330	–	6 MHz	8 MHz	13 MHz	–	High seas

National Bureau of Standards (WWV): from Fort Collins, Colorado, gives synoptic chart, weather report and storm warnings for the North Atlantic, Caribbean Sea and Gulf of Mexico. On 2.5, 5, 10, 15 and 20 MHz at 08 and 09 minutes past each hour.

Bermuda

Bermuda (ZBM): storm warnings, synoptic report and forecast for Western North Atlantic. On VHF channel 27 and 2582 kHz at 1235 and 2035 GMT.

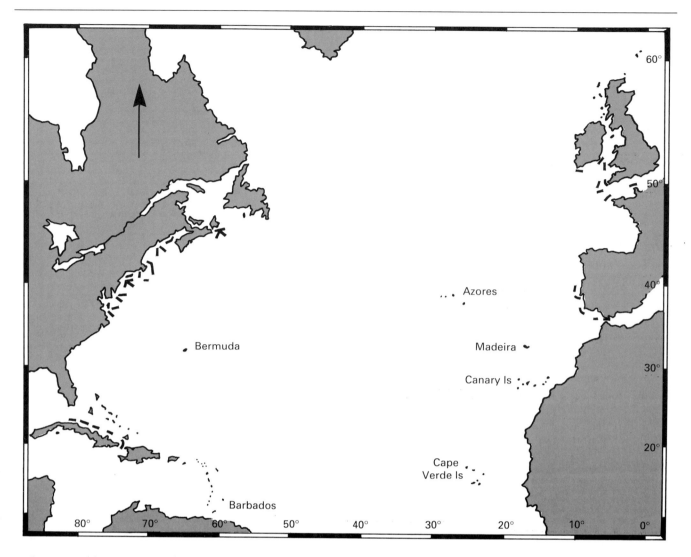

Chart 4 Traffic Separation Schemes in the North Atlantic. Based on information from the International Maritime Organisation. Consult large scale charts for individual details.

Traffic Separation Schemes

In many areas where shipping is heavy – particularly around headlands, where a number of major routes converge and in constricted waters – IMCO Traffic Separation Schemes have been set up. Typically they consist of two lanes down which vessels pass port-to-port, a central separation zone, and usually an inshore traffic zone. The rules governing separation schemes are detailed in the International Regulations for Preventing Collisions at Sea, but so far as yachts are concerned the most important points are as follows:

1 As far as possible avoid crossing traffic lanes, but if obliged to do so cross on a heading as nearly as practicable at right angles to the general direction of traffic flow. (It should be noted that it is the *heading* rather than the *ground* track which is to be at right angles to the traffic flow)

2 Use inshore traffic zones whenever possible

3 Do not impede the safe passage of a power-driven vessel following a traffic lane

Traffic Separation Schemes are nearly always monitored by coast guards or other official bodies, usually by radar, and more than one yachtsman has been prosecuted for ignoring the regulations. It seems that a sailing yacht being unable to comply with the rules without resorting to her engine is not considered any defence. This of course begs the question of the engineless yacht.

11 THE BRITISH AND EUROPEAN COASTS

Regional weather

The Atlantic coast of Europe reaches from 36°N at Gibraltar to the Arctic Circle and beyond, the vast majority of yachts staying south of 60°N. The cruising season around the coasts of Britain and France runs from May until early October, extending later into the year as one progresses south.

From the latitude of northern Spain northwards the prevailing winds blow from the west or south-west, drawing air directly from the Atlantic Ocean. This encourages an unstable weather pattern, and yachtsmen used to the more settled conditions usually found off the east coast of America may be startled by how quickly conditions can change. The BBC shipping forecasts covering the area are generally very accurate and it is important to take them seriously (see Chapter 10).

The Bay of Biscay has long had a reputation for particularly unpleasant weather, dating back to the days of the square-riggers and beyond. While this may not be entirely deserved during the summer months, setting off across Biscay too late in the year is foolhardy. To risk catching a gale without sufficient sea-room and before the crew have settled into their stride is an appalling way to start any long cruise, and all but the largest yachts should think in terms of reaching Spanish waters before the end of August.

A large area of low pressure forms annually over the Iberian Peninsula in early summer, dominating weather patterns until late autumn. The western edge of this depression gives rise to the Portuguese trades, northerly winds which blow parallel to the coast in a band some one hundred miles wide. These winds are most reliable from July through to September or October, and may be augmented near the coast by strong sea breezes, sometimes giving rise to strong or even gale force winds for a short time in the afternoon.

If making a diversion into Gibraltar, the wind may be more variable in both strength and direction after passing Cape St Vincent and, on reaching the Strait of Gibraltar, be blowing either straight in or straight out. There is a constant flow of current from the Atlantic into the Mediterranean, due to the high rate of evaporation in the confined area of the Mediterranean Sea. The speed of this current is affected partly by the tide, which retards or accelerates it, and partly by the wind. In moderate weather there is no difficulty in beating into Gibraltar, but against the levanter (the local name for a strong easterly wind) it may be impossible for a small yacht to make much progress, due to the steep seas kicked up by wind against current. In that case, shelter may be sought in one of the Spanish ports westward of the Strait. A strong westerly or south-westerly wind which reinforces the current can make it virtually impossible for a yacht to get out from Gibraltar and into the Atlantic. Even a very slight easing of the wind strength does, however, make an immediate and remarkable difference and as soon as this happens good progress may be made by hugging the Spanish coast as far as Tarifa, after which the strength of the current falls off rapidly.

Once clear of the coasts of Spain and Portugal, the chances are that a breeze from a northerly quarter may be found to take the yacht towards the Madeiran archipelago or the Canaries.

Currents

The North Atlantic Current divides in two before reaching the British Isles, one part running up the west coast of Scotland towards Scandinavia and the other deflected south-west and then south past the Iberian Peninsula. Smaller branches enter the English Channel and Irish Sea. The relatively warm water of what was previously the Gulf Stream provides a moderating influence on temperatures in western Europe, which tend to be much less extreme than those inland.

The Portuguese Current, again part of the vast clockwise circulation of water in the North Atlantic, runs in a generally southerly direction from Cape Finisterre to the Canary Islands where it becomes known as the Canary Current. It is reinforced by the constant flow through the Strait of Gibraltar mentioned above.

Tides and tidal streams

Both tidal range and strength of stream vary a great deal along the Atlantic coast of Europe. Greatest spring range among the relevant ports listed in Part III is the 6.1 m (20 ft) experienced at Brest, while the least is the 1.1 m (3 ft 7 in) found at Gibraltar. However ranges of 12 m (40 ft) may occur in some areas, notably around the Channel Islands and the adjacent French coast and in the Bristol Channel.

These great ranges naturally give rise to strong tidal streams, including the 'Severn Bore' – an almost vertical wave which may travel up the River Severn at considerable speed – and the infamous 'Alderney Race' between Alderney and the Normandy peninsula which can reach nearly ten knots on the flood. Tidal streams can be particularly strong off headlands, with heavy overfalls. If these are marked on the chart it is important to keep clear of them, but tide rips and overfalls can occur off most headlands and one must always be prepared for this. Strong winds against the stream will aggravate the situation and can create dangerous conditions.

Details of tidal ranges, streams and races will be found in the various local nautical almanacs.

Approach and landfall

Approaching the European coastline there is always the chance of strong onshore winds and poor visibility, and unless equipped with one of the electronic aids discussed in Chapter 5, the yacht's position may be uncertain. If this

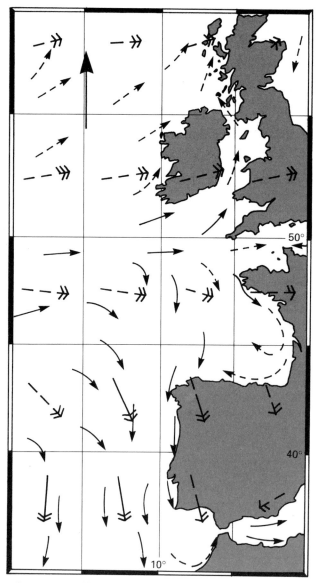

Chart 5 Prevailing winds and currents off the coast of Europe – August. (Winds in feathered arrows, currents in solid arrows.) Based on information from the *Atlantic Pilot Atlas.*

is the case the best action may be to heave-to and await an improvement before closing the coast.

A network of coastal marine DF beacons with ranges of up to 200 miles cover the area, though these are currently undergoing major reorganisation during which some will be discontinued and others retained on changed frequencies. In contrast to many parts of the world the upkeep of lights and buoyage is excellent and it is rare for any major navigational aid to be out of action for more than a few hours.

The Scottish coast
Boats making direct for Scandinavia, and passing round the north of Scotland, should have no problems provided they are well clear of Rockall (57°37′ N 13°41′ W). The St Kilda Island group and the Flannan Islands, 40 miles and 20 miles off the west coast of the Outer Hebrides, should be well clear to starboard, but Sula Sgeir (59°06′ N 6°11′ W) and North Rona (59°08′ N 5°50′ W) could be

close to your route and a hazard to be avoided in thick weather. Both are now lit. The long range DF beacons from Barra Head round to the Orkney and Shetland Islands should enable a vessel to avoid all dangers.

Do not pass through the Pentland Firth, between the north Scottish coast and the Orkney Islands, in conditions of strong winds or poor visibility. Shelter can be sought in the lee of Lewis by passing round the Butt of Lewis, and Stornoway on the east side is an official entry port.

If the prevailing or forecast conditions make it inadvisable to approach the mainland coast, seek shelter on the east coast of the Outer Hebrides by making up to the north, passing east of Barra Head. The best haven would then be Loch Boisdale harbour on South Uist. Strong tidal streams and dangerous overfalls can exist off Barra Head – keep at least three miles off. Bearings on the DF beacon on Oigh Sgeir in conjunction with Barra Head will help locate Loch Boisdale in thick weather. When anchoring in the Hebrides beware of kelp. A fisherman or Herreshoff anchor may prove best.

The Irish coast
If making for Crosshaven in Cork harbour on the south Irish coast, the DF beacon on Mizen Head, and subsequently the beacon on Round Island in the Scilly Isles, both with a range of 200 miles, may be found useful. Early shelter could be sought in Castletown in Bear Haven on the north side of Bantry Bay, but this would need either good visibility or electronic navigation aids, as identifying the coast can be difficult and approaching the wrong bay would be dangerous. In thick weather it would be best to stand off the southern Irish coast until Kinsale DF beacon is picked up (50 miles range). Shelter can be found in the lee of the Old Head of Kinsale and Kinsale Harbour entered or the yacht continue to Crosshaven or Cork.

The English coast
If making for Falmouth or Plymouth, the Bishop Rock lighthouse marking the south-western extremity of the Scilly Isles is the traditional first landfall in good visibility. The DF beacon on Round Island in the Scilly Isles can be picked up 200 miles out and crossed with Mizen Head in southern Ireland to establish a position. Subsequently the beacon at Ushant off the French coast, with 100 mile range, and that at Lizard Point with a 70 miles range, may be found useful.

There can be strong tidal streams off the Bishop Rock, and overfalls on the Pol Bank, three miles to the southwest. There may also be strong streams off Lizard Point and heavy overfalls extending to the south for three miles or more. Give these points a wide berth, and in strong south-westerlies make no attempt to close the coast until well round the Lizard, when a course for Falmouth can be shaped northwards in the lee of the land.

There is often considerable shipping in the vicinity of the Lizard though there is no longer a formal separation zone off the headland. In addition to traffic up and down the English Channel, vessels may also be altering course for Falmouth or Plymouth. The whole situation can be very confusing, especially at night, with the addition of brilliantly lit fishing vessels, often working in fleets and occasionally in pairs. In heavy or thick weather it is safer to keep well clear to the south until able to turn north towards Falmouth and cross the traffic at right-angles.

The English Channel

The English Channel has one of the world's highest concentrations of ship traffic, and it is essential to maintain a good lookout and to proceed with great caution if visibility is poor. Most of the traffic is concentrated on two main routes, one on the northern side running from the Scilly Isles and Land's End towards the Dover Strait, and the other on the southern side, rounding Ushant and the Casquets before again heading east to the Dover Strait. Each of these corridors carries two-way traffic. There are also ferries sailing between England and France, and coastal trading vessels, fishing boats and yachts continually on the move. If at any time after entering the English Channel weather conditions or bad visibility make it advisable to seek shelter, it will generally be found safer to close the English coast rather than the French.

The French coast

The north-west coast of France (the Brittany peninsula) is a particularly dangerous coast to approach in thick or heavy weather because of the many offlying rocks and strong tidal streams. There is also heavy shipping in the separation lanes off Ushant, a turning point where ships often alter course. The Traffic Separation Scheme extends for a lateral distance of 35–40 miles in a general north-westerly direction from Ushant, and it is essential to study an up-to-date chart before approaching this area.

The many dangers are well marked but it is essential to have good visibility, a suitable chart, an awareness of the tidal streams and a reliable and accurate position before closing this coast. If the weather is thick and the marks cannot be seen and identified with certainty, it is far safer to stand well off the land, clear of the strongest tidal streams and shipping lanes, and either await fairer weather or proceed elsewhere.

If making for Cherbourg or further east it is perfectly feasible to proceed up the English Channel in heavy weather if the wind is fair. However conditions may be uncomfortable as Channel seas tend to be short and steep, particularly when there is a strong tidal stream running against the wind. The streams increase in strength as the Channel narrows towards the Cherbourg peninsula and can have a marked effect on both progress and sea state. There is a Traffic Separation scheme off the Casquets.

The Spanish and Portuguese coasts

The coast of Iberia is in some ways safer than that of northern Europe, with relatively few outlying rocks or tidal races. However this is balanced by heavy shipping and frequent poor visibility, both prevalent along a narrow band relatively close inshore. Sudden northerly gales are another feature of the area. Provided an accurate position is known, it may be best to keep well offshore until on the approximate latitude of one's landfall, before crossing the shipping lanes and approaching the coast at right angles. Again there is much commercial fishing, often by large seagoing trawlers which may travel at speed to and from the fishing grounds, and are not always known for the efficiency of their lookout.

Formalities

Both customs and immigration regulations and the formality with which they are applied varies from

For centuries, sailors have breathed a sigh of relief at safely weathering Cape Finisterre on Spain's north-west coast.
Photo: Anne Hammick

The British and European Coasts 59

country to country within Europe. Throughout the UK, France and Portugal the paperwork is taken seriously on both arrival and departure. In Spain the situation is sometimes so relaxed that it is difficult to find anyone to take an interest, but the effort should still be made. Generally speaking, the officials treat yachtsmen very fairly, a situation which will only be maintained so long as the attitude is mutual.

All those ports listed in Part III are official entry/exit ports. Once within the territorial waters of any country the Q flag should be flown and clearance obtained as soon as possible, but most authorities will accept that, in stress of weather, a vessel may have to shelter in the nearest available haven before moving to an official port of entry. In some places, where smuggling or gun-running are not unknown, a yacht entering a remote harbour or anchorage may be treated with suspicion – to allay these fears always contact the authorities, even if only the local police, by radio, telephone or in person. Fly the Q flag and your national colours until cleared.

There is a universal ban on the import of hard drugs, and many countries look carefully at prescribed medicines, which are best accompanied by a letter from the prescribing doctor. Import of fresh meat is forbidden in some European countries including the UK (not a problem for most ocean cruising yachts!) as are growing plants and some fresh vegetables. All countries have limits regarding the import of alcohol and tobacco for personal use – the amount varies and it may be possible to store any excess in bond against departure.

There are very strict regulations in the UK regarding bringing animals of any kind into the country, and if planning to do so it is *essential* to contact the authorities at the intended port of arrival well in advance. It may be possible for animals to be confined below decks while in the UK, but the anti-rabies laws are taken very seriously indeed and any breach will inevitably lead to the destruction of the animal and a heavy fine for the owner.

Facilities

Depending on where the boat is lying, facilities may be anything from top class to non-existent. All European harbours detailed in Part III have adequate facilities, with those in the UK, Ireland and France in general more attuned to yachts than those in Iberia. Full details for each harbour will be found in Part III.

Sailing directions and yachtsmen's guides

The Atlantic coasts of Europe are well covered by both official and unofficial pilots of all kinds. The former are listed in Appendix C, together with charts showing the areas covered by each volume. Admiralty numbers 22, 27, 37, 40, 66 and 67, and US numbers 141, 142, 143 and 191 cover the coasts of Britain and Europe.

Yachtsmen's guides to the area compiled by clubs or individuals and published in English include:

Adlard Coles Pilot Pack, Vol 3, Brian Goulder (ACN)
Ardnamurchan to Cape Wrath, Clyde Cruising Club (CCC)
Atlantic Spain and Portugal, RCC Pilotage Foundation (Oz Robinson/Mike Sadler) (Imray)
Bristol Channel & Severn Pilot, Peter Cumberlidge (ACN)
Brittany and Channel Islands Cruising Guide, David Jefferson (ACN)
Channel Harbours and Anchorages, K Adlard Coles and others (ACN)
Channel Islands Pilot, Malcolm Robson (ACN)
Cruising Association Handbook, Cruising Association (Seventh edition) (CA)
French Pilot Vols 1 to 4, Malcolm Robson (ACN)
Lundy, Fastnet and Irish Sea Pilot, Vols 1 to 3, David Taylor (Imray)
Mull of Kintyre to Ardnamurchan, Clyde Cruising Club (CCC)
Normandy and Channel Islands Pilot, Mark Brackenbury (ACN)
North Biscay Pilot, Nicholas Heath/RCC Pilotage Foundation (ACN)
North Brittany Pilot, RCC Pilotage Foundation (ACN)
Sailing Directions for the East and North Coasts of Ireland, Irish Cruising Club (ICC)
Sailing Directions for the South and West Coasts of Ireland, Irish Cruising Club (ICC)
Scottish West Coast Pilot, Mark Brackenbury (ACN)
Shell Pilot to the English Channel, Vols 1 and 2 – Capt John Coote (Faber & Faber)
South Biscay Pilot, Robin Brandon (ACN)
West Country Cruising, Mark Fishwick (YM)
West Highland Shores, Maldwin Drummond (ACN)
Yachtsman's Pilot to the West Coast of Scotland, Vols 1 to 3, Martin Lawrence (Imray)

Relevant ports covered in Part III

12 SOUTHWARDS IN THE EASTERN ATLANTIC

The prevailing wind and current systems of the eastern Atlantic drive inexorably south, totally in tune with the wishes of the vast majority of European yachtsmen. Thus nearly all cruising yachts leaving Britain and Europe head in this direction, by a variety of routes. There is a wide choice of possible departure and landfall points, and while those chosen are both typical and popular there should be little difficulty in interpolating for other passages.

Passage	Approx distance
Falmouth to Madeira via the coast of Iberia	1300 + miles
Falmouth to Madeira direct	1250 miles
Falmouth to the Azores	1200 miles
Azores to Madeira	500 miles
Madeira to the Canaries	240 miles
Canaries to the Cape Verde Islands	850 miles

Passage planning charts

Latitudes	Admiralty	US
60°20′ N to 48°20′ N	4102 (1:3,500,000)	102 (1:3,500,000)
50°30′ N to 34°40′ N	4103 (1:3,500,000)	103 (1:3,500,000)
38°50′ N to 8°20′ N	4104 (1:3,500,000)	104 (1:3,500,000)

In addition to the small-scale charts listed above, many large-scale charts are published by the Portuguese and Spanish hydrographic offices as well as the British Admiralty and the US Defense Mapping Agency.

Falmouth to Madeira via the coasts of Spain and Portugal

This is one of the pleasantest ways to start an Atlantic circuit cruise. It avoids overlong passages in the initial stages, takes in an attractive and interesting cruising area and meshes perfectly with the seasonal weather patterns.

A yacht intending to depart from British shores before mid-August has time in hand to wait for a good forecast to cross the Bay of Biscay and may spend an enjoyable month or six weeks cruising north-west Spain. La Coruña provides an excellent landfall with a nearby DF beacon if visibility is poor, after which it is possible to day sail as far as Bayona. Allowing a couple of weeks for the Portuguese coast and a further week or ten days on passage to Madeira or the Canaries, the yacht will arrive around the end of October with another month to explore the area and get organised for the Atlantic passage. This is so near to the ideal that it is well worth aiming for if at all possible.

If time is limited two choices are open. By far the better is to sail south in the summer and leave the yacht in some safe port for collection later in the year. Vilamoura, or Puerto Sherry just north of Cadiz, are two possibilities. Gibraltar, although a greater diversion from the route towards Madeira or the Canaries, offers advantages to English speakers and provides easy importation of boat's gear duty-free for vessels in transit (which Spain and Portugal may not). Funchal has limited room for yachts to be left unattended, but several harbours in the Canaries, including Mogan (see page 145), have recently been used by British yacht owners with great success and relatively little expenditure.

The second alternative is to leave the English Channel late in the year and run the gauntlet of the autumn gales in Biscay. This comes a *very* poor second. The incidence of gales in Biscay increases from one day each month in August, to six days each month in October and nine in November. The autumn scenario of yachts gale-bound in Falmouth eager to be on their way, dashing out on an improved forecast only to be caught by a storm in the Bay, is repeated every year. Occasionally there are fatalities.

When crossing the Bay of Biscay French and Spanish fishing vessels are likely to be met and when approaching the northern coast of Spain there may be some shipping heading to and from such ports as Bordeaux and Brest. If the passage includes a diversion into Gibraltar a yacht returning westwards will encounter a high concentration of traffic in the Strait. This fans out as soon as the narrowest part is passed, the merchant shipping dividing into three main streams. One goes westward to St Vincent, one coastwise to the south, and one in the general direction of Madeira and the Canaries. There will, in addition, be large numbers of fishing craft. In twenty-four hours most of this will be left behind and little more will then be seen until the main north/south Atlantic shipping lane is crossed, west of the longitude of Cape St Vincent.

The 500-mile passage from the Portuguese coast towards Madeira or the Canaries is usually a pleasant one, often carrying the north-easterly winds to one's destination. However this is not always the case, and in some years the winds may either fail completely or back into the west as they did in 1987. The first island to be seen will probably be Porto Santo, and in normal conditions if planning to visit it will be best to do so at this stage and avoid the beat back from Madeira.

Falmouth to Madeira direct

Although the direct course from the English Channel to Madeira passes close to the Spanish coast, if the passage is to be made direct it will be worth making enough westing to remain a safe distance off this potential lee shore. The greatest concentrations of traffic will also be found near the coast, an area known for its poor visibility. By staying fifty to one hundred miles offshore one should escape both these problems while still receiving the full benefits of the northerly Portuguese Trades and Portuguese Current.

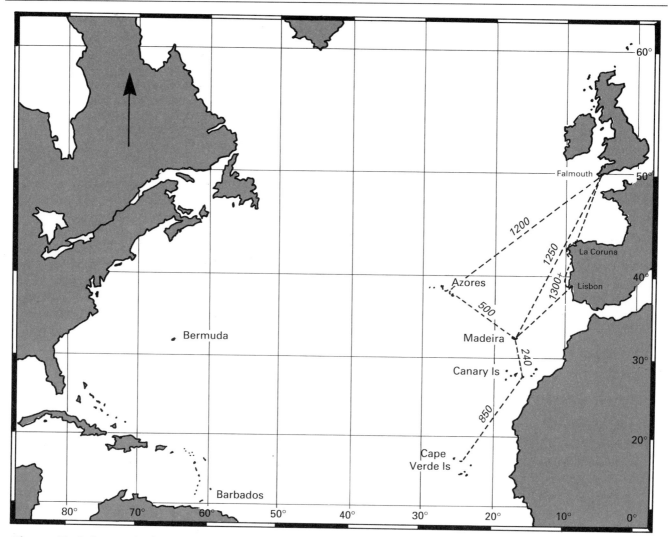

Chart 6 Typical routes in the Eastern Atlantic.

Falmouth to the Azores

This passage might be the first stage of a transatlantic voyage by the middle latitudes, a dog-leg on the way down to Madeira or the Canaries and the trade wind passage, or the outward part of a return cruise from England to the Azores. Timing will probably depend largely on the purpose of the voyage, but any period between late May and early August would be suitable.

Unless it is particularly desired to visit Spain or Portugal *en route*, in which case headwinds will probably have to be faced on the westward passage to the Azores, it is best to keep as near the rhumb line as conditions permit. The current sets south-east and prevailing winds are likely to be between south-west and north-west. There is a good chance of encountering a high pressure system on approaching the islands, and it would be wise to carry enough fuel to motor the last hundred miles or more if necessary.

Azores to Madeira

A pleasant passage can be anticipated, with winds between north-west and north-east backed by a favourable current. There is generally good visibility and relatively little

shipping. Though there may be a temptation to linger in the Azores it would be wise to depart before the middle of September.

Madeira to the Canaries

This passage may be made at any time of the year, but the chances of increased wind and decreased visibility will be greater from November onwards. The south-going current is relatively constant. If intending to cruise the Canary Islands it makes good sense to head for the eastern end of the group; if planning only a brief stop-over before the Atlantic passage, keep further west. The passage from Funchal to Santa Cruz de Las Palmas lies close to the Ilhas Selvagens or Salvage Islands (see Chapter 13), known for the vulnerability of their lights, and unless conditions are perfect it would be wise to keep well off.

Canaries to the Cape Verde Islands

It is debatable whether this passage should not be considered as part of the trade wind route, since many yachts pass near the Cape Verde Islands after leaving the Canaries whether they stop or not. It may also be the first passage of the circuit to be done mainly under downwind rig.

Both current and winds will be favourable, with the latter becoming more reliable as one progresses south. However as the wind picks up so visibility will decrease. This is the *harmattan*, a dust-laden wind from west Africa which may cut visibility at sea level down to a few miles. The sky will still be clear and the horizon apparently solid, rendering sextant sights unreliable and landfalls potentially hazardous if a good watch is not kept. Until very recently several of the islands were incorrectly charted, at up to three miles from their correct positions as established by satellite based systems. A timely reminder to always use current charts and to avoid relying too heavily on electronic navigation systems (other than radar).

13 THE MADEIRAN, CANARY AND CAPE VERDEAN ARCHIPELAGOS

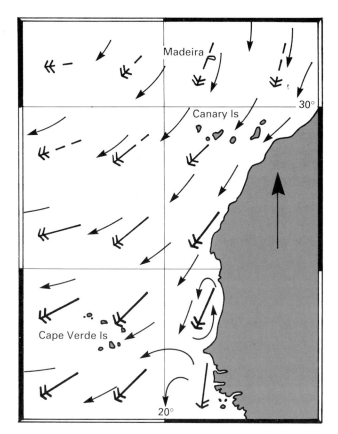

Chart 7 Prevailing winds and currents of the eastern Atlantic between 10°N and 35°N – November. (Winds in feathered arrows, currents in solid arrows.) Based on information from the *Atlantic Pilot Atlas*.

Regional weather

Although the Madeiran, Canary and Cape Verdean archipelagos cover a stretch of ocean more than 1000 miles from north to south, prevailing weather conditions are much less varied than would be the case further north. All lie in the path of the north-east trades, the main difference being that whereas Madeira and the Canaries may be influenced by the southern edge of winter depressions, in the latitude of the Cape Verde Islands the northeast trades hold almost total sway with the only real variation being in wind strength.

Within the Canary Islands a yacht may encounter sudden and gusty increases in wind strength, typically around the south-west and south-east coasts of the higher islands. These 'acceleration zones' can be quite distinct and may produce an increase from less than 5 knots to 25 knots or more within a few hundred metres.

Mention has already been made of the *harmattan* wind, which blows off the African continent south of about 20°N and can carry dust up to 500 miles offshore – or occasionally right across the Atlantic Ocean to the Caribbean. This is not so much a distinct wind as the

visual result of any breeze blowing at 20 knots or more over a period of several days, and can thus be anticipated with reasonable accuracy. Whether or not visibility appears to be bad, if the wind is above 20 knots *harmattan* conditions should be suspected – clear skies and an apparently firm horizon, out of which islands or other vessels may materialise when only a few miles distant.

Currents

Madeira and the Canary Islands lie squarely in the path of the south-west setting Canary Current, which swings somewhat further westward by the latitude of the Cape Verde Islands. In summer the influence of the Equatorial Counter Current may set up south or south-east setting eddies between 10°N and 15°N, but by November or December these have retreated south of 10°N. As in all areas, an ocean current averaging one knot or less may, when constricted between islands, run at considerably greater speeds.

Tides and tidal streams

Tidal rise and fall in the area is relatively slight, the mean spring range decreasing from 2.2 m (7 ft 2 in) at Porto Santo to 0.8 m (2 ft 7 in) in the Cape Verde Islands. Even so, tidal streams in the Cape Verdes can run strongly between the islands, and may reach over three knots when combined with the current.

Approach and landfall

Landfall will most often be made from northwards and should present no particular hazards. With the exception of one or two of the Cape Verdes all the islands are relatively high, some excessively so, and Tenerife in particular may sometimes be seen from 50 or 60 miles away. The vast majority of yachts making the trade wind passage leave from either Madeira, one of the Canary islands or the Cape Verdes, and the passages between the groups are covered in the previous chapter. Each area has its advantages and disadvantages, and all offer some interesting cruising in their own right.

The Madeira group

This group comprises Madeira Grande, Porto Santo lying some 30 miles to the north-east, the two Ilhas Desertas, and the isolated and rocky Ilhas Selvagens just over 150 miles south on the course between Funchal and the western Canaries. Only Madeira and Porto Santo are regularly visited by yachts, though both the other groups have fair-weather anchorages.

First sight of the Madeiras is likely to be of the conical peak of Porto Santo. This is a most satisfying landfall, rising as it does in solitary grandeur, visible in daylight at a distance of 40 miles or more. The islands are well-lit, and there are aero beacons on both Madeira and Porto Santo.

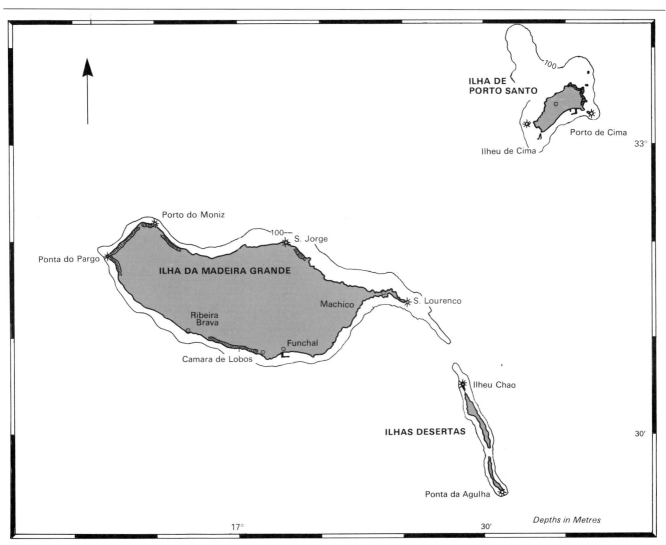

ILHA DE PORTO SANTO

100

Porto de Cima

Ilheu de Cima

33°

Porto do Moniz

100

S. Jorge

Ponta do Pargo

ILHA DA MADEIRA GRANDE

Machico

S. Lourenco

Ribeira Brava

Funchal

Camara de Lobos

Ilheu Chao

ILHAS DESERTAS

30'

Ponta da Agulha

Depths in Metres

17°

30'

Chart 8 The Madeira archipelago. Based on Admiralty Chart No 1831.

If planning a stop at Porto Santo it is wise to do so first to save beating back. It is an official port of entry, but facilities are poor with drinking water a particular problem. Provided the wind stays in the north-east, excellent anchorage will be found off the long sandy beach which forms much of Porto Santo's southern coast, however should the wind back this will quickly become a lee shore. A large harbour exists with room for several dozen yachts to lie at anchor, for which a small charge is made. If the weather appears settled and time not too pressing, Porto Santo is well worth a brief visit.

To most yachtsmen Madeira effectively means Funchal (see page 143), as although there are a number of other possible anchorages none offer remotely comparable facilities. The harbour is well lit and the town quite unmistakable, making it possible to enter at any hour of day or night. It is, however, a busy harbour and in addition to the normal commercial traffic and fishing craft there are often cruise ships on the move.

Many yachts spend a month or more in Funchal, either rafted alongside in the small marina or anchored off (note the caution on page 143), while their crews explore the island. It is arguably the loveliest of any visited on the standard Atlantic circuit, and once outside the tourist area round Funchal is remarkably unspoilt. Local buses provide a cheap and entertaining way to travel.

Funchal has several large supermarkets and a particularly good fruit and vegetable market, with a fish market next door. It is a favourite place to take on stores for the transatlantic passage, though prices in the Canary Islands may be found to be slightly cheaper on some items. The international airport on the south-east coast makes crew changes simple, and if conditions are settled it may be found easiest to anchor off the nearby town of Machico and save on taxi fares.

The Canary Islands

For a long time the Canaries were in disfavour with small boat sailors. La Luz on Gran Canaria and Santa Cruz de Tenerife, the two ports most often used by small craft, were primarily commercial and fishing harbours where foreign yachts were tolerated rather than welcomed. Both suffered frequent oil pollution. However conditions have improved markedly over recent years, and there are now many more yacht harbours, many with marina services.

On making landfall from the north the 3717 m (12,195 ft) volcanic peak of Tenerife will be seen from a great distance in clear weather, often complete with a scattering of snow despite being less than 300 miles outside the tropics. If intending to continue across the Atlantic most yachts will make for the western end of the archipelago; if planning to cruise through the Canary Islands it

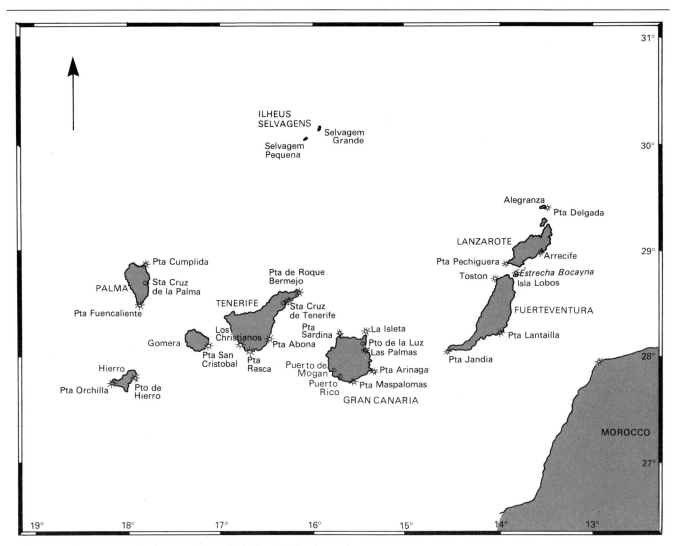

Chart 9 The Canary Islands. Based on Admiralty Publication NP131.

is logical to make one's landfall further east, either at Lanzarote or the small island of Graciosa which lies off its north-eastern tip.

Both harbours detailed in Part III are in effect 'double', with marinas or yacht harbours lying within easy reach of the shopping facilities of a larger town. Either would be good places at which to store up for the Atlantic crossing, though by no means the only ones. Excellent fruit and vegetables are available almost everywhere, and even smaller towns generally have at least one supermarket.

The annual ARC rally currently leaves from Las Palmas, Gran Canaria, where there is a 150 berth marina and excellent facilities. Whether the mushrooming development of tourist resorts is felt to be a plus or a minus, one by-product is that air communications are particularly good in terms of both frequency and value.

The Cape Verde archipelago

The Cape Verde Islands have never figured on many yachts' cruising itineraries, due to a history of poor facilities and lack of available information. However this is changing fast, and the practical advantage of breaking the transatlantic passage in the Cape Verdes is obvious – distance to Barbados is under 2000 miles, compared with 2700 miles from the Canaries, and as the islands are well within the trade wind belt a direct course can usually be steered.

Yachts are expected to make their landfall at either Porto Grande, São Vincente (see page 149), Ilha do Sal (where the international airport is situated) or Porto da Praia on Santiago. Of these Sal ('salt') is potentially the most difficult, being low lying and often lost in the haze until close by, while sand spits extend well offshore. However it does have the advantage of being furthest to windward, allowing other islands to be visited without unnecessary beating. São Vincente is more easily identified, not least because the mountains of neighbouring Santo Antão generally rise above the low-lying *harmattan* band. The same is true of Santiago further south.

All three islands mentioned above have aero DF beacons, but maintenance of all navigation aids throughout the Cape Verde islands is poor and there is no guarantee that these, or even major lights, will be working. A programme is in hand to remedy this situation, but information about changes in light characteristics takes a very long time to reach the Hydrographic Offices of other countries. Do not trust even the most recent charts to be entirely accurate.

The chief appeal of the Cape Verdes lies in the fact that they are largely undeveloped, and nearer in spirit to Africa

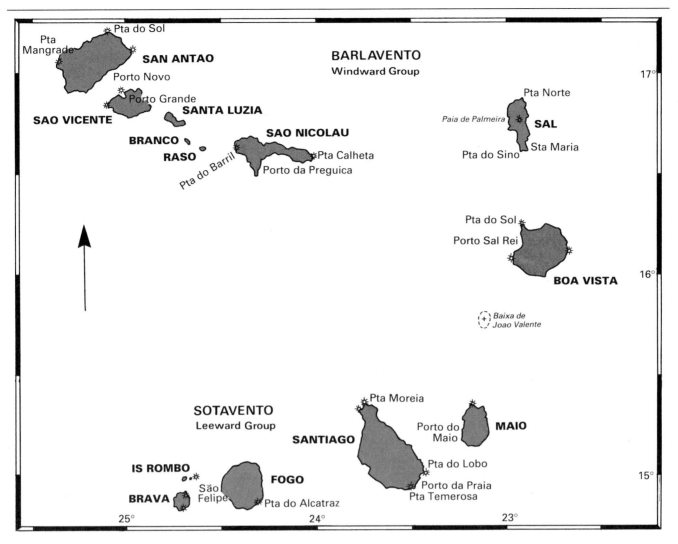

Pta do Sol

Pta Mangrade

SAN ANTAO

Porto Novo

BARLAVENTO
Windward Group

17°

Porto Grande

SAO VICENTE

SANTA LUZIA

BRANCO

RASO

Pta do Barril

SAO NICOLAU

Pta Calheta

Porto da Preguica

Pta Norte

Paia de Palmeira

SAL

Pta do Sino

Sta Maria

Pta do Sol

Porto Sal Rei

BOA VISTA

16°

Baixa de
Joao Valente

Pta Moreia

SOTAVENTO
Leeward Group

SANTIAGO

Porto do
Maio

MAIO

Pta do Lobo

IS ROMBO

BRAVA

FOGO

São
Felipe

Pta do Alcatraz

Porto da Praia
Pta Temerosa

15°

25°

24°

23°

Chart 10 The Cape Verde archipelago. Based on a plan in the *Atlantic Islands*.

(from which much of the population originally came) than to Portugal, the colonial power before independence in 1975. They are also desperately poor, and for this reason precautions should be taken against petty theft. Tourism is still a fairly new concept, though cruise ships call at São Vincente, and the local people are always friendly if sometimes overly curious.

Storing facilities are poor and all food except fresh fish expensive, making it wise to do the bulk of stocking up for the transatlantic passage in Madeira or the Canaries. Good drinking water may also be hard to come by in the dry, northern islands. The southern chain are generally wetter, and both water and fresh stores may be more readily available.

Few visitors remain indifferent to the Cape Verdes. Most are fascinated; a few cannot reconcile themselves to the poverty, dirt and lack of facilities. In comparison the Caribbean islands will seem like the centre of civilisation. Try to visit before the situation changes.

Formalities

Customs and immigration formalities differ between the groups. The Madeiran group, being Portuguese, take paperwork seriously and it is necessary to clear in and out of each island – sometimes each anchorage. In theory, the advent of the EC should mean fewer formalities for EC

owned and registered yachts entering Madeira from another EC country, but this has yet to be proved. The Canaries, though not part of the EC, take the relaxed Spanish attitude, and it may be difficult to get written clearance on leaving for presentation at the next port of call. Fortunately the customs officers in the Lesser Antilles are aware of this. The Cape Verdean authorities also take customs (and particularly immigration) seriously, though the visa requirement for yachtsmen not staying ashore overnight, is waived.

For full details see Part III, port information.

Sailing directions and yachtsmen's guides

Admiralty Pilot NP 1, Volume I and US *Sailing Directions* SD 143 cover the area (see Appendix C). Until recently there was no widely available guide to these islands written primarily for yachts, but this has been rectified by the RCC Pilotage Foundation's *Atlantic Islands*, compiled by Nicholas Heath and the present author and published by Imray Laurie Norie & Wilson Ltd. This gives detailed coverage to all three groups in addition to the Azores.

Relevant ports covered in Part III

The spectacular anchorage at Porto de Faja on Ilha Brava in the Cape Verde Islands. It is worth remembering that in Latin-based languages *Porto* implies merely an entrance or landing place, not a port as we understand the term. *Photo: Charles Watson*

It is a fact that while the actual Atlantic voyage generally receives the bulk of the anticipation and planning, it is often the most trouble-free passage of the entire circuit. The trade wind crossing has not been nicknamed the 'milk run' for nothing. There are a number of possible routes in terms of departure, arrival and distance, but all run pretty well parallel and are governed by the same prevailing conditions. For that reason they will be taken together rather than separately.

Passage	Approx distance
Madeira to Antigua	2900 miles
Canaries to Barbados	2700 miles
Cape Verdes to Barbados	1900 miles

Passage planning charts

Latitudes	Admiralty	US
Southern North Atlantic	4012 (1:10,000,000)	120 (1:6,331,100)

It is important to remember that the amount of magnetic variation differs as one crosses the Atlantic, from approximately 8°30′ W in Madeira and the Canaries to 14°W in the vicinity of the Cape Verdes, 18°W or more in the middle and around 14°W in the Lesser Antilles. All are changing gradually, not necessarily at the same speed. The chart will therefore show nothing but the True compass rose, plus isogonic lines linking the places which have a common

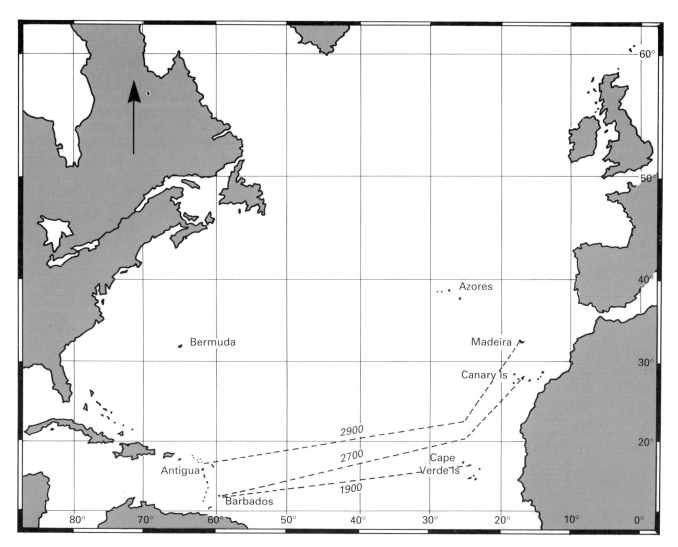

Chart 11 Typical trade wind routes.

amount of variation, and details of annual change. It is worth calculating and applying these accurately, as even a few degrees of error can produce a sizeable divergence over several days' run.

Timing

The majority of yachts make the trade wind crossing in November or December, though this probably has more to do with a desire to be in the Caribbean for Christmas than anything else. Before mid-November the winds may be unreliable and it would plainly be dangerous to arrive before the end of the hurricane season. However there is no good reason why this passage should not be made in January, February or even later, and some of the fastest crossing times have been recorded at this time of year. In general, the later the crossing the stronger the winds are likely to be.

The trade wind belt

Whichever departure point is chosen, the objective is to get well into the belt of the established north-east trades as soon as possible. The northern limit of this belt varies with the seasons – from about 30°N in summer to 25°N in winter – and also from year to year. The fatal mistake is to head west too soon and risk getting caught in the 'light 'n' variables' which predominate towards the centre of the Atlantic's massive high pressure system. Even when established, the trade wind, contrary to popular belief, does not always blow from the same quarter or at the same strength. Sometimes it does not blow at all, and the crew who do not experience a day or two of mid-ocean calm are fortunate. It is, however, less fickle than winds in many other parts of the world. Its strength rarely exceeds force 6 (25 knots) and averages nearer force 4 (15 knots).

As mentioned, the northern limit of the trade wind belt varies from one year to the next. The position 25°N 25°W is often quoted as being the point to make for, and in November 1984 proved good advice – we sailed within a few miles of it after leaving Madeira, turned west on the Great Circle course for Antigua, and had excellent winds nearly all the way. Three years later conditions were quite different, and though it did not affect our passage from the Cape Verde Islands to Barbados it caused problems for yachts leaving from the Canaries, who did not find good winds until south of 20°N. Not even a weatherfax will accurately depict the position of the trade wind frontier, and the best and simplest tactic is to keep heading south-west until steady winds are found, continue on this course for another 300 miles or so (at least 3° of latitude) to get well into the belt, and then set a course for the chosen landfall.

When the trade wind is fully established the sky is usually speckled with small clouds, like puffs of steam from an old-fashioned railway engine. Any large mass of cloud, lower and darker than the rest and coming up astern, is likely to denote a squall. At best this may give the ship a welcome burst of speed, at worst it might make it necessary to shorten sail. Sometimes these squalls bring a sharp downpour of rain, occasionally with thunder and lightning, though the worst of these thunderstorms seem to take place to the north of the trade wind route and one is often a spectator (and thankfully only that) at an impressive but reassuringly distant display.

Ocean currents and swell

The Canary Current, as it approaches the Cape Verde Islands, changes its course and changes its name. It turns increasingly westward and becomes known as the North Equatorial Current. Both movement and reliability tend

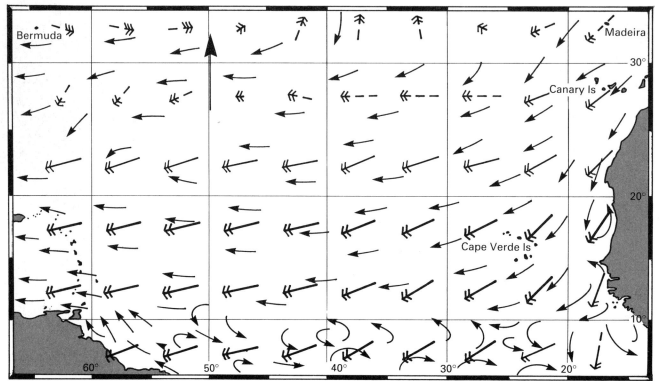

Chart 12 Prevailing winds and currents of the southern North Atlantic – December. (Winds in feathered arrows, currents in solid arrows.) Based on information from the *Atlantic Pilot Atlas.*

to increase throughout the winter season, though speed at any given point can be little more than a guess. Allow for 0.5 knots in the dead reckoning, and check this daily against the plotted position – sometimes there will appear to be virtually no current, at other times it may pick up to nearer a full knot. Allow a generous margin when approaching the islands.

Even an apparently calm ocean is seldom totally without swell, which may suddenly increase for no apparent reason. Usually it arises from a storm many thousands of miles away and is in itself harmless, though if running down from the North Atlantic, as commonly happens, may catch a yacht under running sails on the beam, causing her to roll horrendously. When sizeable swells and locally created seas oppose each other troublesome crests will be created, some of which may come aboard.

If skirting the windward side of an island at the end of a transatlantic passage, making generous allowance for current and leeway takes on particular importance. More than one yacht has driven ashore because forces which had contributed to forward progress during the downwind passage, and therefore went largely unnoticed, were ignored on altering course onto the wind.

Caribbean approach and landfall

The traditional island on which to make landfall after a trade wind crossing is Barbados, not least because it lies more than 80 miles to windward of the rest of the archipelago and to call later would involve a long and tedious beat into the trade wind. The island is well worth a visit, with good shopping and other facilities. Details of the capital, Bridgetown, will be found in Part III on page 157.

Other popular islands on which to make landfall are Martinique, St Lucia and Antigua, with boats coming up from the South Atlantic usually opting for Grenada. Suitable harbours of entry on each of these islands are included in Part III.

Although few Caribbean islands are well lit in terms of navigational aids, considerable ambient light is produced by airports, hotels, domestic and street lighting. This is particularly true of Barbados, Martinique and Antigua, though all three are fringed by windward reefs which could prove hazardous in poor visibility. Usually the weather is clear and heavy rain, which is the only thing likely to cut down visibility, will normally be in the form of short-lived squalls which soon move away. The islands which have major airports also have powerful aeronautical DF beacons.

Many people, years after returning from a one-year Atlantic circuit, remember the trade wind crossing as the high point of the entire cruise. For most it will be the longest ocean passage they ever make. It is as well that it is also usually one of the most enjoyable.

Visions of dropping anchor off a perfect Caribbean white sand beach may be the first step to plans for a trade wind crossing.
Photo: Anne Hammick

It is beyond the scope of this book to cover the South Atlantic in detail, not least because of the relatively small numbers of yachts which cross it each year. Other than those beginning their cruise in South Africa itself, the majority will be circumnavigators making the long haul up from Cape Town to the Caribbean, or occasionally from the Cape to Europe – the latter not technically an Atlantic crossing but nevertheless one of the longest Atlantic passages around.

This chapter therefore contains only a broad outline of South Atlantic weather and currents outside those areas most frequently traversed by yachts, plus brief details of the commonly used 'feeder' routes into the North Atlantic and the islands at which these passages may be broken.

Winds and weather

The South Atlantic, like its northern counterpart, is dominated by a central area of high pressure and the wind and current systems which circulate around it. These run anti-clockwise, and are constrained by both the land masses of the African and South American continents and the prevailing westerlies – the 'Roaring Forties' – which circle the globe south of latitude 40°S. The south-east trades form a belt between the equator and about 20°S, swinging more easterly as they progress westwards, to become north-easterly off the coast of South America. There is less annual movement of this belt than is the case in the North Atlantic, and the south-east trades are also considered

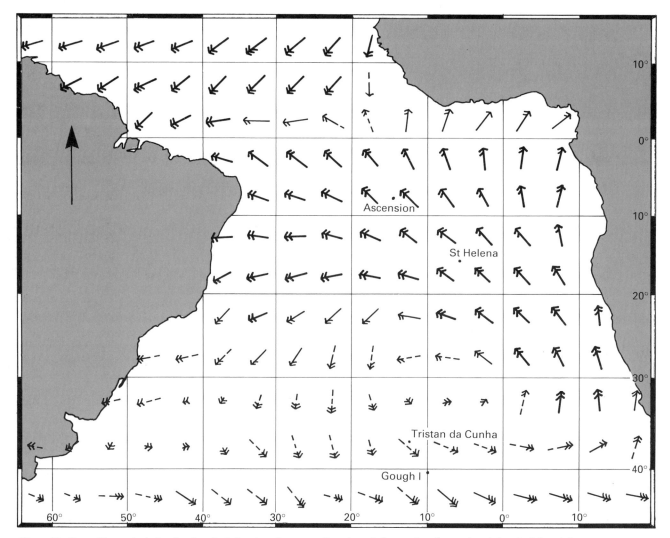

Chart 13 Prevailing winds in the South Atlantic – January. Based on information from the *Atlantic Pilot Atlas*.

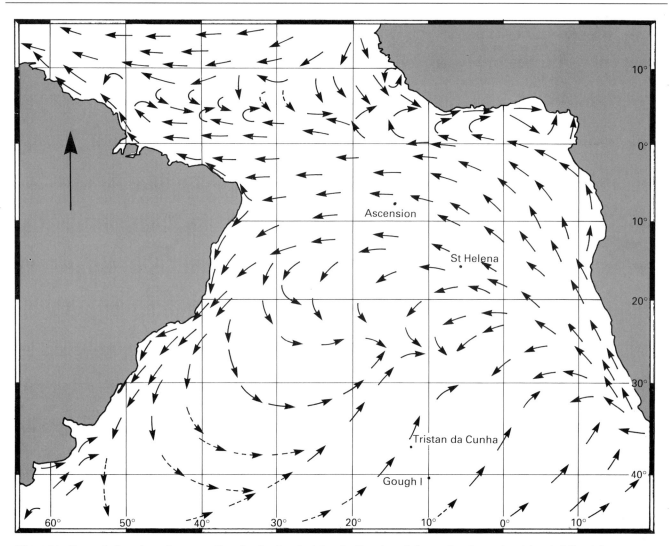

Chart 14 General direction of current flow in the South Atlantic. Based on information from the *Atlantic Pilot Atlas.*

more dependable than their northern counterpart.

Between the two circulating systems of the North and South Atlantic lie the Doldrums, an area of light easterly winds where calms punctuated by occasional squalls are common. The band is considerably wider in the eastern part of the Atlantic, where it may stretch from the Equator to around 10°N, but narrows off further west. Occasionally it may disappear completely near the coast of Brazil allowing yachts to pass directly from the south-east into the north-east trades. Although technically lying in the North Atlantic, the Doldrums are included here as being more relevant to trans-equatorial routes.

One significant difference between the two oceans from the yachtsman's point of view is that tropical hurricanes do not occur in the South Atlantic.

Ocean currents

Current flow in the South Atlantic is affected by the two dominant wind systems – the high pressure circulation outlined above and the strong westerlies further south. Thus while a west-going current is generally to be found north of about 20°S, the east or north-easterly set which sweeps around Cape Horn may sometimes extend beyond 15°N, particularly in the centre of the ocean. Nearer the African coast the west-going Agulhas Current is constricted as it passes around the Cape of Good Hope, and becoming known as the Benguela Current, runs north-westwards up the coast to join the water circulation set up by the south-east trades. As this cold water from the southern latitudes moves northwards it may give rise to fog, though visibility over the rest of the South Atlantic Ocean is generally good.

Sandwiched between the two west-going Equatorial Current systems is the Equatorial Counter Current, a relatively narrow band of east-going water centred around 6°N. It flows most strongly in the eastern Atlantic, fading out westwards where the two more powerful systems combine as they approach the South American continent.

Routes, seasons and timing

The unsettled and often stormy weather to be found around the Cape of Good Hope abates slightly during the southern summer. Thus the majority of yachts arriving in Cape Town (see page 152) do so between December and February. Those heading for the Caribbean usually depart again within a few weeks, but if sailing direct to Europe it may be better to leave slightly later, in order to avoid reaching the Azores before early summer.

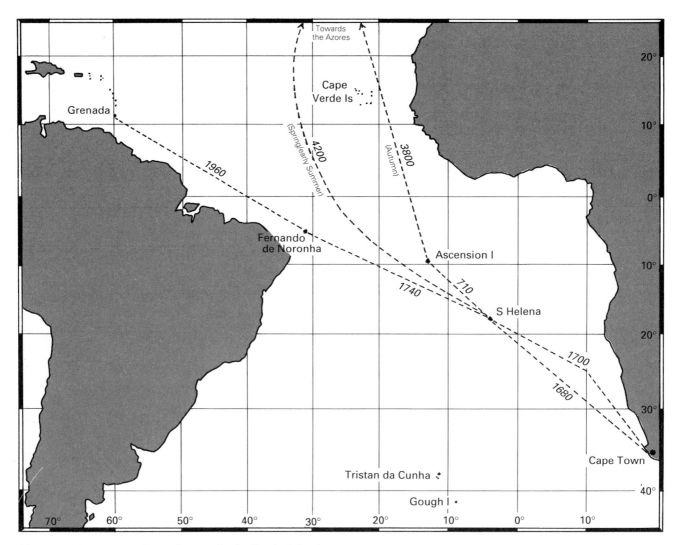

Chart 15 Most commonly used routes in the South Atlantic.

Once again only the most popular passages and landfalls are covered, leaving the skipper to interpolate as necessary.

Passage	Approx distance
Cape Town to St Helena	1680 miles
St Helena to Ascension Island	710 miles
St Helena to Fernando de Noroñha Island, Brazil	1740 miles
Fernando de Noroñha to the Lesser Antilles	1960 miles
St Helena to the Azores	4000 miles

Passage planning charts

Coverage	Admiralty		US	
Northern section	4012	(1:10,000,000)	120	(1:6,331,100)
Central section	4022	(1:10,000,000)	22	(1:10,000,000)
Eastern section	4021	(1:10,000,000)	21	(1:10,000,000)
Western section	4020	(1:10,000,000)	20	(1:10,000,000)
Gnomonic (Great Circle)	5096	(1:13,500,000)	24	(Variable scale)

Cape Town to St Helena

After leaving Cape Town on a favourable forecast the best bet is generally to keep slightly east of the rhumb line at first, to make the most of both wind and current. From a position around 25°S 10°E a direct course can be shaped for St Helena. However as already mentioned, visibility near the coast may be poor, and if south-westerly gales threaten it will obviously be necessary to work offshore in order to maintain searoom. For this reason many yachts simply take the rhumb line, gaining in distance saved what they may lose in speed.

St Helena may often be seen from 50 miles or more, appearing very square and solid rather than formed of individual peaks. Approach round the north coast is generally advised, due to Speery Ledge which lies about 1.5 miles off the southern tip of the island with less than 3 m (10 ft) of water. Due to its position squarely in the path of the south-east trade winds, the only feasible anchorages are on the north-west coast. The chief of these is James Bay – see page 155 in Part III for further details.

St Helena to Ascension Island

This passage should be a straightforward continuation of

the north-westerly route from Cape Town via St Helena with both wind and current favourable, and there is no reason to sail any course other than the rhumb line.

Ascension Island can generally be seen from a good distance, but is bypassed by most yachts largely because its function as a military base and communications centre inevitably means that they are not particularly welcome. The anchorage at Clarence Bay on the north-west coast is particularly rolly, sometimes catching a swell running down from the North Atlantic, and landing dryshod at the Pierhead steps notoriously difficult. Best anchorage is to be found north-east of the pier in about 11 m (36 ft), and on no account should yachts anchor south of the two spar buoys which mark a shoal patch, or anywhere that might obstruct shipping movements.

All formalities are carried out by the Administrator at the Police Office in Georgetown, which gives on to Clarence Bay. Only a brief stop of 48 hours is normally permitted, though this may be extended if necessary re-pairs must be completed. There are few attractions ashore – no bars or cafés, no readily available transport, and a requirement that crews be back aboard by 1900 hours each evening. Both water and fresh stores are likely to be limited, and may be unavailable to yachts even if on sale to islanders. Diesel can normally be obtained through the wharfmaster. There is no civilian airport.

St Helena to Fernando de Noroñha Island, Brazil

Fernando de Noroñha lies some 200 miles off the north-east coast of Brazil, at approximately 3°50′ S 32°20′ W, and conveniently breaks the long passage for yachts heading towards the Caribbean. Both wind and current on this route are generally favourable, though winds are on average lighter than is the case further east. The current sets almost due west, and may on occasion be found to have some south in it.

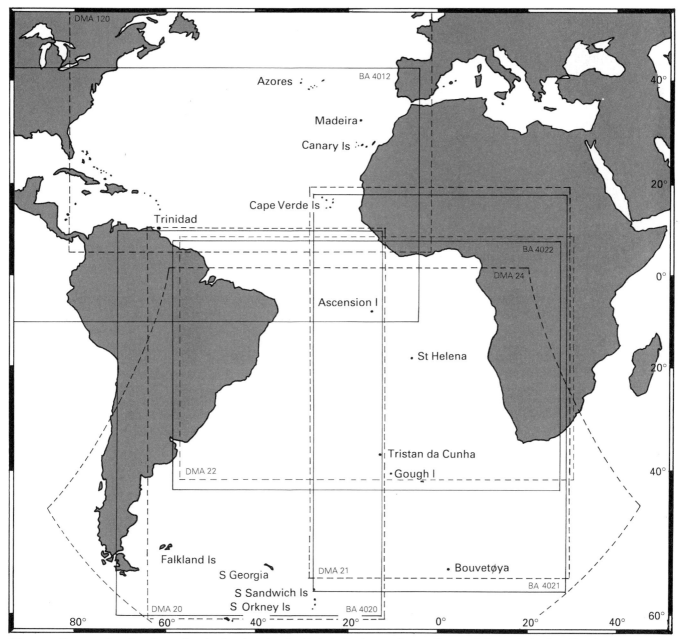

Chart 16 Passage planning charts for the South Atlantic. (Admiralty in continuous lines, US DMA in broken lines.)

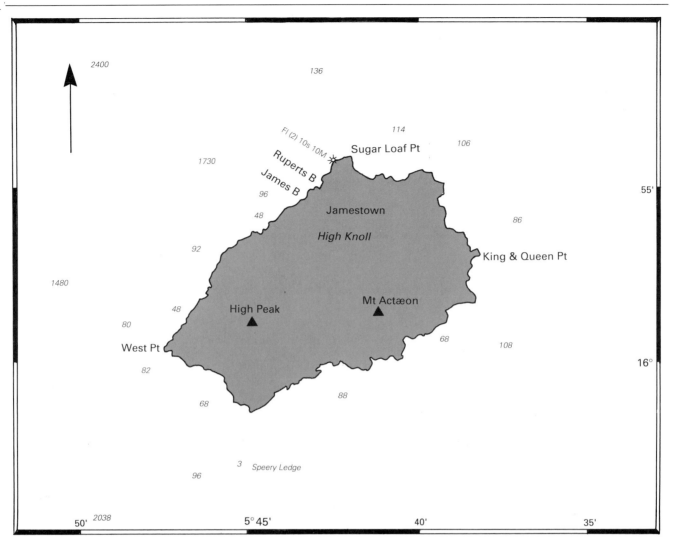

2400

136

Fl (2) 10s 10M

114

106

1730

Sugar Loaf Pt

Ruperts B

James B

96

48

Jamestown

High Knoll

55'

86

92

King & Queen Pt

1480

48

High Peak

Mt Actæon

West Pt

68

108

82

16'

88

68

3 *Speery Ledge*

96

50' 2038

5° 45'

40'

35'

Chart 17 St Helena. Based on Admiralty Chart No 1769.

Although Fernando de Noroñha is not an official entry port for Brazil there are customs and immigration offices about a mile from the yacht anchorage at Santa Antonia Bay, where permits to buy fuel can also be obtained. The anchorage is rolly though reasonably sheltered, and construction of a small breakwater for local craft has greatly eased the problem of landing by dinghy in the surf. The western half of the island is a nature reserve fringed by an underwater park, with restricted access. Both water and fuel are available by can, but fresh stores are very limited.

Fernando de Noroñha to the Lesser Antilles

The last leg of the Cape Town to Caribbean route crosses the Equator and, to the extent that they exist so far west, the Doldrums. Winds can be expected to back from southeast on departure through east into the north-east, making this a generally fast passage except in years when the Doldrums are unusually extensive. Currents are also favourable. On approaching the angular 'corner' of the South American land mass the west-going South Equatorial Current splits, one branch running north-west up the coast towards the Caribbean at speeds of up to two knots while the other follows the land south-west, eventually to rejoin the major circulatory system.

St Helena to the Azores

Although not strictly a transatlantic passage, a number of yachts make the long haul from the Cape to northern Europe each year. Almost all break the voyage at St Helena and again in the Azores, and the first and third legs of this passage are thus covered elsewhere.

The main question must be at what longitude to cross the Equator. Further west there is a better chance of avoiding or at least minimising the Doldrums, extra easting on the other hand will be invaluable once into the north-east trades. In general the best point appears to be between 25°W and 30°W in spring and early summer, further east as the summer progresses, until by the autumn it may even be worth sailing between the Cape Verde Islands and the African mainland. Whatever course is shaped it is inevitable that much of the later part of this passage will be hard on the wind – a wind which may lighten or die entirely both in the Doldrums and further north on approaching the Azores. Currents will also be largely unfavourable. This is the only Atlantic passage likely to take more than a month, and the fifty days taken by a 35 ft ketch in 1990 is not untypical.

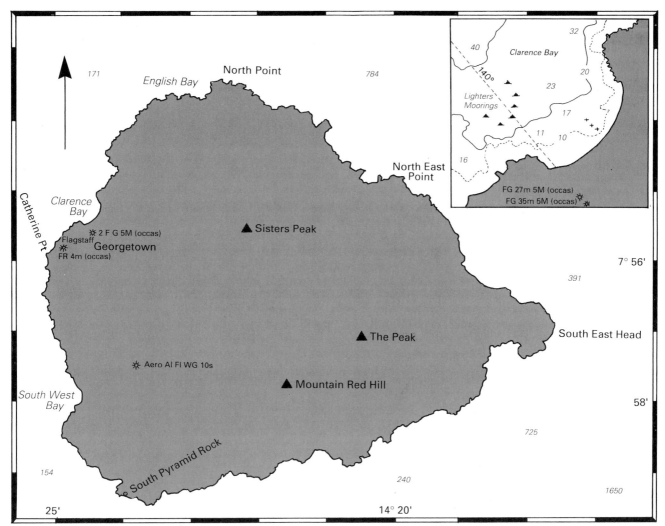

Chart 18 Ascension Island with an inset of Clarence Bay. Based on Admiralty Chart No 1691.

Within the chart:
- North Point
- English Bay
- North East Point
- 171
- 784
- Catherine Pt
- Clarence Bay
- ☀ 2 F G 5M (occas)
- Flagstaff
- ☀
- FR 4m (occas)
- Georgetown
- ▲ Sisters Peak
- 7° 56'
- 391
- ▲ The Peak
- South East Head
- ☀ Aero Al Fl WG 10s
- 58'
- South West Bay
- ▲ Mountain Red Hill
- 725
- South Pyramid Rock
- 154
- 240
- 1650
- 25'
- 14° 20'

Inset (Clarence Bay):
- 40
- 32
- Clarence Bay
- 140°
- 20
- Lighters Moorings
- 23
- 17
- 11
- 10
- 16
- FG 27m 5M (occas)
- FG 35m 5M (occas) ☀

The yacht anchorage and dinghy landing at Santa Antonia Bay, Fernando de Noroñha Island, Brazil. *Photo: Liz Hammick*

Formalities

The above routes cover departure or arrival in the waters of at least six different countries. Formalities vary accordingly, and are covered in the port information in Part III. Where this is not the case – ie Ascension Island and Fernando de Noroñha – very brief details have been included with the passage notes.

Sources of information

Compared to the North Atlantic, the South Atlantic is poorly provided so far as background information is concerned. Though nearly all sources mentioned in Chapter 10 cover both oceans, without exception each devotes considerably more space to north than south. Only the Admiralty *Routeing Charts* (BA Chart 5125, monthly numbers 1–12) are impartial. The US Defense Mapping Agency publishes no South Atlantic equivalent to its *Pilot Chart 16* for northern waters.

Sailing directions and yachtsmen's guides

The coasts fringing the South Atlantic are poorly covered by pilot books so far as yachts are concerned, but the official *Sailing Directions* are more comprehensive. Taken in order clockwise these are Admiralty publications NP 1 Vols I and II, NP 5 and NP 7A; and US DMA publications SD 121, SD 123, SD 124, SD 143 and SD 148. Full details plus area charts will be found in Appendix C.

St Helena including Ascension Island and Tristan da Cunha by Tony Cross (David & Charles) contains much interesting and useful information of a general nature, but is not written specifically for those arriving by yacht.

Relevant ports covered in Part III

17 Cape Town, South Africa   page 152
18 James Bay, St Helena   page 155
19 Bridgetown, Barbados   page 157
20 Prickly Bay, Grenada   page 159

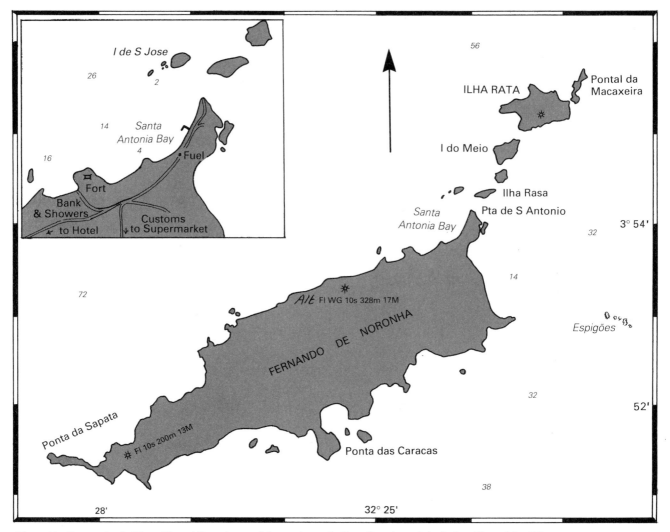

Chart 19 Fernando de Noroñha with an inset of Santa Antonia Bay. Based on Admiralty Chart No 388.

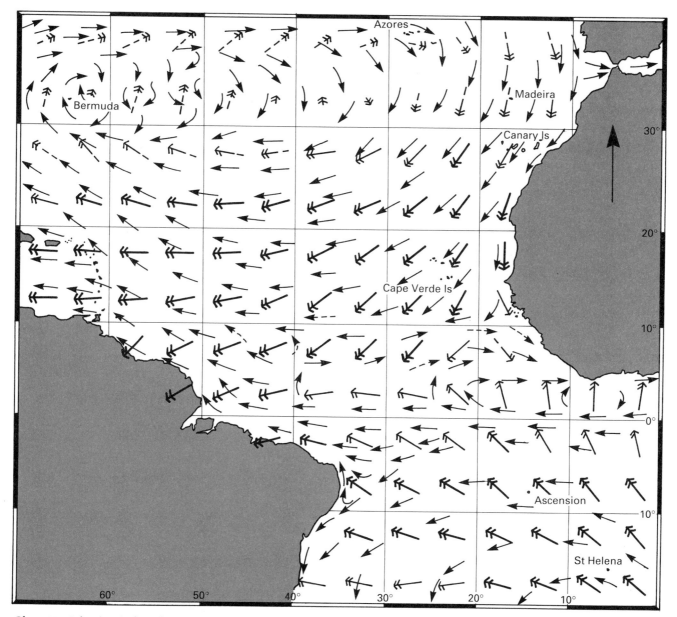

Chart 20 Atlantic winds and currents between 20°S and 40°N – May. (Winds in feathered arrows, currents in solid arrows.) Based on information from the *Atlantic Pilot Atlas.*

For most people, the chance to spend time cruising the Caribbean islands provides the main incentive for an Atlantic circuit. Situated as they are in the trade wind zone and within the Tropic of Cancer, their waters afford some of the world's best sailing conditions.

History

Although the (misnamed) West Indies are often thought of as having been discovered by Columbus, recent archaeological research has proved the existence of much earlier human occupation. The Caribs, who were in possession of much of the Caribbean before the Europeans took over, represented the second or third wave of Indian emigration from South America. In most of the islands they were wiped out within a few hundred years, but some still live in a reserved territory on the windward side of Dominica with a few in northern St Vincent. The vast majority of the local people today are descended from the slaves who were brought over from Africa in the seventeenth and eighteenth centuries to work in the sugar plantations.

Nearly all the islands have small museums, but that in St John's, Antigua, is particularly notable for its comprehensive collection of pre-Columbian artifacts.

The trade wind

Although the trade wind dominates Caribbean weather, there are subtle but important variations throughout the cruising season. From December until early April the winds are remarkably constant in both strength and direction, averaging about 15–20 knots out of the east or north-east. However force may increase dramatically in sudden squalls (usually though not invariably signalled by an advancing line of purple-grey clouds), or where the trade wind funnels down valleys or around the ends of islands. From time to time the entire Caribbean experiences a winter with lighter winds than normal, though during the 1980s winds were generally somewhat stronger than the average. It may be necessary to adapt the itinerary to suit the prevailing conditions, particularly if these had

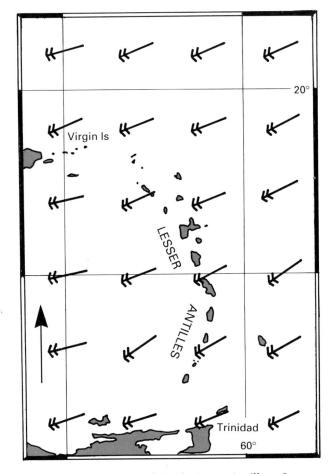

Chart 21 Prevailing winds in the Lesser Antilles – January. Based on information from the *Atlantic Pilot Atlas*.

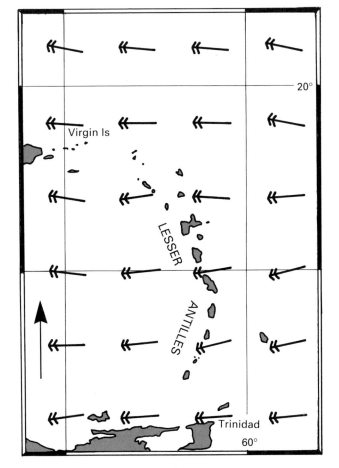

Chart 22 Prevailing winds in the Lesser Antilles – May. Based on information from the *Atlantic Pilot Atlas*.

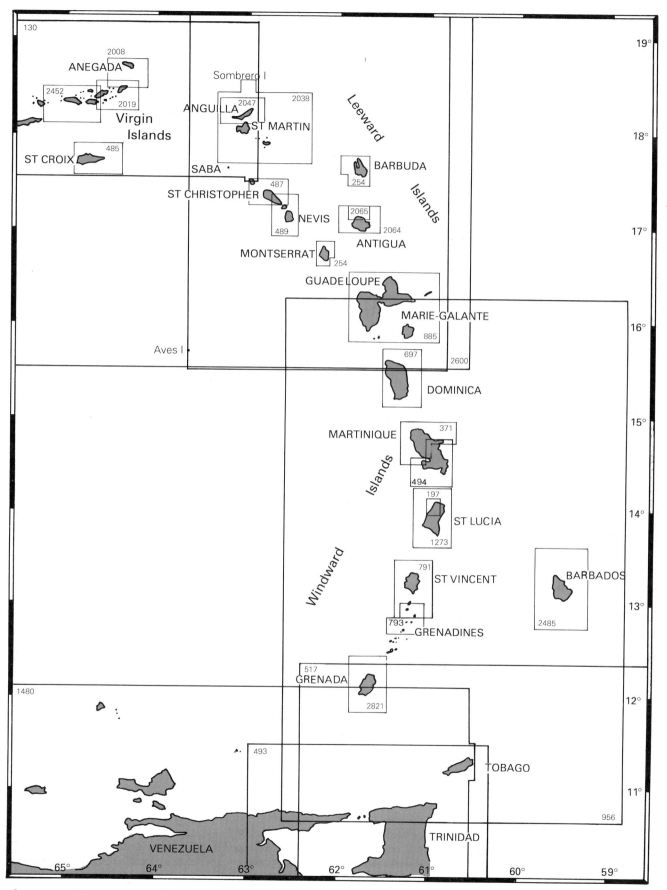

Chart 23 British Admiralty Charts for the Eastern Caribbean. Based on Admiralty Publication NP 131.

included an intention to explore windward reefs such as those fringing Martinique.

From mid April to the beginning of the hurricane season in June or July (see Chapter 10) the winds become less consistent. Antigua Race Week, held at the end of April, is renowned for producing everything from flat calms to gusts resulting in knock-downs, quite often on consecutive days. By May the winds will be definitely lighter, particularly in the northern part of the area. As they moderate they also veer slightly, swinging from north-east through east to slightly south of east, a definite boon for yachts leaving the islands for the United States or Bermuda.

Even when the open water trades are blowing strongly, calms often lurk in the lee of the higher islands – effectively all those of any size between Grenada and Guadeloupe. Most yachts will resort to motoring, but if engineless or a purist the best chance of progress is either to keep as close in as is consistent with safety, or else at least 5 miles offshore. Neither of these are guaranteed, and if in a real hurry it may be worth considering sailing the windward side instead.

Conversely, it is easy to drift towards the end of an island, forgetting that the light breeze and flat sea will be replaced by gusty winds and a sizeable ocean swell within a matter of a few boat's lengths. It may not be overkill to change down headsails (if not equipped with roller-furling) and even put in a reef in anticipation. Coming from under the protection of a high coastline, life will suddenly become very boisterous and anyone working below at chart table or galley deserves due warning.

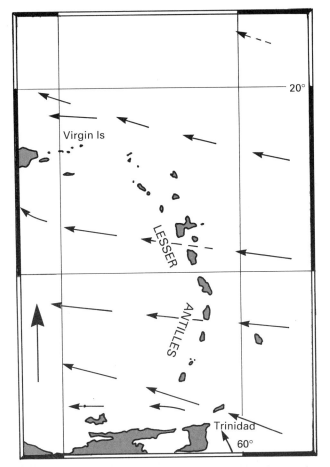

Chart 24 Currents in the Lesser Antilles – March. Based on information from the *Atlantic Pilot Atlas*.

Current and swell

The North Equatorial Current sets westward between the islands, often attaining a knot or more. Though tidal streams may increase or decrease the rate of flow they are seldom strong enough to overcome it completely.

Allowance should also be made for leeway caused by the ocean swell which, after a fetch of nearly 3000 miles, sets on to Atlantic coasts and through the gaps with considerable power.

Navigation and pilotage

Except for Barbados, which lies to the east of the main archipelago, each island is within sight of its immediate neighbours and navigation can be mostly by eye if you are so minded. Navigational aids are few and far between, and may not always be maintained to the same standards that would apply at home, making night sailing, other than well offshore, unwise for the newcomer. Buoyage follows the American IALA B system (red right returning) in all areas other than St Vincent and the Grenadines, which are currently still on the European IALA A. Even the French islands have bowed to the inevitable and made the change, and it can only be a matter of time before St Vincent does likewise.

Another reason for avoiding night sailing is the number of fish-pot floats to be found even well offshore, and often clustered particularly thickly in the approaches to many anchorages. These floats may be of fibreglass or plastic, white or coloured, or simply be stoppered bottles or chunks of expanded polystyrene. Others may be the old traditional bamboo floats, six or eight feet long, and sometimes waterlogged and floating a few inches below the surface. All are a hazard when one is moving under power and a lookout should be stationed at the bow whenever they are met in quantity. A powerful torch will be needed after dark. Under sail they are less of a menace but can still wrap themselves around an exposed rudder or free-turning propeller.

Anchorages

To those used to ever-changing winds and strong reversing tidal streams, it may go against the grain to anchor in a position protected through half the compass or less. However due to the constancy of the trade winds the islands afford a reliable lee on their western coasts and many of the best anchorages are quite open in this direction. The best afford both shelter from the wind and freedom from rolling, but this is not always the case and quite often a certain amount of rolling may have to be endured. This is particularly true of those anchorages chosen more because of shoreside convenience than actual shelter, such as Carlisle Bay, Barbados, and the anchorages off St Pierre, Martinique and Roseau, Dominica – all worth visiting for different reasons.

Formalities

On approaching land, allow time to brush up your knowledge of the entry procedure for the particular island to which you are going. All are different. Except for the French, Dutch and American islands, most have been granted their independence and nearly every island that

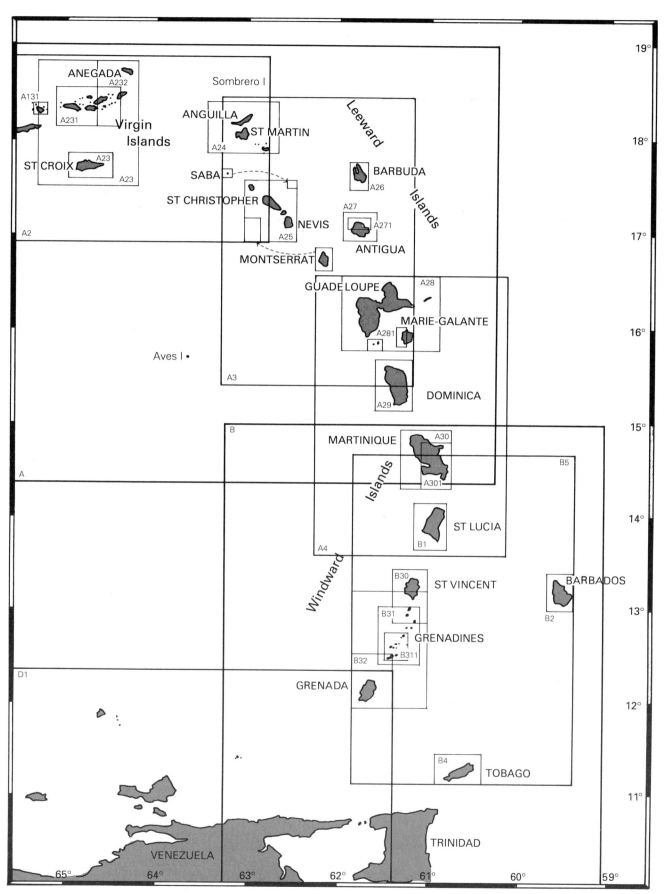

ANEGADA
A232
A131
A231
Virgin
Islands
ST CROIX
A23
A23

Sombrero I
ANGUILLA
A24
ST MARTIN
SABA
ST CHRISTOPHER
A25
NEVIS
MONTSERRAT

Leeward
Islands

BARBUDA
A26
A27
A271
ANTIGUA
A28
GUADELOUPE
MARIE-GALANTE
A281
A3
DOMINICA
A29

Aves I •

A2

B
A
D1

MARTINIQUE
A30
A301
A4
Windward
Islands
ST LUCIA
B1
B30
ST VINCENT
B31
GRENADINES
B311
B32
GRENADA

B5
BARBADOS
B2

B4
TOBAGO

VENEZUELA
TRINIDAD

65°   64°   63°   62°   61°   60°   59°

19°
18°
17°
16°
15°
14°
13°
12°
11°

Chart 25 Imray–Iolaire charts for the Eastern Caribbean. Based on information from Imray Laurie Norie & Wilson.

A typical Caribbean coral anchorage, Clifton Harbour on the eastern (windward) coast of Union Island in the Grenadines. Although the reef forms a natural breakwater, it does nothing to stop the trade winds whistling through – a drawback or a blessing, depending on how you view it. *Photo: Libby Grubb*

was formerly a British possession is now a country in its own right, with its own national colours. For the visiting yacht this means a lot of different courtesy flags as well as a lot of formalities.

Nearly all the islands take entry and clearance procedures seriously. Most authorities will wish to see clearance papers from your last port of call, and in theory failure to produce these could result in being sent back to fetch them. More likely would be a fine, so make a point of obtaining them prior to departure. In some islands there is only one port of entry; in others there are several. All harbours mentioned in Part III are official entry ports.

Procedures vary from island to island. The most common is for the skipper to go ashore alone to report; in a few the boat should be moored or anchored to await the arrival of customs and/or immigration officers. In one or two places vessels are expected to go alongside. Always hoist the Q flag at sea before arrival, and if in doubt about procedure and unable to check with other yachtsmen play safe by anchoring in a conspicuous place. If nobody responds within one hour, the skipper should go ashore alone, taking crew list, ship's papers, passports and money. The latter is particularly important since many islands charge dues of one kind or another on arrival. US dollars will always be accepted in lieu of the local currency *except* in the French islands – which in any case do not charge entry fees at the present time.

Generally speaking the authorities on most of the islands are fair and tolerant in their treatment of yachts.

However the officials – quite naturally – expect to be taken seriously and do not take kindly to anyone who breaks the rules. The implications of this are that if a yacht wishes to leave minus any of the crew who were aboard on arrival it will have to be proved that they either (a) transferred to another yacht which has already left, (b) have already departed by air, or (c) hold a valid air ticket to a country which will accept them. All three are best notified to immigration both on arrival and when they take place. While official interest in drugs is largely confined to the illegal kind, if any member of the crew has medicinal drugs aboard they will need to be declared on arrival and a doctor's certificate should be carried in support of them. Firearms must also be declared, and in most places will be impounded until departure.

Formalities in the US islands

Many yachtsmen expect clearance into Puerto Rico and the US Virgin Islands to differentiate between US citizens and those of other nationalities, but this is not the case.

All yachts must seek clearance into the Commonwealth of Puerto Rico (which includes Culebra and Vieques) on arrival. Having cleared in it is possible to travel freely to the United States if not stopping elsewhere *en route*. Neither is it necessary to clear again on arrival at the US Virgin Islands. However the same does not apply in reverse, and having cleared into the Territory of the US Virgin Islands it is still necessary to go through the procedure again on entering Puerto Rico or the United States.

An equally typical leeward anchorage, in a small bay fringed with mangroves and palm trees. Life will be quieter away from the insistent trade winds, but in the evening the crew may be at the mercy of flies or mosquitoes. *Photo: Philip Allen*

However once cleared into the USVI it is possible to travel freely between the different islands of the territory.

The position regarding visas for foreign yachtsmen (referred to as *aliens* by the US authorities) is currently in a state of flux. In theory UK citizens no longer need visas for the US Virgin Islands, but do need them for Puerto Rico and the United States itself. Some other nationalities still require them for all three. In practice it could do no harm to ensure all crew members have appropriate visas, whether or not they are actually necessary.

Currency

In most of the islands from Grenada to Antigua the Eastern Caribbean dollar (EC) is used, currently pegged to the US dollar at a rate of EC$2.40 to $1US. The only ex-British island to have its own currency is Barbados, with a dollar roughly equal in value to the EC dollar but not acceptable outside Barbados. All the French islands use the French franc, in Dutch St Maarten either Dutch guilders or US dollars are accepted with equal alacrity, while in both the US and British Virgin Islands the US dollar is the official currency.

In point of fact the US dollar is acceptable throughout all the English-speaking islands, and if a price seems particularly reasonable check that you have not been quoted in US. This is particularly important if enquiring the cost of a taxi tour or other service. Most confusion is sheer misunderstanding on both sides, but occasionally the less

scrupulous may ask for payment in US dollars and then attempt to give change, dollar for dollar, in EC.

All but the smallest islands have banks, either the national bank of that particular country or a branch of a major chain, often Barclays International. For this reason a credit card of the Barclaycard/Visa family is the most widely accepted, though American Express and Access/MasterCard may also be useful from time to time. Traveller's cheques are exchangeable at all banks, as well as at many larger hotels. Passports are likely to be required when presenting all the above.

Facilities

Services and facilities of all kinds have improved beyond recognition over the past ten or fifteen years, largely due to the ever-growing charter boat and tourist industries.

All islands other than the very smallest now have reasonable food shops, many have large supermarkets – Barbados, Martinique and the Virgin Islands lead the field here, but competition is growing – and most sport bustling local produce markets which mot only offer variety and good value but are great fun to visit. Hotels, restaurants and cafés of all persuasions and prices have mushroomed, though many of the best are among the old-established. Not surprisingly, true *bon viveurs* will flock to the French islands where the standard of cuisine is claimed to rival that of France itself.

Boatyard facilities have also improved drastically, and

the West Indian harbours detailed in Part III have boatyards capable of hauling and carrying out major work on boats up to 60 feet or so, sometimes larger. However all are likely to be very busy throughout the cruising season, and except in a true emergency it will probably be necessary to book weeks if not months in advance. Fortunately, with the increased effectiveness of modern antifoulings, few owners engaged in the typical one-year circuit expect to haul their yachts while away from home waters. For a British-built boat, Antigua Slipway in English Harbour, Antigua (see page 168) offers the best chance of finding parts and spares for UK manufactured equipment. Those yards used to servicing American-built charter yachts are likely to carry the equivalent US fittings.

Medium and large scale charts

The Lesser Antilles are particularly well covered by medium and large scale charts with, in addition to those published by the British Admiralty (Chart 23, page 81) and US Defense Mapping Agency, the *Imray–Iolaire* series of yachtsmen's charts (Chart 25, page 83) and French publications covering Martinique, Guadeloupe, St Barts and St Martin.

BBA Chart Kit No 10 – *The Virgin Islands* — may also be found useful in that area.

Sailing directions and yachtsmen's guides

Official *Sailing Directions* covering the Caribbean comprise Admiralty publications NP 70 and 71 (the *West Indies Pilot* Vols I and II), together with NP 7A which covers the north coast of South America, and US publications SD 147 and 148 (the *Caribbean Sea* Vols I and II). See Appendix C for areas.

Regarding privately written guides, until recently most yachtsmen relied on those compiled by Donald M Street Jr, who has sailed the Lesser Antilles for many years aboard his venerable yawl *Iolaire*. However in the last few years a wider choice has become available, and as all appear to approach their subject from a different angle there is much to be said for carrying more than one guide to each area.

Cruising Guide to the Caribbean, Michael Marshall (ACN)
Cruising Guide to the Caribbean and the Bahamas, JC Hart and WT Stone (Dodd, Mead) (South and Central American coasts and Greater Antilles)
Cruising Guide to the Leeward Islands, Chris Doyle (Cruising Guide Pubs)
Cruising Guide to the Virgin Islands, Nancy and Simon Scott (Cruising Guide Pubs)
The Lesser Antilles, RCC Pilotage Foundation / Service Hydrographique et Océanographique de la Marine (Imray)
Sailor's Guide to a Venezuela Cruise, Chris Doyle (Cruising Guide Pubs)
Sailor's Guide to the Windward Islands, Chris Doyle (Cruising Guide Pubs)
St Maarten, St Kitts & Nevis Cruising Guide, William Eiman (also covers Anguilla, St Barts, Statia and Saba)
Street's Cruising Guides to the Eastern Caribbean, Vol 2 parts 1 and 2, Vols 3 and 4, DM Street Jr (WW Norton / Imray)
Virgin Anchorages, The Moorings staff (Cruising Guide Pubs)
Yachtsman's Guide to the Virgin Islands, Meredith E Fields (Tropic Isle Pubs)

Relevant ports covered in Part III

The Bahamas, together with the adjoining Turks and Caicos Islands, form an extensive chain of rocky islands surrounded by coral reefs and sand banks. They extend from about 21°N to 27°30′N and from 71°W to 79°W, covering an area of more than 5000 square miles, much of it with depths of less than 1.8 m (6 ft). Columbus made his first landing in the New World at San Salvador in 1492.

The archipelago is best cruised from east to west. Both prevailing winds and currents set this way, and for much of the day the sun will be aft, enabling water colours indicating shoals and coral heads to be most easily read.

Caution

The Bahamas has gained an unenviable reputation for violent crime over the past decade. This is mostly drug-associated, with smugglers using the islands as a base for drug running operations into the United States. Motor yachts have occasionally fallen victim to piracy, and there is always the outside chance of those aboard a cruising yacht witnessing something which endangers them. Until the situation improves it would be wise to avoid remote areas unless in company with at least one other yacht.

The US Coast Guard is charged with the job of surveillance, and frequently board and search private yachts in the course of their work. This is a routine matter which should be accepted as such, and is almost invariably carried out politely and professionally. The Coast Guard has authority from the Bahamian government to search all vessels, so the British owner of a UK-registered yacht should not expect to be exempt.

Weather and currents

Prevailing winds are easterly, with a northerly component from October to January or February and an increasingly southerly trend from June until September. May is the transition month when cold fronts from North America cease and frontal waves from the tropical Atlantic begin. These may cause local but intense weather systems between the Virgin Islands and the Bahamas, and the Bahamas themselves often experience at least one tropical storm during May. Several different weather forecast transmissions cover the area (see Chapter 10) and these should be listened to with care. The Bahamas lie squarely in the hurricane belt and it would therefore be very wise

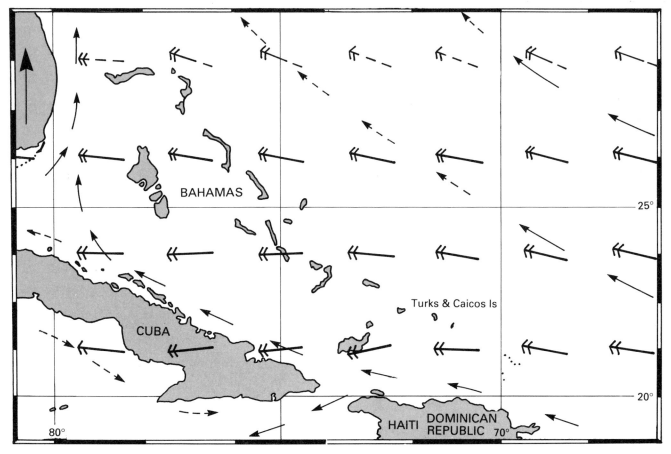

Chart 26 Prevailing winds and currents in the Bahamas – May. (Winds in feathered arrows, currents in solid arrows.) Based on information from the *Atlantic Pilot Atlas*.

to plan to be out of the area by mid or late June.

A north-west going current averaging about 0.5 knots follows the trend of the Bahamas until it merges with the Gulf Stream north of the islands. In places it may run with considerably greater speed, setting onto and across shoals and reefs, and is one more good reason for avoiding passagemaking after dark. In the NW Providence Channel currents are unpredictable and much influenced by the wind. In the Florida Strait the Gulf Stream runs at 3.5 to 4 knots in mid stream, rather less at the edges, and if heading for Miami or Fort Lauderdale allowance must be made.

Tides and tidal streams

Tidal streams in the southern Bahamas set on and off the banks and the appropriate tables and tidal stream atlas will need to be consulted.

Navigation and pilotage

The shallow waters dotted with coral heads and sand banks, combined with unpredictable currents and tidal streams, all call for what is known locally as 'eyeball navigation'. It cannot be emphasized too strongly that errors in these waters may be dangerous and that the greatest care must be exercised. A draught of 1.8 m (6 ft) is the absolute maximum, and 1.5 m (5 ft) would be more comfortable.

Charts are frequently out-of-date or inaccurate, and markers and beacons few and far between. Those with most experience advise as follows:

1 Avoid night passages if possible, but if you find yourself at sea at nightfall heave-to in open water to await daylight
2 Navigating from east to west, try to confine passages across shoal waters to before noon, with the sun at your back so that you can see the submerged coral heads. A person at the spreaders is best able to do this
3 Avoid inter-island passages from west to east, to windward with the sun in your eyes. If forced to go in this direction it may well be better to make an ocean passage
4 Remember that tides and currents may not only be stronger than indicated, but may set in the opposite direction to that which is forecast. Consult local opinion whenever possible, especially among the skippers of fishing and inter-island trading craft

Formalities

Entry must be made at one of 28 official ports – prior to that a yacht may sail through the islands but cannot anchor overnight. The Q flag should be hoisted 3 miles off, and in theory everyone is expected to stay aboard until customs and sometimes immigration officials come out to grant clearance. In practice it may sometimes be necessary for the skipper to go ashore to hunt them up. A Cruising Permit will be issued, which remains valid for up to six months. There are severe penalties for not observing clearance formalities.

Firearms must be declared and kept locked away until departure. Animals need valid rabies inoculation certificates.

Facilities

The Bahamas has its own currency, the Bahamas dollar (B$). This is at par with the US dollar, which is also widely accepted.

Facilities depend almost entirely on where you are. At Nassau on New Providence Island they are excellent, with several marinas and chandleries catering for the yacht owner plus several large supermarkets. The same is true of Freeport on Grand Bahama Island. However some of the outer islands are basic indeed, down to those which are no more than a sand bar supporting a few palm trees. Consult one of the cruising guides.

Sailing directions and yachtsmen's guides

The Bahamas are included in the Admiralty *Sailing Directions* NP 70, Vol I, and US *Sailing Directions* SD 147, Vol I (see Appendix C). Unofficial cruising guides currently include:

Cruising Guide to the Caribbean and the Bahamas, JC Hart and WT Stone (Dodd, Mead & Co)
Boater's Photographic Chartbook to the Bahamas, AirNav Publications
Cruising Guide to The Abacos and North Bahamas, Julius M Wilensky (Barnacle Marine)
Yachtsman's Guide to the Bahamas, Meredith E Fields (Tropic Isle Pubs)

18 NORTH FROM THE LESSER ANTILLES

Most cruising yachts leave the Lesser Antilles in April or May, in order to be well north before the start of the hurricane season in June. The incidence of hurricanes in that month is in fact very low (see Chapter 10), but departure in good time enables yachts to reach their next cruising ground on the North American coast, or make the transatlantic passage back towards Europe, at the best time of year.

Yachts heading for America may follow the Bahamas to Florida, sail direct to some point further north, or make the passage via Bermuda. A few of those returning to Europe will sail directly to the Azores, but most will also call at Bermuda, and then visit the Azores before making their final landfall in the British Islands or mainland Europe. These latter passages are dealt with in Chapter 22. Wherever yachts are headed, nearly all will be aiming for higher latitudes in which summer cruising can be undertaken and tropical storms avoided.

One largely unpublicised problem encountered on passages northwards during early summer by yachts using traditional navigation methods can be in getting a reliable latitude. This is because the declination of the sun draws north of the Virgin Islands in the middle of May, to reach its maximum declination of 23°26′.6N on Midsummer Day, 21 June. Thus any yacht sailing north in this period will at some stage cross the declination of the sun, which will rise due east, pass directly overhead at noon and set due west. For several days on either side it will be impossible to get any indication of latitude from the sun, and moon, planets or stars will have to be used. Navigators who have not previously used these might be wise to get some practice in advance.

Passage	Approx distance
Virgin Islands to Florida via the Bahamas	1000 miles
Virgin Islands to Morehead City, North Carolina	1200 miles
Virgin Islands to Bermuda	850 miles
Antigua to Bermuda	940 miles
Bermuda to Newport, Rhode Island	650 miles
Virgin Islands to the Azores (recommended route)	2500 miles

Passage planning charts

Coverage	Admiralty		US	
BA to 42°N	4012	(1:10,000,000)		
US to 45°N			120	(1:6,331,100)
To 45°N and 60°W	4403	(1:3,500,000)	108	(1:3,500,000)

Virgin Islands to Florida via the Bahamas

This route cuts ocean passagemaking to a minimum, linking as it does with the Intracoastal Waterway running parallel to the Eastern Seaboard of the United States. However with depths throughout much of the Bahamas no more than 1.8 m (6 ft) it calls for meticulous navigation, and both charts and cruising guides will need to be studied with care. See Chapter 17 for further details of the Bahamas.

If time is limited or draught prevents passage through the Bahamas themselves, a second possibility is to sail up the Atlantic side of the chain until Eleuthera is abeam, then pass through the NE and NW Providence Channels and across the Strait of Florida to Miami or Fort Lauderdale.

Both these passages should enjoy favourable winds and currents, though the latter are unpredictable and have caused the loss of more than one yacht. Winds between April and June are predominantly easterly at 10–15 knots, becoming south-east as the season progresses. Unsettled weather is most likely to be encountered during May.

The US Coast Guard monitors all vessels entering US waters, and it is highly likely that a yacht will be boarded at sea and searched for drugs. Reports indicate nothing but courtesy from those charged with this task, though British yachtsmen may be taken aback by the number of guns in evidence. It is as well to remember that if it were not for the many vessels caught running drugs each year their presence would not be necessary.

Virgin Islands to Morehead City, North Carolina

This should be another largely downwind passage, with south-easterly winds veering into the south and a 2.5 knot current following the trend of the coast. If sailing the rhumb line course in May or June there is an outside chance of encountering a hard blow, but a greater percentage likelihood of calms particularly during the mid portion of the passage. Plenty of fuel should be carried. The alternative is to sail a dog-leg, shaping a course to a point near 28°N 37°W before swinging northwards, in order to avoid the edge of the central Atlantic high pressure system with its associated light winds and calms.

If taking the direct route towards Charleston or Morehead City, either aim well south of your destination and allow the Gulf Stream to aid you, or cross it at right angles at a point which will enable you to come out roughly where you wish to make your landfall. At all costs avoid letting it carry you too far north – to return southward against both wind and current would be hard work indeed.

Virgin Islands to Bermuda

Bermuda lies almost due north from the Virgin Islands at just short of 65°W, and is well within the possible path of early season hurricanes. Therefore this is another passage which should be completed before the end of June.

Departing from the Virgin Islands in May or June, south-easterly trade winds should aid the initial stages of

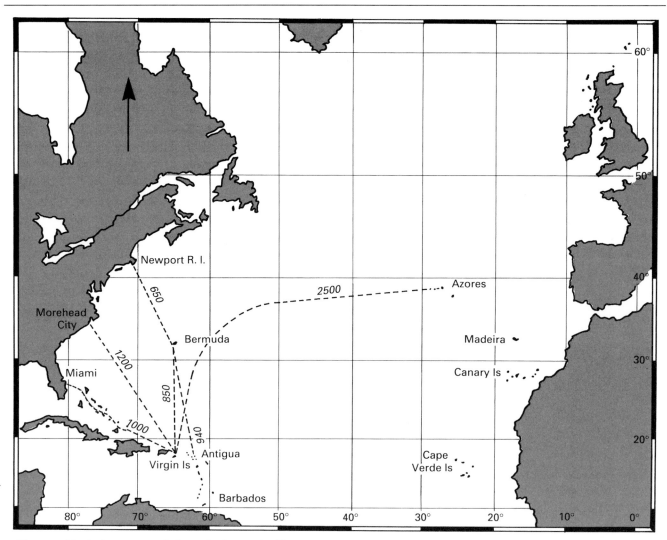

Chart 27 Typical routes north from the Lesser Antilles.

the passage. However as progress is made northwards winds are likely to become less reliable, with a high probability of light variables or calms later in the passage. Occasionally a late-season *norther* may come through, but this is unusual after mid April. Winds associated with cold fronts generally blow up sharply from the north-west, veering through north, east and south to finally blow themselves out in the south-west.

A north-west going current of about 0.5 knots can be expected until within 100 miles of Bermuda, after which it will vary in both speed and direction. Plenty of fuel should be carried, some of which should be earmarked for the final approach. Although Bermuda has a bad name as a landfall because of the extensive coral reefs which surround it, yachts coming from the south have the least difficult approach (see Chapter 20).

The passage between the Virgin Islands and Bermuda traverses the western edge of the Sargasso Sea – technically not a sea at all, but the static area around which the vast North Atlantic current systems sweep. Large carpets of brown Sargasso seaweed will be met with, which though thin are remarkably fibrous and will render towed and impeller logs virtually useless. A reliable latitude will be needed each day to keep a check on progress, and those relying on traditional methods may wish to brush up on moon, planet or star sights for the reasons outlined earlier.

Antigua to Bermuda

Very similar to the above, but typically sailed slightly earlier in the season by yachts departing at the beginning of May after Antigua Week. Winds are likely to be easterly or even north of east on departure, to some extent offsetting the advantage of leaving from a point further to windward. They are likely to veer south of east as progress is made northwards, becoming light and variable. The skipper with a schedule to keep up would be wise to take on additional fuel, in deck-stowed containers if necessary.

Bermuda to Newport, Rhode Island

Although Newport has been chosen as being a frequent destination, remarks concerning this passage could equally apply to the passage from Bermuda to New York or Cape Cod. All lie within the hurricane belt, making landfall by the end of June highly desirable. Winds in that month are likely to be south or south-westerly for much of the passage, though should a cold front move eastwards off the American continent strong west or north-west winds, often accompanied by driving rain, can be expected. Particularly bad seas will be produced where these winds cross the Gulf Stream.

Currents are likely to be variable until around 35°N,

where the full force of the Gulf Stream will be met. Between Bermuda and Newport this sets east or north-east at up to 1.5 knots, in a band some 300 to 400 miles wide. It is subject to considerable variation, and details are transmitted together with the 1600 GMT and 2200 GMT weather forecasts by the US Coast Guard at Portsmouth, Virginia (see Chapter 10).

The last 100 miles or so of the passage will be affected by the cold Labrador Current, which flows past Newfoundland and Nova Scotia, and continues south-west along the coast before petering out around the latitude of the Chesapeake. The northern edge of the Gulf Stream, where it meets the cold Labrador Current flowing south-west, is typically marked by a wall of fog. In June and July visibility of less than two miles can be expected for more than 20 per cent of the time in the later stages of the passage.

Virgin Islands to the Azores

Although the direct course from the Virgin Islands to the Azores is about 2200 miles whereas the recommended route is 300 to 400 miles longer, no vessel should attempt the rhumb line unless she is prepared to do much of the passage under power. To do so would be to cross the very middle of the high pressure area which dominates the Atlantic between Bermuda and the Azores, where light winds and calms are not so much probable as almost guaranteed.

In order to decrease the chance of calms a course should be shaped to pass within 200 to 300 miles of Bermuda before swinging north-eastwards. Exactly how far to continue before heading east is open to argument, and will depend both on the conditions for the year and the preferences of those aboard – sail the rhumb line after reaching 35°N and run the risk of prolonged calms, or keep going to 38°N or 40°N in search of stronger winds and a faster passage? See Chapter 22 for more details on the later part of this route.

In either event it is one more route for which the maximum amount of fuel should be laid in. It may also take considerably longer than anticipated – 30 to 35 days is not unusual – and if the wind fails and an awning cannot be rigged while under way, it may be hotter than at any other time in the Atlantic circuit. As much drinking and washing water as possible should be carried, and its usage monitored carefully.

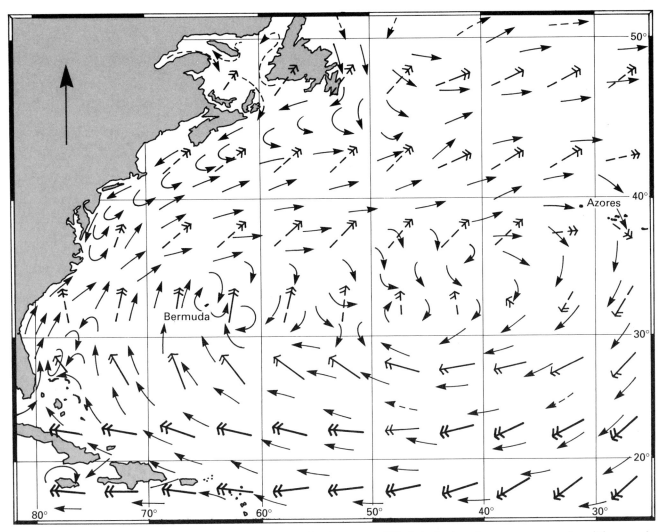

Chart 28 Prevailing winds and currents in the western Atlantic – June. (Winds in feathered arrows, currents in solid arrows.) Based on information from the *Atlantic Pilot Atlas*.

19 THE NORTH AMERICAN COASTLINE

Weather and currents

The continent of North America has a coastline stretching from the Tropic of Cancer to the Arctic Circle, though few yachts venture beyond 60°N. Regional weather patterns and particularly temperature vary accordingly.

One of the few generalisations that can be made is that, during the summer cruising season, winds generally blow either offshore or parallel to the coast. Thus strong on-shore gales, familiar to the European yachtsman, are seldom a problem. A more frequent hazard north of about 40°N is poor visibility, caused by the cold Labrador Current bringing arctic water south in a narrow stream almost to the latitude of Cape Hatteras. As the cold water encounters the warm air, it literally steams, giving rise to the notorious fogs of the Newfoundland Banks, Nova Scotia and Cape Cod. Unlike poor visibility around British or European coasts, which is often associated with high pressure and therefore light winds or calms, thick fog allied with winds of 20–30 knots is not unusual off the American and Canadian coasts.

Visibility is at its worst in summer, with a 20 per cent likelihood of less than two miles in all areas north of Block Island, increasing to a 40 per cent likelihood off Nova Scotia and Newfoundland. There is no doubt that the stranger intending to cruise these waters might ease their task and save themselves much anxiety by fitting radar.

Further south, the warm Gulf Stream parallels the coast, running at up to four knots in the Florida Strait but slowing as it fans out into the Atlantic. When strong northerly winds oppose the north-east-going current particularly vicious seas can form, which have been responsible for the loss of more than one yacht. Although the movements of the Gulf Stream and its associated eddies are unpredictable, the US Coast Guard runs a permanent monitoring system and details are transmitted with their 1600 GMT and 2200 GMT weather forecasts.

Ice

The Labrador Current is also responsible for carrying icebergs south past Newfoundland, sometimes reaching

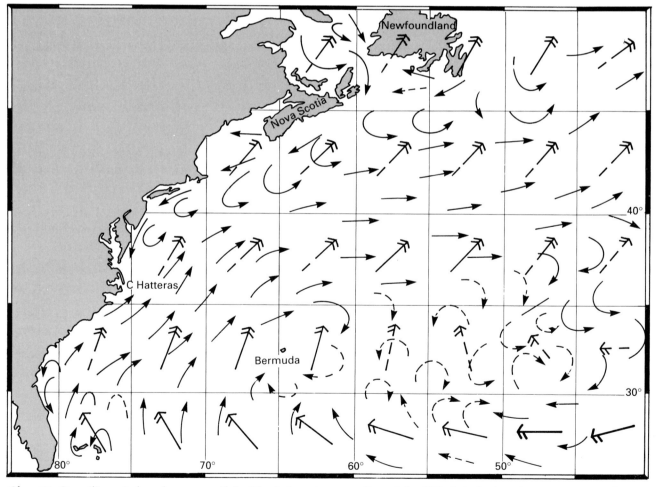

Chart 29 Prevailing winds and currents off the North American coastline – July. (Winds in feathered arrows, currents in solid arrows.) Based on information from the *Atlantic Pilot Atlas*.

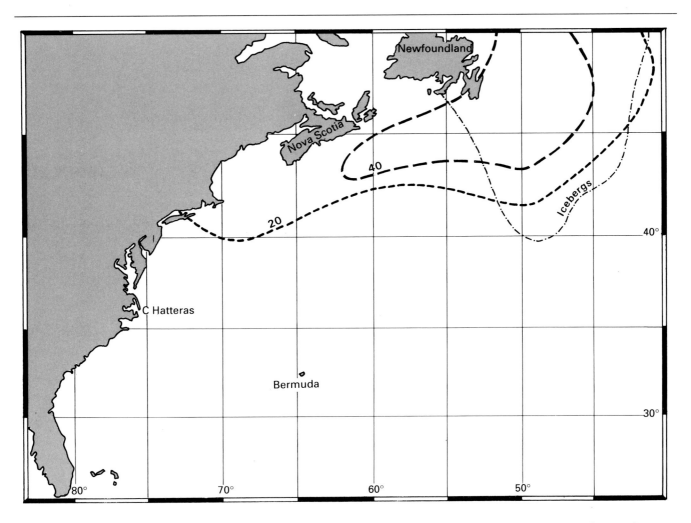

Chart 30 Iceberg limits and percentage likelihood of less than two mile visibility off the North American coastline – July. Based on information from the *Atlantic Pilot Atlas*.

40°N before melting. They are seldom encountered east of 40°W or west of 60°W, their range being most widespread in June and shrinking throughout the late summer and autumn. Rogue bergs have occasionally been found much further south and east, but this is very unusual. There can be a concentration of bergs east of Cape Race, where the big ones go aground on the Grand Banks. As the season progresses and the icebergs begin to melt, they float off and move further south, finally reaching the northern edge of the Gulf Stream where they disperse and melt completely. Ice is therefore most prevalent in the northern and eastern parts of the Grand Banks early in the season, and at the southern end, and perhaps into the edge of the Gulf Stream, later on. The International Ice Patrol co-ordinated by the US and Canadian Coast Guard services broadcasts daily reports of the location and drift of bergs. A report can be obtained before sailing by telephoning (902)426–6030 or (709) 772–2083.

Tides and tidal streams

Tidal influence varies enormously along the North American coastline, from a bare 1.3 m (4 ft) in Florida to the massive 15 m (50 ft) tides of the Bay of Fundy. The US East Coast edition of *Reed's Nautical Almanac* is one of several sources of tide tables and tidal stream atlases which should be consulted as appropriate.

Approach and landfall

Conditions on approaching the coast will be dictated to a great extent by the specific latitude and area chosen. It would plainly be impossible to detail all feasible landfalls, so only those associated with the passages outlined in Chapters 18, 22 and 23 will be covered. The official *Sailing Directions* and/or a suitable yachtsman's guide should be consulted for more detailed information.

Much of the US eastern seaboard is fringed by a wide and relatively shallow continental shelf, with depths of 36 m (120 ft) or less being found 50 miles offshore in many areas. Depths then drop off very suddenly to 3000 m (10,000 ft) or more, and in bad weather very confused seas can result. It is important not to get caught in this area by the onset of heavy weather on approaching the coast, and equally important to make offing as rapidly as possible on departure in order to get into deep water before there is any chance of meeting heavy weather.

The main problem on approaching the Canadian and northern US coasts is the high incidence of fog, and the fact that it can be prolonged. It is thus not practical to stand off and await improved conditions and one must be prepared to continue, with caution, and enter port in bad visibility. It is therefore important to have an accurate position before entering the fog.

Cape Race and the east coast of Newfoundland are

within the iceberg zone in the early part of the season (April to June). This, combined with fog, will call for great caution when approaching this coast. The coasts of Nova Scotia and the United States can generally be regarded as being to the west of the iceberg zone.

The Grand Banks and the waters off Nova Scotia are popular fishing grounds for fleets of trawlers and coastal fishing boats. A sharp lookout should be maintained for them, and also for both nets and lines of pots marked by floats, which may be found well offshore. The gear itself will be submerged, and thus the buoy the only danger. The increasing reliance on radar by shipping means that merchant vessels seldom reduce speed much in poor visibility, even though small craft may not be spotted on the screen. The main concentrations of shipping may be expected off Cape Race, the approaches to Halifax, the Nantucket Light Vessel, and to the north of Cape Cod where the routes to Boston and the Cape Cod Canal will be crossed.

Newfoundland

St John's is the nearest port to Europe and full details of approach and entry are given in Part III. Cape Race (46°39′ N 53°04′ W) may be used as a landfall by those on the Northern or Great Circle routes, and for yachts not carrying Satnav, GPS or Loran C the DF beacons on Cape Race, Cape St Francis and Cape Spear (all 100-mile range) will be found useful on approach. If coming from the east, sounding for Ballard Bank (about eight miles east of the Cape) gives an indication of position if visibility is poor. Virgin Rocks and the nearby Eastern Shoals, lying 100 miles east of Cape Race, are a potential hazard on the approach.

Offshore the current sets southerly at about one knot, but runs westerly around Cape Race. There can be a strong northerly eddy off the south coast of Newfoundland. If close inshore beware of the tides and the possibility of being swept into the bays along the southern coast. Many wrecks have occurred in fog on the south-eastern and southern coasts of Newfoundland, owing to the indraught or to the current setting north-eastward.

Nova Scotia

Sable Island (43°55′ N 59°50′ W), which lies just under 100 miles off the coast of Nova Scotia, has a 200-mile DF beacon which can be useful on approaching the coast. However the island itself must be given a wide berth – it is a graveyard of ships, with strong unpredictable currents and shoal water. Other powerful beacons are situated at Scatarie Island NE Light, Cranberry Island Light and Sambro Island Light, all with ranges of 100 miles or more, and there are many beacons of 50 miles or less which are useful when closer in. However there are no powerful beacons serving the southern part of Nova Scotia, where a strong indraught has been reported off Cape Sable. Oil rigs may be encountered in the area (see Chapter 9).

Halifax is the recommended port for entering Nova Scotia, and full details will be found in Part III.

Nantucket Shoals

Many yachts on passage from Europe or coming up from Bermuda make landfall at the Nantucket Shoals Lanby (40°30′ N 69°26′ W), 50 miles south-east of Nantucket Island with its offlying shoals. Probably the majority con-

tinue to Newport, Rhode Island, for which harbour and final approach details will be found in Part III. Nantucket Shoals Lanby carries a 13-mile range light standing 13 m (43 ft) above sea level, and is also equipped with a horn and 50-mile DF beacon. Care must be taken in the vicinity of the Lanby as it also marks the separation zone for the shipping lanes in and out of New York (see Chapter 10).

The Nantucket Shoals, which stretch more than 30 miles south-east of Nantucket Island, have a least depth of 1.25 m (4 ft) and frequently break in bad weather. Strong tidal streams set over the Shoals, and though they can be crossed in calm weather via the marked channels this is not advised. In any case, only a slight deflection to the west of the rhumb line will be needed if heading for Newport, and none at all for Block Island or further west. If heading northwards the choice is between closing the coast at Buzzards Bay and traversing the Cape Cod Canal, or heading north-east from the Lanby to shape a course between Nantucket Shoal and Georges Bank, where oil rigs may be encountered (see Chapter 9).

Cape Hatteras

While Cape Hatteras (35°15′ N 75°31′ W) may be broadly defined as a target area for yachts coming west from Bermuda or north from the Lesser Antilles or Bahamas, its coastline is highly dangerous with many offlying banks and strong and unpredictable currents. Cape Hatteras itself deserves to be given a wide berth.

A popular route for northbound yachts is to join the Intracoastal Waterway at Morehead City, North Carolina, passing through the Sounds inside Cape Hatteras *en route* to the Chesapeake Bay. DF beacons with ranges of 125 and 150 miles respectively operate from Oregon Inlet and Fort Macon on the Beaufort Inlet, with 50 mile beacons on Diamond Shoals and Frying Pan Shoals. In addition there is a powerful lighthouse at Cape Lookout. The principal requirement when making the approach is to avoid the Lookout Shoals.

Southbound yachts should either stand well offshore around Cape Hatteras, or enter the Chesapeake and thence the Intracoastal Waterway at Norfolk, Virginia. Cape Henry at the southern entrance to the Bay and Chesapeake Light to the north are both equipped with DF beacons (150 and 150 miles respectively) and powerful lights.

Formalities: Canada

Arrival should be made at an official port of entry, and if possible notified by VHF. Otherwise the skipper should go ashore alone to contact customs and immigration. The usual paperwork and details are required, together with (for a foreign yacht) an intended itinerary and approximate departure date. In the case of many nationalities, including British, a cruising permit can then be issued, removing the need to clear again at subsequent ports. Firearms must be declared on arrival, but most single-shot weapons are permitted. Animals must have valid rabies vaccination certificates, but even so are not allowed ashore and will have to remain on board.

Formalities: the United States

Again it is important to clear in at a designated port of entry, and if in doubt the Coast Guard will advise on

Approaching Norfolk, Virginia, from the south via the Intracoastal Waterway. It is possible to sail on many stretches of the Waterway and all bridges either open or lift. *Photo: Tony Vasey*

procedure. Parts of the coast, most notably Florida, have severe problems with drug smugglers and it is worth making a particular effort to seek clearance *immediately* on arrival. Most foreign yachts are boarded for inspection, some before they even make their landfall (though a Coast Guard boarding at sea has nothing to do with inward clearance, which must still be sought in the normal way).

Ship's registration papers, clearance from the previous port and a crew list will be required, and the US is one of the few major countries for which nearly all nationalities (including all Europeans) must have a visa. In addition a detailed stores list may be called for, and many items (including fresh meat, fruit and vegetables) are likely to be confiscated. Canned foods of all types are normally allowed.

Surprisingly for a country with relatively relaxed gun laws, only hunting and sporting firearms may be brought in without restrictions. Animals do not need rabies certificates if arriving from rabies-free countries but will otherwise require them, and rabies *does* exist in some islands of the Lesser Antilles. Pet birds will be put into quarantine. There are also restrictions on various animal products from endangered species – few yachts are likely to have furs aboard, but many people may have bought souvenirs of tortoise or turtle shell jewellery, scrimshaw on whalebone or ivory, or simply have picked up some coral.

Most nationalities, including those of Britain and northern Europe, may apply for a cruising licence. This remains valid for up to one year and exempts the yacht from further clearance until ready for departure.

American-registered yachts returning home must also report arrival to customs, but are less likely to be boarded for inspection. There is no specific requirement for such vessels to clear outwards, though it would be wise to do so since the authorities of most other countries will wish to see evidence regarding date and port of departure.

PS: Not all US officials understand why being referred to as an 'alien' strikes many Britons as so amusing. It may be best to keep a straight face.

The US Coast Guard

Confusion can sometimes arise over the role and responsibilities of the US Coast Guard, which has a much wider brief than the British service of the same name.

Whereas the British Coastguard is largely land-based, the US Coast Guard is very active afloat. Its responsibilities include policing its own and nearby international waters for drug smugglers (in the course of which private yachts are frequently boarded and searched), and generally ensuring that all vessels proceed in an orderly manner. Unlike Britain, where lifeboats are the responsibility of the Royal National Lifeboat Institution, in the USA the Coast Guard also runs its own search and rescue vessels and aircraft. They will respond if a vessel is in immediate danger, but where there is no risk to life or craft the Coast Guard will usually turn the job over to a private contractor for commercial salvage – which is likely to be expensive.

It is standard practice, and in some places mandatory, to call the Coast Guard on VHF channel 16 on approach to harbour. They will give updated chart information if required, but prefer not to give specific directions for entering harbour for reasons of liability. However a skipper who blundered into trouble through not asking for advice would find little sympathy.

Another Coast Guard responsibility is for small craft safety, and if one calls them for assistance, or is boarded for a drug check, they are likely to inspect the safety equipment carried. Their list of requirements includes several items not usually found aboard British and European yachts while other aspects of marine law may also be different on crossing the Atlantic (see Appendix H).

(American yachtsmen may be interested to know the converse regarding safety requirements in European waters. Basically, some European countries including France run similar schemes covering vessels owned by their own nationals, but none affect foreign registered yachts. In Britain there are no regulations at all governing craft for private use – people can, and occasionally do, put to sea in barrels or worse! Only if running a yacht commercially for charter or tuition do stringent safety requirements come into effect.)

Sewage disposal

The Federal Government has charged the US Coast Guard with the inspection of sewage disposal arrangements on yachts. The rules are an amalgam of Federal and State Laws, and are further complicated by local ordinances. The usual recourse for visiting yachts is to fit a 'Y' valve at the heads, in order that sewage can be pumped directly overboard when offshore and into a holding tank at other times. It has been suggested that a large plastic container, suitably plumbed-in, would make an acceptable holding tank, which can then be pumped out periodically at a shore establishment equipped to do so. It may be necessary to seal the valve in the holding tank position on occasion, and provision should be made for this (see Appendix H for further details).

Facilities

America probably offers the best facilities for yachts and their owners to be found anywhere on the globe. The larger yachting centres of Canada are not far behind. Equally, both countries still offer cruising grounds with dozens of miles between loaves of bread.

All those harbours detailed in Part III have good facilities for yachts, though many of the best-known yachting centres – eg Annapolis – are outside the scope of a book concentrating on Atlantic crossings and landfalls. Local guides should be consulted.

Sailing directions and yachtsmen's guides

Official *Sailing Directions* to the North American coast between Newfoundland and Florida comprise Admiralty publications NP 50, NP 59, NP 65, NP 68 and NP 69; US publications SD 140, SD 145 and SD 146; and Canadian Hydrographic Service volumes covering Nova Scotia (SE

coast) and Bay of Fundy, Gulf and River St Lawrence, Newfoundland, and Labrador and Hudson Bay. See Appendix C for the areas covered by each volume.

There are also privately written guides covering every inch of the coast, much of it several times over. These currently include:

Cruise Cape Breton, Cape Breton Development Corporation
Cruising Guide to Eastern Florida, Claiborne Young
Cruising Guide to Labrador, Sandy Weld/Cruising Club of America
Cruising Guide to Maine, Parts 1 and 2, Don Johnson/Julius M Wilensky (Wescott Cove)
Cruising Guide to Narragansett Bay, Lynda and Patrick Childress
Cruising Guide to Newfoundland, Sandy Weld/Cruising Club of America
Cruising Guide to the Chesapeake, Stone, Blanchard & Hays
Cruising Guide to the Florida Keys, Frank Papy
Cruising Guide to the Maine Coast, Hank and Jan Taft (International Marine)
Cruising Guide to the New England Coast, Roger Duncan and John Ware
Cruising Guide to the Nova Scotia Coast, John McKelvy
Cruising Guides to the Coastal Carolinas, Vols 1 and 2, Claiborne S Young
Cruising the Chesapeake: A Gunkholer's Guide, William Shellenberger
Embassy Complete Guide to Long Island Sound, Mark Borton and J Grant
Embassy Complete Guide to Rhode Island and Massachusetts, Mark Borton
Intracoastal Waterway Facilities Guide, RD Smith
Port to Port Guides, Parts 1 to 4 (Maine to Key West), Pilot Publishing
The Intra-Coastal Waterway, Jan and Bill Moeller (Seven Seas)
Waterway Guides (Northern, Mid-Atlantic and Southern), Communication Channels
Yachting Guide to the South Shore of Nova Scotia, Arthur Dechman

Chart kits

BBA Chart Kits (six covering Canadian border to Bahamas via the Intracoastal Waterway)
Waterway Guide Chartbooks (six covering Canadian border to Florida), ES Maloney

Relevant ports covered in Part III

Bermuda is Britain's oldest colony and is self-governing. It has its own currency, the Bermuda dollar, which is at par with the US dollar. Its economy is closely linked to the American tourist trade, and the two currencies are interchangeable. The islands consist of a low-lying group of small coral islets surrounded by extensive reefs, many of which are joined by causeways.

Weather and currents

Weather in Bermuda is influenced by the position of the Azores high, the Gulf Stream, and the weather systems on the eastern seaboard of the United States. Winds typically box the compass during the year, being generally westerly from December through until April, backing into the south around May, and gradually swinging through south-west, west and north from September onwards. In June and July, when the majority of yachts making the Atlantic circuit pass through, an average of 15–20 knots

may be expected though a sudden increase to 30 or 40 knots may accompany the passage of a frontal wave moving from the American coast. The islands lie well within the hurricane belt (see Chapter 10) and passagemaking yachts should endeavour to be out of the area by the end of June. Temperatures vary from around 17°C (62°F) in February to 28°C (82°F) in August.

Currents in the vicinity are unpredictable, though a northerly set is the most common. The islands lie within a few hundred miles of the eastern wall of the Gulf Stream, which frequently sets up large eddies, and though currents seldom exceed 0.5 knots they may reverse direction within a matter of days.

Approach and landfall

Due to the reefs which extend up to ten miles off the north-east, north and west coasts of Bermuda, the only safe approach is from a position south or south-east of the

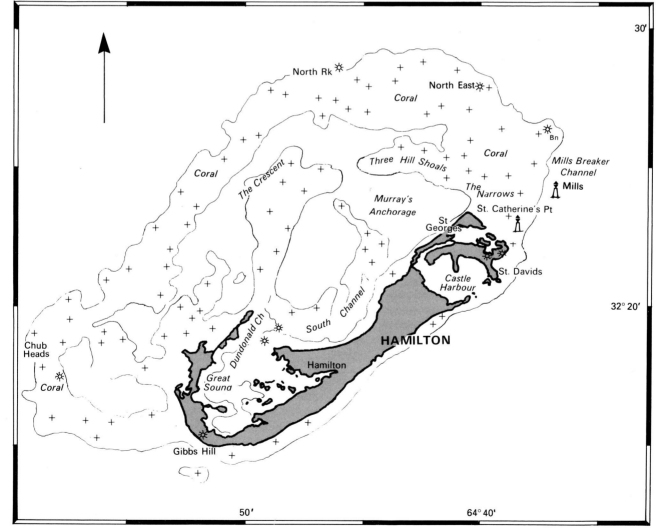

Chart 31 The Bermuda islands. Based on Admiralty Chart No 1073.

group. Here the coast is very steep-to, with the 200 m (650 ft) sounding lying within a mile of the coastline in places. There is also a local magnetic anomaly, which may give a possible error of up to 6° in addition to the normal variation for this zone. There are two DF beacons on the island, with ranges of 100 and 150 miles respectively.

In thick weather, and particularly if not equipped with radar or electronic position systems, it may be advisable to call up Bermuda Harbour Radio (ZBM) on VHF channel 16 or 2182 kHz well in advance of arrival for pilotage information. It is in any case a requirement to contact them before entering the buoyed channel for the narrow Town Cut Channel leading into St George's Harbour. Details of the approach and entry to St George's Harbour will be found in Part III.

Formalities

Clearance into Bermuda is likely to be the most expensive encountered on the entire Atlantic circuit, currently being US$30 per head (including babies and small children) irrespective of the size of yacht. Entry must be made at St George's – full details will be found in Part III. The Q flag should be flown when entering and until pratique has been granted, after which boats may proceed to Hamilton or elsewhere. St George's must again be visited for clearance out prior to departure.

Visitors are normally allowed to remain for an initial period of three weeks, but if a longer stay is desired application must be made to the Department of Immigration. Firearms, including Very pistols and spear guns, must be declared and may be impounded until departure or placed under seal aboard. Medically prescribed drugs must also be declared. There are severe penalties for the possession of illegal drugs.

Facilities

Bermuda is a sophisticated island with all manner of shopping facilities for both the tourist and the yacht owner. All slipping and repair services are available, and bonded stores may be obtained prior to departure. However, almost everything must be imported, making food and other stores extremely expensive. Canned foods are available, but variety may be limited as great reliance locally is placed on chilled and frozen foods. For the yacht without refrigeration this creates a problem, since chilling fruit or vegetables badly impairs their keeping properties. It may be possible by asking around to find a source of locally laid eggs which have been neither washed nor chilled, and some locally grown vegetables.

Sailing directions and yachtsmen's guides

Admiralty Pilot NP 70, Vol I and US *Sailing Directions* SD 147, Vol I cover the area (see Appendix C). There is also the 16-page *Information Sheet* published annually by the Bermuda Department of Tourism (POB HM 465, Hamilton HM BX, Bermuda) which is free on request and includes detailed and useful information on buoyage and navigation, clearance, facilities and other matters. Two privately written guides are available – the *Yachtsman's Guide to the Bermudan Islands* by Michael Voegli and the *Yachting Guide to Bermuda* by Jane and Edward Harris (Bermuda Maritime).

Relevant ports covered in Part III

The Azores form an autonomous region of Portugal (and are thus within the EC), where Portuguese is spoken with an accent which varies from island to island. Currency is the Portuguese escudo.

Compared with other island groups in the Atlantic the Azores are thinly spread. The nine islands lie in three distinct groups stretching over more than 300 miles of ocean, and show surprising diversity in terms of both landscape and populace. All are of volcanic origin, and ancient *caldeira* craters are a feature of nearly every island. Only Pico retains its original cone, the dramatic 2351 m (7713 ft) summit being visible at 50 or 60 miles in clear weather.

Several new harbour developments are taking shape throughout the islands, and though naturally intended primarily for the use of local people, visiting yachtsmen will also benefit. Until recently only Horta on Faial and Ponta Delgada on São Miguel could be regarded as safe under nearly all conditions, but the completion of an extensive double breakwater at Praia da Vitoria on Terceira has added a third harbour to the list. There are also many less well protected bays and harbours where a yacht can lie at anchor in settled conditions.

The Azores have long been regarded by most yachtsmen simply as a convenient place to break the Atlantic passage, and their merits as a cruising ground largely overlooked. Unless other commitments necessitate pressing onwards, try to allow at least two or three weeks in the archipelago – and don't spend them all in Horta.

Weather and currents

During the sailing season, effectively from June until mid September, the climate is dominated by the Azores High. In most years this becomes strongly established, resulting in prolonged periods of light winds or calms, but some-

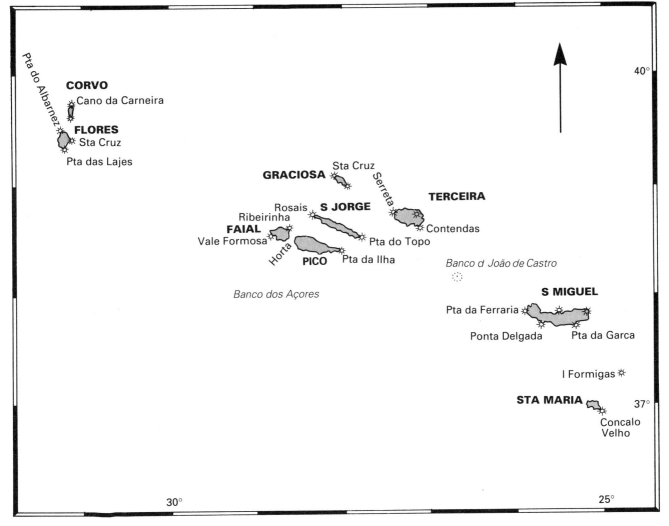

Chart 32 The Azores archipelago. Based on Admiralty Chart No 1950.

times the High remains weak so that windier, more changeable weather predominates as it does at other seasons. Winds between south-west and north are the most common throughout the year, but almost every other direction is likely to be experienced at some time. As in Atlantic Europe, south-easterly winds usually foretell an approaching front. There is a six per cent likelihood of calms between June and August, decreasing to four per cent in September.

Summer temperatures typically rise to around 23°C (74°F), though heat waves can occasionally produce a sizzling 30°C (86°F) for days at a time. However nights can feel chilly, particularly to those who have spent the previous months in the tropics.

Visibility is generally good, though southerly winds may produce hazy conditions which limit the field of view to five miles or so while still apparently giving a sharp horizon. This is particularly common around the western islands of Flores and Corvo. Like the *harmattan* in the Cape Verdes, it can be most misleading and produce problems for traditional navigation.

The Azores are affected by that branch of the North Atlantic Current setting south-east towards the Iberian coast which later becomes the Canary Current. Flow in open waters seldom exceeds half a knot, but this may double around the ends of the larger islands and when ocean and tidal currents combine, races may form. Ocean swell can be a factor when picking an anchorage, as it frequently runs in from the west even when winds are light. For this reason the majority of Azorean harbours are on south or east-facing coasts.

Tides and tidal streams

Tidal range is relatively small throughout the Azores and nowhere exceeds 1.8 m (6 ft). However streams can run

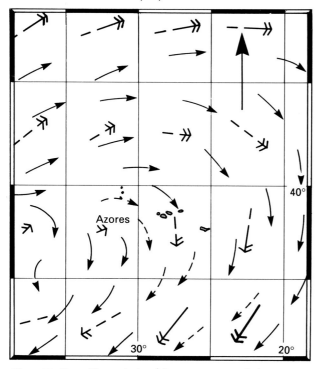

Chart 33 Prevailing winds and currents around the Azores – July. (Winds in feathered arrows, currents in solid arrows.) Based on information from the *Atlantic Pilot Atlas*.

with surprising speed and may reach two knots in the Canal do Faial between Faial and Pico. Tides set north or north-east on the flood, south or south-west on the ebb.

Approach and landfall

Approach to the Azores is straightforward and neither Flores nor Faial, the two most popular landfall islands for transatlantic yachts, have any serious outliers. The usual course is to skirt their southern coasts, and if approaching Faial in darkness it should be noted that the Vale Formoso lighthouse at its western end is widely regarded as being considerably less powerful than stated, with a range of nearer 5 miles than the claimed 13 miles. Yachts approaching from Europe often make landfall on São Miguel, which again is steep-to. All three islands are equipped with powerful DF beacons with ranges exceeding 200 miles.

Buoyage (such as it is) follows the European IALA A system, opposite to that found in North America and the Caribbean.

Caution: Many yachts making the passage from the USA or Bermuda like to call first at the island of Flores, but until harbour facilities are improved this is advisable only in settled weather. If intending to make landfall at Flores (and it is a lovely island well worth visiting) it is strongly advised that a current copy of the RCC Pilotage Foundation's *Atlantic Islands* should be carried aboard.

Formalities

The Portuguese seem to like their paperwork, and entry can be a long drawn-out affair. Furthermore it is necessary to clear in and out of each island individually, though the Q flag need only be flown on first arriving from abroad.

In theory, the advent of the EC should mean fewer formalities for EC owned and registered yachts arriving from mainland Europe, but in practice this represents such a small percentage of total arrivals that it is likely all yachts will be expected to follow the same clearance procedures for some time to come.

On first arrival the skipper should take passports and ship's papers to the *Capitania do Porto* (Port Captain), proceeding to the *Guarda Fiscal* (immigration) office, the *Policia Maritima* and in some cases the *Alfandega* (customs). A *Livrete de Transito* (transit log) will be made out, in which all further movements of the yacht will be recorded until she leaves the islands. It is generally necessary to visit the *Capitania, Policia Maritima* and possibly the *Guarda Fiscal* again before leaving.

Clearance is much less effort in Horta than elsewhere, as all the necessary offices are in one building in the marina (see page 198) whereas in other harbours it may entail a longish walk. Also several of the officials speak excellent English. However even when the language barrier presents almost insurmountable difficulties the officials are invariably courteous, and there is no doubt at all that a smile will speed things along much more effectively than any show of impatience.

A Portuguese courtesy flag should be flown, and many visiting yachtsmen like to hoist the blue, white and gold Azorean flag beneath it.

Facilities

Repair and other facilities for yachts are limited, and all imported spares carry heavy duty which cannot be reclaimed. However, sophisticated fishing boats operate from several of the islands, implying the existence of at least one or two electronics engineers and most skills are available if really desperate. By far the best harbours if work needs to be done are Horta and Ponta Delgada, both of which have small but well run marinas with helpful, English-speaking staff who would almost certainly assist with recommendations and/or translation as necessary. Further details of both these harbours will be found in Part III.

Food shopping has improved considerably over the past decade, though many of the smaller towns still offer little more than the basics. It would be fair to say that while all normal day-to-day needs are likely to be met, it would be unwise to expect to do any major stocking up in the Azores. Nearly all the islands have markets and the fresh produce is excellent – both temperate and tropical fruit and vegetables thrive, and seasonal gluts of plums and figs may test the toughest digestion. Particularly good cheese is also produced, notably on Pico and São Jorge.

Sailing directions and yachtsmen's guides

The Azores are included in Admiralty *Sailing Directions* NP 67 and US publication SD 143 (see Appendix C).

Only one privately written guide is currently available, the *Atlantic Islands*, compiled by Nicholas Heath and the present author for the RCC Pilotage Foundation and published by Imray Laurie Norie & Wilson Ltd. A great deal of original research went into its production, including visits to more than thirty harbours and anchorages throughout the archipelago and the collation of all kinds of background information – and that was just the Azores. The *Atlantic Islands* also covers Madeira, the Canaries and the Cape Verde Islands. Annual supplements are available from the publishers for a small fee – newly purchased copies should already contain them.

Relevant ports covered in Part III

22 TRANSATLANTIC IN THE MIDDLE AND NORTHERN LATITUDES

There is a wide variety of possible routes if sailing from the USA or Canada to the UK and Europe, some of which break the voyage at one or more of the mid Atlantic island groups. Probably the majority of cruising yachts elect to take the voyage in stages. Others make the passage direct, usually keeping further north. It is broadly true to say that eastward routes tend to keep further south so as to make maximum use of the North Atlantic Current. It is certainly more pleasant to cross the northern Atlantic from west to east than vice versa, with a good chance of favourable winds for most of the passage. Yachts heading westwards must either stay well north and face the likelihood of severe weather, or remain further south in the hope of lighter weather but at the expense of mileage lost to the current.

Inevitably, many of the following remarks which refer to one passage will also apply to others with a similar departure point or landfall. It is therefore suggested that readers should study all those passages taking a similar or parallel course, in addition to the one they actually intend to sail.

Passages eastwards	Approx distance
USA to Bermuda	650 to 700 miles
Bermuda to Horta, Azores	1820 miles
Newport, Rhode Island to Horta, Azores	1980 miles
Halifax, Nova Scotia to Horta, Azores	1635 miles
St John's, Newfoundland to Horta, Azores	1240 miles
Horta, Azores to Falmouth, UK	1250 miles
Ponta Delgada, Azores to Spain or Portugal	750 to 820 miles
Ponta Delgada, Azores to Gibraltar	960 miles
Newport, Rhode Island to Falmouth via the mid latitudes	2940 miles
Halifax, Nova Scotia to Falmouth via the mid latitudes	2600 miles
Newport, Rhode Island to Falmouth via the Great Circle	2850 miles
Halifax, Nova Scotia to Falmouth via the Great Circle	2390 miles
St John's, Newfoundland to Falmouth via the Great Circle	1900 miles

Passages westwards	Approx distance
Falmouth, UK to the Azores – see Chapter 12	1200 miles
Horta, Azores to Bermuda	1820 miles
Bermuda to Newport, Rhode Island – see Chapter 18	650 miles
Falmouth to Newport, Rhode Island via the mid latitudes	2940 miles
Falmouth to Halifax, Nova Scotia via the mid latitudes	2600 miles
Falmouth to Newport, Rhode Island via the Great Circle	2850 miles
Falmouth to Halifax, Nova Scotia via the Great Circle	2390 miles
Falmouth to St John's, Newfoundland via the Great Circle	1900 miles
Falmouth to Newport, Rhode Island via the Northern Route	2870 miles
Falmouth to Halifax, Nova Scotia via the Northern Route	2230 miles
Falmouth to St John's, Newfoundland via the Northern Route	2050 miles

NB: many of the above distances are approximations, due to the wide variety of possible routes.

Passage planning charts

Coverage	Admiralty	US
Northern North Atlantic	4011 (1:10,000,000)	120 (1:5,870,000)
Southern North Atlantic	4012 (1:10,000,000)	120 (1:6,331,100)

It is important to note that magnetic variation differs as one crosses the Atlantic, reaching more than 20° of westerly variation near 50°W. The amount of variation fluctuates slowly, rates varying from place to place. Ocean passage charts show isogonic lines, linking those places with equal variation, and also give details of annual changes. Variation should be calculated and applied with great care, the calculation being reworked frequently as progress is made.

Weather patterns

Except in the immediate vicinity of Bermuda, the passages discussed in this chapter lie between 35°N and 55°N or 60°N. Those routes in higher latitudes, perhaps visiting Greenland or Iceland *en route* to Norway, are the preserve of the experienced yachtsman and should be carefully researched using the relevant *Sailing Directions* and Admiralty *Routeing Charts* or US *Pilot Charts*.

The latitudes in which crossings are most often made are dominated by the prevailing westerly and south-westerly winds, created by low pressure to the north and the mid Atlantic High Pressure system to the south. This typically stretches from Bermuda to the Azores throughout the summer, but in some years may remain further south than usual, allowing the passage of depressions also to veer unusually far south. Less frequently, associated cells of high pressure not only form but persist further north, giving light winds and calms over large areas for weeks at a time. Thus while some features – such as fog – tend to be true of a particular area or latitude at all times, others may shift their area of influence from one year to the next.

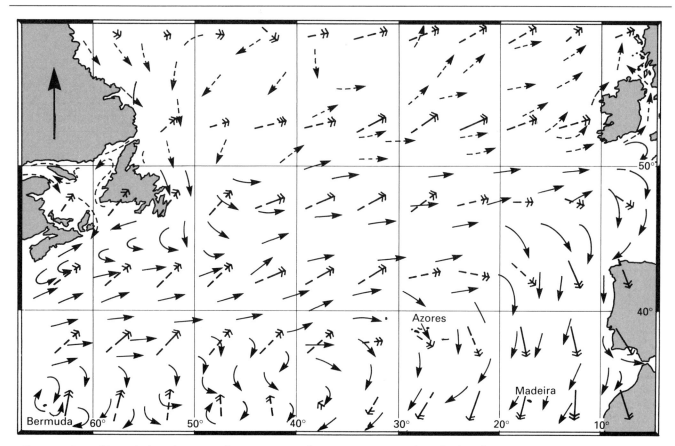

Chart 34 Prevailing winds and currents between 30° and 58°N – June. (Winds in feathered arrows, currents in solid arrows.) Based on information from the *Atlantic Pilot Atlas*.

Whereas the movements of the trade wind belt can be predicted with a fair degree of accuracy, weather affecting all crossings in the middle and northern latitudes owes more than a little to luck.

Short term weather over the entire area is dominated by the west to east passage of Atlantic depressions, as they move from their breeding ground off Nova Scotia towards Britain and Europe. These give rise to those rapidly changing conditions familiar to European yachtsmen – south-east winds veering into the south-west together with a falling barometer as the depression approaches, a period of south-westerlies and heavy rain as the warm front passes, followed by a sudden shift into the north-west as the cold front comes through, often accompanied by sharp, squally showers but soon clearing to give blue skies and clear visibility.

Not only do Atlantic depressions generally move more slowly in summer than in winter, but almost without exception they are much less intense and generate correspondingly less powerful winds. Thus by far the best season for all crossings north of the Atlantic high pressure system is between mid May and mid August. Unfortunately visibility off the coasts of Canada and the northern US is at its worst in July, and the iceberg limit is also at its greatest extent (see Chapter 19). However these drawbacks are far outweighed by the almost certain promise of lighter winds – from a ten per cent plus chance of winds over 35 knots on any one day between October and April (rising to 25 per cent, or a gale every four days, in January), down to an average of only one per cent in

July. Naturally, the chance of encountering a gale is always greater in northern latitudes than further south. Although it is rare for a hurricane to track beyond 40°N 60°W, the possibility should be borne in mind and careful attention paid to weather forecasts.

Ocean currents

The northern North Atlantic is dominated by the vast clockwise circulation described in Chapter 10. The Gulf Stream sets north-east in a clearly defined band off the North American continent, continuing to flow east or slightly north of east at around half a knot over much of the ocean between 35° and 55°N, by which time it is known simply as the North Atlantic Current. On reaching about 20°W this current splits, one arm continuing past Scotland towards Norway and the other setting south-east and then south off the coasts of Spain and Portugal. Minor branches flow into the English Channel and Bay of Biscay.

The only major exception to the generally east-going circulation is the Labrador Current, which sets south or south-west down the coasts of Canada and the northern United States (see Chapter 19). From 50°W westwards the interface between the Gulf Stream and the Labrador Current is known as the Cold Wall and is normally very noticeable because of the change both in water temperature and in colour – the cold Labrador Current is light green whereas the warm Gulf Stream is a deep blue. However do not expect a sharp unbroken line of division at all times – there will be bulges and eddies where the waters mix.

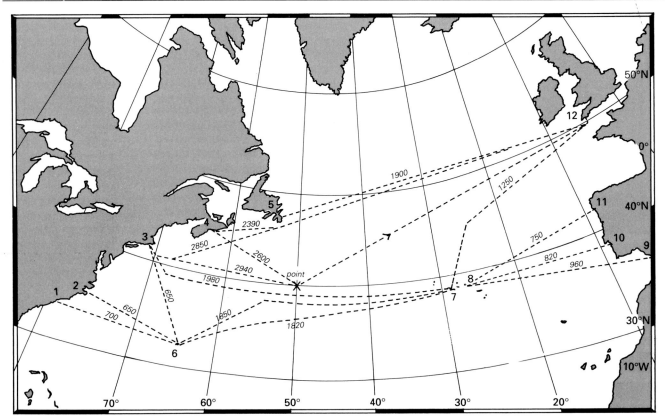

Chart 35 Typical routes eastwards in the middle and northern latitudes. Projection based on Admiralty Chart No 5095. Key to numbered departure/arrival ports: (1) Charleston, S Carolina; (2) Norfolk, Virginia; (3) Newport, Rhode Island; (4) Halifax, Nova Scotia; (5) St John's, Newfoundland; (6) St George's, Bermuda; (7) Horta, Azores; (8) Ponta Delgada, Azores; (9) Gibraltar; (10) Lisbon, Portugal; (11) Bayona, Spain; (12) Falmouth, UK.

USA to Bermuda

Departure can be made from whichever US port is most convenient and a direct course normally sailed. In order to clear the Bermuda area before the onset of the hurricane season many yachts make the passage in May, when south-westerly winds of 15 to 25 knots alternate with stronger winds from the north or north-east. When these oppose the Gulf Stream dangerous seas can be created. By June the incidence of northerlies is less, but the chance of an early season hurricane must be considered.

The further north the departure point the more windward work is likely to be called for, and it may be worth diverging from the rhumb line course in order to cross the Gulf Stream as quickly as possible, having made additional westing while still in the Labrador Current. Although the *Routeing* and *Pilot Charts* show the Gulf Stream in this area as running at an innocuous 1–1½ knots, many observers have experienced much higher rates, together with eddies and offshoots totally uncharted and inexplicable. For comfort – and also for safety – avoid crossing the Stream in a strong northerly wind.

The corridor between Bermuda and the US coast is a favourite hurricane track, those later in the season tending to run further inshore than early season hurricanes, which (though far less likely to start with) have a statistically greater chance of approaching Bermuda itself. Hurricane forecasting has become a fine art, and if you leave the US coast with a favourable forecast, although there is no guarantee of reaching Bermuda unscathed, neither is there any reason to be caught unawares. Both speed and track

become more predictable than is the case earlier in the hurricane's existence, and the meteorologists should give enough warning for evasive action to be taken. Although a hurricane can occur any time between June and November, the worst period is from July to September inclusive. To that extent it would seem reasonable to leave Bermuda, if heading eastwards, by mid or late June.

Details of approach and landfall on Bermuda will be found in Chapter 20. St George's harbour is covered in Part III.

Bermuda to the Azores

There are two choices regarding this passage. The first is to head north-east after departure until 38°N or 40°N is reached, before turning due east for the Azores. Unless a major cell of high pressure has formed much further north than is usually the case (as happened in 1988) this should put one firmly into the belt of the Westerlies. There is also a good chance of a favourable current. The disadvantages are an increased distance to sail, and the fact that gales are not uncommon in these latitudes, particularly in May and June.

The alternative is to sail a course much nearer to the Great Circle, though it would still be wise to make some northing early on. On this route the likelihood of calms is considerably greater, but the likelihood of gales correspondingly less. The current will also be much less predictable, particularly in the earlier stages of the passage. Although the general trend of the North Atlantic Current in this area is between east and south, giant eddies may form, setting at up to half a knot in almost any direction and frequently altering from day to day. Plenty of fuel may be needed if the passage is not to be a slow one. Choice of route will obviously depend on the size of yacht and the strength and priorities of her crew.

The Azores are well known for the extensive calm which often surrounds them, and enough fuel should be kept in reserve to motor the last 50 miles if necessary. A reserve of 100 miles would be even better. Details of the approaches to the islands are given in Chapter 21, and entry details for the harbours of Horta and Ponta Delgada in Part III.

USA or Canada to the Azores

This is most likely to be the choice of yachts leaving from the Chesapeake Bay or further north, and much of what has been said under the previous two headings will apply equally to the direct route.

From south of New York it should be possible to sail a Great Circle course, and enjoy favourable winds and currents most of the way. From further north the standard procedure is to head south-east to make a good offing and get well clear of the Labrador Current with its attendant fogs. Once around 40°N a direct course can be shaped for the Azores, though some skippers may prefer to continue a little further south. The first part of the passage will be within the hurricane zone, and it would be wise to be east of 55°W before the end of June.

Azores to northern Europe

It is often necessary to leave the Azores under engine, and if fuel is limited the wind is most likely to be found first by motoring due north. Even if leaving with a good wind take every opportunity of making northing until at least 45°N, aiming to cross it near 25°W. A direct course from this position should make the most of the east-going current (and avoid the south-east set towards Iberia) and there is also a good chance of favourable winds out of the westerly quadrant. In some years it may be necessary to work even further north to pick up reliable winds before turning north-east – it is worth listening to the BBC shipping forecasts (see Chapter 10) even before entering their area for the Atlantic synopsis.

If at all possible, aim to be making landfall well before the end of August. The south-western approaches to the English Channel – and the rest of northern Europe for that matter – are notorious for the severe gales which often come through early in September. If entering the English Channel in such a gale, which is almost certain to come up from the south-west and later veer into the north-west, by far the best harbour to make for will be Falmouth, tucked behind the shelter of the Lizard peninsula. Details of both Falmouth and Plymouth will be found in Part III.

Azores to Iberia or Gibraltar

There are two likely reasons for heading east from the Azores. Crews from northern Europe who are in no particular hurry may choose to break the passage homewards on the coast of north-west Spain, waiting there for a good forecast before crossing the Bay of Biscay. Others may be planning to cruise the west coast of Iberia before heading east to Gibraltar and thence into the Mediterranean. A few may cruise as far as Vilamoura or even Gibraltar before departing south-west for Madeira, the Canaries and the Trade Wind crossing.

Whatever the reason there is a good chance of this being a pleasant passage, with northerly winds and a south-going current both of which are apt to be quite strong. As the chance of north-easterlies increases on closing the coast it would be wise to keep well to windward of the intended destination, to avoid a last minute slog against both wind and current. If continuing direct to Gibraltar, after rounding Cape St Vincent the current will tend towards the Straits as there is a permanent flow into the Mediterranean caused by the high rate of evaporation in that warm area. Winds may be variable.

There is certain to be considerable shipping off the coasts of Spain and Portugal, where poor visibility may also be encountered – see Chapter 11. There is also heavy traffic through the Straits of Gibraltar, where a Traffic Separation Scheme is in force.

USA or Canada to Europe via the mid latitudes

The mid latitudes, so far as this passage is concerned, may be defined as a track passing south of Sable Island and the Newfoundland Grand Banks but well north of the Azores high pressure system. If the yacht is lying west of Cape Cod, the choice is either to sail south of the Nantucket Shoals or transit the Cape Cod Canal and leave from further north.

In either case, to reduce the time spent in fog and avoid possible icebergs, make for the vicinity of 40°N 50°W – point X on Chart 35. Up-to-date weather and ice reports may make it possible to shift this point further north and reduce the distance to be sailed, but your track could then coincide with the main shipping routes which you may prefer to avoid. Alternatively these reports may force you to continue further south, to avoid a strong southern drift of icebergs.

From point X, a Great Circle course can be sailed for most European destinations. Winds will be predominantly westerly, but may veer right around the compass as depressions pass through. West of 30°W up to one knot of north-easterly progress should be derived from the current, but as one progresses eastwards the current loses both its northerly component and some of its force.

Those remarks regarding landfall made in the section entitled *Azores to northern Europe* apply equally to this passage, and to the following one.

USA or Canada to Europe via the Great Circle

From anywhere in north-eastern United States the Great Circle route to northern Europe runs close past the coast of Nova Scotia (well inside Sable Island) and thence to Cape Race on the south-east tip of Newfoundland. The winds are likely to be fair, but there can be a high incidence of fog and there will also be the weak adverse Labrador Current on this part of the route. St John's Harbour, 60 miles north of Cape Race, makes a good final port for provisions and stores. An up-to-date ice report should also be obtained.

From Cape Race or St John's, a Great Circle course can be shaped. Icebergs and/or fog may have to be contended with until around 40°W (crossed on this route at about 49°N), but east of 40°W normal North Atlantic conditions can be expected with a predominance of fair winds and current. Unfortunately the Atlantic depressions spawned off Nova Scotia also favour the Great Circle route on their way to north-west Europe, and there is a good chance of at least one severe gale if crossing this far north. Larger seas may also be expected for much of the passage than if crossing further south.

Passages westward

Any passage westward in the higher latitudes involves a lot of windward sailing and adverse currents with, in the latter stages, the chance of meeting ice and the certainty of fog on and to the west of the Grand Banks. For this reason few cruising yachtsmen opt to sail directly from northern Europe to Canada or the United States, more often going via the Azores and possibly Bermuda. The direct routes are largely the preserve of entrants in the single and two-handed races run biennially from Plymouth, UK to Newport, Rhode Island, who are in the main experienced yachtsmen well able to decide their own routes and prepared to take their chances with the weather. Whatever route is chosen, gale-force headwinds may be met repeatedly as depressions track past and at least some progress will be lost to the current.

A potential problem further south is the outside chance of encountering a hurricane – see *USA to Bermuda* above. Weather forecasts should be monitored carefully, particularly later in the season, and the yacht should be readied to take evasive action if necessary. Ideally, landfalls on the American coast south of 40°N should be made before the end of June.

Azores to Bermuda

The route from Europe to the Azores (see Chapter 12), and thence either to Bermuda or direct to the United States, is the summer choice of most cruising yachtsmen. Though headwinds and an adverse current are inevitable for much of the passage it will at least be warm, and yachts with a good range under power may consider taking the rhumb line or Great Circle course along the ridge of high pressure which normally lies between Bermuda and the Azores. Extensive calms and flat to glassy seas can be expected on this route, and it will be very hot.

Yachts with less range under power would be wise to head due west, at least until beyond 50°W, only ducking further south if the forecast indicates that reliable winds are likely to be found – certainly both timing and route planning for this passage are easier than they used to be due to better weather forecasting. If departing from Horta, a long-term forecast can usually be obtained from the marina office, otherwise one or more of the short-wave transmissions listed in Chapter 10 should fit the bill.

It must be remembered that Bermuda lies well into the

Weathering storm force winds on passage from Newfoundland to Europe in a Rival 41. Choosing to cross by a northerly route increases the likelihood of heavy weather, but shortens the distance to be sailed. *Photo: Jill Vasey*

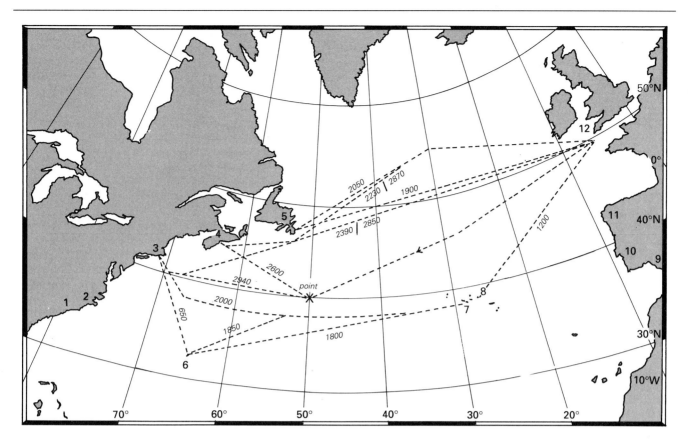

Chart 36 Typical routes westwards in the middle and northern latitudes. Projection based on Admiralty Chart No 5095. Key to numbered departure/arrival ports: (1) Charleston, S Carolina; (2) Norfolk, Virginia; (3) Newport, Rhode Island; (4) Halifax, Nova Scotia; (5) St John's, Newfoundland; (6) St George's, Bermuda; (7) Horta, Azores; (8) Ponta Delgada, Azores; (9) Gibraltar; (10) Lisbon, Portugal; (11) Bayona, Spain; (12) Falmouth, UK.

hurricane belt, as does the area between Bermuda and the North American mainland. The passage should be timed accordingly.

Details of the approaches to Bermuda will be found in Chapter 20, with St George's harbour covered in Part III. Onward routes are considered in Chapter 18.

Azores to USA or Canada

Unless the destination is very far north, the first part of this route will be much the same as if heading for Bermuda. The best bet is to remain at around 38°N until south or south-east of one's landfall in order to minimise time spent in fog and the chance of meeting icebergs. Expect a long, slow beat into headwinds and current, and load up with plenty of fuel and other stores before departure. Details of approach and landfall on the US and Canadian coasts are given in Chapter 19, but see also the following passages and interpolate as necessary.

Europe to USA or Canada via the mid latitudes

This passage follows much the same route as its reciprocal from west to east. Its objects are also largely the same – to keep well north of the Azores high pressure system, but south of the Grand Banks and Sable island. If the destination is west of Cape Cod the Nantucket Shoals should either be left well to starboard or landfall made north of the Cape and the passage continued close down the coast

and through the Cape Cod Canal.

Exactly what route is taken in order to reach 40°N 50°W – point X on Chart 36 – will depend on individual choice. The shortest will obviously be the Great Circle, but many cruising yachtsmen will opt to keep further south in the hope of avoiding some of the strong headwinds likely to be found near 50°N. However do not head too far south early on and risk getting caught in the calms which so often surround the Azores – it would be wiser to keep at least 300 miles north of the islands. The passage will be largely to windward, butting into an opposing current, at whatever latitude is chosen.

While 40°N 50°W is quoted as a suitable point from which an onward course can be shaped to the final destination, this could be altered in the light of up-to-date ice reports. While the temptation will always be to get out of the opposing Gulf Stream and into the favourable Labrador Current as soon as the ice situation permits, this also means heading into the worst of the fog. Again, an individual swings-and-roundabouts decision.

Europe to USA or Canada via the Great Circle

To sail the Great Circle from one's departure port to Cape Race at the south-western extremity of Newfoundland will be the shortest route in terms of distance, but not necessarily the fastest option and certainly not the most pleasant. Winds will be mainly from between north-west and south-west, and there is a high probability of heavy weather as Atlantic depressions track towards Europe. Landfall is likely to be made in poor visibility (Cape Race has a 40 percent incidence of visibility under two miles in July) and from 40°W onwards ice may be encountered.

Europe to USA or Canada via the northern route

This cold, windy route is largely the preserve of entrants in the biennial transatlantic races – and the average cruising person would probably consider them welcome to it. The object is to go north of the succession of lows which track across the Atlantic from west to east, in the hope of picking up easterly winds on their northern perimeters. A typical point to head for is 55°N 30°W, after which a Great Circle can be shaped to Cape Race, Newfoundland and beyond, giving Sable Island a wide berth. The gamble depends on being able to keep north of the centres of the lows. It is likely to be cold and the weather heavier than on the more southerly routes, but offers the potential of a fast passage.

The latter part of the voyage goes straight through the centre of the fog and iceberg zones, and many competitors in the transatlantic races have spoken of sudden and unnerving sightings. There is also a considerable amount of traffic, both merchant ships and fishing vessels. Radar would be extremely useful and some form of electronic position fixing system almost essential. Jock McLeod, an intrepid singlehander with many ocean races to his credit including several OSTARS, has this to say about the northerly route: 'It could be described as a long thrash to windward with a permanently foul tide, and should not be undertaken lightly'.

PART III – PORT INFORMATION

Selection

The following ports have been selected primarily as being suitable for landfall or departure, and most also have reasonable facilities for yachts. No attempt has been made to cover all viable harbours, for which local cruising guides should be consulted. Where possible ports have been chosen which, with due caution, may be approached and entered even in bad conditions.

Coordinates

The coordinates given for each port correspond with current charts and the appropriate port plan. However, users of satellite based position fixing systems should be aware that there may occasionally be a considerable discrepancy between the charted position of any feature and that confirmed by their instrument. Bearings, where given are in true.

Local time

Local time, in relation to Greenwich Mean Time, is quoted for each port. In many places, including Great Britain, clocks are advanced during the summer months. The dates when this operates are decided by the government of each country and may vary from year to year. The times quoted are therefore subject to the appropriate adjustment for local 'summer' time if applicable.

Tides

Tidal heights quoted are Mean Level above Datum, as listed in *Reed's Nautical Almanac* and *British Admiralty Tide Tables* NP202, Vol 2. All heights are given in metres.

Charts

For most ports only British Admiralty and US Defense Mapping Agency charts are listed, together with the Imray-Iolaire Caribbean series where applicable and Canadian charts for Nova Scotia and Newfoundland. Others, sometimes on a larger scale, may be produced by the hydrographic office of the country concerned but are often difficult to obtain. Chart numbers change from time to time with the publication of new editions and an up-to-date Catalogue of Charts should be consulted before placing an order.

Where a chart is listed twice with different scales this indicates a relevant larger scale insert on a chart of an overall smaller scale.

Buoyage

The IALA A system (red to port, green to starboard, plus cardinals) is standard in European waters, including the offshore islands. The IALA B system (green to port, red to starboard, plus cardinals) is used throughout American waters, including Bermuda and the Caribbean. The only exception is in St Vincent and the Grenadines, currently using IALA A but likely to change to IALA B in the near future.

Chartlets and harbour plans

The chartlets and harbour plans in this book should not be used for navigation: they are intended only to illustrate the text. In many areas developments are being made which could render information out of date at any time. Current charts, pilot books and yachtsmen's guides should be consulted before attempting to enter any harbour for the first time.

Caution

Ocean cruising yachtsmen should be aware that maintenance of navigation aids is poor in some parts of the Atlantic, and even major lights may sometimes be out of service for long periods. Where a change is notified, it may also take several months for it to appear in *Notices to Mariners* and on newly bought charts. If approaching in darkness and in any doubt at all about entry it is always prudent to stand off until daylight.

VHF radio frequencies

Some of the frequencies allocated to numbered channels vary between Europe and the USA. Channel 16 is common to both. (See Appendix E.)

Definitions

In the following pages, the word *marina* indicates the existence of custom-built berthing arrangements for yachts, although the quality of accommodation and services may vary widely. *Yacht harbour* indicates the existence of an area within which yachts may lie, or may be directed to lie.

Mailing addresses

It is always wise to arrange mailing addresses in advance, though in most cases mail will also be held for all yachts. Poste restante is used in Europe, General Delivery in American-influenced areas, and the words 'please hold for arrival' can do no harm. Wording should be kept clear and simple, without titles or honorifics, and the sender's address always given on the envelope (though by no means all uncollected letters will be returned).

Ports

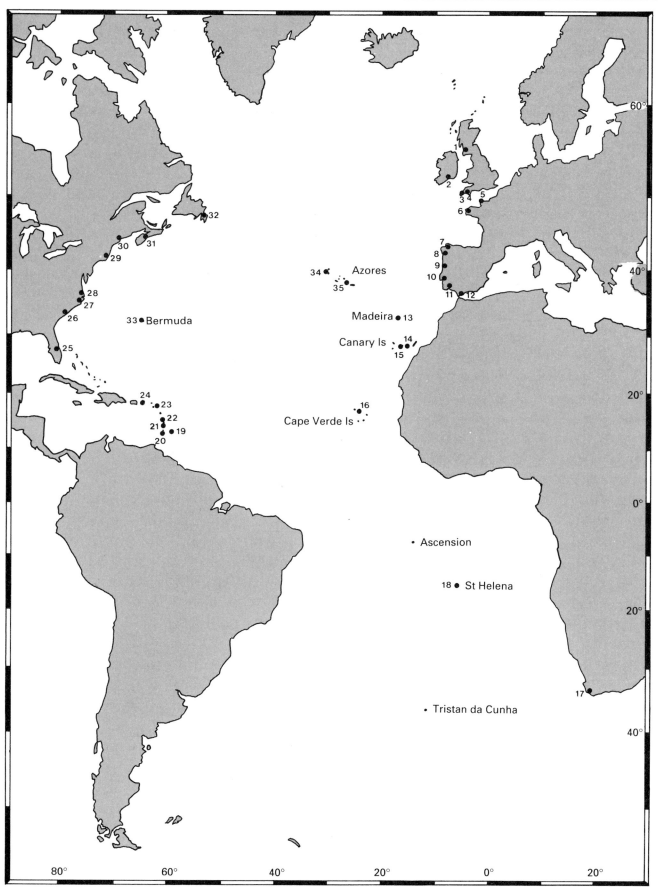

Chart 37 The North and South Atlantic showing ports covered in Part III.

Charts	Admiralty		US	
General	2724	(1:200,000)	35299	(1:200,000)
Approach	2126	(1:75,000)	36103	(1:75,000)
Harbour	1864	(1:12,500)	36102	(1:12,500)

Springs: 3.5 m/11 ft
Neaps: 2.9 m/9 ft 5 in

Flag: British (Red Ensign)
Currency: £ sterling

General

Campbeltown lies near the mouth of the Clyde, a large sheltered estuary midway up the west coast of Scotland. The area as a whole makes an excellent departure or arrival point for any voyage to or from America by one of the more northerly routes, or for a cruise to Ireland or Scandinavia. In its own right the Clyde forms a superb cruising ground with miles of semi-sheltered waters, good anchorages and no crowding.

Although marinas are on the increase in the Clyde and good facilities for yachts are to be found at Troon, Largs, Rhu and Kip on its eastern shores, Campbeltown is a convenient landfall harbour and official port of entry.

Approach

Approach to the Firth of Clyde lies through the North Channel between the north coast of Ireland and the island of Islay, the latter being the most southerly major island off the west coast of Scotland. The DF beacons at Barra Head and Eagle Island, plus that at Tory Island off the north-west coast of Ireland, may be useful at this stage.

After rounding Rathlin Island the narrowest part of the North Channel is reached – the 11 miles separating the Mull of Kintyre from Fair Head in Ireland. There is a Traffic Separation Scheme in force in the area. On both sides the land is high, and only in the poorest visibility is it not apparent. The main aids to navigation are the light on Altacarry Head at the north-east end of Rathlin Island

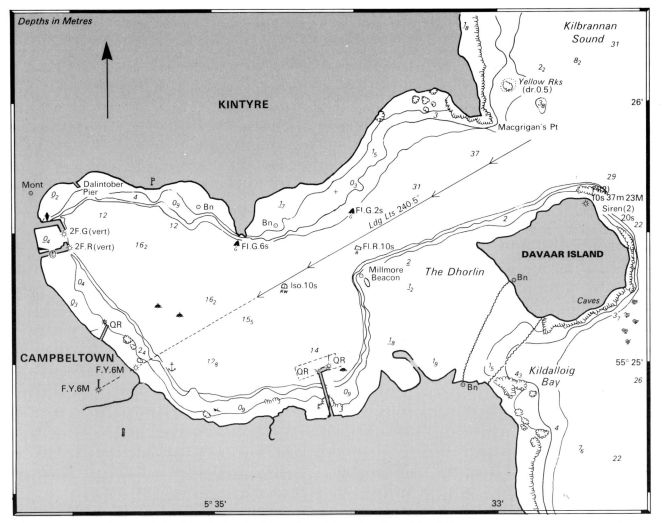

Chart 38 Campbeltown, Firth of Clyde, Scotland. Based on Admiralty Chart No 1864.

[Fl(4) 20s 22M], and the Mull of Kintyre light [Fl(2) 20s 29M] at the extreme south-west of the Kintyre peninsula.

In this area of the North Channel the tide can run at up to five knots in places, and when wind and tide are opposed severe races can form. In these conditions the Mull of Kintyre should be given a wide berth. Those unfamiliar with the area are advised to pass south of Sanda Island [FlW/R 24s 19/16M], about 1.5 miles offshore. The Patterson Rock, close to its eastern end, is marked by a buoy.

On turning northwards for Campbeltown the Patterson Rock should be given a wide berth. A close watch should also be kept on the tidal situation in Sanda Sound, particularly during the strong south and west-going ebb. The shore is quite clean to the entrance to Campbeltown Loch.

Radio

The principal Coastguard base for the area is at Greenock and watch is kept over the whole area on VHF channels 16 and 67. Clyde Radio is the main communications link in the area and uses VHF channel 26. The Campbeltown harbour authorities monitor VHF channel 16, with 12 and 14 as working channels.

Entrance

No attempt should be made to cut inside Davaar Island, which protects the entrance to Campbeltown Loch from the south-east, as the island is attached to the mainland by a shingle spit which dries at low water. The entrance is between Davaar Light and Macringan's Point, a distance of about 750 m, with leading lights bearing 240.5°. Thereafter keep to the buoyed channel.

Anchorage and moorings

It is possible to anchor near the harbour entrance for access to the town, but it is more comfortable in northerly winds to anchor to the east of the sailing club, clear of private moorings. In general the holding is good, and shelter is fine from all directions. However, strong winds gust over the hills to the south-west when the wind is in that direction.

Berthing and marinas

For clearing customs and easy shore-going, tie up inside the harbour at the new quay and see the harbourmaster. The harbour is dredged periodically and some steps have been taken to improve facilities for visiting yachtsmen. The lifeboat, fishing boats and small craft use the western side of the main pier and there is generally quite a lot of fishing traffic. The harbour is exposed and uncomfortable in easterly and south-easterly winds.

Formalities

Entry requirements may be waived in the case of an EC owned and registered yacht arriving direct from another EC country (including the Azores), but if in any doubt it would be wise to check procedure with customs. In the case of a non EC owned vessel, or if arriving from a non EC country the Q flag should be hoisted on entering territorial waters. If customs officials do not arrive within a reasonable period after the yacht has berthed, the skipper should go ashore to telephone them at the Customs House in Campbeltown.

Facilities

Campbeltown cannot equal the facilities offered to yachts by a purpose-built marina and, after landfall and customs clearance, many crews may wish to push on to one of the marinas on the east coast of the estuary. Running from south to north these are: Troon (0292 315553), Largs (0457 675333), Rhu (0436 820238/820652), Kip (0475 521485). Troon has customs facilities and is only two miles from Prestwick international airport.

Boatyard/engineers The yard at Campbeltown builds large fishing vessels and has a substantial slip
Sailmaker None in Campbeltown, but three elsewhere in the Clyde
Chandlery In Campbeltown
Sailing club Near the anchorage
Diesel/water In the fishing harbour
Bottled gas Camping Gaz and Calor Gas exchanges
Laundry/launderette In the town
Banks The usual, with credit card facilities
General shopping Good
Provisioning Several supermarkets, groceries, etc
Restaurants/hotels Several near the harbour
Medical services A health centre and cottage hospital at Campbeltown and an air ambulance to Glasgow

Communications

Mailing address C/o the post office
Post Office/telephones In the town
Bus/rail service Regular bus service (though distances are such that serious travel by bus would be tedious)
Taxis/car hire Available locally
Air services Machrihanish airport, a major NATO base with a civil airport installation at its eastern end, is just over two miles from the harbour. Frequent daily services operate to Glasgow, linking with national and international flights

Springs: 4.2 m/13 ft 10 in   *Flag*: Republic of Ireland
Neaps: 3.3 m/10 ft 10 in   *Currency*: Punt (Irish pound)

Charts	Admiralty		US	
General	2424	(1:150,000)	35400	(1:150,000)
Approach	1765	(1:50,000)	35424	(1:50,000)
Harbour	1777	(1:12,500)	35421	(1:12,500)

General

On the south coast of Ireland and 60 miles east of Fastnet Rock, Cork Harbour is one of the world's finest natural harbours and a busy commercial port. Crosshaven on the Owenboy River is on the west side of the entrance. It is the home of the Royal Cork Yacht Club, and offers good shelter in all weathers. It is said that Sir Francis Drake once

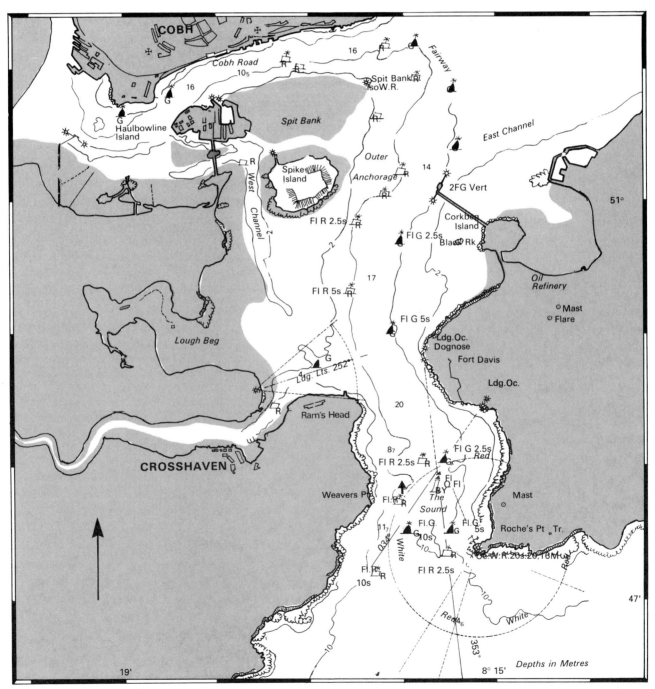

Chart 39 Cork Harbour, Ireland. Based on Admiralty Chart No 1777.

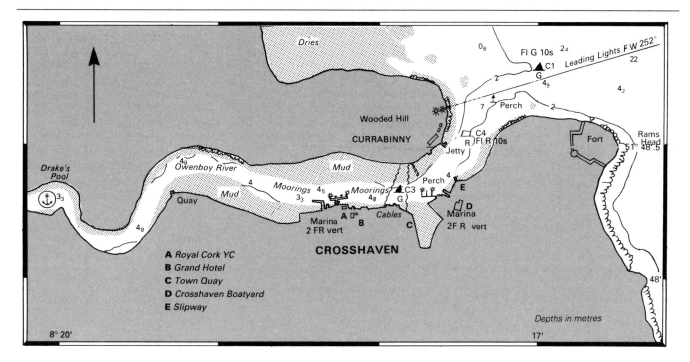

Chart 40 Crosshaven, Ireland. Based on Admiralty Chart No 1777.

evaded the Spanish fleet by taking his ships up the Owen-boy River to Drake's Pool.

Buoyage follows the European IALA A system.

Approach

The distinctive promontory known as the Old Head of Kinsale [Fl(2) 10s 72m 25M] lies some 15 miles south-west of Cork entrance and is easily identified if closing the coast from the south or south-west. There is a DF beacon on the headland. On approaching Cork Harbour itself landfall marks are a 24 m (79 ft) high hammer-headed water tower about 1.5 miles east of Roches Point, and a high chimney with red and white horizontal bands and vertical red lights north-east of Corkbeg which shows clearly east of Roches Point. A pillar buoy marking safe water is situated some five miles south of the entrance.

Dangers

Pollack Rock with a least depth of 7.6 m (25 ft) lies 1.25 miles east-south-east of Power Head, itself 3.25 miles east of the entrance to Cork harbour. The rock is marked by a red can bell buoy and is covered by a red sector of Roches Point Light.

Daunt Rock with a least depth of 3.5 m (11 ft) lies nearly five miles south-south-west of Roches Point. It too is marked by a red can buoy and covered by a red sector of Roches Point light.

Radio

Cork Harbour Radio monitors VHF channel 16, working channel 12. The Royal Cork Yacht Club monitors channel 37 during daylight hours in the summer. Valencia Radio uses channels 16, 23 and 67, plus 85 for link calls.

Entrance

Entry is between Weaver Point and Roches Point, on a heading slightly west of north. At this point the entrance is about three quarters of a mile wide, narrowing to half a mile between Fort Meagher and Fort Davis. There are two well buoyed channels divided by Harbour Rock, but as this has a least depth of 5.2 m (17 ft) both buoyed channels and leading lights (two sets) can safely be ignored by yachts. Rock ledges extend up to 180 m (600 ft) offshore on either side. Tidal streams can run strongly in the entrance, reaching two knots at springs. Two rocks, the Cow which always shows and the Calf which dries 1.3 m (4 ft), extend 180 m (600 ft) south of Roches Point.

On reaching Fort Meagher, allow at least 180 m (600 ft) clearance around Ram's Head before altering course westwards for the Owenboy River, passing close to the green cone buoy which marks the east end of the spit dividing the west channel from the Crosshaven channel. The latter is narrow, and no liberties should be taken with the buoyage or unlit perches. If approaching at night and unfamiliar with the area it would be wise to anchor and await daylight.

Anchorage and moorings

There is no good anchorage in the lower river, which is crowded and has cables and numerous old chains fouling the bottom, but a mooring may be available through the Crosshaven Boat Yard (021 831161) or the Royal Cork Yacht Club (021 831023). The yellow mooring buoys between the town quay and the Yacht Club are available from Salve Engineering (021 831145). Drakes Pool, 1.5 miles up the river, offers secure anchorage in delightful surroundings but has no facilities.

Berthing and marinas

There are two marinas, run (progressing upstream) by the Crosshaven Boat Yard and the Royal Cork Yacht Club.

Both are on the south side of the river with depths of 2.0 m (6 ft) or more, and usually have berths available for visitors.

Formalities

Entry requirements may be waived in the case of an EC owned and registered yacht arriving direct from another EC country (including the Azores), but if in any doubt it would be wise to check procedure with customs. In the case of a non EC owned vesel, or if arriving from a non EC country, hoist the Q flag on closing the land. Customs and immigration may be contacted through the Royal Cork Yacht Club or through the police station situated across the road from the Yacht Club.

Facilities

Boatyard The Crosshaven Boat Yard has a boat lift for hauling out, covered and open boat storage areas, and can handle most repairs and maintenance including rigging

Engineers Salve Engineering

Sailmaker McWilliams Sails (021 831505) do first-class work

Chandlery Several in Cork

Chart agent Union Chandlery, Anderson's Quay, Cork (021 271643)

Compass adjusters In Cork

Yacht club The Royal Cork Yacht Club is the oldest in existence, having been founded in 1720. It has a fine clubhouse on the river and an established reputation for hospitality to visiting yachtsmen

Diesel At both marinas

Water At both marinas and the town quay

Bottled gas Camping Gaz exchanges locally, consult marina dockmaster about Calor Gas or other refills

Showers At the Royal Cork Yacht Club

Laundry/launderette In Cork

Banks Numerous in Cork, but no bank in Crosshaven itself

General shopping Limited in Crosshaven, but excellent in Cork some 12 miles away

Provisioning There is a supermarket in Carrigaline four miles away on the bus route to Cork

Bonded stores In Cork

Restaurants/hotels Several locally, and a wide choice in Cork and the surrounding countryside

Medical services Hospitals in Cork

Communications

Mailing address C/o the Royal Cork Yacht Club, Crosshaven, Co Cork, Republic of Ireland, by pre-arrangement with the secretary/manager
Mark mail 'to await arrival'

Post Office In Crosshaven

Telephones At the Yacht Club

Bus/rail services Buses to Cork, linking with the rail network

Ferry services Car ferry to Swansea in South Wales and to Roscoff in Brittany

Taxis Available by telephone

Car hire In Cork

Air services Cork airport with flights to the UK and the Continent about ten miles distant. Train from Cork to Limerick for Shannon airport and transatlantic flights

Charts	Admiralty	US
General	2565 (1:150,000)	36140 (1:200,000)
Approach	154 (1:35,000)	37041 (1:35,000)
Harbour	32 (1:12,500)	37042 (1:12,500)

Springs: 5.3 m/17 ft 4 in   *Flag:* British (Red Ensign)
Neaps: 4.2 m/13 ft 9 in   *Currency:* £ sterling

General

Falmouth is the most westerly of the larger English Channel ports and is convenient for departure and landfall for passages south and west. It is one of the finest natural harbours in Europe, with much sheltered deep water and several inlets and creeks. There are infrequent ship movements (tug assisted) entering and leaving the dock area, and also some commercial fishing. The entrance is well marked and safe under all conditions.

Approach

After passing the Lizard [Fl 3s 70m 29M] the only danger is the group of rocks known as the Manacles, clearly marked on the chart and with an East Cardinal buoy to seaward. An easterly wind combined with a flood tide can produce a race between Black Head and the Manacles on the direct course to Falmouth. In these conditions, after rounding the Lizard, head towards the Lowland Buoy in about 50°N 5° W and thence east of the race towards Falmouth. Lobster pot marker buoys may be encountered anywhere in the area, either singly or in attached strings, and may be found well offshore. They are often poorly marked and constitute a hazard to a yacht under power, particularly at night.

Radio

Call Falmouth Harbour Radio on VHF channel 16, working channel 12. In emergency call Falmouth Coastguard on channel 16, working channel 67. For a commercial radio-telephone link call Pendennis Radio on working channel 62.

Falmouth harbour, looking northwest. The commercial docks are on the right, with the river (buoyed as far as Falmouth Yacht Marina) winding up towards Penryn. *Photo: Falmouth Harbour Commissioners*

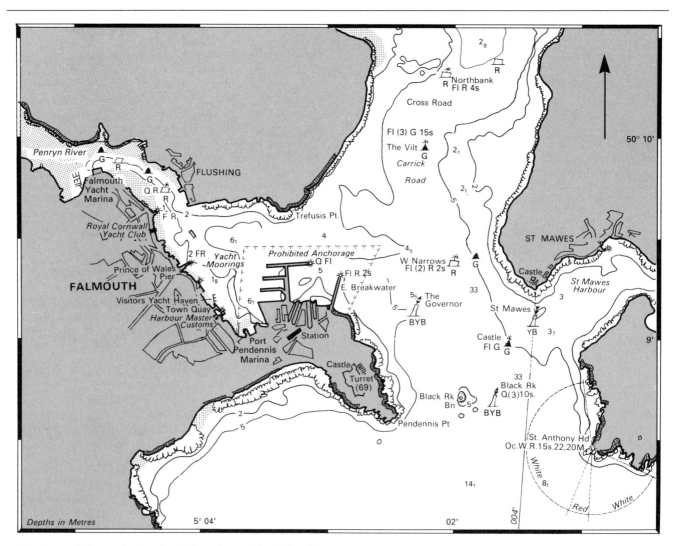

Chart 41 Falmouth, England. Based on Admiralty Chart No 32.

Entrance

The entrance is passable under all conditions – even with a southerly gale and ebb tide a yacht can enter in safety though not in comfort.

The main channel lies between St Anthony Head and the East Cardinal buoy marking the unlit Black Rock Beacon, and should be used after dark. In daylight a yacht can safely pass either side of Black Rock at 100 m (350 ft) distance, though lobster pots are frequently laid between Black Rock and Pendennis Point. Inside there is adequate water for large yachts over the whole of the roads.

There is local racing in Carrick Roads two or three afternoons each week in summer. This is taken very seriously, particularly by the skippers of the gaff-rigged Falmouth Working Boats, and it would be most unwise to cut through the racing fleet.

Anchorage and moorings

The main yacht anchorage is in the south-west of the harbour off the Town Quay. Holding is generally good in firm mud, though there are a few soft patches, and protec-

tion adequate. There are twelve green mooring buoys set aside for visiting yachts, most of them situated off the Royal Cornwall Yacht Club. A detached pontoon for the use of visitors may also be moored in this area.

Land either at the Visitors' Yacht Haven or the Royal Cornwall Yacht Club.

Berthing and marinas

There are two marinas in Falmouth in addition to the smaller Visitors Yacht Haven (0326 312285) which can take up to forty yachts, maximum 12 m (40 ft) LOA and 2.0 m (6 ft) draft. It is in place between April and October and has piped water, a refuse skip, toilets and free hot showers nearby but no access to mains electricity.

Falmouth Yacht Marina (0326 316620) is situated about three quarters of a mile up the Penryn River. The approach channel carries 2 m at all states of the tide, but though the river is buoyed the dredged channel at the marina is narrow and the beacons must be followed. Moor to the clearly marked reception pontoon until directed to a berth by marina staff. All normal marina and boatyard facilities are available, and it is a pleasant marina in which to winter. Falmouth Yacht Marina monitors VHF channels 37 and 80.

Port Pendennis Marina (0326 211819), a marina village development with limited space for visiting yachts, lies in the southern part of the harbour between the docks and the town. It is enclosed within a single tidal barrier, with access for about half the tide. A reception pontoon is moored in the western side of the entrance. Port Pendennis Marina monitors VHF channel 80.

Formalities

Entry requirements may be waived in the case of an EC owned and registered yacht arriving direct from another EC country (including the Azores), but if in any doubt it would be wise to check procedure by calling 'Falmouth Customs' on VHF channel 16 prior to arrival. In the case of a non EC owned vessel, or if arriving from a non EC country, hoist the Q flag at sea, notify 'Falmouth Customs' and then remain aboard until customs and immigration arrive. If berthed alongside it is permissible for the skipper only to go ashore to telephone the Customs House (0326 314156).

Facilities

Falmouth has excellent facilities for yachts, and is a good place to make final preparations for an Atlantic cruise. All the following companies are in or near Falmouth itself – others exist elsewhere on the estuary.

Boatyards Falmouth Boat Construction Ltd, Flushing (0326 374309); Port Falmouth Boat Yard Ltd (0326 313248); Falmouth Yacht Marina (0326 316620) and others. All have haulage facilities and can arrange any repairs or servicing likely to be required
Electronics Seacom Electronics Ltd (0326 376565)
Sailmakers South West Sails, Penryn (0326 375291); Penrose Sailmakers (0326 312705) who also specialise in traditional sails
Chandleries Bosun's Locker (0326 312595); a branch of the Boat House at Falmouth Yacht Marina

Admiralty chart agent/compass adjusters Marine Instruments (0326 312414)
Yacht club The Royal Cornwall Yacht Club, Greenbank, Falmouth, Cornwall TR11 2SW (0326 311105/312126) welcomes visiting yachtsmen and women. It has a dinghy landing, showers, a bar and an excellent restaurant
Diesel Falmouth Yacht Marina and Visitors' Yacht Haven. The fuelling barge *Ulster Industry* is usually moored south-west of Trefusis Point
Petrol Falmouth Yacht Marina and Visitors Yacht Haven
Water Falmouth Yacht Marina, Port Pendennis Marina and Visitors' Yacht Haven
Shore power Falmouth Yacht Marina and Port Pendennis Marina
Bottled gas Falmouth Yacht Marina, Visitors' Yacht Haven, Bosun's Locker Chandlery
Ice The Galley Stores at Falmouth Yacht Marina
Showers Falmouth Yacht Marina, Port Pendennis Marina, Visitors' Yacht Haven and Royal Cornwall Yacht Club
Banks Several, with encashment facilities for all major credit cards
General shopping Reasonable – anything lacking can generally be found in Truro about ten miles away
Provisioning Excellent fresh stores available, but supermarkets somewhat limited
Bonded stores A E Monson (0326 373581)
Restaurants/hotels Dozens, at all levels
Medical services Falmouth Hospital (0326 315522) plus many doctors, dentists and opticians

Communications

Mailing addresses C/o Royal Cornwall Yacht Club by pre-arrangement or either marina if booked in
Post Offices Several
Telephones Numerous, both coin and card operated
Bus/rail services Buses to Truro and other nearby towns. Trains to Truro for connections to London, etc
Taxis Many private companies
Car hire AVIS (0326 211511) at Falmouth Yacht Marina
Air services Daily flights to London from Newquay airport about 30 miles away

Springs: 5.5 m/18 ft		*Flag*: British (Red Ensign)		
Neaps: 4.4 m/14 ft 5 in		*Currency*: £ sterling		

Charts	Admiralty		US	
General	442	(1:150,000)	37060	(1:150,000)
Approach	1267	(1:75,000)	37043	(1:75,000)
Harbour	30	(1:12,500)	37044/5	(1:12,500)

General

Plymouth is one of England's larger maritime cities with excellent facilities for yachtsmen and good communications. Local yards and suppliers are accustomed to meeting the needs of long distance voyagers of all nationalities. Plymouth is a busy naval, commercial and fishing port but this does not conflict with the yachtsman's needs.

Approach

The Eddystone Lighthouse [Fl(2) 10s 41m 24M] marks a small area of breaking rocks ten miles south-south-west of Plymouth. It is conspicuous by day or night and can be passed on either side at a distance of 500 m (0.3 miles). Rame Head and Penlee Point to the west of the entrance and the Mewstone to the east are prominent features. In clear weather, the high land of Dartmoor to the north east and the radio masts on Staddon Heights on the eastern shore of the Sound assist identification. There is a gunnery range to the east of the entrance – call Wembury Range on VHF channels 16, 11, 12 or 14 to check firing times.

Radio

Plymouth is under the jurisdiction of the Queen's Harbour Master – call Longroom Port Control on VHF channels 16, 14, 12 or 8. In an emergency call Brixham Coastguard on channel 16, working channel 67. For a commercial radio-telephone link call Start Point Radio on working channels 26, 60 or 65.

Entrance

Plymouth Sound is nearly two miles wide at its entrance, over half of this being blocked by a detached stone breakwater. Although the breakwater is lit at both ends it would not be impossible for a stranger entering in bad conditions to spot the large fort in the middle, mistake it for one of the ends and run up on the breakwater. The Western Channel can be used in all conditions, though gales from a southerly quarter may cause sizeable breaking seas off the breakwater end. Thence the recommended approach lies north-east across the Sound leaving Drake's Island to port. The whole area is very well buoyed.

Bridge Channel to the west of Drake's Island makes a convenient short cut if heading for the Mayflower Marina, but should not be attempted without either local knowledge or a large-scale chart.

Anchorage and moorings

There are no protected anchorages convenient to the city itself, though quiet anchorages and good shelter, depending upon wind direction, can be found in Cawsand Bay to the west of the detached breakwater, Jennycliff Bay beneath the prominent Staddon Heights radio masts and Barn Pool to the west of Drake's Island. The Tamar and Lynher Rivers afford some interesting exploring and many protected but remote anchorages. There are very few moorings available to visitors.

Berthing and marinas

There are four marinas in Plymouth itself plus several others further up the River Tamar. All monitor VHF channel 80.

Longest established is the Mayflower International Marina (0752 556633/567106), which can take deep draught yachts up to 30 m (100 ft). The staff are helpful and security excellent but it is some distance from the city. Tidal streams run strongly across the approach, and in severe south-westerly gales the marina can become uncomfortable.

Millbay Marina Village, in the eastern entrance to the old Millbay Dock opposite the Brittany Ferries terminal, is a residential development with berthing for property owners and has limited space for visiting yachts.

Queen Anne's Battery Marina (0752 671142) on the northern shore of the Cattewater can take yachts up to 45 m (150 ft) and 4.5 m (15 ft) draught. The landward approach is through a rather scruffy commercial area, but a passenger ferry crosses to the Mayflower Steps in the historic area of the city. The Royal Western Yacht Club of England has recently moved to premises overlooking the marina, which hosts a number of its major races.

Sutton Yacht Harbour (0752 664186) lies north of Queen Anne's Battery Marina. It is convenient, but has a limited number of visitors berths and is unsuitable for yachts of more than 14 m (45 ft) overall.

Formalities

Entry requirements may be waived in the case of an EC owned and registered yacht arriving direct from another EC country (including the Azores), but if in doubt check procedure by calling 'Plymouth Customs' on VHF channel 16 before arrival. In the case of a non EC owned vessel, or if arriving from a non EC country, hoist the Q flag off the Eddystone, notify 'Plymouth Customs' and then remain aboard until customs and immigration arrive. If berthed alongside it is permissible for the skipper only to go ashore to telephone Customs – dial 100 and ask for Freephone Customs Yachts, or call them on 0752 669811.

Facilities

Many historic voyages have begun or ended in Plymouth, from the time of the Pilgrim Fathers onwards. It is hard to

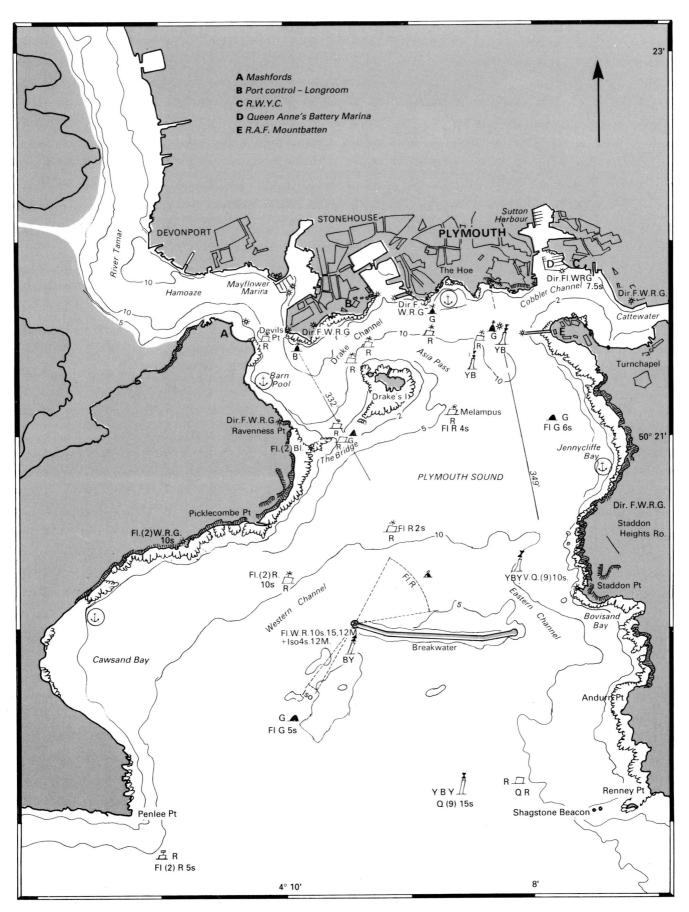

A *Mashfords*
B *Port control – Longroom*
C *R.W.Y.C.*
D *Queen Anne's Battery Marina*
E *R.A.F. Mountbatten*

23'

DEVONPORT

STONEHOUSE

PLYMOUTH

Sutton Herbour

River Tamar

Hamoaze

10

10

5

Mayflower Marina

The Hoe

D

C

Dir.Fl.WRG

Cobbler Channel 7.5s

Dir.F.W.R.G.

Cattewater

A

Devils Pt

Dir.F.W.R.G.

B

Dir.F.W.R.G.

Drake Channel

10

Asia Pass

G

R

G

YB

R

YB

E

Turnchapel

Barn Pool

R

R

Drake's I

2

10

Dir.F.W.R.G.
Ravenness Pt

R

G

R

The Bridge

2

Melampus
R
Fl R 4s

5

G
Fl G 6s

50° 21'

Jennycliffe Bay

Fl.(2)Bl.

PLYMOUTH SOUND

349°

Dir. F.W.R.G.

Staddon Heights Ro.

Picklecombe Pt

Fl.(2)W.R.G.
10s

Fl R 2s
R

10

YBY V.Q.(9)10s.

Staddon Pt

Fl.(2)R.
10s
R

Western Channel

Fl R

5

Eastern Channel

Bovisand Bay

332

Cawsand Bay

Fl.W.R.10s.15,12M.
+Iso4s.12M.

BY

Breakwater

so

Andurn Pt

G
Fl G 5s

YBY
Q (9) 15s

R
Q R

Renney Pt

Shagstone Beacon

Penlee Pt

R
Fl (2) R 5s

4° 10'

8'

Chart 42 Plymouth, England. Based on Admiralty Chart Nos 30 and 1967.

imagine anything a yacht might require which could not easily be found.

Boatyards Mashford Brothers Ltd at Cremyll (0752 822232) is the largest yacht yard with slip facilities and capacity to service yachts up to 250 tons, 37 m (120 ft) LOA, 7.0 m (23 ft) beam and 3.5 m (12 ft) draught. There are also yards at both Mayflower International Marina and Queen Anne's Battery Marina, plus numerous smaller yards. Specialised services of all kinds are available

Electronics Greenham Marine (0752 228114) and Marconi Marine (0752 665759) at Queen Anne's Battery Marina; Ocean Marine Services (0752 500977) at Mayflower International Marina, plus others

Sailmakers The Sail Locker, QAB Marina (0752 670156) and Clements (0752 562465)

Chandleries No less than eight, including at least one at each marina

Admiralty chart agent The Sea Chest, Queen Anne's Battery (0752 222012)

Yacht clubs Royal Western Yacht Club of England, Queen Anne's Battery, Plymouth (0752 660077); Royal Plymouth Corinthian YC, Madeira Walk, The Hoe, Plymouth PL1 2NY (0752 664327)

Weather forecast 48-hour Atlantic weather forecast available by telephone from RAF Mountbatten (0752 402534)

Diesel All marinas and Mashfords Boatyard

Petrol As above

Water As above

Shore power All marinas

Bottled gas Mayflower and QAB marinas

Showers All marinas

Launderettes Mayflower and QAB marinas, and in Plymouth itself

Banks All major British banks, with cashpoint facilities

General shopping Excellent, as befits a major city

Provisioning Excellent

Bonded stores A E Monson (0752 665384)

Restaurants/hotels Numerous at all prices

Medical services Freedom Fields Hospital (0752 668080). Many doctors, dentists and opticians

Communications

Mailing address C/o any of the marinas or yacht clubs by pre-arrangement

Post Offices Several

Telephones At all marinas and in the city

Bus/rail services Local bus services, coaches and mainline trains to London and elsewhere

Ferries Services to Brittany and northern Spain

Taxis Numerous private firms

Car hire All major agencies

Air services Plymouth airport, with regular services to London and the Continent

| *Springs*: 6.3 m/20 ft 8 in | *Flag*: France |
| *Neaps*: 5 m/16 ft 5 in | *Currency*: French franc |

Charts	Admiralty		US	
General	2656	(1:325,000)	37090	(1:200,000)
Approach	1106	(1:50,000)	37263	(1:44,400)
Harbour	2602	(1:10,000)	37281	(1:10,000)

General

Cherbourg is one of the major ports of northern France for both commercial shipping and yachts, and is also a destination for cross-Channel ferries. It is well sheltered and offers first class services.

Approach

Cherbourg lies almost exactly in the middle of the northern coast of the Cotentin peninsula. If landfall is made from northwards after dark, the powerful light on Cap Barfleur [Fl(2) 10s 72m 27M] may be useful until obscured when bearing 088°. If approaching from the west or northwest, Cap de la Hague [Fl 5s 48m 24M] should be visible. Cap Barfleur also has a DF beacon.

Both ebb and flood tides run fast along the northern coast of the Cotentin peninsula, and generous allowance should be made for the stream to avoid being swept past the entrances (and even possibly into either the Barfleur or Alderney Races).

Radio

French coastal stations do not answer an initial call on VHF channel 16 unless it is a Mayday call. Contact Cherbourg Harbour on VHF channels 21 or 27. The yacht harbour monitors VHF channel 9.

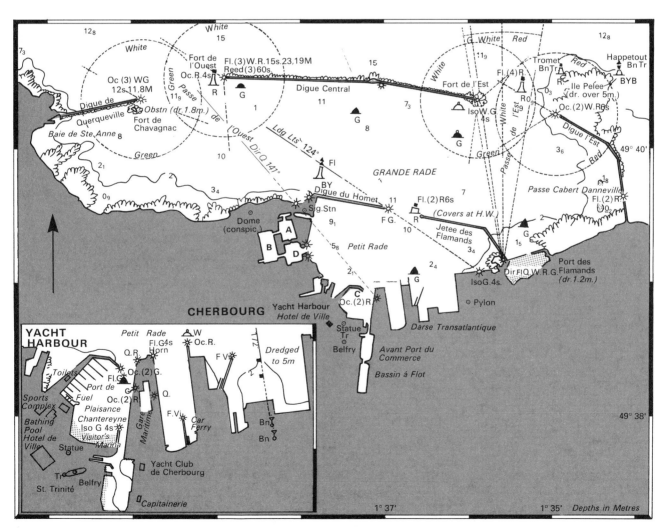

Chart 43 Cherbourg, France. Based on a plan by the previous editor, Philip Allen.

Entrance

The western entrance (Passe de l'Ouest) is straight-forward. There are two sets of leading lights, and while the directional quick flashing pair on 141° stand out well enough, the pair on 124° (fixed green and isophase green) can be confused with other harbour and shore lights until close to.

The eastern entrance (Passe de l'Est) is obstructed on its east side by the drying rock plateau of the Ile Pelée, the extremities of which are marked by two unlit beacon towers. At night, an approach along the division line between the white and red sectors of the directional light on Port des Flamands gives a safe line through the Passe de l'Est.

Entering the Petite Rade near high water, bear in mind that the eastern breakwater, the Jetée des Flamands, covers at high water. Its western end is marked by a red can buoy which must be left to port.

Anchorage and moorings

There is a small yacht anchorage just north of the yacht harbour.

Berthing and marinas

The yacht harbour or Port de Plaisance Chantereyne (33 53 75 16) is situated just west of the conspicuous Gare Maritime and ferry terminal. It is accessible at all states of the tide, but is exposed to winds from the northerly quadrant which can make berthing difficult or even dangerous. Suitable for yachts of up to 15 m (LOA) and 2 m draught, it has more than 800 berths. A new visitors' marina has recently been opened in the southern part of the Port de Plaisance Chantereyne.

Larger yachts should continue south past the Gare Maritime into the Avant-Port de Commerce (available at all tides and in any weather) and thence through a swing bridge into the Bassin à Flot, the gates of which open from two hours before to one hour after high water.

The Harbourmaster's office (33 44 00 13) is in the yacht harbour buildings.

Formalities

It is not necessary for a British yacht to report to customs if arriving from another EC country (including the Azores), but failure to do so implies a formal declaration that the vessel complies with all the detailed customs and health regulations. If required, the customs office (33 44 16 00) will be found in the Capitainerie building to the east of the Avant-Port de Commerce.

All yachts must carry some form of registration, and it is currently forbidden for one skipper to hand over to another unless the hand-over is between co-owners or immediate family. Customs may visit yachts, sometimes boarding at sea.

Facilities

Boatyard With engineers/electronics/sail repairs and 30-tonne travelling crane at the Port de Plaisance Chantereyne

Chandlery/chart agent At the Port de Plaisance Chantereyne

Yacht club The Yacht Club de Cherbourg (33 52 02 83), formerly situated to the east of the Avant-Port de Commerce, now has a clubhouse in the yacht harbour buildings

Diesel/petrol At the Port de Plaisance Chantereyne. The fuelling berth is open between 0800 and 2000 and is accessible three hours either side of high water

Water On pontoons at the Port de Plaisance Chantereyne

Shore power On pontoons at the Port de Plaisance Chantereyne (220V 10A)

Bottled gas At the Port de Plaisance Chantereyne, and many places in the city (Camping Gaz only available)

Showers At the Port de Plaisance Chantereyne and the Yacht Club de Cherbourg

Laundry/launderette In the city

Banks Numerous

General shopping Excellent

Provisioning Wide variety of groceries and delicatessen at the Port de Plaisance Chantereyne and in the city. Outdoor markets on Tuesday, Thursday and Saturday

Restaurants/hotels Numerous at all levels

Medical services Good, as befits a large city

Communications

Mailing address C/o Port de Plaisance Chantereyne or Yacht Club de Cherbourg by pre-arrangement

Post Office/telephones Numerous

Bus/rail service Frequent trains to Paris and elsewhere

Ferry service To Portsmouth and Southampton

Taxis/car hire Plentiful

Air services Cherbourg airport (12 km from harbour) has regular flights to England as well as internal routes

Springs: 7.5 m/24 ft 7 in	*Flag*: France		
Neaps: 5.9 m/19 ft 5 in	*Currency*: French franc		

Charts	Admiralty		US	
General	2643	(1:200,000)	37320	(1:200,000)
Approach	798	(1:60,000)	37322	(1:45,700)
	3427	(1:30,000)		
Harbour	3428	(1:15,000)	37325	(1:15,000)

General

Brest has long been France's primary naval base, no doubt partly due to its protected and easily defensible position inside the relatively narrow Goulet de Brest some ten miles from the open sea. The Rade de Brest makes an interesting cruising ground, though some parts are reserved for naval use with the movement of yachts restricted and anchoring prohibited.

Brest is a large city of considerable historic interest, with excellent facilities.

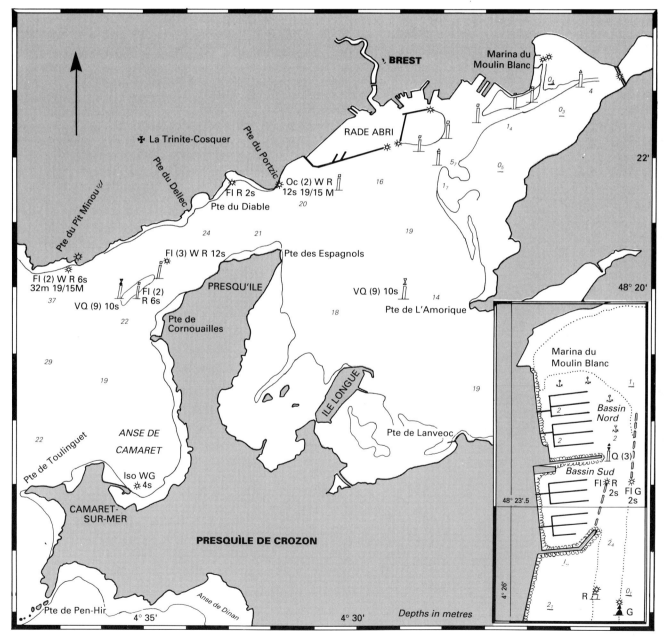

Chart 44 Brest, France. Based on Imray Chart No C36.

Approach

If approaching from northwards down the Chenal du Four, after rounding Pointe de St Mathieu Les Vieux Moines tower, Le Coq and Charles Martel buoys should all be left to port. The twin light towers of Le Petit Minou [Fl(2) WR 6s 32m 19/15M] should by then be visible, and be brought in transit with the grey tower of Pointe du Portzic [Oc(2) WR 12s 56m 19/15M] on 086°. Veer to starboard on approaching Le Petit Minou, but remain on the northern side of the Goulet to clear the Plateau des Fillettes shoal in mid-channel, well marked with buoys and beacons.

If entering from the south-west the Plateau des Fillettes shoal may be left to port, but good clearance must be allowed around the Pointe des Espagnols to clear La Cormorandiere wreck and white beacon.

Radio

French coastal stations do not answer an initial call on VHF channel 16 unless it is a Mayday call. The port working channel is VHF channel 8. The Marina du Moulin Blanc may be contacted on VHF channels 9 or 16 (in English if necessary).

Entrance

On approaching Pointe du Portzic the city, together with the large naval and commercial port complex, will be seen some two miles beyond. Yachts are unwelcome here, and should continue the further three miles to the Marina du Moulin Blanc, on the eastern edge of reclaimed land near the mouth of the Elorn River. The marina is approached via a narrow dredged channel, and the buoyage should be observed. A minimum of 2.5 m is carried even at low water springs.

Anchorage and moorings

There are many sheltered anchorages within the Rade de Brest, but not adjacent to the port of Brest itself where anchoring is generally either forbidden, or the water too shallow.

Berthing and marinas

The Marina du Moulin Blanc (98 02 20 02) is a large and relatively new marina complex containing nearly 1200 berths. One hundred of these are reserved for visiting yachts of up to 30 m, most of them in the northern basin. A central breakwater divides the marina into two parts, with reception and fuelling pontoons on its northern side. The Capitainerie (harbour office) is near the root of the mole.

Formalities

It is not necessary for a British yacht to report to customs if arriving from another EC country (including Azores), but failure to do so implies a formal declaration that the vessel complies with all the detailed customs and health regulations. All yachts must carry some form of registration, and it is currently forbidden for one skipper to hand over to another unless the hand-over is between co-owners or immediate family. Customs may visit yachts, sometimes boarding at sea.

Facilities

Boatyard With 14-tonne travel lift and six-tonne crane at the Marina du Moulin Blanc
Engineers/electronics At the Marina du Moulin Blanc and the Port du Commerce
Sailmaker At the Port du Commerce and at the Marina du Moulin Blanc
Chandlery At the Marina du Moulin Blanc and the Port du Commerce
Chart agent At the Port du Commerce
Compass adjusters At the Port du Commerce
Weather forecast Posted daily at the Harbour Office
Diesel/petrol At the Marina du Moulin Blanc
Water On pontoons at the Marina du Moulin Blanc
Shore power On pontoons at the Marina du Moulin Blanc
Bottled gas At the Marina du Moulin Blanc, and many places in the city (Camping Gaz only available)
Ice At the Marina du Moulin Blanc
Showers At the Marina du Moulin Blanc
Laundry/launderette At the Marina du Moulin Blanc
Banks Currency exchange available at the harbour office, many banks in the city
General shopping Shops of all varieties in the city
Provisioning Small grocery in the marina, a large supermarket on the road into Brest plus many others
Bonded stores M Fournier at the Port du Commerce and at the marina
Restaurants/hotels Restaurant in the marina complex, plus many others
Medical services Good, as befits a large city

Communications

Mailing address C/o Marina du Moulin Blanc by prior arrangement
Post Office In the city
Telephones Kiosks at the marina and in the city
Bus/rail service Frequent buses into the city (although the marina lies 3 miles beyond the Port du Commerce, it is little more than a mile from the city by land). Trains to Brest to Morlaix, Rennes and beyond
Taxis/car hire Agency at the marina, plus bicycle hire
Air services Twice daily flights to Paris (not Sundays). Guipavas airport 10 km from city centre

Charts	Admiralty		US	
General	–		37035	(1:350,000)
Approach	1111	(1:200,000)	37505	(1:156,800)
Harbour	1114	(1:25,000)	37506	(1:25,000)

Springs: 3.6 m/11 ft 10 in   *Flag*: Spain
Neaps: 2.8 m/9 ft 2 in   *Currency*: Spanish peseta

General

La Coruña is a major city of Galicia with roots going back to Roman times, and although the newer parts of the city are largely commercial the older quarters are very picturesque and well worth exploring. La Coruña is a busy fishing and commercial port, also visited by cruise ships, and facilities are in general good.

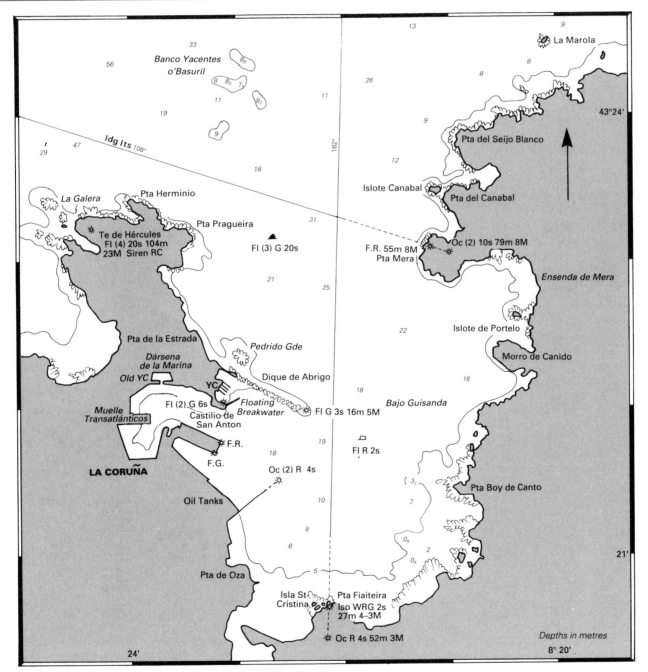

Chart 45 La Coruña, Spain. Based on a plan in *Atlantic Spain and Portugal*.

Approach

Yachts on passage southwards across the Bay of Biscay may make landfall anywhere on the coast between Pta Estaca de Bares [Fl(2) 7.5s 99m 25M] nearly 40 miles to the north-east of La Coruña and Islas Sisargas [Fl(3) 15s 108m 23M] just over 20 miles to the west. An even better landfall would be Cabo Prior [Fl (1+2) 15s 105m 24M], about ten miles north of La Coruña entrance. The Torre de Hércules [Fl(4) 20s 104m 23M], which stands on the peninsula to the west of the harbour, was originally built by the Romans and is the world's oldest operational lighthouse. Its DF beacon can be useful in the poor visibility characteristic of the Spanish coast. There are various banks and shoals in the approaches which, although not of depths to trouble yachts, can cause the seas to break severely in bad weather. In these conditions approach is best made from the west, on a bearing of no more than 145° on the Torre de Hércules.

Radio

The Darsena Radio Torre de Hércules monitors VHF channel 16 and working channel 12.

Entrance

The entrance is straightforward by day or night, with leading lights and marks easily seen. The Dique de Abrigo is a solid affair, visible from some distance and lit at its eastern end. A floating breakwater some 200 m long is now in place off the Castillo de San Anton, running on an axis of 065°–245°. It is intended to protect the yacht anchorage and pontoons from wash, but is low in the water and may be difficult to see, particularly at night.

Anchorage and moorings

Reasonably protected anchorage is to be found between the Dique de Abrigo and the Castillo de San Anton. There is good holding in mud, but it would be wise to use a tripping line. There are also a limited number of mooring buoys, administered by the two yacht clubs. Various other anchorages exist in the Ria de la Coruña, but none are convenient to the city.

Berthing and marinas

A pontoon berth may be available off the new yacht club between Dique de Abrigo and the Castillo de San Anton, but the marina is small and usually filled with local boats. It is also shallow, with at least one rocky patch within the berthing area – check from the dinghy at low tide before final berthing. There appears to be no objection to landing by dinghy on the pontoons, provided it is not left in the way.

The various harbours to the west of the Castillo de San Anton, including the Darsena de la Marina, are used by fishing and commercial vessels. Yachts are generally not welcome, and they tend in any case to be unpleasantly oily and dirty.

Formalities

Formalities in Spain are distinctly relaxed, but fly the Q flag if arriving from foreign. The steward in the new yacht club will produce a form to be completed, which he will then pass on to the appropriate authorities – apparently all that is required.

Facilities

Boatyard With 25-tonne travel lift at the new yacht club

Engineers/electronics To the east side of the Darsena de la Marina

Yacht clubs The old yacht club – the Real Club Nautico – is situated to the west of the Darsena de la Marina. However, of more interest to yachtsmen are the new yacht club (c 1982) near the root of the Dique de Abrigo and that opened in the last few years as an offshoot of the Casino

Diesel/petrol/water From pumps on the quay at the new yacht club. Check depths, which may be no more than one metre at low water springs

Water As above, and also at pontoon berths

Bottled gas Camping Gaz readily available in the city. Calor Gas cylinders must be taken to a plant some miles to the south for refilling

Showers In the new yacht club

Laundry/launderette In the new yacht club

Banks Many in La Coruña, most with credit card encashment facilities

General shopping Excellent

Provisioning For a major stock-up it may be worth taking a taxi to the *Hipermercado* outside town. Otherwise there is good provisioning in town, plus a particularly outstanding fruit, vegetable and fish market just a few minutes' walk from the new yacht club

Restaurants/hotels Many and varied

Medical services Hospital outside the city

Communications

Mailing address C/o the main post office (the poste restante office has a separate entrance around the back). Otherwise c/o the Yacht Club by pre-arrangement

Post Office This imposing building is on the main thoroughfare leading past the Darsena de la Marina

Telephones At the new yacht club and throughout the city

Bus/rail service Local buses, trains to Madrid and elsewhere

Taxis/car hire No problem

Air services The airport at Santiago de Compostela handles international flights, and is about an hour away by bus or less by taxi (60 km)

Springs: 3.5 m/11 ft 6 in	*Flag*: Spain
Neaps: 2.7 m/ 8 ft 11 in	*Currency*: Spanish peseta

Charts	Admiralty		US	
General	3633	(1:200,000)	51100	(1:200,740)
Approach	2548	(1:42,000)	–	

General

Although the town is relatively small, Bayona is one of the most popular and useful harbours on this coast for the cruising yachtsman. The surrounding area is attractive with some pleasant walks, and the town contains many old buildings. The city of Vigo lies less than eight miles away as the crow flies (though considerably further by road), and any requirement that cannot be satisfied in Bayona can probably be met in Vigo.

Approach

Approach may either be made from the north, passing inside the Islas Cies and with Cabo de Home and Punta Robaleira [Fl(2) WR 7.5s 25m 11/9M] to port, or from the west, to the south of the Islas Cies and leaving the Islote Boerio (or Agoeiro) [F2(2) R 8s 22m 6M] to port.

If coming from south of west Cabo Silleiro [Fl(2 + 1) 15s 83m 24M] may be the landfall. This also has a DF beacon, but it should be noted that both lighthouse and beacon are situated nearly a mile south of the headland of the same name, from which offlying rocks extend some distance northwards.

Radio

The yacht club, which runs its own marina, maintains intermittent watch on VHF channel 16.

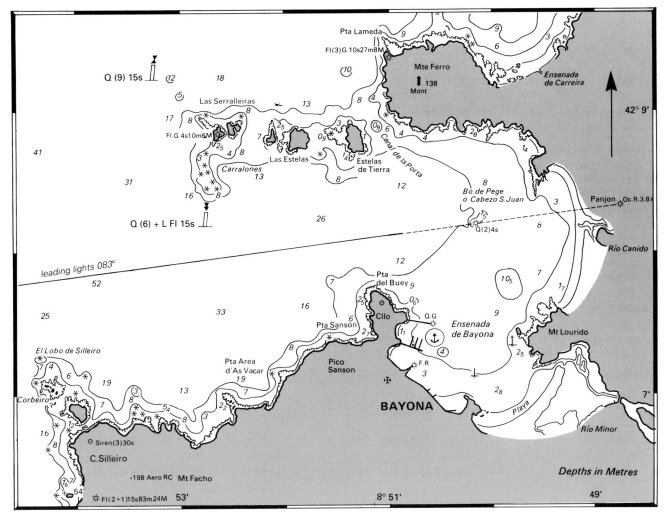

Chart 46 Bayona, Spain. Based on Spanish Hydrographic Office Chart No 9241.

Entrance

If approaching from inside the Islas Cies, the intrepid may wish to try a passage, known as the Canal de la Porta, which leads between Monte Ferro and the easternmost of the three Estelas islands. However it shoals to 0.9 m in the centre of the channel, so keep to the western side. A large scale chart should be consulted.

Most yachtsmen will prefer to use the main entrance, leaving Las Serralleiras [FlG 4s 10m 6M] and its attendant buoys marking the western extremity of the Ilas las Estelas well to port. The leading lights then bear 083°, the front one, Cabezo de San Juan, being on a shoal almost in the centre of the bay. In daylight both Pta da Buey and the breakwater head can be left close to starboard.

Anchorage and moorings

The yacht anchorage is to the south and south-west of the mole, outside the moorings buoys. Holding is excellent – in October 1984 a number of yachts sat out hurricane force winds which veered from south-east right around to the north-west and very few had problems.

The fairway leading to the fishermen's mole south of the marina should be avoided. The moorings (for which a fee is charged) are administered by the Yacht Club – consult their Berthing Master. It has recently been reported that the Yacht Club have objected to dinghies being left at their pontoons – it may be better to land on the beach.

Berthing and marinas

The marina pontoons are owned by the Yacht Club. The reception and fuelling berths are on the south side of the main jetty, and though much of the marina is occupied by local boats the Berthing Master may be able to arrange a visitor's berth.

Formalities

The Yacht Club handles formalities. The Berthing Master will deliver a form which must be completed and returned to the Yacht Club office.

Facilities

Boatyards Repair facilities and a 15-tonne travel lift at the Yacht Club. For major work, try Astilleros Lagos, Avda de Eduardo Cabello 24, Vigo (986 232626), a family-run boatyard with a high reputation for quality

Engineers/electronics Some facilities at the Yacht Club, but for major work it may be necessary to go to Vigo where several are located

Chandlery In Vigo

Yacht club The Real Club Nautico occupies an imposing building overlooking the marina and bay. It has a large and comfortable bar, with a good restaurant and snacks always available

Diesel/petrol From the Yacht Club pontoon. (Yachts are no longer able to fill up at the fishermen's pier, due to rules regarding subsidised fuel)

Water From the Yacht Club pontoon, and on the marina

Bottled gas Camping Gaz available in the town. Calor Gas cylinders must be taken some distance away for refilling

Showers At the Yacht Club

Banks Several in the town, most accepting credit cards

General shopping Somewhat limited – Bayona is a tourist resort rather than a commercial centre or major town

Provisioning Several grocery stores plus a fresh produce market. Quite adequate to replenish supplies, but unsuitable for a major stocking-up

Restaurants/hotels Numerous. The *Parador*, a hotel converted from the Castillo de Monte Real, has attractive walks, a restaurant and a bar, all open to non-residents

Medical services Limited – best to go to Vigo if possible

Communications

Mailing address C/o the Yacht Club by prior arrangement

Post Office In the town

Telephones Booths at the Yacht Club and in town

Bus/rail service Buses to Vigo, linking with the rail network

Taxis/car hire Enquire at the Yacht Club

Air services National airport at Vigo, or international flights from Santiago de Compostela

Springs: 3.5 m/11 ft 6 in	*Flag*: Portugal	
Neaps: 2.7 m/8 ft 11 in	*Currency*: Portuguese escudo	

Charts	Admiralty		US	
General	3634	(1:200,000)	51100	(1:200,740)
			51120	(1:206,900)
Approach	3254	(1:50,000)	51109	(1:50,000)
Harbour	3254	(1:10,000)	51109	(1:15,000)

General

Leixões with its well protected entrance is by far the best port of refuge on this stretch of the coast and can be entered in any weather. It appears to be a grim oil, fishing and general commercial port but this impression is countered by the interest of its maritime activity and by the friendliness and helpfulness of the Yacht Club.

Leixões lies only a few miles north of the ancient city of Oporto (Porto) on the Rio Douro, the approach to which can be dangerous in onshore winds or swell.

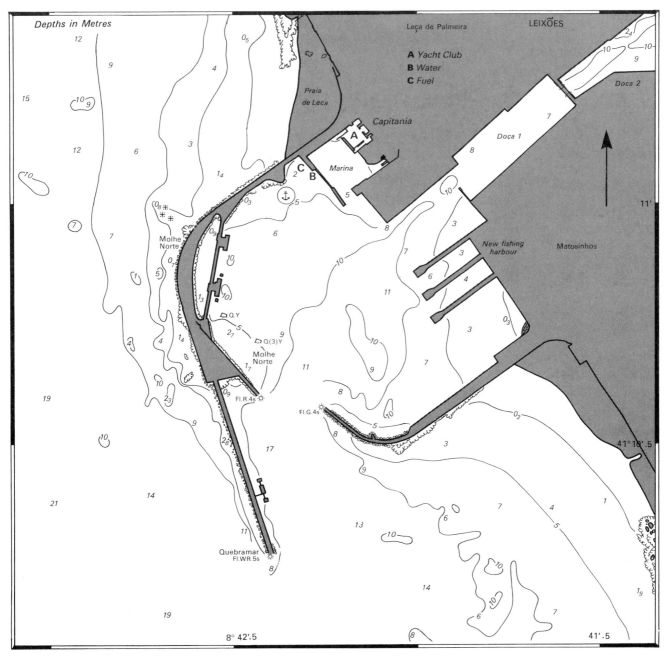

Chart 47 Leixões, Portugal. Based on Portuguese Hydrographic Office Chart No 58.

Leixões, an aerial view looking north. *Photo: Oz Robinson*

Approach

Compared to the coastline further north, the area around Leixões is somewhat featureless. The oil refinery 1.5 miles to the north is a good mark by day or night, with the powerful Leça light [Fl(3) 15s 57m 28M] lying between it and the town. South of Leixões, the city of Oporto gives an indication of latitude.

Radio

The Radar Station controls navigation within 18 miles of the port approaches, working on VHF channels 11, 12, 13, 16, 20 and 68. Port control uses VHF channels 06, 08, 09, 11, 12, 13, 14, 16, 18, 20, 22 and 68 and the pilots VHF channels 14 and 16.

Entrance

If approaching from the north, harbour regulations state that vessels must give the northern breakwater a berth of at least one mile. Not all fishing boats observe this, though there are dangers 200 m to its seaward side. During westerly gales the swell at the entrance may be heavy, but this is lost once within the breakwater. Head for the middle of the passage between the two inner moles on about 355°. At night the breakwater light may be difficult to identify against the bright shore lights, but from south of Leixões the Leça light on 350° leads through the inner moles.

Anchorage and moorings

The yacht anchorage is in the extreme north of the harbour, in the angle formed by the south-west wall of the old fishing harbour and the northern breakwater. Keep well away from the fishing harbour wall, which is used as a naval berth.

A marina has been built in the old fishing harbour, and though crowded with local boats there are often berths available. Ask at the Yacht Club, which overlooks it.

Formalities

The advent of the EC should mean fewer formalities for EC owned and registered yachts arriving from another EC country, but if in any doubt you should check with the *Capitania do Porto*. If it is a non EC owned vessel, or if arriving from a non EC country, the skipper should first visit the *Capitania do Porto* (Port Captain) taking the ship's papers and all passports. A *Livrete de Transito* (transit log), which remains valid while the yacht is in Portugal, will be issued on payment of a small fee. The *Guarda Fiscal* (immigration) and *Alfandega* (customs) must also be seen.

Facilities

Boatyards/engineers/electronics Practically any repair can be made, though yards are geared to fishing vessels rather than yachts. Best to ask at the Yacht Club

Sailmaker In Oporto

Yacht club Overlooking the new marina in the northern corner of the main harbour

Diesel On the south-western wall of the old fishing harbour

Petrol By can from filling stations

Water South-western wall of the old fishing harbour

Bottled gas Camping Gas available in the town

Showers At the Clube Vela Atlantico, near the Yacht Club

Banks In the town

General shopping Reasonable, but better in Oporto

Provisioning As above. There is a market at Matosinhos, best reached by taxi

Restaurants/hotels The Clube Vela Atlantico serves meals, but much more choice in Oporto

Medical services Best to go to Oporto if possible

Communications

Post Office/telephones In Leixões

Bus/rail service The 44 bus runs from behind the Yacht Club into Oporto, and links with the rail network

Taxis Readily available

Car hire In Oporto

Air services International airport at Oporto

Springs: 3.8 m/12 ft 6 in		*Flag*: Portugal	
Neaps: 3.0 m/9 ft 10 in		*Currency*: Portuguese escudo	

Charts	Admiralty		US	
General	3635	(1:200,000)	51140	(1:212,800)
Approach	3263	(1:25,000)	51141	(1:40,000)
Harbour	3264	(1:25,000)	51141	(1:25,000)

General

Lisbon has been the capital of Portugal for more than 700 years. It occupies a splendid site on the north bank of the Rio Tejo (River Tagus) which allows sizeable ships to berth in front of one of the main squares, and is an intriguing city with Arabic undertones and a history of seafaring and exploration. The maritime museum (just inland from the Torre de Belém) is particularly fascinating and not to be missed.

Provision for yachts in Lisbon is improving, and any shortcomings are more than compensated for by the sheer interest of berthing in the heart of one of Europe's more handsome capital cities.

Approach

If making landfall from north or west, the high cliffs of Cabo de Roca [Fl(4) 20s 164m 26M] are likely to be the first indication that the latitude of Lisbon has nearly been reached. In poor visibility Cabo de Roca DF beacon may also be useful. Some five miles further south the lower headland of Cabo Raso [Fl(3) 15s 22m 20M] is rounded to port, the town of Cascais soon becoming visible. In settled conditions there is a pleasant anchorage off Cascais, but it is exposed to wind or swell from south or west and is frequently rolly.

Radio

Lisbon Port Control operates on VHF channels 11, 13, 16, 22 and 63. Navigation and storm warnings on VHF channel 11 and pilots on VHF channel 14.

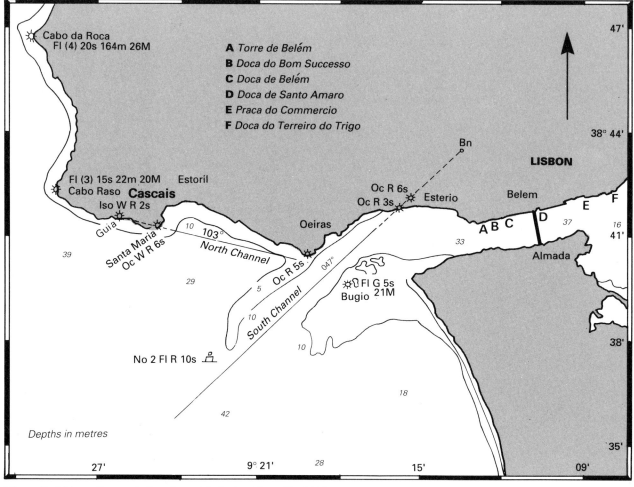

Chart 48 Lisbon, Portugal. Based on Admiralty Chart No 3263.

The fairytale Torre de Belém near the mouth of the River Tagus at Lisbon. *Photo: Anne Hammick*

Entrance

The Rio Tejo is entered between Fort São Julião on the north bank and Fort Bugio to the south-east. The main channel lies on a bearing of about 050° from No 2 buoy, or follow the leading lights of Gibalta and Esteiro up 047°. Do not be tempted to cut Fort Bugio too close or turn too soon – best water is found near the northern bank. Tidal streams run at three knots at springs (more on the ebb after heavy rain) and in strong south-westerly winds there may be rollers on the bar.

There is a second channel close under Fort São Julião much used by fishing boats and other small vessels, particularly in thick weather or if stemming an ebb tide. However, the sandbanks of the bar may shift from time to time, and in addition to current large-scale charts one eye should be kept on the depth sounder. Once inside the mouth, the Rio Tejo is deep with no unmarked hazards. The Ponte 25 de Abril suspension bridge has a clearance of 70 m (220 ft) – unlikely to worry any yacht!

Anchorage and moorings

There is no yacht anchorage convenient to Lisbon itself, though there are a number of possible areas further up-river where it widens into the Mar de Palha (literally 'Sea of Straw', or reeds).

Berthing and marinas

The situation regarding foreign yachts berthing in Lisbon appears to alter relatively frequently. Four possibilities were listed in the previous edition, and though currently (1992) yachts are advised to berth in the Doca do Terreiro do Trigo, the furthest upstream of the four, details of the other three are still included against the possibility that the situation will change again.

Beware the tide setting across the entrances of all these docks – not only will it set you sideways, but it may also tend to slew the boat round during those seconds when the bow is in the calm water of the entrance and the stern still in the moving river.

Taken in the order they will be seen, those docks used by yachts comprise:

1 The Doca do Bom Successo, just upstream of the ornate (and largely original) Torre de Belém which is floodlit at night. This used to be the preferred berth for foreign yachts but is currently full of local boats. It is claimed to be dredged to 3.0 m but this may be optimistic.
2 The Doca de Belém, just beyond the striking monument to Prince Henry the Navigator, which is also floodlit. This dock is reserved for the use of Portuguese yachts and carries 1.5 m or less.
3 Doca de Santo Amaro, just east of the suspension bridge (which can make it noisy). Depths shoal from 4.0 m at the entrance to 0.5 m at the back. Convenient to the authorities, but with no facilities nearby.
4 The Doca do Terreiro do Trigo, considerably further upstream near the old part of the city. It is actually one of a pair of docks, the western being reserved for naval use. The eastern arm is run by the Aporvela, the Portuguese Sail Training Organisation, and is currently the recommended berth for foreign yachts. (It is also a

The entrance to the Doca do Terreiro do Trigo in Lisbon. The cathedral dome makes an excellent landmark.
Photo: Anne Hammick

possible place where a yacht could be left in safety for longer periods). Although claimed to be dredged to 4.0 m there is nearer 2.0 m at low water springs, though the bottom is such soft mud that it hardly matters. There is a pontoon at the north-east end from which fuel and water are available, but mooring is otherwise of the 'bow to the wall, stern to a buoy' variety (or vice versa). Proof of insurance coverage may be required.

Formalities

The advent of the EC should mean fewer formalities for EC owned and registered yachts arriving from another EC country, but if in any doubt it would be wise to check with the *Capitania do Porto*. In the case of a non EC owned vessel, or if arriving from a non EC country, it is likely that all the formalities will have to be observed.

If berthed in the Doca do Terreiro do Trigo the *Guarda Fiscal* (immigration) will visit the yacht, but the *Capitania do Porto* (Port Captain) and *Alfandega* (customs) must be visited in their offices near the Doca de Alcantara. The ship's papers and all passports will be required. If arriving from foreign a *Livrete de Transito* (transit log) will be issued on payment of a small fee. This remains valid until the yacht leaves Portugal. Even if clearance has already been obtained at another port it is still necessary to get the *Livrete* stamped by the *Capitania* and *Guarda Fiscal*.

A port control launch may intercept the yacht while entering Lisbon and officials come aboard. It would be as well to have all necessary paperwork to hand. This does not exempt the skipper from formal clearance once berthed.

Official addresses

British Embassy: 35–37 Rua de Sao Domingos à Lapa (66 11 91 and 66 11 22). Embassy of the USA: Avenida Duque de Loule 39 (57 01 02)

Facilities

Boatyards/engineers/electronics Good facilities are available in Lisbon, though two of the yards, Estaleiro Venancio at Amora and Estaleiro Jose Gouveia at Porto Brandao, are on the south bank of the Tejo. There are many others – ask harbour staff or enquire at the Associacao Naval de Lisboa (the yacht club) at the Doca de Belém
Ramp/drying grid In the Doca de Belém
Sailmaker Velarte, Rua Giestal
Chandlery Garraio, Avenida 24 Julho 2, and Godhino, both in the Cais Sodré area near the Estoril train terminal. Also Pronave, Beco de Arciprestas 6a, Bico 1200
Charts The Instituto Hidrografico, Rua das Trinas 49 (the shop door is on the side of the building, on Rua Garoa de Orta), publishes Portuguese charts and pilots. Also Godhino and Garraio (see above), or G Vieria, Travessa do Carvalho 15-1, 1200 for US DMA charts
Yacht club The Associacao Naval de Lisboa has premises overlooking the Doca de Belém
Diesel/water At all the docks
Bottled gas Camping Gaz readily available in Lisbon; Calor Gas bottles must be taken to the filling plant outside the city

Showers At the Doca de Belém and Doca do Terreiro do Trigo, and also at the yacht club

Laundry/launderette Several in the city

Banks Many, with credit card facilities. Banking hours 0830–1200 and 1345–1430

General shopping Excellent

Provisioning Very good – there are several large supermarkets in the city, and a hypermarket on the road to Cascais

Restaurants/hotels Many and varied. Some bars and restaurants feature live *Fado* singing

Medical services The British Hospital, Rua Saraiva de Carvalho 49 (36 31 61)

Communications

Mailing address There is an entire building adjacent to the main post office given over to nothing but poste restante. Otherwise c/o the Associacao Naval de Lisboa or Aporvela by prior arrangement

Post Office/telephones Many. Stamps can be bought at any shop displaying the green *Correio* sign

Bus/tram/rail service Frequent buses and trams between the Belém area and central Lisbon. Trains to Cascais every 30 minutes via Belém and Estoril

Taxis/car hire No problem

Air services Lisbon has an international airport

| *Springs*: 3.6 m/11 ft 10 in | *Flag*: Portugal |
| *Neaps*: 2.8 m/9 ft 2 in | *Currency*: Portuguese escudo |

Charts	Admiralty		US	
General	89	(1:175,000)	51160	(1:355,190)
	–		51155	(1:150,000)

General

Vilamoura is one of Portugal's few purpose-built marinas, dredged in a lagoon just inside the coastline. It is fringed by a large development of villas, hotels, a casino and a golf course and cannot be considered particularly attractive. However it is a popular and relatively safe place to leave a yacht – possibly between a summer passage southwards

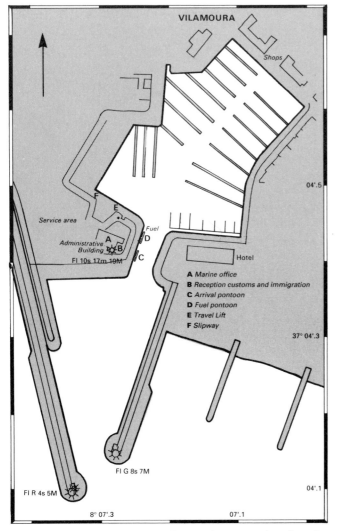

Chart 49 Vilamoura, Portugal. Based on a plan by the Marina de Vilamoura.

and the late autumn passage to Madeira, the Canaries and beyond – and though break-ins are not unknown they are uncommon and there is reason to believe that other yachtsmen are responsible. Security is not very effective, but there are plenty of customs guards about who do instil some respect.

Approach

The Algarve coast is low and relatively featureless, but the white Hotel Dom Pedro building just to the east of the entrance may be visible from some distance. Further east are the tower blocks of Quarteira and Faro airport. Vilamoura has its own powerful light [Fl 10s 17m 19M], and is bracketed by Ponta de Alfanzina [Fl(2) 15s 61m 29M] some 17 miles to the west and Cabo de Santa Maria [Fl(4) 17s 49m 25M] about 12 miles to the south-east.

Radio

Harbour control operates on VHF channels 16, 20 and 62. English is spoken.

Entrance

Two 500 m moles converge to form an entrance 100 m wide and facing south-east. Although the moles are lit, the many moored fishing boats and empty moorings in the outer harbour are not. The entrance to the inner harbour is about 60 m wide, with the reception pontoon on its western side under the control tower (from which Vilamoura light operates). Secure to the reception pontoon on arrival and report to the Administration Office.

Anchorage and moorings

All berths are alongside.

Berthing and marinas

A numbered berth will be allocated by the marina staff. Depths vary from 3.3 m to 2.0 m, and booking may be advisable in the high season. The marina can be contacted by telex 56843 MARINA P, or telephone (89) 32023 or 32043.

Formalities

In theory the advent of the EC should mean fewer formalities for EC owned and registered yachts arriving from another EC country, but if in any doubt check with the *Capitania do Porto*. In the case of a non EC owned vessel, or if arriving from a non EC country, it is likely that all the formalities will have to be observed. If arriving from a foreign port the *Capitania do Porto* (Port Captain) will issue a *Livrete de Transito* (transit log), which remains valid while the yacht is in Portugal. The

Vilamoura, an aerial view looking north. The arrival and fuelling berths can be seen on the port hand in the entrance channel to the marina, which has filled up considerably since this photograph was taken. *Photo: Marina de Vilamoura*

Guarda Fiscal (immigration) and *Alfandega* (customs) must also be visited. The latter is particularly strict – liquor is sealed and a refundable deposit charged on ship's stores in transit. Duty is charged on goods not declared. Even if clearance has already been obtained at another port it is still necessary to get the *Livrete* stamped by the *Capitania* and *Guarda Fiscal*.

There has been at least one case of a customs official in Vilamoura refusing to accept *any* evidence of VAT status other than the Single Administrative Document (SAD), and not recognising a Certificate of Registry as evidence of a yacht's age (See Paperwork in Chapter 8). It would therefore be wise to carry the correct document if intending to visit Vilamoura.

Facilities

Boatyard With 30-tonne travel lift and 5-tonne mobile crane. Yachts can be laid up ashore but there are no undercover facilities

Ramp/drying grid Tidal grid for boats drawing less than 2 m/6 ft 6 in, or dry out on the beach in the south-west corner of the marina. Check at low water first

Engineers/electronics/sailmaker At the marina repair department. Most diesel engine manufacturers have agents at Faro or Portimão

Chandlery In the commercial area on the north side of the marina

Diesel At the fuel pontoon just north of the reception pontoon

Water At the fuel pontoon and at berths

Shore power At individual berths

Bottled gas At the chandlery. Camping Gaz exchanges and Calor Gas cylinders refilled

Ice In Quarteira, ten minutes' walk eastwards along the beach

Showers/launderette In the commercial area on the north side of the marina

Banks In the commercial area

General shopping Various shops surround the marina complex

Provisioning Supermarkets in the commercial area and on the Aldeia do Mar, plus a large market in Quarteira

Restaurants/hotels All around the marina itself, and in Quarteria

Medical services English-speaking doctor(s) in Faro

Communications

Mailing address C/o the marina by prior arrangement. Address: Marina Vilamoura, 8125 Quarteira, Algarve, Portugal

Post Office In Quarteira

Telephones In the commercial area

Bus/rail service Bus services to Faro (40 minutes) and Lisbon (4½ hours)

Taxis/car hire In the commercial area or from the Hotel Dom Pedro to the east of the marina entrance

Air services Faro international airport is 20 minutes by taxi, 40 minutes by bus

Springs: 1 m/3 ft 3 in	Flag: British (Red Ensign)
Neaps: 0.7 m/2 ft 3 in	Currency: £ Gibraltar and £ sterling

Charts	Admiralty		US	
General	92	(1:400,000)	51160	(1:355,190)
	773	(1:300,000)		
Approach	142	(1:100,000)	52039	(1:100,000)
Harbour	1448	(1:25,000)	52043	(1:15,000)

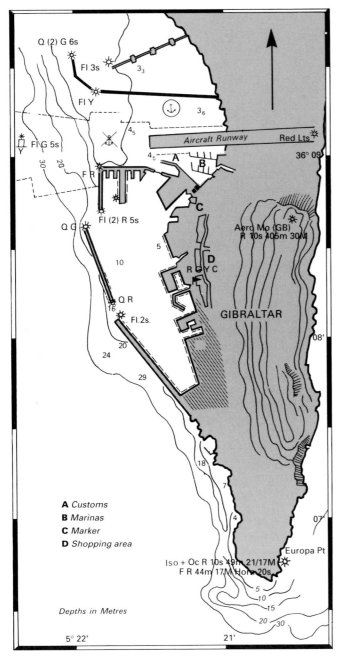

A Customs
B Marinas
C Marker
D Shopping area

Depths in Metres

Chart 50 Gibraltar. Based on Admiralty Chart No 144.

General

Gibraltar is a British colony, self-governing through an elected House of Assembly. It has withstood a number of Spanish sieges, but since 1985 the border with Spain has been open on both sides. Tourism is the major industry, though its importance in banking and as a tax haven is growing. The population is an ethnic mixture of all the Mediterranean races as well as British, and while English is the official language much Spanish is also spoken.

Though somewhat off the beaten track so far as the average Atlantic cruise is concerned, Gibraltar is a good place for major repairs or to lay up. It is considerably easier to get imported items through customs than in the rest of Iberia, and it may well be cheaper to have equipment flown in as ship's stores in transit than to buy locally. The benefits of carrying out major repairs or alterations in an English-speaking area are obvious.

Approach

The Rock of Gibraltar is totally unmistakable from both west and east. After dark the Aeromarine light flashes the letters GB in Morse from high on the rock itself [R 10s 405m 30M], with the sectored Europa Point light [Iso 10s 49m 21M, Oc R 10s 17M, FR 44m 17M] near its southern tip. The airport, just to the north of the customs berth and marinas, is also well lit.

Gibraltar Bay has deep water everywhere except for the offshore reefs on its western side, from Pta Carnero to just south of Algeciras. Depths in the area north of the airstrip also shelve gradually.

Radio

Port control operates on VHF channels 06, 12, 13, 14 and 16, and the pilots on 12, 14 and 16. All the marinas monitor VHF channel 16 during office hours – Sheppard's use channel 77 as its working channel and Marina Bay either channel 9 or 73.

Entrance

Head north-east into Gibraltar Bay, past the long breakwaters of the naval and commercial port. Yachts must berth on arrival at the Customs quay, beyond the ferry berth on the northern side of the inner mole and just south of the end of the runway. This can be approached in any normal weather, though there may be some swell.

Anchorage and moorings

There is an anchorage north of the runway, subject to various restricted areas (see current charts).

Gibraltar, looking northwest, showing the marinas tucked in to the south of the runway. *Photo: Gibraltar Tourist Office*

Berthing and marinas

Sheppard's Marina and Marina Bay lie just to the east of the customs berth. Both tend to be full, and it is worth booking in advance. Otherwise contact via VHF during the approach or before leaving the Customs berth.

Marina Bay (73300/74322) has 200 berths with a maximum draught of 4 m. Sheppard's Marina (77183) has 120 berths, with 24 reserved for visitors. Maximum draught is 2.2 m. Telex 2324 WATERPORT GIBRALTAR.

There is a new marina at Queensway Quay (between Coaling Island and Gun Wharf).

Formalities

Gibraltar is not a part of the EC. On arrival yachts must first call at the reporting station (WATERPORT) on the North Mole opposite the western end of the airport runway. The station flies the 'Q' flag by day and has an illuminated sign at night. Normal particulars of vessel and crew will be required. Any crew member leaving the yacht, whether to move ashore, to another vessel or to leave by air, must be reported by the skipper to the police and the crew list amended accordingly. The same applies to new arrivals. Yacht departures are notified to the marina which informs the relevant authorities. Quarantine restrictions no longer apply to animals aboard yachts, though they must be declared on arrival.

Duty free imports

Yacht equipment sent from abroad addressed to the yacht and marked 'In Transit' will normally be admitted duty free. Personal imports are subject to duty. Customs procedure in both cases is simple and quick.

Facilities

Boatyards Gun Wharf Ltd (further south inside the main commercial harbour) can handle vessels up to 200 tonnes. It has an excellent reputation but is not cheap. Sheppard's Marina has a 44-tonne hoist but most work is handled by sub-contractors. The Gibraltar Yacht Centre can handle up to 60 tonnes and allows owners to do their own work

Engineers/electronics/sailmaker At the marinas

Chandlery Dawlay Co Ltd in Irish Town (78417), The Yachtsman at Marina Bay and a good stock at Sheppard's Marina

Chart agent Gibraltar Chart Agency, 4 Bayside, Gibraltar (76293). There is also an excellent British Admiralty chart depot within the Admiralty Dockyard. This holds a full stock of British Admiralty charts, *Sailing Directions* etc but no unofficial material. Admission is by passport only

Compass adjusters In the naval/commercial harbour

Yacht club The old-established Royal Gibraltar Yacht Club welcomes bona fide visiting yachtsmen as honorary members while in port

Weather forecast Posted at the marinas, and read out on the Gibraltar Broadcasting Corporation and the British Forces Broadcasting Service every few hours

Diesel At the Shell jetty near the customs office

Water At the Shell jetty and at marina berths

Bottled gas Camping Gaz exchanges in town. Calor Gas cylinders (butane) can be refilled at four hours' notice at the Shell jetty. Tanks over five years old require a test certificate

Ice At the marinas

Showers At the marinas

Laundry/launderette At Marina Bay marina and in the town

Banks Barclays International and others with credit card facilities

General shopping A wide range of shops, many shutting between 1300 and 1500. A ferry trip across the Straits to Ceuta on the north African coast makes for variety

Provisioning Several branches of Lipton's Supermarket plus Charles Rodriguez in Marina Bay. Other shops specialise in Spanish and Mediterranean foods

Bonded stores Available at reasonable prices and can be delivered aboard under the eye of customs. Prices are as low or lower in the free port of Ceuta where there are no customs problems

Restaurants/hotels Wide choice at all prices

Medical services St Bernards Hospital, (casualty: 73941). Health Clinic, Casement Square (78337/77603)

Communications

Mailing address C/o the post office, or either of the marinas by prior arrangement

Post Office On Main Street

Telephones At the marinas and in town

Bus/rail service Buses to La Linea, connecting with Spanish bus and railway services

Ferry service Regular ferries to Tangier

Taxis Plentiful

Car hire Several agencies. Hire cars can be taken across the border into Spain

Air services Gibraltar Airport has several flights daily to the UK, and hourly flights to Tangier in summer. There are no flights to Spain – better to take a bus to Malaga Airport

Springs: 2.4 m/7 ft 11 in	*Flag*: Portugal
Neaps: 1.9 m/ 6 ft 3 in	*Currency*: Portuguese escudo

Charts	Admiralty		US	
General	1831	(1:150,000)	51261	(1:150,000)
Approach	1689	(1:15,000)	51263	(1:10,000)
Harbour	1689	(1:7,500)	51263	(1:5,000)

General

Funchal is a favourite harbour with many ocean cruising yachtsmen, and with the construction of the new marina offers shelter from almost any weather. The city of Funchal is somewhat touristy, but the island itself quite beautiful and well worth exploring.

Approach

Most yachts will approach from the east around Pta de Garajau, topped by a huge statue of Christ which is floodlit at night. The city and harbour are totally unmistakable by day or night, and Funchal Bay has deep water everywhere.

Entrance

Very straightforward, though it would be unwise to cut the end of the main breakwater too close. If entering at night there are a great many shore lights which could cause confusion, but on the other hand the ambient light will be helpful in spotting unlit mooring buoys or anchored yachts.

Anchorage and moorings

Yachts may anchor to the east of the *Cais* in a somewhat exposed position, untenable in strong onshore winds when the only adequate shelter would be inside the marina. Depths of 10 m or more are found close inshore and the holding is variable. A First World War wreck lies directly off the easternmost of the two small river mouths some 400 m east of the *Cais* and the area should be avoided.

Caution: Particular care must be taken if anchoring, as the prevailing north-easterly wind eddies around the mountains and frequently blows parallel to the south coast, generally from the west but occasionally from the east. If combined with an onshore sea breeze during the

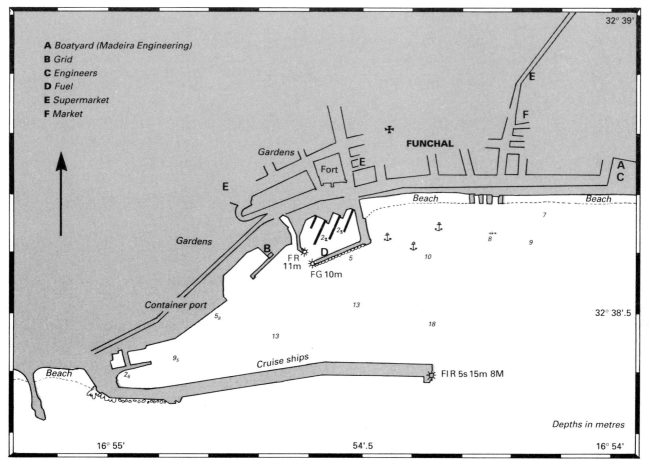

Chart 51 Funchal, Madeira. Based on a plan in the *Atlantic Islands*.

afternoon this will take on a southerly component, which will not only swing yachts through 360° each day but may set them ashore should they drag.

Berthing and marinas

The construction of a marina in the mid 1980s was much welcomed by visiting yachtsmen, but since then the administration has not always been of the best. Four jetties with finger pontoons provide berths for around 160 local craft, but visiting yachts lie alongside the southern wall, frequently six or eight abreast. Depending on wind direction, the marina can collect floating debris and warps may become oily. Charges are relatively high, but recent reports suggest that facilities have been improved to match.

Formalities

The advent of the EC should mean fewer formalities for EC owned and registered yachts arriving from another EC country, but recent reports suggest that full formalities are still observed in Madeira.

All authorities are at the marina. Start at the marina office and work through the *Capitania do Porto*, the *Guarda Fiscal* and the *Alfandega*. Crew arrivals and/or departures while the yacht is in Madeira must be documented through the *Policia Maritima*. All three offices must be visited again before departure.

Duty free imports

Yacht equipment marked with the boat's name and the words 'in transit' is theoretically admissible, but in practice there may be delay and difficulty. The post office has its own customs office at the airport, which deals with goods arriving by parcel post.

Facilities

Boatyard/engineers/electronics Madeira Engineering Lda, at the eastern end of Avenida do Mar, has a good reputation and some employees speak English. It would be wise to get a firm quotation in advance
Ramp/drying grid Inside the mole at the Regional Quay, capable of handling yachts up to about 11 m/36 ft (LOA) and draught 2.0 m
Sailmaker Senor Franco, skipper of one of the pilot launches
Chandlery There is no longer a chandlery in the marina complex but the Brendle hardware store now has a chandlery section at 25 Rue Fontes nearby.
Compass adjustment The chief pilot will undertake this by arrangement with the harbourmaster's office. Alternatively, an owner may swing his own compass by using the following bearings:

1 The eastern end of the breakwater and the eastern end of the harbour office are in line on a bearing of true north
2 From a position east of the breakwater, the lamp standards are in line on a bearing of true west

Yacht club The Clube Naval do Funchal (CNF) has its clubhouse two miles west of Funchal at Quinta Calaca. It welcomes visiting yachtsmen if not too swamped by numbers
Weather forecast Posted daily in the window of the *Capitania do Porto* office and at around noon from the marina office
Diesel At the western end of the marina wall
Petrol By can from the filling station near the roundabout
Water At the marina wall. Madeiran water is exceptionally pure and sweet
Shore power A few power points on the marina wall (220v 50Hz)
Bottled gas Camping Gaz available in town. CORAMA at the GALP service station about one kilometre up Rua Dr Manuel Pestana Jr (beside the eastern of the two small rivers) handles refills of Calor Gas, etc
Ice From the fish dock at the western end of the harbour
Showers In the marina complex. Access is now by key
Laundry/launderette Two in the town
Banks Many, open 0830–1145 and 1300–1445 weekdays only. The Banco Pinto e Sotto Mayor on Rua C Pestana has a VISA card facility
General shopping Good and varied, though with a strong bias towards tourist items
Provisioning Several well-stocked and reasonably priced supermarkets. The fresh produce market in the eastern part of the town is particularly notable – flowers, vegetables and fruit on two levels, with a busy fish market at the rear. Take your own egg boxes and plastic bags
Restaurants/hotels Very wide choice at all levels
Medical services There is a health service information centre for visitors at 1 Rua das Pretas, plus several well-equipped hospitals

Communications

Mailing address C/o the main post office
Post Office on Avenida Zarco. Open 0830–2000 weekdays, 0900–1230 Saturdays
Telephones International calls must be made from an office beyond the post office, with a separate entrance. Open 0830–2400 weekdays, 0900–1230 Saturdays
Bus service Cheap and reliable. A timetable is available from the tourist office
Ferry service Regular ferries to Porto Santo
Taxis/car hire Wide choice
Air services Direct flights to London and Portugal. Santa Cruz Airport 20 km from Funchal

| Springs: 2.5 m/8 ft 2 in | Flag: Spain |
| Neaps: 1.9 m/6 ft 3 in | Currency: Spanish peseta |

Charts	Admiralty	US
General	1869 (1:300,000)	51260 (1:300,000)

General

Although the harbours of Puerto Rico and Puerto de Mogan lie three miles from one another, they are taken here as a pair since each offers benefits the other lacks. Puerto Rico is a major holiday resort – something many yachtsmen may prefer to avoid – while Puerto de Mogan has less infrastructure ashore, though this is growing. Puerto de Mogan is a particularly popular place to leave a yacht unattended, and several owners who have left boats there for months or even years have expressed great satisfaction with the caretaking service available.

Approach

The south-west coast of Gran Canaria is generally steep-to and offers good shelter from the prevailing north-easterly winds, though squalls may occur in the lee of the land. It is not particularly well marked or lit in terms of formal navigation aids, but the many brightly illuminated hotel and villa developments offer a workable substitute. By day the grey buildings and chimneys of the cement works at Punta Taozo, 2.5 miles south-east of Puerto Rico, provide an unmistakable landmark.

Puerto Rico is identified by its backdrop of white buildings but Puerto de Mogan, with low green-roofed buildings behind a high breakwater, may be less easy to spot.

Entrance

Puerto Rico: visitors use the eastern of the two marinas, and apart from the possibility of confusing the two red light towers that mark the western arms of both marinas, entrance is straightforward. Make fast alongside the main wharf until a berth is allocated by the staff. The harbour office is at the root of the main breakwater.

Puerto de Mogan: again entry is straightforward. The reception berth is to starboard immediately after entering, alongside the port office building. The port authorities monitor VHF channel 16 and work on channel 6. Local fishing vessels use the inner section of the marina.

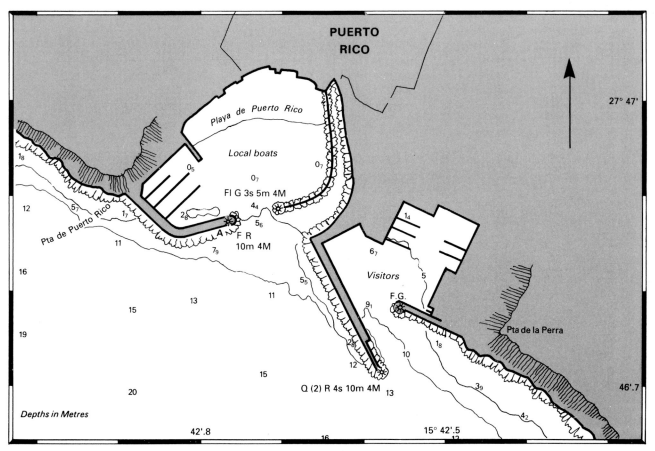

Chart 52 Puerto Rico, Gran Canaria. Based on a plan in the *Atlantic Islands*.

Puerto de Mogan, looking northwest. *Photo: Oz Robinson*

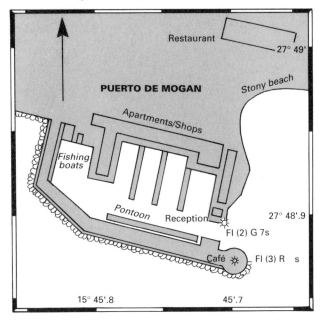

Chart 53 Puerto de Mogan, Gran Canaria. Based on a plan in the *Atlantic Islands*.

Formalities

In both marinas, ship's papers and passports should be taken to the harbour office for inspection. If arriving from abroad fly the Q flag on entry.

Facilities

Boatyards There are yards with travel lifts in both marina complexes. That at Puerto Rico can handle up to 30 tonnes

Engineers/electronics Cortios at Puerto de Mogan and others at Arguineguin and Las Palmas

Chandlery Top Yachting at Puerto de Mogan

Weather forecast Puerto de Mogan harbour office

Diesel Available in both marinas

Water Laid on at the berths in both marinas

Shore power Laid on at the berths in both marinas

Bottled gas Camping Gaz readily available, enquire at the harbour office regarding Calor or other refills

Showers In both marinas

Laundry/launderette In both towns

Banks In Puerto Rico there are banks in the small shopping centre near the beach. In Puerto de Mogan there is a bank in the marina complex

General shopping Good shopping in both towns

Provisioning In the marina complex at Puerto de Mogan and at both the shopping centres at Puerto Rico

Restaurants/hotels A wide choice, particularly in Puerto Rico. At Puerto de Mogan there is a restaurant on the breakwater head

Medical services The doctors at the British–American Clinic (74 57 47) at Puerto Rico speak English

Communications

Mailing address C/o either marina by pre-arrangement

Post Office/telephones Convenient to both marinas

Bus service Linking the two towns, and to Arguineguin, Las Palmas, etc

Taxis/car hire Readily available

Air services The airport is about 25 miles away and can be reached by bus or taxi

Springs: 2.2 m/7 ft 2 in		*Flag*: Spain	
Neaps: 1.7 m/5 ft 7 in		*Currency*: Spanish peseta	

Charts	Admiralty		US	
General	1869	(1:300,000)	51260	(1:300,000)

General

Los Cristianos is easier to approach than Puerto de Colon, some four miles to the north, but is open to the south and south-east whereas Puerto de Colon is more exposed to the north-east. It is principally an anchorage, with limited provision for yachts to lie alongside. Formerly a fishing port and still the terminal for the ferry to Gomera, Los Cristianos has been transformed as a tourist centre with high-rise apartment blocks and good shops and facilities.

Puerto de Colon is a new marina built as part of the larger development of Playa de las Americas. It too has good facilities and better shelter from the south than Los Cristianos.

Approach

Los Cristianos: seen from north-west to south-west the three mile long line of high-rise buildings is conspicuous. At the extreme southern end is an isolated tower block. Further south there are cliffs with a small development, Palm-Mar, followed by Punta Rasca, a low lying point with a light tower 50 m high. Steer for the isolated tower block until the harbour entrance has opened to the north. Approaching from the south after rounding Punta Rasca the entrance will be obvious.

Puerto de Colon: the surrounding shoreline is low and the entrance not particularly easy to identify from seaward. The marina lies near the northern end of the Playa de las Americas development.

If moving between the two harbours, keep at least a mile offshore to clear reefs which fringe the low lying coast. The Spanish charts mark groynes, placed there to retain the sand for bathers.

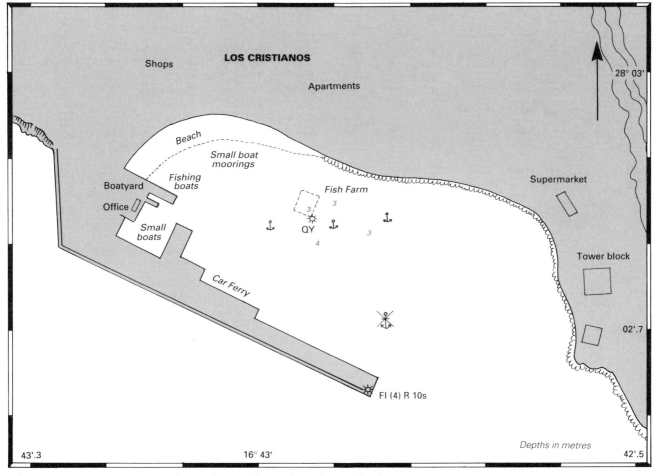

Chart 54 Los Cristianos, Tenerife. Based on a plan in the *Atlantic Islands*.

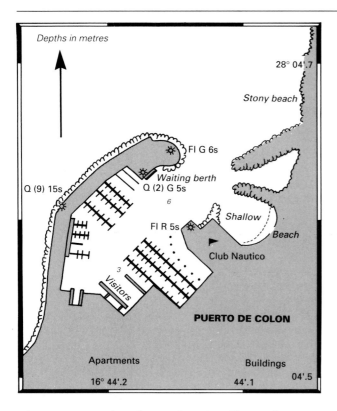

Depths in metres

28° 04'.7

Stony beach

Fl G 6s

Waiting berth

Q (9) 15s

Q (2) G 5s

6

Shallow

Fl R 5s

Beach

Club Nautico

Visitors

3

PUERTO DE COLON

Apartments

Buildings

16° 44'.2

44'.1

04'.5

Chart 55 Puerto de Colon Marina, Tenerife. Based on a plan in the *Atlantic Islands*.

Entrance

Los Cristianos: entry is straightforward and the harbour spacious. The harbour mouth is some 400 m (1300 ft) wide. If entering at night unlit moorings and anchored yachts should be anticipated.

Puerto de Colon: a much smaller marina development with an entrance some 70 m wide. Once identified, approach the entrance on a course at right angles to the coast before turning to starboard. The reception pontoon is on the starboard hand on entering.

Anchorage and moorings

Los Cristianos: visiting yachts are expected to anchor bow and stern in the bay (four metres over sand, but with at least one rock which has fouled anchors). It is essential to remain inshore of a line between the harbour office and a conspicuous low red-roofed building with a pagoda type tower at the south-east end of the bay. Anchoring outside this line obstructs the manoeuvring of the ferry, and can result in a heavy fine if an instruction to move is not obeyed. It is unwise to leave yachts unattended for long periods due to the surge.

There is no anchorage at Puerto de Colon.

Berthing and marinas

Los Cristianos: the small inner harbour is full of local boats, but for a fee yachts may raft along the outer end of

the harbour mole if there is space. Beware of surge from the swell and the wash of incoming ferries – good warps and springs are essential. In the event of very bad weather the harbour officials allow yachts into the inner harbour where they raft together.

Puerto de Colon: Some of the finger pontoons are occupied by local yachts, but there is plenty of space for visitors. Large yachts may have to moor bow or stern-to near the marina office.

Formalities

In both harbours, ship's papers and passports should be taken to the harbour office for inspection. If arriving from abroad fly the Q flag on entry.

Facilities

Boatyard Both harbours have travel lifts, and areas ashore where owners can prepare yachts for the Atlantic crossing

Engineers Bill Emerson, owner of the Jardine Lavandaria at Los Cristianos (opposite the *telefonica* on the esplanade) is a qualified engineer and may be able to arrange for work to be done

Chandlery Jose Miguel Gonzales Banios, Calle El Cabezo 10 (79 01 21), runs a chandlery/ironmongers with a fairly comprehensive stock at Los Cristianos (in the street between the harbour and the post office)

Yacht club The Clube Nautico at Puerto de Colon is located opposite the entrance

Diesel Fuelling berths near the harbour office in Los Cristianos and the reception pontoon in Puerto de Colon

Water At the fuelling berth in Los Cristianos, on the pontoons in Puerto de Colon

Shore power On the pontoons in Puerto de Colon

Bottled gas Camping Gaz readily available; enquire at the harbour office regarding Calor or other refills

Showers Puerto de Colon

Laundry/launderette Los Cristianos

Banks In both towns

General shopping/provisioning Better in Los Cristianos than at Puerto de Colon

Restaurants/hotels Wide choice

Medical services Los Cristianos

Communications

Mailing address C/o either harbour office by pre-arrangement

Post Office/telephones In both towns

Bus service Linking the two towns, and to Santa Cruz, etc

Taxis/car hire Readily available

Air services The main airport of the island, Tenerife Sur, lies about 10 miles east of Los Cristianos and has international connections

Charts	Admiralty		US	
General	366	(1:500,000)	51500	(1:250,000)
Approach	367	(1:150,000)	–	
Harbour	367	(1:17,500)	51500	(1:20,000)

Springs: 1.2 m/3 ft 11 in *Flag*: Republic of Cape Verde
Neaps: 1.0 m/3 ft 3 in *Currency*: Cape Verde escudo

General

After years of receiving a bad press – if mentioned at all – the Cape Verde Islands are at last being recognised as an interesting port of call on the Atlantic circuit. Porto Grande (also known as Mindelo) is an excellent natural harbour and facilities for yachts are very gradually improving. Many of the local people are desperately poor, and sensible precautions should be taken against petty theft.

Approach

Most yachts will approach from the north through the Canal de São Vincente. The small and rocky Ilheu do Passaros [Fl(3) 13s 86m 14M] can be passed on either side.

Caution: refer to the warnings in Chapters 12 and 13 regarding frequent poor visibility and the unreliability of lights and other navigational aids.

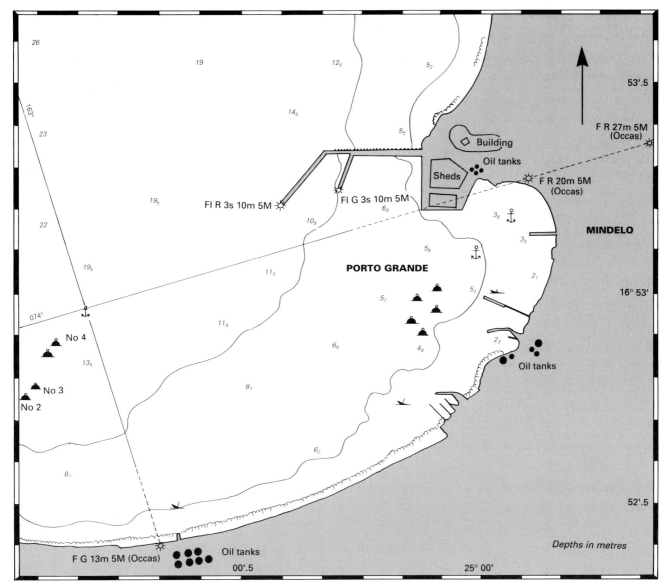

Chart 56 Porto Grande, São Vincente, Cape Verdes. Based on Admiralty Chart No 367.

Porto Grande, São Vincente, looking south-east. An uncharacteristic south-westerly breeze was blowing at the time.
Photo: Anne Hammick

Entrance

Very straightforward both by day and night, with good depths throughout the northern part of the bay. Several wrecks lie off the southern shore. The grey stone breakwaters are deep close-to, and well lit. Once around the outer breakwater a course of 095° leads into the yacht anchorage, though the old leading lights are no longer in operation.

Anchorage and moorings

The yacht anchorage is in the north-east corner of Porto Grande Bay, with good holding in sand. Depths of 5–6 m in the outer part of the anchorage shoal gradually towards the beach. No moorings.

Berthing

It may be possible to lie alongside in the inner harbour, though the east side of the inner breakwater is used by ferries. No yacht lying alongside should ever be left without a watchman being employed.

Formalities

Fly the Q flag on arrival. Officials from the Port Captain's office and immigration may board the yacht or it may be necessary to seek them out ashore – try and ascertain current procedure from earlier arrivals. Visiting yachts-men are not required to have visas. If a courtesy flag is not already hoisted they will be delighted to sell you one.

Ship's papers and passports are held ashore until departure, an unsatisfactory but unavoidable situation, though passports can be reclaimed temporarily in order to cash travellers' cheques. Fees are low and all the officials courteous and efficient.

Facilities

Facilities are distinctly limited, but like most islanders the Cape Verdeans are very ingenious and used to adapting whatever is available. Unless someone on board speaks good Portuguese the services of a local 'Mr Fixit' will prove invaluable. Several are likely to present themselves, and may have written references from other yachtsmen.

Boatyard/engineering/electronics The CABNAVE ship-yard in the bay north of Porto Grande has good facilities though geared more towards ships than yachts. Several of the senior management speak English. ONAVE and INTERBASE are more used to fishing and commercial vessels, but could haul a yacht if necessary

Sailmaker None as such, though a local seamstress might be able to repair lightweight sails

Chandlery Very limited stock at 12 Traversa da Praia

Yacht club The Clube Nautico occupies the low white building with two gables immediately opposite the anchorage and beach. It is welcoming to foreign yachtsmen; dinghies and other items can be left there in safety and rubbish dumped

Diesel Available alongside, by pre-arrangement with the Shell office, or from filling stations in the town

Petrol From filling stations in the town

Water A major problem whenever the water-making plant breaks down. When water is running yachts can fill up by arrangement in the docks, or collect small quantities by can from the Clube Nautico. Quality is variable, and it would be wise to conserve Madeiran or Canaries water for the Atlantic crossing

Bottled gas Camping Gaz cylinders can be exchanged at the Shell garage, and other bottles taken to ENACOL just south of town for refilling

Ice From the fish-freezing plant in the dock area

Showers Sometimes available at the yacht club

Laundry/launderette Launderette at 56 Avenida Unidade Africana, or via the local 'helper' or the Clube Nautico (arrange a price in advance). When there is a water shortage laundry may be a problem

Banks No problems in changing travellers' cheques, US dollars or sterling, but no credit card facilities

General shopping Limited, with prices often twice those in Madeira or the Canary Islands

Provisioning One small supermarket with canned goods and staples but almost no perishables, and two small markets offering a reasonable variety of fresh produce. Prices are high – do not plan on buying more in the Cape Verde Islands than absolutely necessary. The fish market is good, or fish may be bought directly from the boats

Restaurants/hotels Several, at reasonable prices

Medical services There is a hospital to the east of the town, said to be adequate but little more

Communications

Mailing address C/o the post office

Post Office/telephones One block back from the beach

Bus service Services link different parts of the island, but may not return the same day

Ferry service The regular inter-island service employs two purpose-built vessels

Taxis/car hire Readily available, but rates should always be negotiated in advance and include hidden extras such as tax, mileage and fuel

Air services Daily flights from the small airfield at San Pedro to Ilha do Sal, from which there are international services

| *Springs*: 1.8 m/5 ft 11 in | *Flag*: Republic of South Africa |
| *Neaps*: 1.3 m/4 ft 3 in | *Currency*: South African rand |

Charts	*Admiralty*		*US*	
General	2082	(1:300,000)	57480	(1:249,000)
Approach	636	(1:100,000)	57484	(1:36,000)
	1920	(1:37,500)		(1:37,500)
Harbour	1846	(1:10,000)	57488	(1:10,000)

General

Cape Town is one of South Africa's oldest settlements, and vessels have been using the harbour under Table Mountain since the days of the Portuguese explorers. It is now visited by everything from yachts through supertankers to cruise liners, and has facilities to match. It is possible to get almost anything done in Cape Town.

Approach

Cape Town will most often be approached from the south via Cape Agulhas and the Cape of Good Hope, the latter marked by Cape Point light [Fl(2 + 1) 30s 86m 34M] plus a DF beacon. It should be given generous clearance as shoal water extends more than two miles offshore.

Cape Town lies some 25 miles north of the Cape itself, but do not turn northwards until Slangkop Point light [Fl(4) 30s 40m 33M] can be seen, bearing 338°. The coast can then be followed at a distance of at least 0.5 miles to clear all hazards, passing Twelve Apostles and Lion's Head mountains before turning eastwards into Table Bay harbour.

Buoyage is on the European IALA A system.

Radio

On approach to the harbour yachts should contact Cape Town Port Control on VHF channel 16, to request permission to proceed to the yacht basin.

Entrance

The harbour entrance is clear and well lit. Follow a course of about 200° through the outer harbour, turning to port once inside the inner harbour (Duncan Dock). The yacht basin is in the southeastern corner. Upon entering the yacht basin, turn immediately to starboard and proceed along the marina to the floating fuel dock until a slip can be organised.

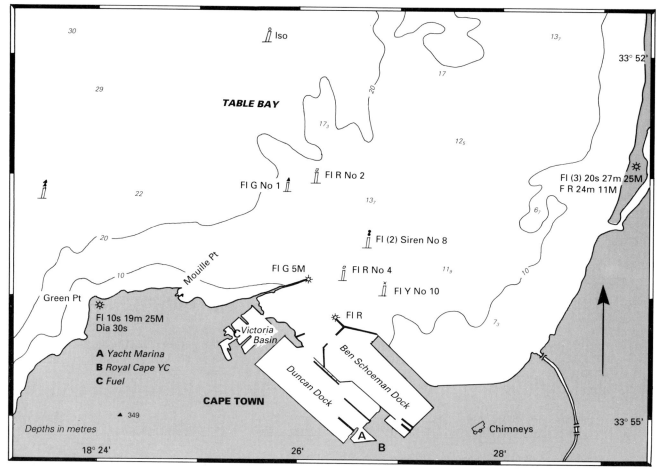

Chart 57 Cape Town, South Africa. Based on Admiralty Chart No 1920.

Cape Town harbour, South Africa, seen from Table Mountain. *Photo: Liz Hammick*

Anchorage and moorings

Anchoring is not permitted in Cape Town harbour.

Berthing and marinas

The Royal Cape Yacht Club, whose office is open during normal business hours (21 1254, 21 1355), can arrange berthing in their marina. The first five days are free, after which a charge is made. Alternatively free berthing can be obtained by securing to the concrete wall of the 'Globe' opposite the Yacht Club marina. For a nominal weekly charge the facilities of the yacht club (ie showers) can be used.

There are minimal harbour dues after one month in all South African ports, unless one stays at the Yacht Club.

Formalities

Whether arriving from another South African port or coming from foreign, customs and immigration should be notified and will come down to the yacht club to process the necessary paperwork. If staying at the Royal Cape Yacht Club they will contact customs and immigration for you. A South African stamp in one's passport has, until recently, made visits to most other African countries difficult – most immigration officials are willing to stamp a loose piece of paper which can later be removed.

To clear out one must first obtain a clearance certificate from the Royal Cape Yacht Club. Take this first to immigration (passport control) and then to the Harbour Revenue Office, both in the Customs and Excise Building

immediately outside Adderley Street Customs Gate, Rooms 535 and 340 respectively. The last stop is customs, located at the Adderley Street entrance where a port clearance will be issued. A yacht leaving at the weekend must obtain port clearance by 1200 on Friday.

Duty free imports

Equipment or supplies shipped from abroad for a visiting foreign yacht in transit are tax exempt. Clearance through customs is easily handled, but it is worth checking the current regulations concerning paperwork, labelling and notification.

Facilities

Boatyards, Several, with good (and cheap) haulage facilities
Engineers/electronics/sailmaker/chandlery Enquire at the Yacht Club for recommendations
Chart agent Chandling International, 53 Carlisle Street, Paardeneiland, Cape Town 7405 (021 512336)
Compass adjusters Enquire at the Yacht Club
Yacht club The Royal Cape Yacht Club overlooks the yacht basin in the inner harbour, and welcomes visiting yachtsmen
Weather forecast At the Yacht Club
Diesel Duty free fuel can be obtained at nearly half price from the Joint Bunkering Services in the Victoria and Alfred Basin, across from Bertie's Landing. Open Monday to Friday 0800 to 1600. The ship's (foreign) registration papers must be produced, but port clearance is not required. Exact change is necessary

Water On the Yacht Club marina pontoons
Shore power On the Yacht Club marina pontoons (220V 50Hz)
Bottled gas Enquire at the Yacht Club
Showers At the Yacht Club
Laundry/launderette In the city
Banks Many in Cape Town, with credit card facilities
General shopping Excellent
Provisioning Particularly good. The larger supermarkets will give a tax refund on the spot for major purchases, on production of the ship's registration papers. Given a day's notice the Tableview Pick-n-Pay Superstore will deliver down to the Yacht Club, and will attempt to order any items which are not on the shelves
Bonded stores Available from the commercial ship chandlers by case lots only, and delivered 48 hours prior to departure
Restaurants/hotels A wide choice at all levels and prices

Medical services Excellent. The District Surgeon on Plein Street can organise yellow fever immunisation, necessary if planning to visit Brazil

Communications

Mailing address C/o the Royal Cape Yacht Club, PO Box 772, Cape Town 8000, Republic of South Africa. They will hold or forward on request
Post Office In the city
Telephones At the Yacht Club and in the city
Rail service Connections throughout South Africa
Taxis/car hire Widely available
Air services Direct flights to Europe from Cape Town (D F Malan) international airport. Air services to the US are currently via London or Rio de Janeiro, but with the lifting of sanctions this is likely to change

Springs: 1.6 m/5 ft 3 in	*Flag*: British (Red Ensign)	
Neaps: 1.1 m/3 ft 7 in	*Currency*: St Helenian £ and	
	£ sterling	

Charts	Admiralty		US	
General	1771	(1:200,000)	57485	(1:200,000)
Approach	1771	(1:25,000)	57485	(1:26,530)
Harbour	1769	(1:7,500)	–	

General

St Helena is a favourite staging post for yachts crossing the South Atlantic from Cape Town to Brazil or the Lesser Antilles. It has been variously described as 'fascinating', 'unusual' and 'friendly', though to many people it will always remain famous primarily as the island to which Napoleon was exiled after defeat at Waterloo.

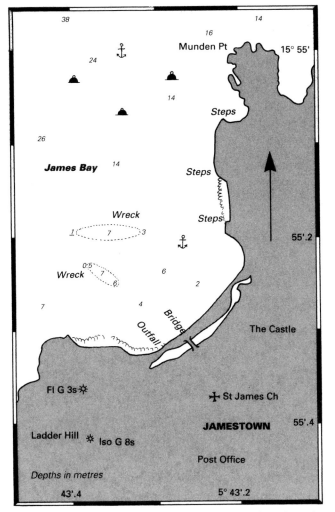

Chart 58 James Bay, St Helena. Based on Admiralty Chart No 1769.

St Helena has long been a British colony. There is only one settlement of any size, at Jamestown on the north-west coast.

Approach

Details of the approach to St Helena together with a plan of the island will be found in Chapter 15, under the heading *Cape Town to St Helena*. It is not well lit, the only powerful lighthouse being at Buttermilk Point [Fl(2) 10s 37m 10M] just west of Sugar Loaf Point, the most northerly promontory. There is an aero beacon situated to the south-west of Jamestown.

Radio

Radio St Helena monitors VHF channel 16 between 0800–2000, 1900 on Sundays.

Entrance

After rounding Buttermilk Point, first Ruperts Bay and then James Bay will be sighted. Both are open anchorages but the buildings of Jamestown make the latter unmistakable. The leading lights for James Bay bear 171°, but it can safely be entered on any course between west and north. The 1910 wreck of the steamship *Pamanui* lies in the centre of the bay, her sternpost still above the water, and there is at least one other wreck plus a number of unlit ships' mooring buoys.

Anchorage and moorings

The yacht anchorage is in the eastern corner of the bay. There are also some large steel drum moorings available which require a stern anchor to be set. Even so, one generally lies beam on to the swell and some rolling is inevitable. This can be minimised by tucking as close in to the beach as prudence and the moored fishing boats allow.

The dinghy landing is often subject to surge, and getting ashore dry can be a challenge. Tenders must be hauled out, making an inflatable the best bet. There is also a small ferry which operates 24 hours a day, primarily for the fishermen.

Formalities

Fly the Q flag on arrival. Ship's papers, passports and previous port clearance papers should be taken to the Harbour Master (the pale blue building on the wharf) and customs and immigration (at the police station in the main square). There is currently a 72 hour maximum stay limitation in force, though extensions are easily obtained. Clearance fees (1992) are £16 for the vessel and £5 per person. Passports may be held at the police station until departure, and firearms, spear guns and scuba gear will be

Anchored off the landing at James Bay in St Helena. *Photo: Liz Hammick*

impounded against departure. Animals are not allowed ashore under any circumstances.

Facilities

Boatyard None as such, but in an extreme emergency the harbour crane can lift up to 30 tonnes

Engineers/electronics Try the workshop which maintains the local boats

Sailmaker None, but local dressmakers are willing to machine light sails (See page 15)

Diesel Small quantities available by container from the filling station in the town, larger quantities – 200 litres (44 gallons) or more – from the fuel barge

Water By container from a tap on the quay

Bottled gas Cylinders can be refilled at the Shell service station

Showers Near the landing steps

Laundry/launderette DIY facilities on the quay, or by machine at Anne's Place, through the public gardens

Banks Cheques accepted but not credit cards

General shopping Limited

Provisioning Several grocery shops and supermarkets. Canned goods, dry staples, bread and eggs can usually be found. Fresh fruit and vegetables from the market on Thursday afternoons from 1400, but get there early. Occasional problems with the regular shipping service from South Africa may affect the availability of food, to which (quite reasonably) local people get first access

Restaurants/hotels Anne's Place is highly recommended for quality and value (book in advance). The Consulate Hotel Bar serves snacks and locally-made draught beer

Medical services Small general hospital in Jamestown and also a dental surgery

Communications

Mailing address Limited use as a mailing address as there is no airmail service

Post Office/telephones On the main street. There is direct dialling to most countries, plus a fax machine (290 2206) at the Cable & Wireless office

Bus service No buses, but lifts are freely offered

Taxis Island tours can be arranged at very modest cost

Car hire None

Air services None. The ship calls every six weeks or so

| *Springs*: 0.8 m/2 ft 7 in | *Flag*: Barbados |
| *Neaps*: 0.7 m/2 ft 3 in | *Currency*: Barbados dollar |

Charts	Admiralty	US	Imray–Iolaire
General	956 (1:644,000)	–	B5 (1:510,700)
Approach	2485 (1:100,000)	25485 (1:100,000)	B2 (1:56,900)
Harbour	502 (1:12,500)	25485 (1:25,000)	B2 (Inset)

General

Barbados has long been one of the more popular islands for an Atlantic landfall – it is reasonably well lit, offers probably the best general shopping of any ex-British island in the West Indies and has direct flights to Britain, the USA and Canada among other countries. In the early 1980s Bridgetown gained a poor reputation for expensive and inefficient clearance procedures, with yachts taking a very definite second place to the large numbers of cruise ship passengers cleared every day, but this appears to have changed and more yachts are now calling.

There is also the fact that, with Barbados lying nearly 100 miles to the east of the main chain of islands, if it is to be visited at all it is logical to do so first. Boats do occasionally beat out from Martinique or St Lucia, but it is not to be recommended. The obvious corollary is that a call at Barbados cuts at least a day off the Atlantic passage.

Approach

Barbados differs from most West Indian islands in that it is low lying with only one high point, Mount Misery, 329 m (1069 ft). Bridgetown lies near the south-west tip of Barbados and is most often approached around the south of the island, though there is no reason why it should not be approached from either end. Along parts of the south-east coast depths shoal rapidly, from 100 m or more to breaking reef in considerably less than 0.5 miles, and if approaching after dark it is unwise to close the windward coast. The airport has an aero DF beacon and is well lit, as is South Point [Fl(3) 30s 44m 17M], and once these have been identified the course should be altered to remain south of the latter by at least a mile, an offing maintained until off Bridgetown.

A large bank known as The Shallows, with a least depth of 60 m (200 ft) lies about four miles south-east of South Point. This area can be very rough when a westerly swell meets an east-going current and should be avoided.

Radio

Barbados Radio monitors VHF channel 16 and uses channel 12 as its working channel.

Entrance

On arrival yachts must pass the main anchorage at Carlisle Bay and go straight to the Deepwater Harbour to clear. The most convenient berth is in the far south-eastern corner, opposite the customs and immigration office, but the quayside is rough and large fenders will be needed.

Anchorage and moorings

After clearance has been granted most yachts return to anchor in Carlisle Bay, in good holding with 10 m or less over sand. Although in some ways a classic Caribbean anchorage, with clear blue water backed by a long sandy beach, Carlisle Bay frequently suffers from swell, causing monohulls to roll and making landing by dinghy a distinctly wet affair. If surf is breaking on the beach Knowles Marine Boatyard jetty is the best bet, though at other times it is possible to land on the beach north of the Holiday Inn, at the Barbados Yacht Club or further south at the Barbados Cruising Club. Until you've got the measure of it, avoid carrying cameras (except the waterproof kind) or other valuables, and transport money, shoes etc in sealed polythene bags.

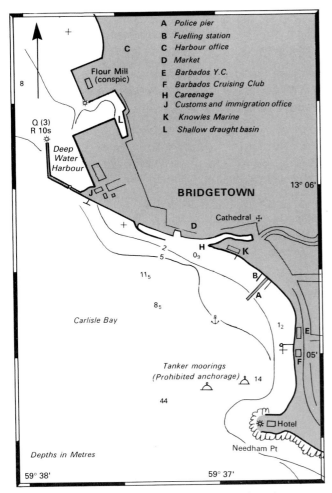

A	Police pier
B	Fuelling station
C	Harbour office
D	Market
E	Barbados Y.C.
F	Barbados Cruising Club
H	Careenage
J	Customs and immigration office
K	Knowles Marine
L	Shallow draught basin

Chart 59 Bridgetown, Barbados. Based on Admiralty Chart No 502.

Berthing and marinas

Yachts are sometimes allowed to lie in the Shallow Water Harbour to the north of the town (several ARC rallies have terminated here) but it is dusty, inconvenient, and generally reserved for local use. Another possibility is to berth in the Careenage, for which permission will be needed from the Barbados Port Authority (436 6883), though the frequent surge will put severe strain on warps and fenders. However most crews will want to celebrate their arrival in the Caribbean by swimming from the boat, impossible in either of the above.

There is talk of building a marina, but until this happens, if lying alongside is important to you it is probably best to head directly for a harbour such as Rodney Bay, St Lucia, which offers full marina facilities.

Formalities

Fly the Q flag on approaching Barbados. As already mentioned, yachts must go into the Deep Water Harbour to clear customs and immigration. Call Bridgetown Harbour Signal Station on VHF channel 12 for clearance to enter the harbour or, if out of hours, to anchor in the quarantine holding area south of the Careenage Molehead.

Customs and immigration are housed in a large building just to the south of the Deep Water Harbour and function from 0600 to 2200 seven days a week. The usual papers, including outward clearance from the previous port, will be required and charges are currently US $25 inclusive, covering boat and crew.

It is necessary to return to the Deep Water Harbour *with the yacht* to obtain outward clearance, which remains valid for 24 hours, but once cleared the yacht must leave directly to sea towards her next port of call and cannot return to the anchorage. If planning to leave at the weekend start the ball rolling by 2100 on Friday.

Coastal cruising

Customs clearance is required to cruise northwards along the coast and dues may also be payable. If intending to do this check the procedure either on arrival or through the Coast Guard on VHF channel 16.

Facilities

Boatyard Knowles Marine on Carlisle Bay has superb contacts, though they do not have haulage facilities which are only available in the main harbour. Whatever your problem, the Knowles brothers can probably help
Engineers/electronics Enquire at Knowles Marine
Sailmaker Enquire at Knowles Marine or the Barbados Yacht Club

Chandlery Two in Bridgetown
Chart agent Mannings in Bridgetown
Yacht club Both the Barbados Yacht Club and the Barbados Cruising Club are friendly and helpful towards visiting yachtsmen
Diesel In the Shallow Water Harbour or, if the surge allows, alongside the Shell jetty just north of the Police Pier
Water By hose in the Careenage and the Shallow Water Harbour. Unless large quantities are required it may be easier to carry it by can from Knowles Marine. Water is scarce in Barbados so a small charge is made
Shore power Possibly in the Careenage
Bottled gas Knowles Marine, or the Texaco tank farm north of Deep Water Harbour. Propane only available
Ice Knowles Marine and most filling stations
Showers Knowles Marine
Laundry/launderette Knowles Marine
Banks Several, including Barclays International, with credit cards a way of life. Both Barbados and US dollars are used, but the former are not accepted elsewhere in the Caribbean so change any remaining for US before departure
General shopping Particularly good by Caribbean standards, though inevitably slanted towards the thousands of cruise ship and hotel tourists
Provisioning Several large supermarkets, mostly stocking American brands, plus a good produce market
Restaurants/hotels A vast choice. The bar/restaurant at Knowles Marine is a favourite evening venue with the cruising people, and there are dozens more in Bridgetown
Medical services A small private hospital, The Diagnostic Clinic, is situated within walking distance of the Barbados Yacht Club. There is a large modern hospital just outside Bridgetown

Communications

Mailing address C/o General Delivery at the main post office (a passport will be required on collection), or c/o either the Yacht Club or the Cruising Club by prior arrangement
Post Office A large building with General Delivery occupying its own floor
Telephones At the post office and elsewhere
Bus service Buses all over the island – a cheap, fun, way to travel
Taxis Plentiful until a cruise ship arrives, when they vanish
Car hire Several agencies. Driving is on the left
Air services International air services to Europe and the Americas, and local air services to eastern Caribbean islands. Grantley Adams airport is 20.8 km from Bridgetown

Springs: 0.7 m/2 ft 3 in		*Flag*: Grenada		
Neaps: 0.6 m/2 ft		*Currency*: EC dollar		

Charts	Admiralty	US	Imray–Iolaire	
General	956 (1:644,000)	25400 (1:250,000)	B5	(1:510,700)
Approach	2821 (1:71,500)	25481 (1:72,560)	B3	(1:162,000)
			B32	(1:91,000)
Harbour	2821 (1:24,200)	25481 (1:24,320)		

General

Prickly Bay, also known as L'anse aux Epines, is one of the few recommended harbours which does not have a town, or at least a village, nearby. However, it is only a short bus or taxi ride from the capital, St George's, and until facilities improve in that harbour Prickly Bay offers a far preferable port of call for yachts. It is particularly attractive even by the high standards of the Caribbean, and is an official port of entry.

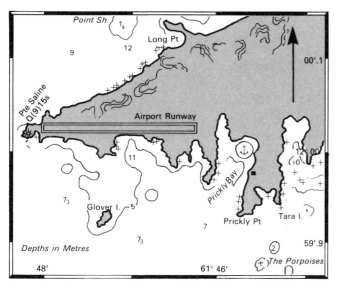

Chart 60 The south-west coast of Grenada. Based on Admiralty Chart No 2821.

Approach

The majority of yachts approach from the north, down the western (lee) side of Grenada. If a course is shaped directly for Point Salines at the Western extremity of the island all outliers will be cleared, but if coming from the direction of St George's, Long Point Shoal to the northwest of Long Point (itself at the western end of the spectacular Grande Anse beach) carries less than one metre. The old, striped lighthouse at Point Salines fell victim to the airport development and the replacement

[Q(9) 15s 7M] is a poor substitute. After rounding Point Salines, Prickly Point to the east of Prickly Bay should be seen about 2.5 miles distant, extending further south than the intermediate headlands. Glover Island can be left on either side.

If approaching from eastwards, or from the south, the chief hazard is The Porpoises, a group of breaking rocks about 0.7 miles south of Prickly Point. They are unmarked and unlit, and have claimed at least one yacht. In fact lights along this entire coast are poor, and if approaching in darkness there is much to be said for taking the traditional line and heaving-to until daylight.

Radio

Spice Island Marine Boatyard monitors VHF channel 16.

Entrance

There are reefs close to both sides of the entrance, but these generally present no problem. More dangerous is the isolated coral patch in the centre of the bay, west of Spice Island Marine, which is *sometimes* marked by an inconspicuous buoy. The water in Prickly Bay though clean is often cloudy, but even so the brownish shoal tinge should be visible in good sunlight. If in doubt keep well east, towards the Spice Island Marine pontoon. There is a second shoal close inshore on the eastern part of the bay just north of the boatyard.

Anchorage and moorings

Most yachts anchor either in the north-east corner of the bay or off the Boatyard, the best place for landing by dinghy. Otherwise take your pick in 10m or so over mud and sand. Anchoring within 100 m (300 ft) of the beach at the Calabash Hotel at the head of the bay is forbidden. Some swell may find its way in from the south, but Prickly Bay is often both flat and breezy – the best possible Caribbean combination. As with all Caribbean anchorages, keep a careful watch for swimmers if going ashore by outboard-powered dinghy.

Berthing and marinas

Spice Island Marine has a length of wall and a small pontoon where it may be possible to lie stern-to. Enquire in the office.

Formalities

Customs and immigration inhabit the upper floor of the building just to the north of the disused slipway. All the usual documents are required, but the attitude is reasonably pleasant and relaxed. Overtime is payable outside 0800–1600 weekdays, and as this is likely to be accompanied by separate taxi fares for several officials the charge can mount dramatically.

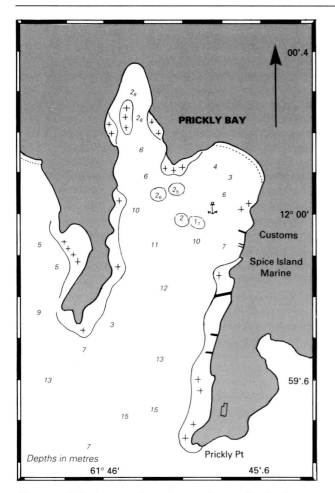

Chart 61 Prickly Bay, Grenada. Based on a plan in the *Lesser Antilles*.

Facilities

Boatyard Spice Island Marine Boatyard (444 4257/4342) has a new travel lift which can handle up to 65 ft (LOA) and 34 tonnes, and though booking generally needs to be made in advance they will pull out all the stops in a genuine emergency. Work can be DIY, or local labour hired

Engineers/electronics At Spice Island Marine Boatyard

Sailmaker Michael at Spice Island Marine Boatyard. Jeff Fisher (440 2556) is agent for a Hong Kong concern which claims to deliver new sails to Grenada within six weeks

Chandlery Good stock at the boatyard

Chart agent Imray-Iolaire Caribbean charts stocked at the chandlery

Yacht club The Grenada Yacht Club remains one of the few reasons for taking a yacht to St George's. Their buildings overlook the Careenage and Lagoon and are famed as a venue from which to see the 'Green Flash'

Diesel On the pontoon at Spice Island Marine

Water On the pontoon at Spice Island Marine, plus taps elsewhere in the boatyard. Although Grenada has some of the sweetest water in the Lesser Antilles, Spice Island Marine uses a cistern to which chemicals must be added, sometimes to its detriment

Shore power Available if berthed stern-to

Bottled gas Propane refills available at the boatyard or at Huggins on the Careenage in St George's. Since an explosion a few years ago they may (rightly) refuse to fill butane cylinders with propane

Ice At the boatyard

Showers At the boatyard. A small charge is made

Laundry/launderette At the boatyard

Banks Several banks in St George's. Barclays International has a VISA card facility

General shopping Essentials Mini Market at Spice Island Marine, and a wide variety of shops in St George's

Provisioning Essentials Mini Market sells the basics, backed up by several supermarkets in town and at the Grande Anse shopping centre. Local ladies sometimes bring baskets of fresh produce out to the boatyard, but nothing rivals the excellent and colourful market in the centre of St George's – take a camera and several bags

Restaurants Pleasant bar/restaurant at Spice Island Marine, or the Red Crab is just up the road. In town the Nutmeg, overlooking the Careenage, deserves a visit – try their calaloo soup and rotis. For a truly ethnic eating experience dine at Mama's, on the road from Spice Island to St George's

Hotels Many at all levels

Medical services Hospital outside St George's

Communications

Mailing address C/o General Delivery at the main post office, or c/o Spice Island Marine Boatyard, PO Box 449, St George's, Grenada. Mail is pigeon-holed in the office

Post Office On the waterfront in St George's

Telephones At Spice Island Marine, or via Cable & Wireless on the Careenage in St George's

Bus service Irregular buses from the boatyard, or walk up the road to the T junction for more frequent services. Lifts are frequently offered. Consider taking the bus (preferably one of the old converted lorry types) across the island to Grenville for the day

Taxis Plenty, both cars and mini-buses. Many of the drivers happily double as tour guides

Car hire Available, but the roads are poor and it may be better to organise a taxi. Driving is on the left

Air services The new airport at Point Salines has direct flights to the UK, USA and Canada, with others via Barbados

Springs: 0.6 m/2 ft		*Flag*: St Lucia	
Neaps: 0.5 m/1 ft 8 in		*Currency*: EC dollar	

Charts	Admiralty	US	Imray-Iolaire
General	956 (1:644,000)	–	B5 (1:510,700)
Approach	1273 (1:72,000)	25521 (1:72,620)	B1 (1:72,000)
Harbour	197 (1:24,100)	25521 (1:25,000)	B1 (Inset)

General

The new development of Rodney Bay Marina, St Lucia, inside the lagoon at Rodney Bay (also known as Gros Islet Bay) has become a popular Atlantic landfall over the last few years. Certainly the range of on-the-spot facilities is the widest in the southern Antilles, and several large charter fleets are based here. It is currently the arrival port for the annual ARC rally.

The marina's most obvious disadvantages are in being some way from Castries and even further from the international airport. The protection offered by the narrow lagoon entrance also means that the water inside is semi-stagnant and uninviting for swimming, though admittedly it is only a short walk to the beach. It all comes down to priorities.

Approach

Rodney Bay lies within a couple of miles of the northern end of St Lucia, one of the more mountainous of the

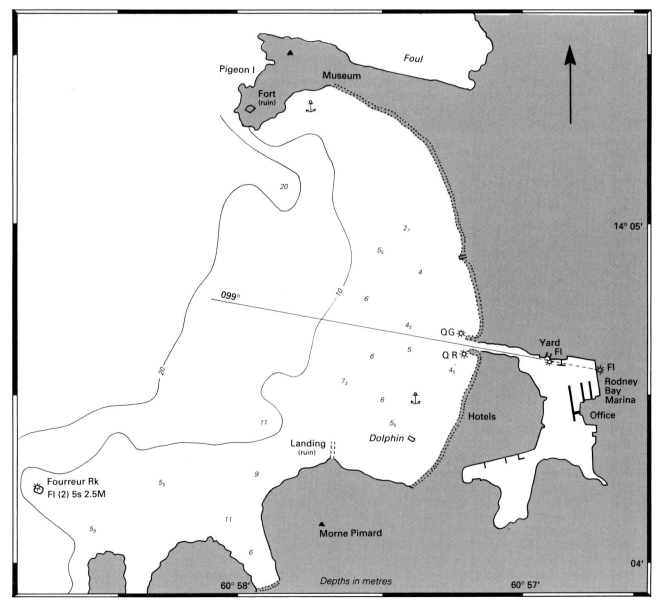

Chart 62 Rodney Bay, St Lucia. Based on a plan in the *Lesser Antilles*.

Lesser Antilles. Although Pointe du Cap at the extreme north of the island has no outlying hazards neither is it lit, and the light at Cape Marquis [Fl(2) 20s] three miles further south on the windward coast is of unspecified range.

Having rounded Pointe du Cap, Pigeon Island will be seen rising to over 100 m (356 ft) at the end of a low artificial causeway. Beyond is Rodney Bay, where fish traps with their associated floats and lines can be a hazard.

Radio

Rodney Bay Marina monitors VHF channel 16.

Entrance

The entrance to the lagoon lies near the middle of the bay, between Gros Islet village to the north and Reduit Beach to the south. It is not hard to identify by daylight and is lit at night, but the channel is narrow and if approaching after dark the first time visitor might do better to anchor outside and enter in daylight. There is 2.5 m (8 ft) or more in the entrance channel and in much of the lagoon itself.

Anchorage and moorings

It is possible to anchor to the south of the marina in the main lagoon, or in the slightly shallower inner lagoon to the south-west. Both offer reasonable holding in mud and a guaranteed escape from rolling, but can be buggy if the wind is down. The alternative is to return to the outer bay after completing formalities and anchor either off Reduit Beach or to the south-east of Pigeon Island, but both may be subject to swell.

Berthing and marinas

If intending to berth at Rodney Bay Marina (809 452 0185) it is best to call up on VHF channel 16 or landline before arrival. Otherwise (if making landfall) secure at the customs berth on the outer pontoon and a more permanent spot can be organised at the same time as dealing with officialdom.

The smaller A-Frame Marina (28725) is situated to the south of the larger marina, with most berths stern-to.

Formalities

Rodney Bay is one of four ports of entry in St Lucia. If staying in the marina it is not necessary to go to the customs berth first – the skipper can take the usual papers and go on foot – but if planning to anchor off it is necessary to secure here first. The office is manned between 0800–1200 and 1400–1800, but overtime is charged after 1630.

Facilities

Boatyard/engineers Rodney Bay Marina has the best boatyard facilities in St Lucia including a 50-tonne hoist and large lay-up area. DIY, or hire local labour

Electronics In the marina complex

Sailmaker Simon's Top Sail (27773) does both repairs and new work, and though not situated at the marina are willing to collect and deliver. A speedy repair service is available at extra cost

Chandlery At the boatyard and in the marina complex

Chart agent Imray-Iolaire charts at the marina chandlery

Diesel On the fuel dock to the north of the marina

Water On pontoon berths and at the fuel dock, also at the A-Frame Marina

Shore power On pontoon berths (220V 50Hz) and stern-to at the A-Frame Marina

Bottled gas At Sunsail Stevens Charters in the marina

Ice From the liquor shop and the Mortar & Pestle supermarket. Also at the fuel dock

Showers In the marina complex

Laundry/launderette At Sunsail Stevens

Banks In the marina complex. Barclays International has a VISA facility

General shopping Plenty of tourist shops, boutiques etc locally, but for wider variety go to Castries

Provisioning Several supermarkets. Bakery etc in the marina complex plus one at the Mortar & Pestle. For the best fresh produce visit the market in Castries

Restaurants Dozens within walking or dinghy distance

Hotels Many, scattered throughout the island

Medical services Various clinics, plus a hospital south of Castries

Communications

Mailing address C/o Rodney Bay Marina, PO Box 1538, Castries, St Lucia

Post Office In Castries

Telephones In the marina complex and elsewhere

Bus service Buses to Castries

Taxis/car hire Lots. Driving is on the left

Air services Small airport at Castries, but most international flights use Hewannora airport, adjacent to Vieux Fort at the south end of the island

Charts	Admiralty	US	Imray–Iolaire
General	956 (1:644,000)	–	A4 (1:388,000)
Approach	494 (1:75,000)	25526 (1:60,000)	A30 (1:92,000)
	371 (1:75,000)	25524 (1:60,000)	
	371 (1:25,000)		
Harbour	371 (1:15,000)	25527 (1:12,500)	A30 (Inset)

Springs: 0.8 m/2 ft 7 in
Neaps: 0.6 m/2 ft

Flag: France
Currency: French franc

General

Fort de France is one of the very few cities in the Lesser Antilles which truly merits the title in terms of both size and atmosphere. It became the capital of Martinique in 1902 following the eruption of Mt Pelée and destruction of the previous capital, St Pierre, and has more than made up for lost time. Facilities are generally excellent, and not surprisingly landfalls in Martinique, and to a lesser extent Guadeloupe, are very popular among French-speaking yachtsmen.

All the French islands of the Lesser Antilles are technically part of France and receive large subsidies from their parent country, some of which appears to go into the comprehensive and generally well maintained system of buoys and lights. Much of the infrastructure comes from France, along with the legal and education systems plus, somehow, that indefinable chic in dress and bearing which so many French West Indian ladies share with their Parisienne counterparts. Not for nothing did Napoleon's Empress Josephine come from Martinique.

Approach

Martinique is one of the more mountainous islands of the Lesser Antilles, and Fort de France lies on the northern shores of a large bay somewhat south of its centre. If making landfall there after a transatlantic passage it there-

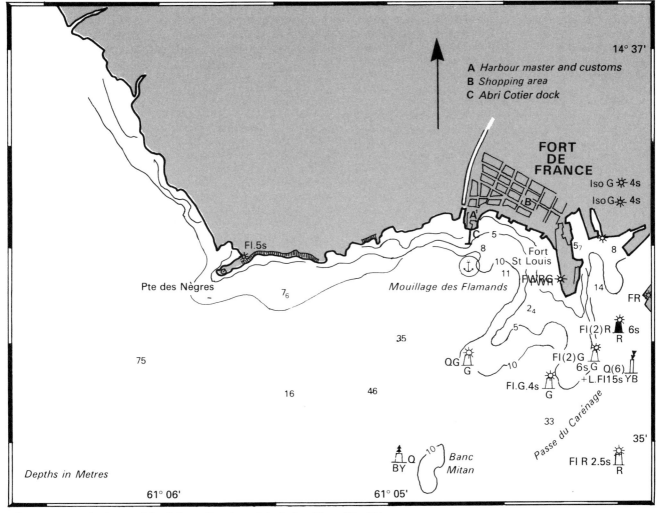

Chart 63 Fort de France, Martinique. Based on Admiralty Chart No 494.

fore makes sense to approach around the southern end of the island, if only to avoid the long and often windless stretch from Pte du Macouba in the extreme north. Reefs and offlying islets fringe much of the windward coast, which should be given a wide berth.

If approaching around the south, Ilet Cabrit [FlR 5s 42m 16M] can be cleared at a mile or so and Rocher du Diamant (Diamond Rock) at the same distance. This will avoid the 4.0 m (13 ft) Banc du Diamant shoal where the seas can be rough. The south-west coast has no outlying hazards.

Radio

Fort de France Radio monitors VHF channel 16 and uses channel 26 as its working channel. Also MF 2545, 2182 kHz.

Entrance

The entrance to the Baie de Fort de France is more than three miles wide, between Pta des Negres [Fl 5s 36m 27M] in the north and Ilet a Ramiers (unlit) in the south. An unlit red buoy, Banc du Gros Ilet, lies almost in the centre of the mouth to mark shoals carrying a least depth of 3.5 m (11 ft). Other buoys, mostly lit, mark other shoals to the east of the main yacht anchorage. The IALA B system is in use.

Anchorage and moorings

The most popular yacht anchorage is in the Mouillage des Flamands, to the west of Fort Saint Louis and directly off the city and public gardens. Moorings have been laid in the area, contributing to the crowding which frequently exists. It may be possible for a smaller yacht to find space close inshore (making sure not to impede the ferry channel), but crews of larger yachts (or those needing scope for a nylon anchor rode) may be faced with a long dinghy ride. Dinghies can be left free of charge at the floating pontoon near the Abri Cotier dock.

Winds from south of east make the Mouillage des Flamands uncomfortable, and an alternative is to cross to Anse Mitan, sheltered by Pte du Bout on the southern shore. A regular ferry service runs to Fort de France.

It may be possible to lie stern-to at the Abri Cotier dock, but this is usually occupied by charter boats. Fort du France is primarily an anchorage.

Formalities

The customs and immigration office lies just behind the Abri Cotier buildings. Hours are 0800–1100 and 1500–1700 seven days a week, with the usual papers required. An attempt to speak some French is appreciated.

Facilities

Boatyards The Ship Shop at Quai Quest (73 73 99) has a 40-tonne travel lift, and Grant's in the military and commercial port a marine railway. Polymar (70 62 88) next to the Ship Shop slipway specialises in GRP yachts, and Chalmesin (60 03 75) in welding

Engineers Madia Boat (63 10 61) are agents for some manufactures, Grand Jean Nautique (60 26 66) for others and Martinique Diesel (51 16 13) for yet more

Electronics Shipelec (60 25 68) for electronics, and Cadet Petit (63 79 18) for electrical work

Sailmaker R Helenon (60 22 05) is local agent for North Sails; also West Indies Sails (63 04 08) and Tasker (63 58 09) local branch of a large French concern

Chandlery The Ship Shop (71 43 40) is one of the best chandleries in the Lesser Antilles, but try also Sea Services (70 26 69) who also have a rigging workshop

Chart agent The Ship Shop stock Imray-Iolaire and French charts

Yacht club The Yacht Club de la Martinique is situated in the military and commercial port on the eastern side of the Fort St Louis peninsula, with its own small marina (vacant berths are extremely rare). Evidence of membership of a recognised yacht club may be requested before facilities can be used

Diesel/petrol At the Abri Cotier dock

Water At the Abri Cotier dock

Bottled gas Camping Gaz (butane) is available, by exchange only, in many places including the Abri Cotier dock. Try Sea Services for getting other bottles refilled, but be prepared for disappointment

Ice At the Abri Cotier dock or Glaciers Modernes

Showers At the Abri Cotier dock and at the yacht club

Laundry/launderette In the city

Banks Many, with credit card facilities, plus a couple of Bureaux de Change

General shopping Excellent – the place to treat yourself

Provisioning Up to the best French standards, with cheese and paté abounding, and a good place to stock up on wine which is very expensive in the ex-British islands. Several of the larger supermarkets, including Super H, make daily deliveries to the Abri Cotier dock. Don't miss the large covered produce market, and the fish market on the banks of the Riviere Madame

Bonded stores Vatier (70 11 39) can deliver to the Abri Cotier dock (where they also sell fuel), but outward clearance must be obtained before taking delivery

Restaurants Many and excellent

Hotels At all levels

Medical services Large modern hospital outside the city

Communications

Mailing address C/o Ship Shop, 6 Rue Joseph Compere, Fort de France, Martinique, or c/o poste restante at the main post office (from which it may have to be collected by the addressee in person, complete with passport or other identification)

Post Office On the main road opposite the attractive Place de la Savanne public gardens

Telephones Many around the city, using cards bought in post offices. There is also an international telephone bureau near the main post office

Bus service Minibuses run all over the island from the square next to the customs office

Ferry service Regular ferries to Anse Mitan

Taxis From the same square as the minibuses. Communal taxis are the norm, and very economical – you specify where you want to go, but the driver can then pick up more passengers en route. Sole use taxis are expensive

Car hire Several agencies. Driving is on the right, of course

Air services International airport to the east of the Baie de Fort de France; flights to USA, Canada and Europe

23 ENGLISH HARBOUR/ FALMOUTH BAY, Antigua

17°0′.4N   61°45′.7W   GMT − 4

Springs: 0.6 m/2 ft
Neaps: 0.4 m/1 ft 4 in

Flag: Antigua
Currency: EC dollar

Charts	Admiralty	US	Imray–Iolaire
General	955 (1:475,000)	25550 (1:150,000)	A3 (1:394,000)
Approach	2064 (1:50,000)	25570 (1:75,000)	A27 (1:57,000)
Harbour	2064 (1:20,000)	–	A27 (Inset)

General

As Fort de France is to French yachtsmen, so English Harbour, Antigua, features high on the list for most British and Americans. Semi-derelict until the 1950s, Nelson's Dockyard and its surrounds are now one of the busiest yachting centres in the Lesser Antilles, particularly during Antigua Race Week at the end of April. Probably less than a quarter of the yachts present actually race but there is plenty going on ashore and, if you don't mind crowds, it provides a fun contrast to the 'deserted beaches' aspect of the Caribbean. (If you can't stand crowds and adore deserted beaches, clear in at Antigua and then sail on to Barbuda, its smaller and much less developed sister island to the north.)

English Harbour is never deserted. Until a decade or so ago most visiting yachts used the same small protected anchorage favoured by the eighteenth-century British

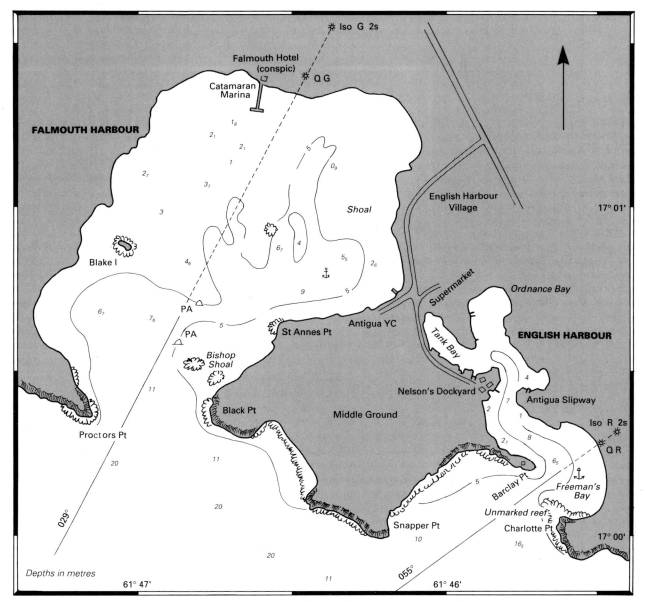

Chart 64 English Harbour/Falmouth Bay, Antigua. Based on a plan in the *Lesser Antilles*.

English Harbour/Falmouth Bay, Antigua   165

Approaching English Harbour from the south, with the distinctive 'Pillars of Hercules' on the east side of the entrance.
Photo: Anne Hammick

fleet, but since then ever-increasing numbers have turned the adjoining Falmouth Bay into something of an overflow area. Many claim to prefer the open, breezy anchorage of Falmouth to its more enclosed neighbour, though few would dispute that English Harbour provides one of the best hurricane holes in the Lesser Antilles. Take your pick.

Almost all the development fringing both harbours is yacht or tourist related, and with nearly all requirements met locally it would be possible, though a pity, to spend several weeks in Antigua without ever visiting the capital, St John's, or venturing more than a mile from one's boat.

Approach

At one time Antigua had a poor reputation as an Atlantic landfall, not least because its vicious windward reefs are unmarked by lights of any kind. While this is still true, the bright lights of V C Bird International Airport in the north of the island now effectively announce Antigua's presence from afar. They appear to burn all night, and should be quite sufficient to prevent the unwary from running up on the island unawares. There is also an aero beacon at the airport. If Antigua is sighted at dusk consideration should be given to reducing speed or even heaving-to for the night, but this might be said of many Caribbean landfalls.

The entrances to English Harbour and Falmouth Bay lie almost in the centre of the south coast, somewhat easier to identify when approaching from eastwards than from the

south. Coming in from the east in daylight the bluff promontory of Cape Shirley [Fl(4) 20s 150m 20M] is unmistakable, though the light atop may be unreliable. This headland is the place to close the coast, and a mile or so onwards the entrances first to English Harbour and then to Falmouth Bay will open up.

From the south the approach is straightforward although the entrances are not always easy to pinpoint. Inland there are rolling hills, but the lower, slightly darker patch in front is Middle Ground, which separates the two entrances. On closer approach the sandstone cliffs of Cape Shirley and Shirley Heights will be seen to terminate at their western end (Charlotte Point) in some unusual vertical columns, aptly named The Pillars of Hercules. If coming in from the south be careful not to get set too far to the west – Middle and Cade Reefs lurk off the southwest tip of Antigua and have claimed several yachts.

Radio

There is no government-run VHF station and no need for one while Nicholson's Yacht Charters operate English Harbour Radio on VHF channel 68. This is monitored by a great many other concerns, and it is possible to order anything from a taxi to a pizza over the airways. Should help of any kind be required you are talking to fellow yachtsmen who know the island and its waters in detail. Channels 6, 12, 14 and 16 may also be used.

Entrance

English Harbour: to the north-west the low crenellations of Barclay Point are unmistakable from nearby, while to the south-east Charlotte Point is marked by the equally distinctive Pillars of Hercules. A reef extends north-west from Charlotte Point directly towards Barclay Point, and best depths will be found by keeping between half and three quarters of the way across the gap – ie nearer to Barclay Point.

Although leading lights exist they should not be relied upon, and first time entry after dark (except perhaps by a very bright moon) is best avoided.

Falmouth Bay: although much larger, wide stretches of Falmouth Bay are shallow and there are several isolated coral patches. Bishop Shoal extends nearly 0.5 mile offshore on the starboard hand soon after entering and often breaks, the central shoal (supposedly buoyed) does not. There are leading lights but they do not always work. As a stranger, do not enter the bay in darkness.

Anchorage and moorings

English Harbour: pick any spot that offers swinging room and does not impede the channel to Antigua Slipway and Nelson's Dockyard. Some prefer the breeze and cleaner water of Freeman's Bay, some the greater convenience of being nearer the Dockyard, perhaps in Ordnance Bay on its northern side. Dinghies can be landed on the beach in Freeman's Bay, at a small pier on the eastern side of Barclay Point, or at the purpose-built dinghy landing by the boundary wall of the old Dockyard. Until recently new arrivals were expected to anchor in Freeman's Bay until cleared by customs inwards, but this is no longer the case.

Falmouth Bay: again a case of finding a convenient spot, though the majority of yachts favour the south-east corner of the bay near the Antigua Yacht Club. Dinghies can be left at the pontoon near the customs building.

Berthing and marinas

English Harbour: a limited number of yachts can lie stern-to at Nelson's Dockyard (463 1053), but space is not always available. Call up on VHF channel 68 before arrival. A few yachts can lie alongside at Antigua Slipway (463 1056) on the eastern shore but this is usually reserved for boats undergoing work.

Falmouth Bay: The long-established Antigua Yacht Club (463 1444) has recently branched out into the marina business, with a new pontoon to which about thirty yachts can moor stern-to. The Catamaran Club (463 1036) runs a marina in the northern part of the bay, but it is usually full and is isolated from many of the shoreside facilities available.

The much-photographed view over English Harbour, Antigua, looking northwest from Shirley Heights. Falmouth Bay is to the right. *Photo: Anne Hammick*

English Harbour/Falmouth Bay, Antigua   167

Formalities

Until recently the only customs in the area were in English Harbour – they came out by launch and long waits were not uncommon. Then the whole operation moved ashore with the Harbour Office, customs and immigration in different buildings with a hot walk between. At last common sense has prevailed, and after entering with the Q flag hoisted the skipper goes ashore bearing ship's papers, passports and previous port clearance to a combined office at the eastern end of the balconied Officers' Quarters building. Hours are 0800–1800 daily, with daily dues payable for anchoring and for a cruising permit (whether or not you plan to cruise the island). Before departure a receipt must be obtained from the Harbour Office before outward clearance will be granted.

Falmouth Bay has its own customs and immigration offices near the small pier in the south-east corner of the bay.

Duty free imports

Yacht equipment is allowed in duty free if marked with the yacht's name and 'In transit'. Normally the owner is required to collect personally from St John's, but an agent can be appointed. Nicholson's will advise.

Facilities

Boatyards Antigua Slipway can haul yachts up to 120 tons, plus a travel hoist for the rest of us. Their reputation is high but they do not normally allow DIY work. Crabbs Marina (460 2113) at Parham Harbour on the north coast have a 50-tonne travel lift and do allow DIY work

Engineers Antigua Slipway, and Pumps & Power (460 1242) at the head of Falmouth Bay

Electronics The Signal Locker (460 1528) has an excellent reputation and is the local agent for a wide variety of British and US manufacturers. Marionics (460 1780) operate from the Catamaran Club

Sailmaker Antigua Sails make and repair sails in their loft on the road behind Carib Marine Supermarket. A&F Sails (460 1522) are conveniently situated in the Dockyard but do repairs only, plus canvas work such as awnings, etc

Chandlery Good stock upstairs at Antigua Slipway, also The Chandlery at Falmouth (near Pumps & Power) and at Crabbs Marina

Chart agent The Map Shop (462 3993) on St Mary's Street in St John's stocks BA, US DMA and Imray-Iolaire charts plus local cruising guides. The chandlery at Antigua Slipway also holds Imray-Iolaire charts

Yacht club Antigua Yacht Club on Falmouth Bay organises evening racing throughout the winter season, and has a relaxed bar (plus book swap) above the ground floor restaurant

Weather forecast Broadcast by English Harbour Radio on VHF channel 6 at 0900 local time following an announcement on channel 68

Diesel/petrol Antigua Slipway, the fuel dock in the southeast of Falmouth Bay and at the Catamaran Club

Water At all the above, plus hoses to yachts lying stern-to at the Dockyard or the Antigua Yacht Club Marina

Shore power Wherever yachts can get close enough

Bottled gas Pumps & Power – propane only, and allow several days

Ice Carib Marine Supermarket, Antigua Slipway, Antigua Yacht Club Marina and the Catamaran Club

Showers Shower blocks in Nelson's Dockyard and at Falmouth

Laundry/launderette Sam & Dave at Falmouth, plus several local ladies who can be found in the Dockyard. DIY facilities (sinks ex-plugs) near the Dockyard showers. Don't leave prized clothes on the lines provided – things occasionally disappear

Banks Barclays International just outside the Dockyard gates, with others in St John's. VISA card advances no problem

General shopping Mostly tourist shops locally, but a wider selection in St John's

Provisioning Carib Marine Supermarket at the head of Tank Bay covers most wants, but also try Mrs Malone's store nearly opposite. She is a Seventh Day Adventist and is open on Sunday. Several larger supermarkets in St John's, plus a produce market opposite the bus terminal

Restaurants Spoilt for choice. The Admiral's Inn has the atmosphere, The Lookout on Shirley Heights the view but neither are cheap

Hotels At least three overlooking English Harbour with many more throughout the rest of the island. Antigua's economy depends heavily on tourism

Medical services Doctors and dentists in St John's, plus a modern hospital outside the town

Communications

Mailing address C/o either Nicholson's Yacht Services, English Harbour, Antigua (on the promontory between Tank and Ordnance bays) or English Harbour Post Office. Neither return uncollected mail

Post Office In the building just outside the Dockyard gates and in St John's

Telephones Outside the Dockyard gates (where there is also a Cable & Wireless office), at Nicholson's Yacht Services and elsewhere

Bus service Minibuses to St John's from the car park outside the Dockyard gates

Taxis Plentiful but not cheap

Car hire Several agencies nearby. Driving is on the left

Air services Direct flights from E C Bird International Airport to the UK, US, Canada, etc

Springs: 0.6 m/2 ft			*Flag*: British Virgin Islands		
Neaps: 0.4 m/1 ft 4 in			*Currency*: US dollar		

Charts	Admiralty		US		Imray-Iolaire	
General	150	(1:282,000)	25600	(1:250,000)	A2	(1:395,000)
Approach	2019	(1:75,000)	25609	(1:80,000)	A231	(1:88,300)
			25611	(1:30,000)	A232	(1:88,300)
Harbour	2020	(1:15,000)	25611	(1:15,000)	A231/2	(Inset)

General

Unlike anchorages such as English Harbour, Fort de France, etc, where many cruising yachtsmen stay for several weeks, once cleared into the British Virgin Islands few yachts will stay in one harbour long – the whole appeal is to explore by water.

Road Town is the capital of the British Virgin Islands and a centre for bareboat charters, but it offers an indifferent anchorage and is not particularly welcoming to cruising yachts. Many skippers prefer to clear at one of the other ports in the area, only visiting Road Town for essential shopping. The IALA B buoyage system is used throughout the British Virgin Islands.

Approach

If coming from eastwards – ie St Martin or Anguilla – aim to arrive at dawn and enter through Round Rock Passage, between Ginger Island [Fl 5s 152m 14M] and the jumbled rocks known as Fallen Jersualem off the south end of Virgin Gorda (unlit). Then either head north for Virgin Gorda Yacht Harbour or continue down the Sir Francis Drake Channel towards Road Town, about half way along the south coast of Tortola.

Landfall from northwards – ie Bermuda or the US – is more of a problem because of the dangers posed by the low-lying island of Anegada. Come in from the north-west and be certain to arrive in daylight. If coming from this direction it may be convenient to clear into the BVI at Great Harbour on Jost Van Dyke.

Radio

British Virgin Islands Radio at Tortola monitors VHF channel 16 and uses channel 27 as its working channel. Most marinas also monitor channel 16.

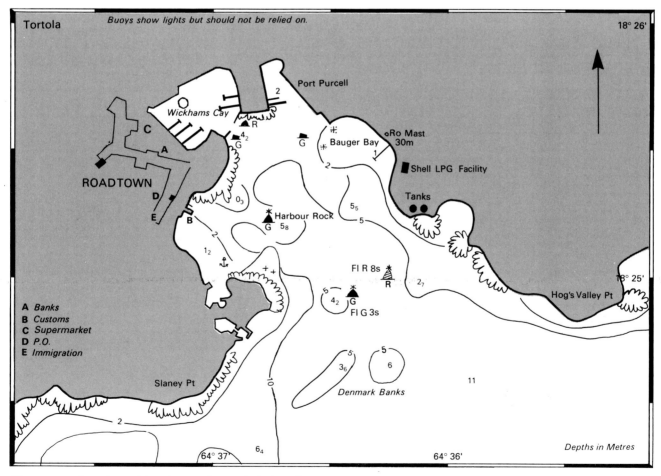

Chart 65 Road Harbour, Tortola. Based on Admiralty Chart No 2020.

Entrance

Road Town: Road Bay is unmistakable, with many buildings and a large fuel depot near its head. Although various shoal patches dot the entrance all carry at least 2.5 m (8 ft) so can be ignored by the majority of yachts. However avoid approaching Fort Burk Point too closely, and beware of Harbour Spit which runs south-east towards the middle of the harbour, supposedly marked by a lit buoy. If continuing into Wickhams Cay at the north end of the bay keep carefully to the channel – it is narrow with a distinct dog-leg but well buoyed.

Virgin Gorda Yacht Harbour: north of the famous Baths on the west coast of the island. The channel is buoyed, with a sharp turn first to the south and then eastwards into the marina proper.

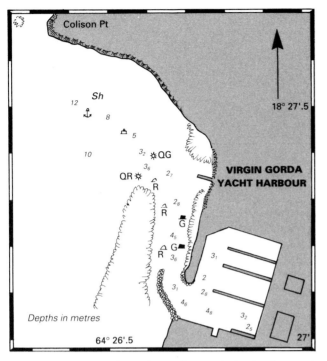

Chart 66 Virgin Gorda Yacht Harbour, Virgin Gorda. Based on a plan in the *Lesser Antilles*.

Anchorage and moorings

Road Town: yachts anchor along the western shores of the outer harbour, with dinghy landing at the ferry pier in the north-west corner. More protected but often buggy is Wickhams Cay – anchor in the northern part being careful not to impede access to the several marinas. A notice forbidding yachts to anchor may be visible, but no one seems to take much notice.

Virgin Gorda Yacht Harbour: St Thomas Bay, in 6.0 m (20 ft) or more over sand, provides pleasant temporary anchorage while clearing in, etc. For both safety and comfort keep well north of the approach to the ferry pier.

Berthing and marinas

Road Town: The Moorings (42331/2/3) and Village Cay Marina (44502) at Wickhams Cay are largely occupied by

The Virgin Islands are a popular place to haul for maintenance or antifouling before the passage north. The travel lift at Tortola Yacht Services in Road Town makes light of the 40 ft *Tehari II*, but may need to be booked well in advance.
Photo: Sepha Wood

charter yachts but a berth may be available. Their reception pontoons are clearly marked.

Virgin Gorda Yacht Harbour (55555): The reception pontoon is nearly opposite the entrance and again well marked. Not much room to manoeuvre once inside, so if short on crew go in with lines and fenders ready (port side to).

Formalities

Fly the Q flag on arrival. The skipper should go ashore to customs and immigration taking all the usual papers plus clearance from the last port of call. In Road Town the offices are at the head of the ferry and customs pier, in Virgin Gorda YH in the main administration block, and hours are 0830–1530. Outward clearance is valid for 24 hours, but if you admit that you intend to depart outside working hours you *may* be charged overtime!

Facilities

Boatyards/engineers/electronics At all the marinas. Virgin Gorda YH has a 60-tonne travel lift and the marine railway at West End on Tortola can handle up to 200 tonnes. Enquire on booking whether DIY work is permitted. Virgin Gorda YH is a popular place to lay up yachts during the hurricane season

Chandlery At most of the marinas, including Virgin Gorda YH

Diesel/water At all the marinas. Water is scarce in the BVI and a charge will be made

Shore power At all the marinas

Bottled gas Refills with propane only. Enquire at the nearest marina

Ice At all the marinas and at many shops and filling stations

Showers At the marinas. It may be possible for crews from yachts anchored off to use marina showers by arrangement, but expect to pay

Laundry/launderette At the marinas and in Road Town

Banks Barclays International in Road Town and in the Virgin Gorda YH buildings. VISA cards accepted

General shopping Not brilliant even in Road Town, though normal needs can generally be met

Provisioning Several large supermarkets in Road Town, to the west of Wickhams Cay. Everything in Virgin Gorda must be brought over on the ferry, so although the store in the marina complex is well stocked prices are high

Restaurants Dozens, both tourist and local

Hotels Everything from small guest houses to five-star developments

Medical services Doctors on Tortola and Virgin Gorda, hospital outside Road Town

Communications

Mailing address C/o Road Town Post Office (not recommended) or one of the marinas by prior arrangement

Post Office Near the customs building in Road Town

Telephones At the post office, marinas and elsewhere

Bus service Buses to Beef Island airport and other destinations

Ferry service Frequent ferries between Road Town and Virgin Gorda

Taxis/car hire No problem. Driving is on the left

Air services Beef Island airport, Tortola (about ten miles from Road Town) has links with other Caribbean islands including Antigua and Puerto Rico, but no long-haul flights. There is a convenient anchorage in nearby Trellis Bay. Virgin Gorda has a small airstrip, but having seen it most yachtsmen would probably rather go by water

PORTS ON THE INTRACOASTAL WATERWAY

The following four ports, Fort Lauderdale (Florida), Charleston (South Carolina), Morehead City (North Carolina) and Norfolk (Virginia) are popular places at which to join or leave the Intracoastal Waterway, that combination of canal, river and lagoon which links the Chesapeake Bay to southern Florida.

All four harbours have multiple marinas offering excellent facilities, and are covered in detail in one or more of the relevant guides (see Chapter 19 and Appendix B). It can generally be assumed that all normal requirements will be met, and for that reason less space is devoted to listing facilities than is the case elsewhere.

25 FORT LAUDERDALE, Florida, USA   26°05′N 80°07′W GMT–5

| *Springs*: 0.8 m/2 ft 7 in | *Flag*: USA |
| *Neaps*: 0.7 m/2 ft 3 in | *Currency*: US dollar |

Charts	Admiralty		US	
General	2866	(1:500,000)	11460	(1:466,940)
Approach	–		11466	(1:80,000)
Harbour	3684	(1:20,000)	11470	(1:10,000)

General

Most yachts approaching Fort Lauderdale – or more correctly Port Everglades – will be doing so to enter the Intracoastal Waterway, which runs northwards for more than 1000 miles to Norfolk, Virginia. There is considerable commercial activity in the port, and priority must always be given to ships when entering or leaving.

Approach

The east coast of Florida shelves gently with no offlying hazards in the Fort Lauderdale area. However nearly all the shoreline is built up, and it may be difficult to pinpoint the narrow entrance to Port Everglades from offshore, particularly in daylight. At night Port Everglades light [Fl 5s 106m 19M] on a building just north of the entrance should help with identification, allied to fixed and flashing red lights on chimneys about a mile further south.

Radio

The US Coast Guard monitors VHF channel 16. See page 55 for HF frequencies.

Entrance

The outer fairway buoy, marked '1', lies about 1.5 miles due east of the harbour entrance. The first pair of channel

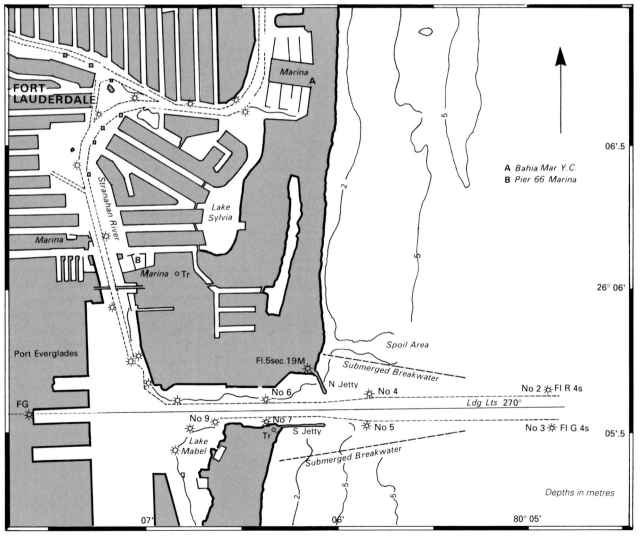

Chart 67 Fort Lauderdale, Florida. Based on US Chart No 11470.

markers – '2' to starboard and '3' to port – will be found about a mile offshore and from then on the channel, known as Outer Bar Cut, is clearly marked. Submerged breakwaters run from each side of the entrance out towards these buoys, and any yacht tempted to take a short cut should do so only with the aid of large scale charts. Green leading lights on 270° mark the centre of the fairway.

The entrance to Port Everglades is relatively narrow, and protected by the North and South Jetties. Inside is the large Turning Basin with wharves on the western side. The marked channel turns sharply northwards, hugging the eastern shore and passing under a high bridge to join the Stranahan River. About 0.5 mile further on this converges with the New River and the Intracoastal Waterway proper.

Berthing and marinas

Pier 66 Marina and Lauderdale Marina are both situated immediately north of the bridge which marks the end of the Turning Basin, with Bahia Mar a mile or so further up the Intracoastal Waterway. There are many others. Call ahead on VHF channel 16 to enquire about a berth.

Formalities

Even if the yacht has been boarded by the US Coast Guard while still at sea, as is becoming increasingly common, she should still arrive flying the Q flag if coming from outside the US, and once ashore all formalities must be dealt with in the usual way. Florida is particularly sensitive to the drugs problem, and all incoming yachts must call at one of the twenty-six official entry points. These include the three marinas listed above, where a yacht *may* be allowed to lie alongside without charge while formalities are completed. All have direct phone lines to the nearest customs and immigration office, whose instructions must be followed to the letter. Ship's papers, passports (with visas as appropriate) and previous port clearance will be required – see Chapter 19. Foreign yachts will also need to apply for a Cruising Licence, if eligible.

Facilities

Excellent but not cheap (see page 96 for details of guide books).

Springs: 1.7 m/5 ft 7 in	*Flag*: USA	
Neaps: 1.4 m/4 ft 7 in	*Currency*: US dollar	

Charts	Admiralty		US	
General	2865	(1:500,000)	11520	(1:432,720)
Approach	2803	(1:80,000)	11521	(1:80,000)
Harbour	2806	(1:40,000)	11523/4	(1:20,000)

General

The city of Charleston is of great historic interest and well worth exploring. Unfortunately it suffered severely during Hurricane *Hugo* in 1989 when not only many town buildings but also the marinas were badly damaged, but repairs are now largely complete. The harbour appears wide, but much of it is shallow and commercial shipping restricted to the dredged channels must not be impeded. The Intracoastal Waterway crosses the harbour on a west/east axis.

Ferries run out to Fort Sumter National Monument where the first shots of the Civil War were fired – essential visiting for anyone with the least interest in American history.

Approach

The coastline surrounding Charleston is generally low and somewhat featureless, with depths shoaling very gradually offshore for a distance of 30 miles or more. However it is well marked, with the outer fairway buoy [Fl R 6s] some eight miles off the harbour mouth. The powerful Charleston light [Fl(2) 30s 50m 26M] is shown from a triangular tower near the root of the North Jetty, and if approaching from southward the lights of Charleston Airport [Aero AltFl W/G 10s 21m 25/22M] some 12 miles to the south-west may also be seen.

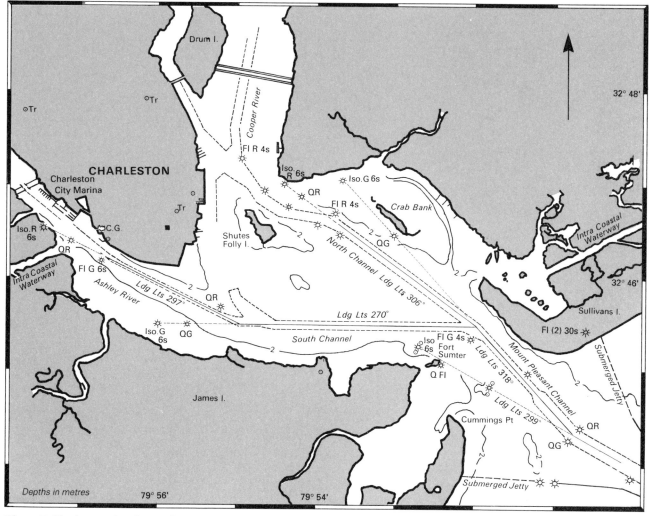

Chart 68 Charleston, South Carolina. Based on US Chart No 11524.

Radio

The US Coast Guard monitors VHF channel 16. See page 55 for HF frequencies.

Entrance

The approach channel, known as Fort Sumter Range, is marked by pairs of buoys. Numbers 13 and 14 also indicate the extremities of the North and South jetties, only the seaward ends of which are above water, and on no account should any short cuts be attempted inside this line. Leading lights (the rear one on Fort Sumter) indicate the middle of the channel on 299°, but these are abandoned before reaching the entrance proper to follow a second, third or fourth pair depending on final destination.

A fixed bridge with 16.7 m (55 ft) clearance has recently been built just beyond the Coast Guard base on the Ashley River (the two lower bascule bridges beyond both open on demand), limiting access for larger sailing yachts.

Anchorage and moorings

The strong tides and frequent chop can make anchoring uncomfortable, and a marina berth may be preferable. However possible sites are between the Coast Guard base and the Charleston City Marina on the northern side of the Ashley River, or just north of Ripley Light Marina almost opposite. Holding is said to be good, but neither anchorage is deep. If distance to town is not a consideration there are many other possible anchorages around the harbour depending on wind direction.

Berthing and marinas

Marinas and other facilities for yachts are mostly concentrated on the Ashley River to the south-west of the city. The Charleston City Marina (724 7356) and Ashley Marina (722 1996) on the town shore both have visitors' berths and are within walking distance of the city centre. The Charleston Yacht Club is nearby. Ripley Light Marina (766 2100) on the opposite shore also has visitors' berths but is further from town. All monitor VHF channels 16 and/or 68.

Tides run strongly in the Ashley River, especially on the ebb, and must be taken into account when manoeuvring.

Formalities

Fly the Q flag if entering from foreign, and if possible advise of your arrival by VHF. Otherwise telephone customs and immigration on 723 1272 immediately after berthing and follow their instructions. Ship's papers, passports (with visas as appropriate) and previous port clearance will be required – see Chapter 19. Foreign yachts will also need to apply for a Cruising Licence, if eligible.

Facilities

Pretty well everything (see page 96 for details of guide books).

| *Springs*: 0.9 m/2 ft 11 in | *Flag*: USA |
| *Neaps*: 0.8 m/2 ft 7 in | *Currency*: US dollar |

Charts	Admiralty	US
General	2864 (1:500,000)	11520 (1:432,720)
Approach	–	11543/4 (1:80,000)
		11545 (1:40,000)
Harbour	2864 (1:40,000)	11547 (1:12,500)

General

Morehead City and its twin town of Beaufort to the east are popular both as stops on the Intracoastal Waterway and as an entry point for yachts heading north and wishing to avoid Cape Hatteras. The North Carolina Maritime Museum (919 728 7317) is situated in Beaufort and is prepared to handle cruising yachts' mail.

Approach

For details of Cape Hatteras some 70 miles to the north-east see Chapter 19. The later approaches to Beaufort Inlet receive good protection from Cape Lookout, just under ten miles to the south-east, though the vicinity of the Cape and its offlying shoals is dangerous and should be given wide clearance. It should further be noted that the powerful light [Fl 15s 48m 25M] is displayed from a tower about 1.5 miles *north* of the point itself. The coast to the west of Beaufort Inlet runs on an almost east/west axis, with good water within 0.5 mile or less of the shore.

Radio

The US Coast Guard monitors VHF channel 16. See page 55 for HF frequencies.

Entrance

The Beaufort Inlet Channel is buoyed from a point more than two miles offshore and entered on a bearing of 011° with leading lights at night. Once close off Shackleford Point this bearing is abandoned for one on 340°, which leads up Fort Macon Reach and into the well buoyed Morehead City Channel. Fort Macon, on the port hand when entering, is unlit.

Tidal streams in the Beaufort Inlet Channel may run at 2–3 knots and an opposing wind will cause steep seas. In the vicinity of the Port Authority Terminal the stream can reach more than four knots at springs.

Anchorage and moorings

The two best anchorages are on the south side of Taylor Creek, in a marked area opposite the Beaufort Docks, or in Town Creek to the north of Beaufort. The latter anchorage is quieter, and still convenient for the town.

Berthing and marinas

There are many marinas in the area, but those with most visitors' berths are the Dockside Marina (247 4890) and Morehead City Yacht Basin (726 6862), both just west of the Port Authority Terminal, and Town Creek Marina (728 6111), Beaufort Docks (728 2503) and Inlet Inn (728 3600) on the Beaufort side. Morehead City Yacht Basin is approached via an opening bascule bridge and a fixed bridge with 20 m (65 ft) air height, and Town Creek via an opening bascule bridge. Both bascule bridges carry the railway – check opening times with your destination marina, all of which monitor VHF channel 16.

Formalities

Fly the Q flag if entering from foreign, and if possible advise of your arrival by VHF. Otherwise telephone customs and immigration on 726 5845, 726 3561 or 726 2034 immediately after berthing and follow their instructions. Ship's papers, passports (with visas as appropriate) and previous port clearance will be required – see Chapter 19. Foreign yachts will also need to apply for a Cruising Licence, if eligible.

Facilities

There are good facilities for yachts in the Morehead City/Beaufort area, with more along the Intracoastal Waterway to the west of the city (see page 96 for details of guide books).

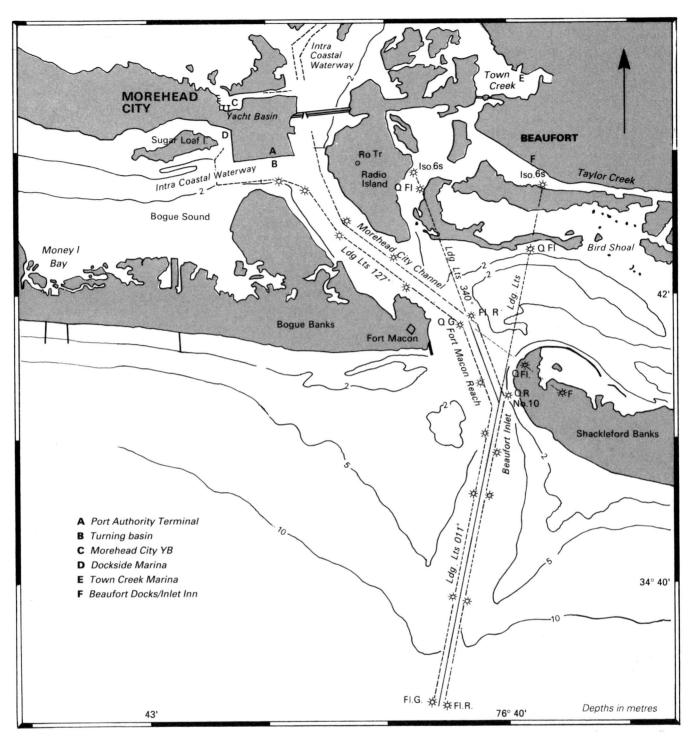

Chart 69 Morehead City/Beaufort, North Carolina. Based on US Chart No 11547 and Admiralty Chart No 2864.

Charts	Admiralty		US	
General	–		12200	(1:416,944)
Approach	2919	(1:80,000)	12221	(1:80,000)
			12222	(1:40,000)
Harbour	2813/4	(1:20,000)	12253	(1:20,000)

Springs: 0.8 m/2 ft 7 in
Neaps: 0.7 m/2 ft 3 in

Flag: USA
Currency: US dollar

General

Norfolk lies at the mouth of the Elizabeth River and marks the emergence of the Intracoastal Waterway into the Chesapeake Bay, and most yachts passing through Norfolk will be either joining or leaving the Waterway. The seaward approach is via Newport Roads – the lower stretches of the James River – where a bridge-tunnel combination links Norfolk with Hampton and Newport News on the northern shore. Hampton Roads is a busy area for both naval and commercial shipping, and the Norfolk Naval Base the largest in the world (tours of the base are run daily in summer).

Approach

Norfolk may be approached from further north up the bay, or from the Atlantic via the Chesapeake Bay Channel between Cape Charles [Fl 5s 55m 24M] on the northern shore and Cape Henry [Mo(U) W/R 20s 50m 17/15M] to the south ('U' in Morse Code is ..—). Six miles

to the east of Cape Henry lies the Chesapeake Bay Bridge Tunnel Complex, with the well buoyed Thimble Shoal Channel leading through it just over three miles from the southern shore. Strong currents can run in the area, sometimes exceeding three knots, and particular care must be taken in the vicinity of the bridge. The Thimble Shoal Channel extends a further six miles west-north-west towards Old Point Comfort [LFl(2) W/R 12s 16m 16/14M] and the northern end of the bridge-tunnel combination linking Norfolk and Hampton. Fort Wool [Fl 4s 8s 8M] marks the southern side of the navigable area.

Radio

The US Coast Guard monitors VHF channel 16. See page 55 for HF frequencies.

Entrance

A direct course can be shaped from the tunnel area past the narrow but well marked channel for Willoughby Bay and thence south-west down Entrance Reach towards Sewells Point. Norfolk Harbor Reach then leads south past the Naval Base into the Elizabeth River. The wide mouthed Lafayette River flows in from the east, before the channel narrows into the Southern Branch and the Waterway proper. The entire area is extremely well buoyed.

Anchorage and moorings

There are several possible anchorages. The northernmost – and deepest – is on the west side of the channel

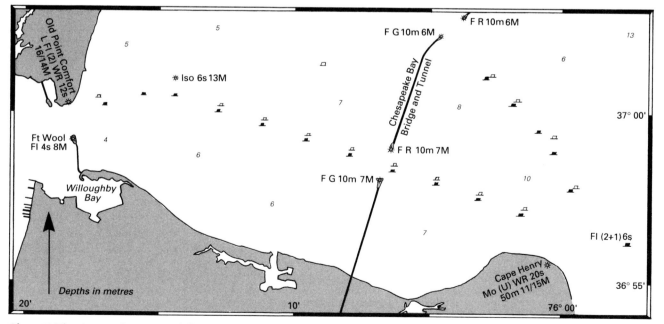

Chart 70 The Approaches to Norfolk, Virginia. Based on Admiralty Chart No 2919.

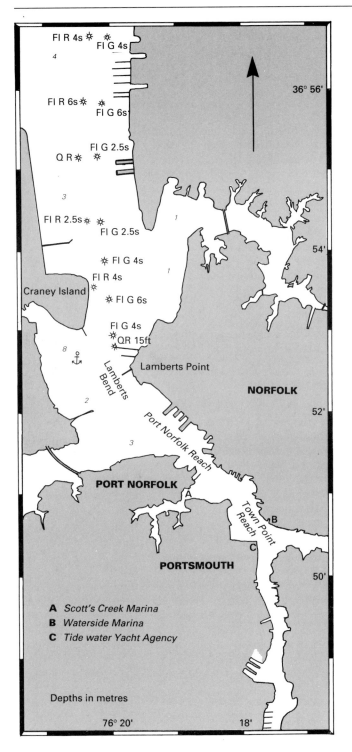

opposite Lamberts Point in 8.0 m (26 ft) or so, with others just south of Lamberts Point on the eastern side or between the two entrances to the Western Branch.

Berthing and marinas

Willoughby Harbor (583 4150) is situated on the north side of Willoughby Bay very near the bridge takeoff, but although there are good facilities for yachts locally it is a long way from the city centre.

Further south, Scotts Creek Marina (399 2628) lies on an inlet off the western side of the main channel, with Waterside Marina (441 2222) and Tidewater Yacht Agency (393 2525) near the entrance to the Eastern Branch. Of these, Tidewater Yacht Agency can take the largest vessels and has the greatest number of berths reserved for transients. All monitor VHF channel 16.

Formalities

Norfolk is an unlikely port at which to arrive from abroad, though customs and immigration can be contacted on 441 6741 if required. Non-US yachts may sometimes be boarded for inspection even if travelling within the country, and in these circumstances the usual ship's papers and passports (with visas as appropriate) will be required in addition to a valid Cruising Licence – see Chapter 19.

Facilities

Very good (see page 96 for details of guide books).

Chart 71 Norfolk Harbour and the Elizabeth River, Virginia. Based on Admiralty Chart No 2814.

Berthed in Norfolk, Virginia, with US Naval vessels in the background. *Photo: Sepha Wood*

Charts	Admiralty	US
General	2860 (1:500,000)	12300 (1:400,000)
Approach	2890 (1:100,000)	13218 (1:80,000)
		13221 (1:40,000)
Harbour	2730 (1:20,000)	13223 (1:20,000)

Springs: 1.2 m/3 ft 11 in
Neaps: 0.9 m/2 ft 11 in

Flag: USA
Currency: US dollar

General

Newport, Rhode Island, lies to the east of the main entrance channel to Narragansett Bay. It has long been an important yachting centre and for many years was the venue for the America's Cup races. It is also the destination of the single and doublehanded transatlantic races run from Plymouth, England, every two years and a favourite landfall for yachts heading north from Bermuda. Newport offers excellent facilities of all kinds for the yachtsman and is an official port of entry.

Approach

The coast between Cape Cod and Newport is low lying, with shoal water and low islands to the south of Cape Cod. The area is very prone to fog and it can be difficult to identify the coast. If coming from the south-east or south it is advisable to make first landfall at Nantucket Shoals

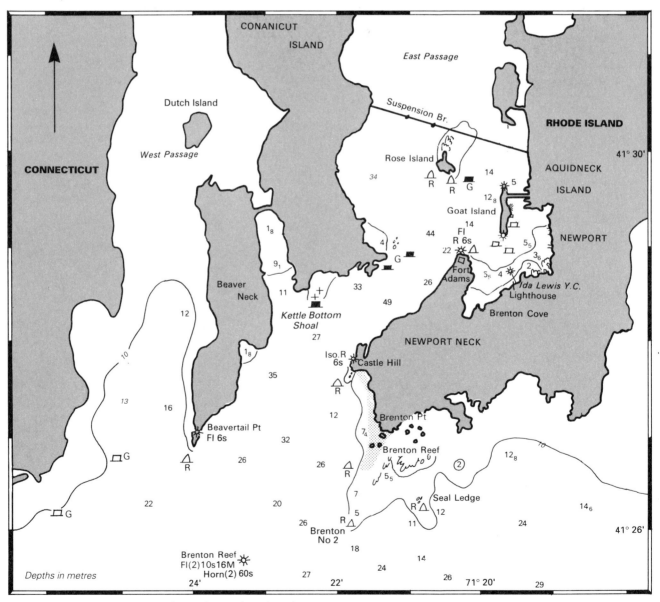

Chart 72 Newport, Rhode Island. Based on Admiralty Chart No 2890.

Lanby (see Chapter 19), thus keeping well south of the shoals themselves and ensuring an exact position from which to close the land. If approaching from the north-east most yachts will use the Cape Cod Canal, which leads into a dredged channel at the north-east end of Buzzard's Bay. A middle route, through Nantucket Sound and Vineyard Sound, is possible but not recommended.

Heavy concentrations of shipping are likely to be encountered on the way to Newport – fishing vessels around the various banks, and commercial traffic *en route* to New York, Narragansett Bay and Boston.

The entrance to Narragansett Bay is well bracketed by lights, including Buzzards Bay light [Fl 2.5s 31m 22M] sixteen miles to the east, Point Judith light [Oc(3) 15s 20m 16M] six miles to the south-west and Block Island SE light [Fl G 5s 79m 24M] eighteen miles south-south-west. All have DF beacons and foghorns.

Most useful is Brenton Reef Tower [Fl(2) 10s 27m 16M] about 1.5 miles directly south of the entrance. It is a square red structure standing on four black legs, complete with foghorn and low-powered DF beacon. It should be noted that Brenton Reef Tower is a *starboard* hand mark for the entrance to Narragansett Bay, warning of rocks running southwards from Brenton Point. Although there is plenty of room to cut between the two (and the shoal is buoyed) this is not a headland to approach too closely. It is possible that Brenton Reef Tower may shortly be demolished and replaced with a buoy.

There have been reports of a Loran anomaly near the entrance to Narragansett Bay which has the effect of placing one some 180 m (600 ft) further to the west than indicated, but this has not been substantiated.

Radio

Castle Hill Coast Guard station maintains a 24-hour watch on VHF channel 16, but can also be called direct on Channel 71. See page 55 for HF frequencies.

Entrance

The outer entrance lies between Beavertail Point to the west and Brenton Point to the east, passing Castle Hill close on the starboard hand. A buoyed channel then leads between Fort Adams and Goat Island into Newport Harbor.

Anchorage and moorings

The two former anchorages (in Brenton Cove at the south-western corner of the harbour and between Goat Island and the town waterfront further north) have been taken over by moorings and a new transient yacht anchorage established just north of the Ida Lewis Yacht Club. Many of these moorings are operated by Old Port Marine, which can be contacted on VHF channel 68. They also run an excellent launch service between 0800 and midnight which will pick up and deposit anywhere in the harbour for a modest fee – again contact on channel 68. Dinghies can be left at the Municipal Dock.

Berthing and marinas

There are many marinas in the Newport area. The largest is at Goat Island, situated about half way along that island's eastern shore, but it has few visitors' berths and is some way from the town. Best for the visiting yachtsman are the Newport Yachting Centre and Old Port Marine, both on the eastern side of the harbour and convenient for the town. Marina charges are high.

Formalities

The Q flag should be hoisted on closing the coast. Arrival must be reported by the skipper within 24 hours and formal entry made within 48 hours. No one may board or leave the yacht (except to report arrival) until customs give permission. The authorities may be telephoned from any marina – normal office hours are 0800–1700, excluding Saturdays, Sundays and holidays. Fees are charged for customs services, and a standard overtime charge is made for services outside these hours.

Facilities

Boatyards/engineers/electronics There are no longer many yards on the town waterfront, but plenty in the Narragansett Bay area. Enquire at the nearest marina for advice

Sailmaker Several in the town

Chandlery Several, including at least one at each marina

Chart agent The Armchair Sailor Bookstore (847 4252)

Yacht club The Ida Lewis Yacht Club, host to many America's Cup races, has its premises on the southern shores of the harbour

Diesel Fuelling berths at the marinas

Water At all marinas

Shore power Alongside at all marinas

Bottled gas LPC bottles can be refilled (propane only)

Ice At all marinas

Showers At all marinas

Laundry/launderette At Goat Island Marina and Newport Yachting Centre

Banks Plenty in the town. All cards accepted

General shopping Good if slightly tourist orientated

Provisioning Several large supermarkets and many delicatessens etc

Restaurants/hotels Wide choice at all levels

Medical services Readily available, but expensive

Communications

Mailing address C/o General Delivery at the main post office or any of the marinas by pre-arrangement

Post Office In the town

Telephones At the marinas and elsewhere

Bus/rail service Buses and trains to Providence, Rhode Island, with connections to Boston, New York, etc

Taxis/car hire No problem

Air services From Providence to international destinations

| | *Springs*: 3.2 m/10 ft 6 in *Neaps*: 2.7 m/8 ft 10 in | *Flag*: USA *Currency*: US dollar |

Charts	Admiralty	US
General	2492 (1:677,000)	13260 (1:378,838)
Approach	–	13302 (1:80,000)
		13305 (1:40,000)
Harbour	–	13307 (1:20,000)

General

Camden is a most attractive harbour which is deservedly very popular – and often very full. It is well protected other than from the south-east. Services and facilities are excellent, and the town of interest in its own right. The inner harbour is home to many historic vessels – schooners and windjammers were built there in the nineteenth and early twentieth centuries and a number still sail commercially from the harbour, carrying passengers rather than cargo.

Camden is not an obvious choice for an Atlantic landfall, unless by a local yacht returning home, but could be a good departure point if leaving for the eastward Atlantic passage by one of the northerly routes (see Chapter 22).

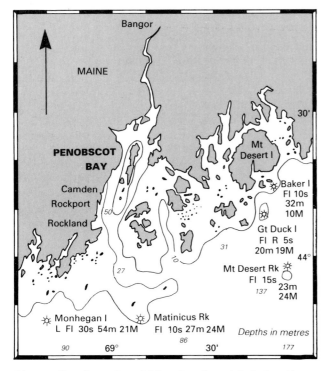

Chart 73 Penobscot Bay, Maine. Based on Admiralty Chart No 2670.

Approach

Camden lies on the western shore of Penobscot Bay, approximately 150 miles from the northern entrance to the Cape Cod Canal, and about the same distance west of Cape Sable at the south-west tip of Nova Scotia.

If approaching from the south, landfall is probably best made at Matinicus Rock [Fl 10s 27m 24M], the southernmost of the many reefs, rocks and islands scattered throughout Penobscot Bay and its approaches. The bare granite rock stands 17 m (56 ft) above water level and carries the remains of an old lighthouse in addition to the circular grey tower used today. From the east, Mt Desert Rock [Fl 15s 23m 24M] is the most likely landfall. Penobscot Bay is well buoyed and lit, and a suitable large-scale chart should be consulted for the passage up the western arm of the bay towards Camden.

The approach to Camden itself is marked to the south by The Graves, a heap of barren rocks surmounted by a green light structure. The Graves can be left on either side, with generous clearance to allow for submerged outliers, but if in doubt is best passed to seaward.

Radio

The Camden Harbor authorities monitor VHF channel 16 and the Camden Marine Operator monitors channel 26 and 84. Routine calling is on channel 9.

Entrance

Heavily wooded Curtis Island [FG] marks the entrance to Camden Harbor and must be left to port on entry, together with the green can buoy No 7 off its northern end. On the starboard hand two ledges (submerged at high tide) fringe Northeast Point [Fl R 4s 6m 5M], marked by a pair of red buoys, No 4 and No 6. There is a narrow inner passage close around Northeast Point used by local boats, but first time visitors would be wise to stick to the main entrance.

Anchorage and moorings

Camden Harbor comprises two distinct parts: the larger outer harbour, which is more exposed, and the protected – and very crowded – inner harbour. Moorings occupy much of the outer harbour, but it is still possible to anchor in the extreme north in Sherman Cove. Anchoring is not permitted in the inner harbour. Fairway channels in both parts of the harbour are marked by large circular red and green buoys.

Wayfarer Marine (236 4378, or VHF channels 16 and 9) maintains many rental moorings, marked *WMC-RENTAL* and bearing a maximum boat length. Camden Yacht Club (236 3014) monitors VHF channel 68, and may be able to advise visitors about unoccupied private moorings. Several of the boatyards, including PG Willey Wharf (236 3256), also have moorings which may be available for hire by arrangement. The Camden Yacht Club runs a launch service in summer, for which there is a small charge, summoned either on VHF channel 68 or by three blasts on the horn.

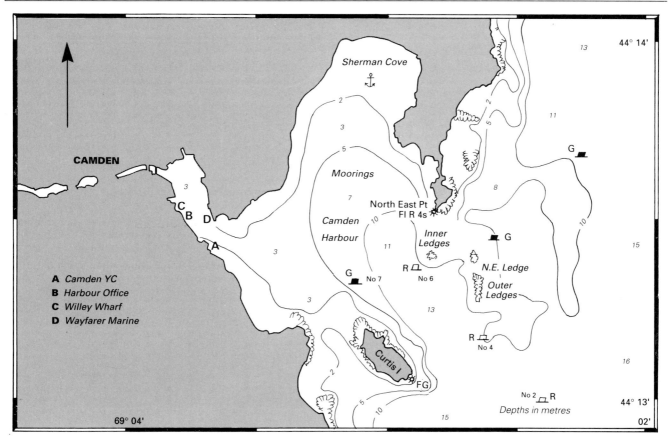

Chart 74 Camden, Maine. Based on US Chart No 13307.

Berthing and marinas

The best bet is likely to be Wayfarer Marine, seen on the starboard hand on entering the inner harbour, but expect to raft several boats abreast at peak periods. It may also be possible to berth alongside at Sun Yacht Charters (south side, inner harbour) when their charter fleet is away, or overnight at the town pier on application to the Harbor Master (236 7969 or VHF channel 16).

Formalities

Camden is not an official port of entry though it is possible to clear in by pre-arrangement. If the Camden Marine Operator can be contacted on VHF channels 26 or 84 before arrival he will forewarn the authorities. A Q flag is not obligatory, but may help to identify your boat amongst the throng.

The nearest customs office is in Belfast, near the head of Penobscot Bay (338 3954). One working day's notice will be required to arrange a visit, and in the case of a foreign yacht a cruising licence or permit will be issued if eligible (see Chapter 19). The Immigration and Naturalization Service is located at Bangor (945 0334). All the officials are most helpful, and arranging outward clearance from Camden should not be a problem.

The Harbor Master's office is near the head of the inner harbour, in the Chamber of Commerce building.

Facilities

Boatyards Several, including Wayfarer Marine on the north side of the entrance to the inner harbour

Ramp/drying grid Alongside the wall at the Camden Yacht Club, by pre-arrangement. The wall is marked to indicate exactly where the boat should lie and tie-down rings are provided in the lawn

Cranes/engineers/electronics Wayfarer Marine

Sailmaker E S Bohndell & Co (236 3549) in nearby Rockport

Chandlery The Downeast Trading Co (236 8763), near the public landing at the head of the inner harbour, also Harborside West (236 3264) and Wayfarer Marine (Store: 236 8486)

Chart agent The Owl and Turtle Bookstore, Bayview Street

Yacht club The Camden Yacht Club, on the south side of the inner harbour entrance, welcomes visiting yachtsmen. Their short-stay pontoon is a convenient place to take on water

Diesel Wayfarer Marine or PG Willey Wharf

Water Camden Yacht Club, Harborside West, Wayfarer Marine or PG Willey Wharf

Shore power Harborside West, Wayfarer Marine or PG Willey Wharf

Bottled gas (propane) Wayfarer Marine or PG Willey Wharf

Ice Harborside West, Wayfarer Marine, PG Willey Wharf and several places in town

Showers Wayfarer Marine, PG Willey Wharf and the Harbour Office

Laundry/launderette Wayfarer Marine, plus at least one in the town

Banks Several

General shopping All usual town shops

Provisioning Several good grocery stores and delicatessen in Camden itself, but for major provisioning it might be worth getting a taxi to the QGA Supermarket or the Megunticook Corner Market, both a few miles outside the town

Bonded stores Not available

Restaurants To suit all palates and pockets. Several specialise in seafood and local chowders

Medical services The Penobscot Bay Medical Center is situated about six miles south of Camden

Communications

Mailing address General Delivery at the post office, or c/o Camden Yacht Club by pre-arrangement

Post Office On Chestnut Street, near the public landing

Telephones At the public landing and elsewhere in the town

Taxis At the main intersection

Car hire Smith's Garage at Rockport (236 2320). Bicycles can be hired from Maine Sport, on Camden's Main Street

	Flag: Canada
Springs: 1.8 m/11 ft in	
Neaps: 1.5 m/4 ft 11 in	*Currency*: Canadian dollar

Charts	Admiralty	US	Canadian
General	1651 (1:725,000)	14005 (1:300,000)	4003 (1:1,000,000)
		14014 (1:350,000)	4012/3 (1:350,000)
Approach	729 (1:256,000)	14083 (1:145,000)	4320 (1:145,000)
	2410 (1:50,000)	14087 (1:36,480)	4385 (1:36,500)
Harbour	2028 (1:10,000)	14091 (1:12,000)	4203 (1:10,000)
	2029 (1:10,000)	14089 (1:12,000)	4202 (1:10,000)

General

Halifax is the capital of the Canadian province of Nova Scotia. It is a large commercial port and a naval base, and an official port of entry. North West Arm, a long narrow bay branching off just inside the main entrance and before the city and waterfront is reached, is the centre of yachting activity in the area.

Approach

The coastline of Nova Scotia is somewhat rugged and hilly with many inlets, and off-lying rocks and small islands extend up to five miles from the coast in places. It is well buoyed, but subject to fog during summer months, particularly with onshore winds. In clear weather the land will be visible well before any dangers are approached, but in poor visibility it is essential to exercise great caution when closing the coast.

If approaching from west of 63°30′ W care must be taken when off Pennant Point and Sambro Island. This is an area of shoal water and isolated rocks, many of which dry or are awash, and in bad weather the sea breaks fiercely. Although it is well buoyed these may be missed in thick weather. Sambro island has a powerful DF beacon which can be of great value on the approach.

The final approach to Halifax is made between Chebucto Head on the western side, a 30 m (100 ft) headland of whitish granite with a light [Fl 20s 49m 16M] shown from a white tower close to the north, and Devils Island [Fl 10s 16m 13M] off Hartlen Point to the northeast. Between them lie Portuguese Shoal and Rock Head Shoal, both of which are buoyed. Additionally there are numerous other buoys and leading lights on the final approach, and to identify these an up-to-date chart is essential.

Radio

'Halifax Traffic' located at Chebucto Head operates a Vessel Traffic Management System on VHF for all vessels over 20 m (65 ft) and will advise smaller craft on the proximity of shipping. They monitor VHF channel 16 and use channel 14 as their working channel. The Canadian Coast Guard also listens on channel 16.

Entrance

Final entrance lies between Sandwich Point and Macnab's Island. Best water is found close to the western shore from Chebucto Head inwards to Sandwich Point and on towards Purcell's Cove, where Point Pleasant divides North West Arm from the main harbour.

Anchorage and moorings

There are many yacht moorings in North West Arm and care must be taken if entering at night or in thick weather. Anchorage is prohibited in the southern part of the inlet. The clubhouse of the Royal Nova Scotia Yacht Squadron lies on the port side, about 0.5 mile up North West Arm, with moorings off it. Visitors can anchor off, or may go alongside the floating pontoons or the stone quay if space permits. Armdale Yacht Club is situated on Melville Island near the head of North West Arm, with moorings off it and pontoon berths and jetties round the island's shore. Beware a rocky shoal patch 60 m (200 ft) off the western end of Melville Island.

Berthing and marinas

As well as pontoons at both yacht clubs it is also possible to moor for limited periods alongside a jetty near the centre of the city about 0.5 mile east of the Citadel and convenient for customs and shopping.

The Maritime Museum of the Atlantic may also be able to arrange free mooring for up to a week in the main harbour.

Formalities

The Q flag should be hoisted on approaching the land. If possible notice should be given of imminent arrival, otherwise it will probably be necessary for the skipper to go ashore to telephone the authorities, who work office hours (0900–1700) and charge a heavy fee if summoned to clear a vessel at other times. However if entry is made outside these hours or between 1200 Saturday and 0900 Monday, clearance may be held over until normal office hours provided neither crew nor yacht leave port in the meantime.

Facilities

Boatyard Both yacht clubs have facilities for slipping and repair work, and will advise visitors about alternative yards if they cannot offer the necessary service
Engineers/electronics/sailmaker Enquire at one of the yacht clubs
Chandlery In the city
Chart agent US charts from The Binnacle (423 6464) or Gabriel Aero-Marine Instruments (450 5030)

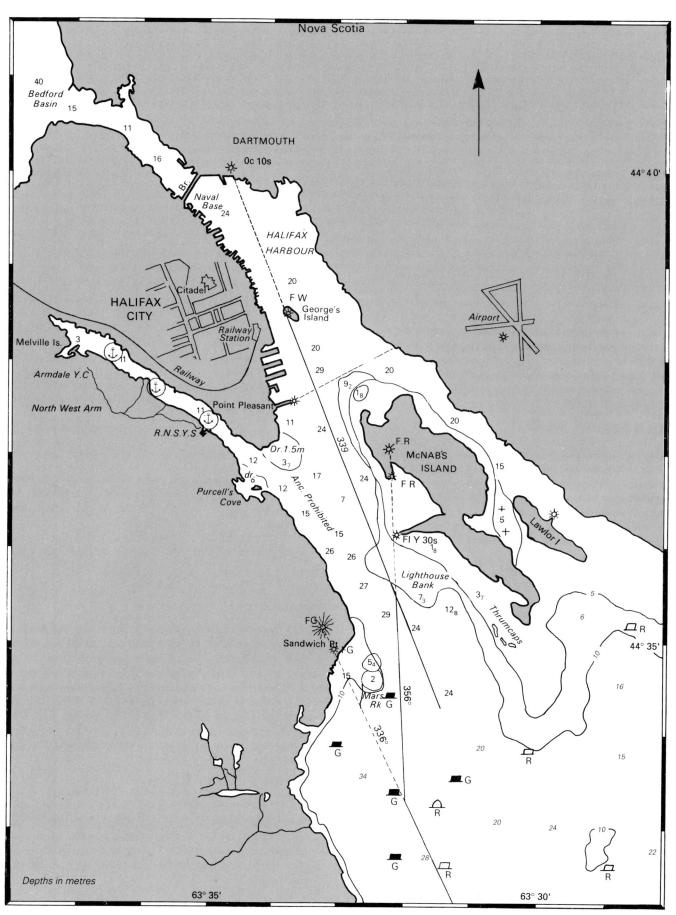

Chart 75 Halifax, Nova Scotia. Based on Admiralty Chart No 2410.

Yacht clubs The Royal Nova Scotia Yacht Squadron and the Armdale Yacht Club both have good facilities and welcome visiting yachtsmen

Diesel Available at both yacht clubs

Water Available at both yacht clubs

Bottled gas Refills (propane only) may be a problem – enquire at one of the yacht clubs

Showers At both yacht clubs at the discretion of the staff

Laundry/launderette Near the head of North West Arm

Banks Several in the city

General shopping Halifax is a large city with all the usual stores

Provisioning Good – supermarkets in the city and in the suburbs near the head of North West Arm, but very little close to the anchorages themselves

Restaurants Many, including at both yacht clubs

Hotels Wide choice

Medical services Hospital in the city

Communications

Mailing address C/o General Delivery at either of the two yacht clubs by prior arrangement

Post Office In the city, plus a sub-post office in the suburbs near the head of North West Arm

Telephones At both yacht clubs and elsewhere

Bus service A local bus route serves the area of the anchorages

Rail service Halifax is served by the Canadian National Railway system. The main station is near the southern end of the docks

Taxis/car hire Plentiful

Air services The new airport is some 25 miles north of the city and offers flights to destinations within Canada, the US and Europe

| Springs: 1.3 m/4 ft 3 in | Flag: Canada |
| Neaps: 0.9 m/2 ft 11 in | Currency: Canadian dollar |

Charts	Admiralty	US	Canadian
General	232A(1:565,700)	14024 (1:720,240)	4001 (1:3,500,000)
		14360 (1:284,330)	4016/7 (1:350,000)
Approach	2902 (1:75,000)	14373 (1:75,000)	4846 (1:60,000)
		14364 (1:37,500)	
Harbour	298 (1:6,090)	14365 (1:3,600)	4846 (1:5,000)

General

St John's is the capital and principal port of Newfoundland, situated on the Atlantic coast of the Avalon Peninsula near the south-east corner of the island. The harbour is landlocked and well sheltered, but is purely commercial with no real provision for small boats. Its principal importance to the transatlantic yachtsman is in being the nearest port to Europe. It is an official port of entry.

Approach

The approaches to Newfoundland lie in one of the foggiest areas in the world. However it is often clear within a few miles of the shore even when there is thick fog further out. There are DF beacons on Cape Race and Cape St Francis which can be of great help. Icebergs carried south by the Labrador current may pose a further hazard (see Chapters 10 and 19).

The coastline is generally very steep, rising directly to

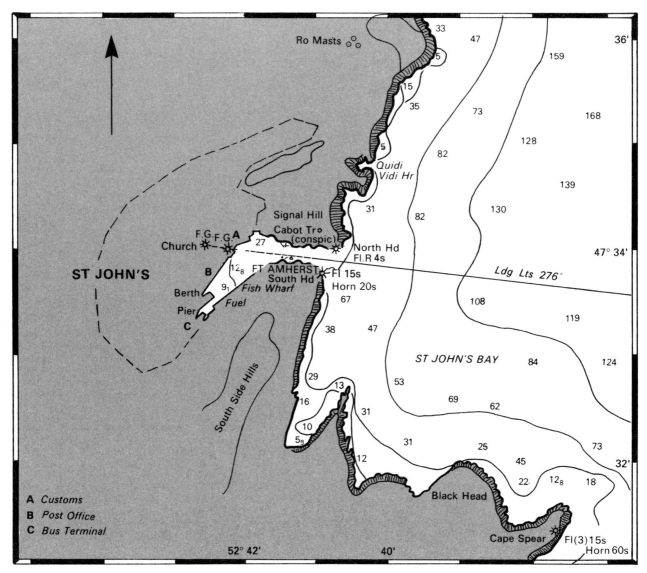

Chart 76 St John's, Newfoundland. Based on Admiralty Chart No 2902.

60 m (200 ft) in many places, with a somewhat barren appearance and few signs of habitation. Hills of 150 m to 250 m (500 ft to 800 ft) lie close inland and identification of the exact landfall can be difficult. The bluff coastline can also result in squally winds or wind shadows when close inshore. The shore is generally steep-to and clear of underwater rocks, and in thick weather can be approached using the depth sounder. The 40 m (130 ft) line lies between 0.25 and 0.5 mile offshore. Sugarloaf Head three miles north of St John's is conspicuous – 150 m (500 ft) high with a sheer cliff face. It appears wedge-shaped when seen from north of north-east, but as a truncated cone from east-north-east round to the south-east. Cape Spear, 3.5 miles south-east of St John's, is a promontory some 60 m (200 ft) high, projecting north-eastward from the coast. A light is shown [Fl(3) 15s 71m 20M] from a lighthouse 14 m (45 ft) in height on its eastern face.

Radio

St John's Radio broadcasts weather forecasts and ice reports as well as providing radio communications. They may be called up on VHF channel 16. A Traffic Management System is administered from Signal Hill and may be contacted on VHF channel 11 or 14 as 'St John's Traffic'. The Canadian Coast Guard monitors VHF channel 16.

Entrance

The entrance to St John's lies between North and South Head, and is very narrow – about 300 m (1000 ft). It is not easily identified from a distance but becomes clearer as the land is closed. North Head is a steep headland of 72 m (235 ft) rising to 150 m (500 ft) immediately to its north-west as Signal Hill, topped by the conspicuous Cabot Tower. A light [Fl R 4s] is shown at a height of 24 m (78 ft) from a very small, white 'pepper pot' structure on the southern shore of North Head.

South Head may be identified by Fort Amherst Light [FL 15s 40m 13M], shown from a low tower attached to a white building built on bare reddish rock just below the vegetation line. There is also a fog horn. The final approach is straightforward with no offlying dangers other than Vestal Rock, 4.0 m (13 ft) high and lying some 137 m (450 ft) east of Fort Amherst light. However in thick weather care must be taken not to mistake the entrance to Quidi Vidi harbour a mile further north for that of St John's. Quidi Vidi has no lighthouses or fog signals.

Enter between the two headlands on a course of 276°, keeping slightly to the north of the centre. There are leading lights [FG] with daymarks which lead in through the channel on this bearing, but they are difficult to identify. The twin towers of the Roman Catholic Cathedral break the skyline behind St John's – the rear light and daymark is just to the north of these towers and almost level with their bases. If the leading line cannot be identified continue on 276° until 100 m (330 ft) clear of North Head, observing the buoys and lights which mark shoals on both sides of the channel. At the western end of the channel the harbour opens up to the south-west. The harbour is busy and anchoring is only allowed under the direction of the Harbour Master. There is good holding in mud.

Berthing and marinas

The harbour is entirely surrounded by wharves, most of which are used by commercial and fishing vessels. The recommended berth is at the south-western end of the long straight wharf which forms the western side of the harbour, in an area used by small craft. The wharf face can be oily and some protection for fenders may be required, otherwise secure alongside another vessel. The Harbour Master may redirect a yacht to an alternative berth.

Formalities

The Q flag should be hoisted on closing the coast. The customs officers in St John's are on duty from 0800–2400 including holidays. A yacht arriving between 2400 and 0800 need take no action and will be contacted by an official when the office opens – should clearance be essential between these times it can be arranged but a substantial fee will be charged. No one may go ashore until the yacht is cleared.

Duty free imports

Equipment to be fitted or used on a foreign registered yacht may be imported duty free through St John's customs office. Enquire about current procedures before despatch.

Facilities

Boatyards There are no yacht yards at St John's, though there are a few yards which build and maintain small fishing boats and similar craft which might be able to assist in an emergency. There is a small boatyard with a mobile lift at the port of Harbour Grace on the west side of Conception Bay, about 40 miles by sea from St John's

Engineers D F Barnes (579 5041)

Electronics Radar and radio technicians who service the fishing boats

Sailmaker United Sail Works (754 2131)

Chandlery IMP Group (722 4221) and Windshift Marine (753 3892)

Chart agent Campbells Ships Supplies (726 6932)

Compass adjuster Capt Wilf Blackmore (579 0567)

Yacht club The Royal Newfoundland Yacht Club, which welcomes visiting yachtsmen, is situated at Long Pond on the western shores of the Avalon Peninsula

Diesel The fuel wharves are in the southern part of the harbour. Although more accustomed to bunkering ships by the ton some do have pumps suitable for small boats

Water No provision for taking on small quantities by hose, though it might be possible at the fish wharves in the south of the harbour. Otherwise carry by can from a convenient tap

Bottled gas Bottles cannot be refilled or exchanged

Ice Try the fish wharves in the south of the harbour

Showers Negotiate with a hotel

Laundry/launderette In the main shopping area

Banks In the main shopping area

General shopping Good

Provisioning Several large supermarkets in the south west outskirts of the town

Bonded stores Campbells Ships Supplies (726 6932)

Restaurants/hotels A reasonable choice

Medical services Good modern hospital in St John's

Communications

Mailing address C/o General Delivery, Main Postal Station 'C', 354 Water Street, St John's, Newfoundland, Canada AIC 5YI

Post Office In the main shopping area

Telephones At the post office and elsewhere

Bus service Daily bus service to Port-aux-Basques (14 hours) for the ferry to Sydney, Nova Scotia

Taxis/car hire No problem

Air services St John's airport has direct flights to the UK and Europe as well as links within Canada and the USA

Charts	Admiralty		US	
General	360	(1:200,000)	26340	(1:200,000)
Approach	334	(1:60,000)	26341	(1:50,000)
	868	(1:17,500)	26342	(1:17,500)
Harbour	1315	(1:6,200)	26343	(1:6,200)

Springs: 1.1 /3 ft 7 in   *Flag*: British (Red Ensign)
Neaps: 0.9 m/2 ft 11 in   *Currency*: Bermudian dollar

General

St George's is Bermuda's second town, considerably smaller than the capital, Hamilton. Distances are such that travel is easy between the two, and certainly storing before departure is best done in Hamilton. There is some interesting cruising to be had around Bermuda, with many isolated and attractive anchorages.

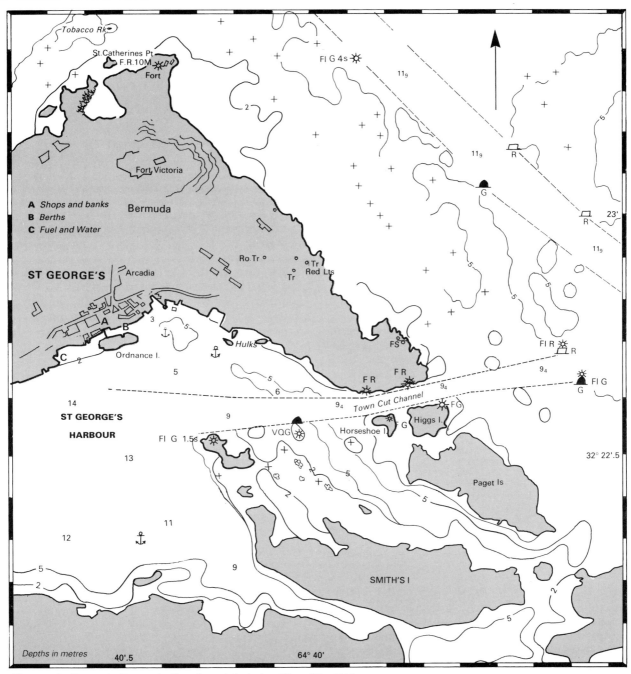

Chart 77 St George's, Bermuda. Based on Admiralty Chart No 1315.

Entering the Town Cut Channel at St George's, Bermuda. The (lit) pylons are visible from well offshore. *Photo: Anne Hammick*

Buoyage follows the IALA B system as used in the US and much of the Caribbean.

Approach

Details of the approaches to Bermuda will be found in Chapter 20.

St George's harbour is situated at the extreme eastern end of the island and is approached via a well buoyed channel, one branch leading north-west around the island towards Hamilton and the other through the Town Cut Channel into the harbour. The powerful St David's Island light [Fl(2) 20s 65m 15M, FR/G 20M] lies about a mile to the south. All vessels must contact Bermuda Harbour Radio *before* entering the buoyed channel, as should a cruise liner or other large vessel be departing a one-way traffic system will be in operation.

Radio

Bermuda Harbour Radio station (ZBM) monitors VHF channel 16.

Entrance

Although the Town Cut is narrow, entry with a reliable engine is not difficult. If faced with beating in under sail it might be wise to consider the alternative of a tow, which Bermuda Harbour Radio can arrange. In poor visibility, including heavy rain squalls, the Harbour Radio can monitor progress on radar. Although it has been said that entry after dark should be avoided, the Town Cut and its approaches are well lit and many yachts arrive at night and make their way into the harbour without problems – as always, the final decision lies with the skipper.

Once through the Cut the harbour opens out, with good water to starboard. If entering after dark keep watch for anchored yachts, which may be unlit, and beware of straying southwards out of the dredged channel.

Anchorage and moorings

The main yacht anchorage is to the north of the dredged channel and to the east of Ordnance Island, in depths of 2–5 m. Holding is good, but there are various old chains etc littering the bottom and a trip line may be advisable. Larger yachts will find greater depths in the southern part of the harbour, but it is a long dinghy ride ashore. Dinghies can be left at the steps inside Ordnance Island.

Berthing and marinas

Berthing alongside is on a strictly first come first served basis, with yachts rafting on the northern side of Ordnance Island and at Somers Wharf and Hunters Wharf further west. Other wharves are reserved for shipping. None of the yacht berths are very deep, and as there is neither any charge nor any restriction on length of stay it is unusual to find one free.

Formalities

All yachts must proceed to the customs berth at the eastern end of Ordnance Island immediately upon arrival.

It is manned 24 hours a day, the officials being forewarned by Bermuda Harbour Radio. Two copies each of crew list and stores list will be required, plus ship's papers, passports and previous port clearance. Only after the formalities are complete may a yacht move out to anchor or continue to Hamilton. Entry charges are high – see Chapter 20.

In theory it is necessary to revisit the dock to obtain outward clearance, but in practice it may be acceptable for the skipper to deal with the paperwork while the yacht remains out at anchor – enquire on arrival.

Duty free imports

Yacht equipment addressed to the boat and marked 'in transit' may be imported free of duty. All other imports are subject to tax.

Facilities

Boatyards Six or more, all with haulage facilities. Consult Bermuda Harbour Radio for recommendations, which may vary according to size of yacht and the type of work required

Engineers Meyer Industries Ltd, who can also haul yachts up to 60 m (200 ft)

Electronics Electronic Communications Ltd, Marine Communications, Marine Electronic and Telecommunications (Bermuda & West Indies) Ltd

Sailmaker Ocean Sails/Doyle, or Dockyard Canvas Co (repairs only)

Chandlery At marinas and boatyards elsewhere on the island

Chart agent Pearman, Watlington & Co Ltd at Pitt's Bay Boat Co (53232)

Yacht clubs The St George's Dinghy Club has waterside premises on the road leading to the Town Cut and is friendly towards visitors. The Royal Bermuda Yacht Club occupies a large pink building on Front Street in Hamilton, and though welcoming to bona fide yachts-men applies various restrictions where yachtswomen are concerned

Weather forecast Via radio (Chapter 10) or telephone the Naval Oceanography Command Facility Weather Office (293 5491) for a 48-hour forecast. A Yacht Pre-Sail Weather Packet can be arranged on request, for which 12 hours' notice is required

Diesel/petrol/water At St George's Boatyard to the west of Ordnance Island. There is a shallow spot just off the berth

Bottled gas Propane is in general use in Bermuda. Butane, apart from Camping Gaz, is not obtainable

Ice St George's Boatyard and several of the supermarkets

Showers At yacht and dinghy clubs

Laundry/launderette In St George's

Banks In St George's and Hamilton

General shopping Limited in St George's but good in Hamilton

Provisioning More difficult than one might expect for a yacht without refrigeration – see Chapter 20. Nearly all food must be imported, and is therefore expensive

Bonded stores Arrangements must be made several days in advance. The shop will then deliver in bond to customs, who will turn the purchase over to the yacht on clearance

Restaurants/hotels Many and various. Tourism plays a major part in Bermuda's economy

Medical services The King Edward VII Memorial Hospital at Paget, near Hamilton, plus many doctors and dentists

Communications

Mailing address C/o the post office

Post Office/telephones St George's and Hamilton

Bus service Regular buses to Hamilton, Ireland Island at the west end of Bermuda and elsewhere

Taxis Easily available

Care hire No car hire – mopeds are available instead

Air services Daily air services to the US, Canada and Europe

Springs: 1.6 m / 5 ft 3 in	*Flag*: Portugal
Neaps: 1.2 m / 3 ft 11 in	*Currency*: Portuguese escudo

Charts	Admiralty		US	
General	1855	(1:150,000)	51061	(1:250,000)
Approach	1957	(1:37,500)	51062	(1:50,000)
Harbour	1957	(1:10,000)	51062	(1:10,000)

General

Horta is the only town of any size on Faial, with a history reaching back to the mid-fifteenth century. The harbour is probably the best in the islands and has been a favourite with yachtsmen since Joshua Slocum visited in 1895 – he commented then on the friendliness and hospitality of the local people, and things have changed little.

No visit to Horta would be complete without a beer (or a coffee) in the Café Sport, run by the Azevedo family for three generations. Neither would it be wise to tempt the fates by neglecting to add a painting, or at least the yacht's name, to the hundreds which already cover the harbour and marina walls. Many famous yachts feature here.

Approach

Approach and landfall on the Azores archipelago is covered in Chapter 21. However it should be repeated that the stated range of the light at Vale Formoso [LFl(2) 10s 113m 11M] near the western tip of the island is optimistic and may be nearer to five miles. The only other major light is at Pta da Ribeirinha [Fl(3) 20s 147m 29M] on the east coast north of Horta.

Faial has few offlying dangers and the coast may safely be closed to within half a mile or so. If approaching from south-east the Baixa do Sul (also known as Chapman's Rocks) with 7.0 m depths should be avoided if any sea is running. Horta lies near the south-east corner of the island, facing Pico across the Canal do Faial.

Radio

The marina staff (who speak English, French and Spanish as well as Portuguese) monitor VHF channels 11 and 16.

Entrance

If approaching from westwards, Horta harbour will not be seen until the last headland is rounded, when a course

The marina at Horta, Faial, seen from high ground to the south. The main harbour breakwater is out of the picture on the right. *Photo: Anne Hammick*

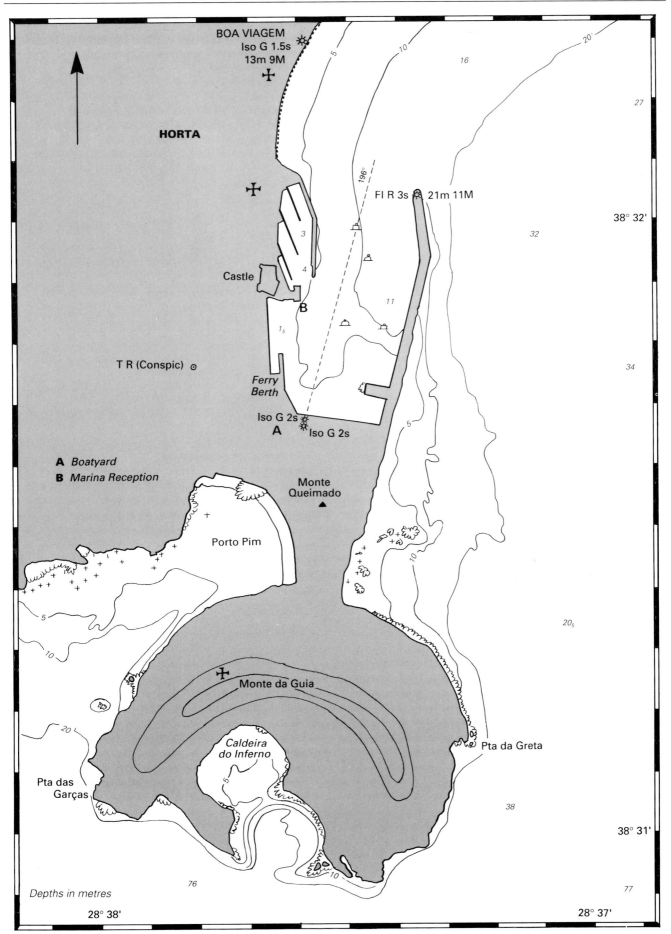

BOA VIAGEM
Iso G 1.5s
13m 9M

HORTA

FI R 3s ☼ 21m 11M

196°

Castle

B

1₅

T R (Conspic) ⊚

*Ferry
Berth*

Iso G 2s ☼
A ☼ Iso G 2s

A *Boatyard*
B *Marina Reception*

Monte
Queimado ▲

Porto Pim

Monte da Guia

*Caldeira
do Inferno*

Pta da Greta

Pta das
Garças

Depths in metres

38° 32'

32

34

20₅

38

38° 31'

27

76   77

28° 38'   28° 37'

Chart 78 Horta, Faial, Azores. Based on a plan in the *Atlantic Islands*.

can be steered directly for the breakwater head which has good depths close in. However avoid rounding it too tightly – the Pico ferry leaves at speed and tends to cut it fine. At night the breakwater light will probably be seen first, as the light of Boa Viagem tends to be overshadowed by town lights. The marina entrance is not lit; visiting yachts should secure to the reception/fuel berth on the western side of the entrance until assigned a berth.

There is at least one unlit steel ship's mooring buoy in the harbour, and if approaching the reception quay in darkness care must also be taken to avoid the yacht moorings laid opposite.

Anchorage and moorings

Anchoring in the harbour is no longer allowed. A double row of yacht mooring buoys has been laid to the east of the marina entrance, intended to take the overflow in busy periods. Consult the marina staff.

Berthing and marinas

Horta marina opened in 1986 and is an object lesson in how such a facility should be maintained and run. The majority of yachts are allotted finger pontoons, with the larger ones rafting up against the wall. Only the very largest yachts (over 30 m and with draught exceeding 4.0 m) berth in the outer harbour alongside the breakwater.

Horta marina is probably the best place in the archipelago to ride out storm or hurricane force winds since the outer harbour faces north-east and the marina entrance south.

Formalities

The advent of the EC should mean fewer formalities for EC owned and registered yachts arriving from mainland Europe, but in practice this represents such a small percentage of total arrivals that it is likely all yachts will be expected to follow the same clearance procedures for some time to come.

Fly the Q flag on arrival unless this is from another Azorean island. In Horta the officials to see are the *Policia Maritima* and *Alfandega* (customs) whose offices flank that of the berthing master on the reception quay. A *Livrete de Transito* (transit log) which remains valid until the yacht leaves Portugal will be issued on payment of a small fee. On departure both offices must again be visited, taking the receipted marina bill and the *Livrete* for re-stamping. Office hours are 0800 to 1230 and 1400 to 2000 and outward clearance remains valid for 24 hours.

Facilities

Boatyard Capable of rough but serviceable repairs to steel, aluminium and wood, but no facilities for major fibreglass repairs. A 25-tonne mobile crane operates on the breakwater, but slings and a cradle might be a problem

Engineers Bensaude & Cia Lda, Rua Vasco da Gama 42, have a good reputation for engineering repairs at reasonable prices
Electronics Enquire at Bensaude
Chandlery Limited stock available from the corner shop almost opposite the marina steps. Chandlery carries high import duty which is not reclaimable
Yacht club The Clube Naval occupies the new building on the water front south of the marina.
Weather forecast A daily forecast and synoptic chart is displayed outside the *Capitania* (near the Pico ferry berth), with a copy posted in the marina office
Diesel From a pump at the marina reception quay, 0800–1200 and 1300–2000
Petrol By can from the diesel pump attendant or from filling stations in town
Water On the marina pontoons
Shore power On the pontoons (220 V 50 Hz). Yachts must provide their own cable and plug, plus adaptor if necessary
Bottled gas Camping Gaz readily available in town. Bensaude & Cia Lda will refill Calor Gas and other non-standard cylinders. Allow several days
Ice Sometimes available from the fish freezing plant at the head of the main harbour
Showers In the semi-circular building in the north-west corner of the marina area
Laundry/launderette In the shower block. Attendant service by machine, or DIY at large sinks
Banks Several in the town, at least one with a VISA card facility. Small quantities of currency can be exchanged at the Café Sport
General shopping Surprisingly good
Provisioning Three supermarkets, with good stocks by Azorean standards. There is a small fruit and vegetable market at the northern end of the town with a fish market beyond
Restaurants A wide variety at very reasonable prices. Many accept Eurocheques or credit cards
Hotels Four star downwards
Medical services Hospital outside the town

Communications

Mailing address Either c/o Peter Azevedo at the Café Sport or c/o the Marina Office
Post Office At the northern end of the town, open 0830–1830
Telephones At the main post office, Café Sport and others
Bus service Circular route around the island. The tourist office will supply a timetable on request
Ferry service Several times daily to Pico, and also to the other islands of the 'central' group – details from the tourist office
Taxis Taxi rank outside the Estalagem de Santa Cruz
Car hire Choice of several
Air services National, inter-island and international flights, though most UK flights are via Lisbon

Charts	Admiralty		US	
General	1854	(1:150,000)	51081	(1:250,000)
Approach			51082	(1:50,000)
Harbour	1854	(1:12,000)	51082	(1:10,000)

Springs: 1.7 m/5 ft 7 in *Flag*: Portugal
Neaps: 1.3 m/4 ft 3 in *Currency*: Portuguese escudo

General

Ponta Delgada is the largest town in the Azores, with a busy naval and commercial harbour. Other than Horta and Praia da Vitoria (Terceira) it is the only place which can be considered safe for yachts in almost all conditions, though winds between east and south can send a heavy swell into the harbour. It also offers the best shopping and provisioning in the Azores. The island of São Miguel is particularly beautiful, with spectacular lakes and hot springs, and well worth exploring.

A new marina was opened early in 1993 in the northeast of the harbour. Nearby are several open air swimming pools, cafes and restaurants.

Approach

Much of São Miguel is high and often visible from many miles away. The coastline is largely steep-to, with few offlying dangers, but many of the headlands are fringed by rocks and all should be given at least 500 m clearance. If approaching from the west, Baixa da Negra lies about 0.5 miles south of the Airport Control Tower [Alt FlWG 10s 83m W28M/G23M] and should be given a wide berth. The island is relatively well lit, with powerful lights at Pta da Ferraria [Fl(3) 20s 106m 27M] at its western end and Pta do Arnel [Fl 5s 67m 25M] to the east. Santa Clara [LFl 15s 26m 15M] marks the headland to the west of Ponta Delgada.

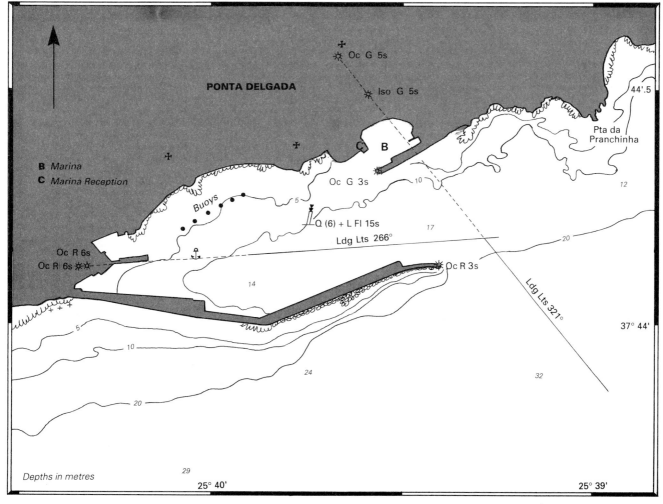

Chart 79 Ponta Delgada, São Miguel, Azores. Based on a plan in the *Atlantic Islands*.

Entrance

Final approach and entrance is straightforward, though the grey stone breakwater may blend with the concrete esplanade if approaching on a bearing of less than 325°. There are good depths close to the breakwater end. At present yachts berth in the western part of the harbour, passing south of the South Cardinal buoy marking Baixa de S Pedro, but when the marina is completed this will be passed to the east. There are two sets of leading lights, both of them easily visible against the many shore lights behind, but if entering at night beware the scattered mooring buoys, many of which trail floating lines, and unlit yachts and fishing boats which may be anchored on the leading line.

Anchorage and moorings

The best anchorage is in the west of the harbour, near the end of the old yacht pontoon in 8–10 m over sand. Various pink and orange plastic mooring buoys have been laid for visiting yachts, or one of the large orange metal buoys further out may be free – but possibly with a fishing boat due to return.

Berthing and marinas

The new marina has already gained an excellent reputation. On arrival yachts should berth at the reception quay, to visit the offices of local officials and be assigned a berth. The marina office is open 0900–1800 daily and monitors VHF channel 16 during working hours. The western most of the three pontoons is reserved for visitors, and is reported to have some 2.7 m (9 ft) at LWS. Large yachts lie inside the marina mole.

Formalities

The advent of the EC should mean fewer formalities for EC owned and registered yachts arriving from mainland Europe, but in practice it is likely all yachts will be expected to follow the same clearance procedures for some time to come. All officials now have offices in the marina area. The skipper should visit the *Policia Maritima* bearing ship's papers, passports and insurance documents to be issued with a *Livrete* and be advised of the other officials to be seen. On departure the marina office must be visited first to settle the bill, and it may then be necessary to present copies of the receipt to the *Policia Maritima* before the *Livrete* will be stamped for departure.

Facilities

Boatyards Several yards where wooden fishing boats are built and steel repaired. One at the western end of the harbour, plus Cos Bensaude (222005) and Sofopel (26751). It is possible for yachts to be craned out on the breakwater though slings and/or cradle might need to be made up

Engineers/electronics Jose Gonçal Ves Cerqueira Lda (24763/98400), though more used to fishing vessels

Yacht club The *Clube Naval de Ponta Delgada*, which has recently moved from its old premises at the head of the harbour into a new building near the root of the marina mole, is friendly and helpful towards visiting yachtsmen

Weather forecast A forecast and synoptic chart is posted daily on the notice board in the marina. This normally covers the nexty 48 hours, but a one-week forecast can be prepared on request

Diesel A fuel berth was under construction in August 1993 and should be operational by 1994

Petrol From filling stations in town

Water On marina pontoons. Hoses need special connectors (available in town if not already carried)

Electricity On marina pontoons (220v 50Hz). Again a locally available connector is needed, and yachts must provide their own cable and plug, plus adaptor if necessary

Bottled gas Camping Gaz exchanges, but no refilling of other cylinders

Showers In the marina complex

Launderette Under construction in the marina during 1993

Banks Several. The Banco Pinto e Sotto Major has a VISA card facility

General shopping Good for most needs

Provisioning Two well-stocked supermarkets, plus a large fruit and vegetable market with fish market attached

Restaurants/hotels Wide choice at all levels

Medical services A hospital near the harbour, plus several medical centres

Communications

Mailing address C/o the marina office or Clube Naval

Post Office Open 0830 to 1830, but usually busy with long delays. Stamps can be bought at any shop displaying the green *Correio* sign

Telephones At the marina office, which also has a fax receiving service, and at the post office

Bus service Good network, with a reputation for running early. Timetable from the tourist office

Taxis/car hire No problem. Mopeds and cycles can also be hired

Air services Daily flights to Lisbon and the other islands

The following suggestions for further reading are indexed by chapter for easy reference. It is certainly not implied that every book under each heading need be consulted – all books (and authors) tend to have their individual strengths and weaknesses, and in many cases parts of the subject matter may overlap between one title and the next. All should be available in bookshops, chandleries or through mail order catalogues. Which books will be carried on board, and which read before departure and then left at home, must depend on the size of the yacht and the priorities of her skipper.

Lists of British Admiralty and US Defense Mapping Agency *Sailing Directions* and of the many yachtsmen's guides and pilots covering the Atlantic margins will be found in separate Appendices. Appropriate manufacturers' handbooks should also be carried, but for obvious reasons cannot be listed here.

Preparations
(relevant to several chapters in Part I)

Cruising Under Sail, incorporating Voyaging Under Sail, Eric Hiscock (ACN; IMP)
Handbook of Offshore Cruising, Jim Howard (ACN; SH)
Around the World Rally, Jimmy Cornell (ACN)
Ocean Cruising Countdown, Geoff Pack (D&C)
Ocean Cruising on a Budget, Anne Hammick (ACN; IMP)
Sell Up and Sail, Bill and Laurel Cooper (ACN)

The philosophy of ocean cruising
Sensible Cruising: The Thoreau Approach, Don Casey and Lew Hackler (IMP)
Cruising as a Way of Life, Thomas Colvin (OP)
Voyaging on a Small Income, Annie Hill, (WB)

The boat and her permanent fittings
Seaworthiness: The Forgotten Factor, CA Marchaj (ACN)
Desirable and Undesirable Characteristics of Offshore Yachts, Technical Committee of the Cruising Club of America (WWN)
The Ocean Sailing Yacht, Vols 1 and 2, Donald M Street Jr (WWN)
The Capable Cruiser, Lin and Larry Pardey (ABB)
The Cruising Multihull, Chris White (IMP)
Multihulls for Cruising and Racing (ACN; IMP)
Upgrading the Cruising Sailboat, Dan Spurr (IMP)
Comfort in the Cruising Yacht, Ian Nicolson (ACN)
Cruising in Comfort, Jim Skoog (IMP)
Rigging, Enrico Sala (ACN)
Understanding Rigs and Rigging, Richard Henderson (ACN; IMP)
Refrigeration for Pleasureboats, Nigel Calder (IMP)
Boat Engines, Dick Hewitt (FH)
Troubleshooting and Maintenance of Boat Engines, Peter Bowyer (ACN)
The Care and Repair of Small Marine Diesels, Chris Thompson (ACN)

Marine Diesel Engines, Nigel Calder (AP; IMP)
Boat Owner's Mechanical and Electrical Manual, Nigel Calder (ACN; IMP)
Boatowner's Wiring Manual, Charles Wing (ACN; IMP)
Marine Electrical and Electronics Bible, John Payne (ACN; SH)
Marine Electrics, Geoffrey O'Connell (AP)
Boat Electrical Systems, Dag Pike (ACN)
The 12-Volt Bible for Boats, Miner Brotherton (WB; IMP)

Equipment for ocean and warm climate cruising
Anchoring and Mooring Techniques Illustrated, Alain Grée (ACN)
Sails, Jeremy Howard-Williams (ACN)
Boatowner's Energy Planner, Kevin and Nan Jeffrey (IMP)
Canvas Work, Jeremy Howard-Williams (AP)
Canvas and Rope Craft, Frank Rosenow (ACN)

Ocean navigation
Celestial Navigation for Yachtsmen, Mary Blewitt (ACN)
Basic Astro Navigation, Conrad Dixon (ACN)
Ocean Navigator, Kenneth Wilkes, Revised by Pat Langley-Price and Philip Ouvry (ACN)
Sky and Sextant, John P Budlong (VNR)
The Sextant Handbook, Bruce Bauer (AP; IMP)
The Sextant Simplified, Captain O M Watts (TRP)

Radio and electronics
A Guide to Small Boat Radio, Mike Harris (ACN)
Electronics Afloat, Dag Pike (ACN)
Mariners Guide to Single Sideband, Frederick Graves (ABB)
Using GPS, Conrad Dixon (ACN; SH)
Understanding Weatherfax, Mike Harris (ACN: 1996)

The crew
The Hitch-Hiker's Guide to the Oceans, Alison Muir Bennett and Clare Davis (ACN; IMP)
The Cruising Mate's Handbook, Joyce Sleightholme (ACN)
Cruising with Children, Gwenda Cornell (ACN; SH)

Provisioning
The Care and Feeding of the Offshore Crew, Lin and Larry Pardey (ABB)
The Happy Ship, Kitty Hampton (F&F)
Sailing the Farm, Ken Neumeyer (ABB)

The mechanics of ocean cruising
Living Afloat, Claire Allcard (ACN; ABB)
Managing your Escape, Katy Burke (IMP)
Collin's Gems: Guide to Flags, Collins
Yachtsman's 10 Language Dictionary, Barbara Webb with the Cruising Association (ACN; SH)

Safety
Bluewater Handbook, Steve Dashew (ABB)
Reading the Weather, Alan Watts (ACN)
The Yachtsman's Weather Guide, Ingrid Holford (IMP)

Weather at Sea, David Houton and Fred Sanders (IMP)
Heavy Weather Sailing, K Adlard Coles, revised by Peter
  Bruce (ACN; IMP)
This is Rough Weather Cruising, Erroll Bruce (ACN)
Heather Weather Cruising, Tom Cunliffe (FH)
Aground, James Minnoch (IMP)
Rapairs at Sea, Nigel Calder (IMP)
First Aid for the Cruising Yachtsman (RYA)
Advanced First Aid Afloat, Peter F Eastman (ABB)
The Ship's Captain's Medical Guide (HMSO)
First Aid at Sea, Douglas Justins and Colin Berry (ACN)

The North Atlantic – Background
Ocean Passages for the World, NP 136 (BAHD)
Atlantic Pilot Atlas, James Clarke (ACN)
World Cruising Handbook, Jimmy Cornell (ACN; IMP)
World Cruising Routes, Jimmy Cornell (ACN; IMP)

The Lesser Antilles (West Indies)
Cruising in Tropical Waters and Coral, Alan Lucas (ACN;
  IMP)

Publishers

ABB	–	Armchair Bookstore Booklist
ACN	–	Adlard Coles Nautical
AP	–	Ashford Press
BAHD	–	British Admiralty Hydrographic Department
D&C	–	David & Charles
F&F	–	Faber & Faber
FH	–	Fernhurst Books
HMSO	–	Her Majesty's Stationery Office
IMP	–	International Marine Publishing
RYA	–	Royal Yachting Association
SH	–	Sheridan House
SS	–	Seven Seas
TRP	–	Thomas Reed Publications
VNR	–	Van Nostrand Reinhold
WB	–	Waterline Books
WWN	–	W W Norton, New York

APPENDIX B – Yachtsmen's Guides and Pilots

Please note: inclusion of a book in the following list merely signifies its existence. It does not necessarily imply any endorsement regarding content or accuracy.

Adlard Coles Pilot Pack, Vol 3, Brian Goulder (ACN)

Ardnamurchan to Cape Wrath, Clyde Cruising Club (CCC)

Atlantic Islands, Anne Hammick and Nicholas Heath/ RCC Pilotage Foundation (Imray)

Atlantic Spain and Portugal, RCC Pilotage Foundation (Oz Robinson/Mike Sadler) (Imray)

BBA Chart Kit No 10 – The Virgin Islands, Better Boating Association

BBA Chart Kits (six covering Canadian border to Bahamas via the Intracoastal Waterway), Better Boating Association

Boater's Photographic Chartbook to the Bahamas, AirNav Publications

Bristol Channel & Severn Pilot, Peter Cumberlidge (ACN)

Brittany and Channel Islands Cruising Guide, David Jefferson (ACN)

Canary Islands Cruising Guide, Guia Nautica de Canarias (World Cruising Pubs)

Channel Harbours and Anchorages, K Adlard Coles and others (ACN)

Channel Islands Pilot, Malcolm Robson (ACN)

Cruise Cape Breton, Cape Breton Development Corporation

Cruising Association Handbook, Cruising Association (Seventh edition) (CA)

Cruising Guide to Eastern Florida, Claiborne Young

Cruising Guide to Labrador, Sandy Weld/Cruising Club of America

Cruising Guide to Maine, Parts 1 and 2, Don Johnson/ Julius M Wilensky (Wescott Cove)

Cruising Guide to Narragansett Bay, Lynda and Patrick Childress (Int Marine)

Cruising Guide to Newfoundland, Sandy Weld/Cruising Club of America

Cruising Guide to The Abacos and North Bahamas, Julius M Wilensky (Wescott Cove)

Cruising Guide to the Caribbean, Michael Marshall (ACN)

Cruising Guide to the Caribbean and the Bahamas, JC Hart and W T Stone (Dodd, Mead & Co) (includes South and Central American coasts and Greater Antilles)

Cruising Guide to the Caribbean and the Bahamas, JC Hart and WT Stone (Dodd, Mead & Co)

Cruising Guide to the Chesapeake, Stone, Blanchard and Hays (Putnam, New York)

Cruising Guide to the Florida Keys, Frank Papy

Cruising Guide to the Leeward Islands, Chris Doyle (Cruising Guide Pubs)

Cruising Guide to the Maine Coast, Hank and Jan Taft (Int Marine)

Cruising Guide to the New England Coast, Roger Duncan and John Ware (Putnam, New York)

Cruising Guide to the Nova Scotia Coast, John McKelvy

Cruising Guide to the Virgin Islands, Nancy and Simon Scott (Cruising Guide Publications)

Cruising Guide, Block Island to Nantucket, Better Boating Association

Cruising Guide, Long Island Sound, Better Boating Association

Cruising Guides to the Coastal Carolinas, Vols 1 and 2, Claiborne S Young

Cruising the Chesapeake: A Gunkholer's Guide, William Shellenberger (Int Marine)

Embassy Complete Guide to Long Island Sound, Mark Borton and J Grant

Embassy Complete Guide to Rhode Island and Massachusetts, Mark Borton

French Pilot Vols 1 to 4, Malcolm Robson (ACN)

Intracoastal Waterway Facilities Guide, RD Smith

Lundy, Fastnet and Irish Sea Pilot, Vols 1 to 3, David Taylor (Imray)

Mull of Kintyre to Ardnamurchan, Clyde Cruising Club (CCC)

Normandy and Channel Islands Pilot, Mark Brackenbury (ACN)

North Biscay Pilot, Nicholas Heath/RCC Pilotage Foundation (ACN)

North Brittany Pilot, RCC Pilotage Foundation (ACN)

Port to Port Guides, Parts 1 to 4 (Maine to Key West), Pilot Publishing

Sailing Directions for the East and North Coasts of Ireland, Irish Cruising Club (ICC)

Sailing Directions for the South and West Coasts of Ireland, Irish Cruising Club (ICC)

Sailor's Guide to a Venezuela Cruise, Chris Doyle (Cruising Guide Pubs)

Sailor's Guide to the Windward Islands, Chris Doyle (Cruising Guide Pubs)

Scottish West Coast Pilot, Mark Brackenbury (ACN)

Shell Pilot to the English Channel, Vols 1 and 2, Capt John Coote (Faber & Faber)

South Biscay Pilot, Robin Brandon (ACN)

St Helena including Ascension Island and Tristan da Cunha, Tony Cross (David & Charles) (general information rather than a pilot book)

St Maarten, St Kitts & Nevis Cruising Guide, William Eiman (also covers Anguilla, St Barts, Statia and Saba)

Street's Cruising Guides to the Eastern Caribbean, Vol 2, parts 1 and 2, Vols 3 and 4, DM Street Jr (WW Norton/Imray)

The Intra-Coastal Waterway, Norfolk to Miami, Jan and Bill Moeller (Int Marine)

The Lesser Antilles, RCC Pilotage Foundation/Service Hydrographique et Océanographique de la Marine (Imray)

Virgin Anchorages, The Moorings staff (Cruising Guide Pubs)

Waterway Guide Chartbooks (six covering Canadian border to Florida), ES Maloney

Waterway Guides (Northern, Mid-Atlantic and Southern), Communication Channels
West Country Cruising, Mark Fishwick (YM)
West Highland Shores, Maldwin Drummond (ACN)
Yachting Guide to Bermuda, Jane and Edward Harris (Bermuda Maritime)
Yachting Guide to the South Shore of Nova Scotia, Arthur Dechman

Yachtsman's Guide to the Bahamas, Meredith E Fields (Tropic Isle Pubs)
Yachtsman's Guide to the Bermudan Islands, Michael Voegli
Yachtsman's Guide to the Virgin Islands, Meredith E Fields (Tropic Isle Publishers)
Yachtsman's Pilot to the West Coast of Scotland, Vols 1 to 3, Martin Lawrence (Imray)

APPENDIX C – British Admiralty, US Defense Mapping Agency and Canadian Hydrographic Service *Sailing Directions*

Admiralty *Sailing Directions*

NP 1 *Africa Pilot* Vol I (Madeiras, Canaries, Cape Verdes and west coast of Africa from Cabo Espartel to the Bakasi Peninsula)

NP 1, *Africa Pilot* Vol II (the Bakasi Peninsula to Cape Agulhas, St Helena and Ascension islands, Tristan da Cunha group)

NP 5 *South America Pilot*, Vol I (Northeast and eastern coasts of South America, Cabo Orange to Cabo Tres Puntas)

NP 7A *South America Pilot*, Vol IV (North coast of South America including Trinidad and Tobago)

NP 22 *Bay of Biscay Pilot* (Pointe de Penmarc'h to Cabo Ortegal)

NP 27 *Channel Pilot* (Cape Cornwall and Isles of Scilly to Bognor Regis, and Pointe de Penmarc'h to Cap d'Antifer)

NP 37 *West Coasts of England and Wales Pilot* (Cape Cornwall to Mull of Galloway)

NP 40 *Irish Coast Pilot*

NP 50 *Newfoundland Pilot*

NP 59 *Nova Scotia and Bay of Fundy Pilot*

NP 65 *St Lawrence Pilot* (including east coast of Cape Breton Island)

NP 66 *West Coasts of Scotland Pilot* (Mull of Galloway to Cape Wrath)

NP 67 *West Coasts of Spain and Portugal Pilot* (Cabo Ortegal to Gibraltar, including the Azores

NP 68 *East Coast of United States Pilot*, Vol I (Western Head to Barnegat Inlet)

NP 69 *East Coast of United States Pilot*, Vol II (Barnegat Inlet to Cape Canaveral)

NP 70 *West Indies Pilot*, Vol I (Bermuda, Bahamas and Greater Antilles)

NP 71 *West Indies Pilot*, Vol II (Lesser Antilles, Puerto Rico to Grenada)

US Defense Mapping Agency *Sailing Directions*

SD 121 *South Atlantic Ocean* (Planning Guide)

SD 123 *Southwest Coast of Africa*

SD 124 *East Coast of South America*

SD 140 *North Atlantic Ocean* (Planning Guide)

SD 141 *Scotland*

SD 142 *Ireland and the West Coast of England*

SD 143 *West Coast of Europe and Northwest Africa*

SD 145 *Nova Scotia and the St Lawrence*

SD 146 *Newfoundland, Labrador and Hudson Bay*

SD 147 *Caribbean Sea, Vol I – Bermuda, Bahamas and the Islands*

SD 148 *Caribbean Sea, Vol II – Venezuela, Colombia and Central America*

SD 191 *English Channel*

Canadian Hydrographic Service *Sailing Directions*

Nova Scotia (SE coast) and Bay of Fundy
Gulf and River St Lawrence
Newfoundland
Labrador and Hudson Bay

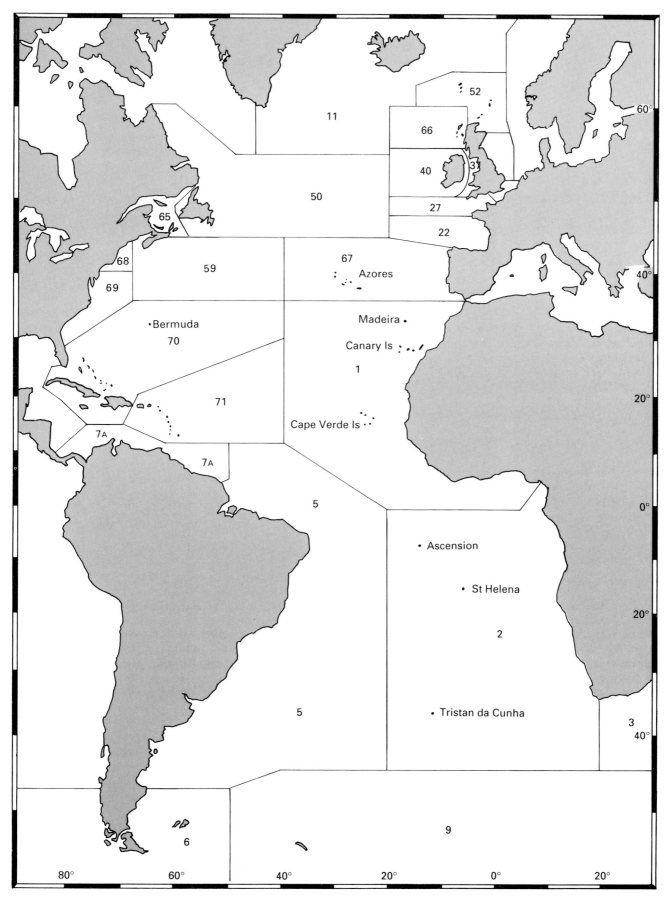

Chart 80 British Admiralty *Sailing Directions* for the Atlantic Ocean. Based on Admiralty Publication NP 131.

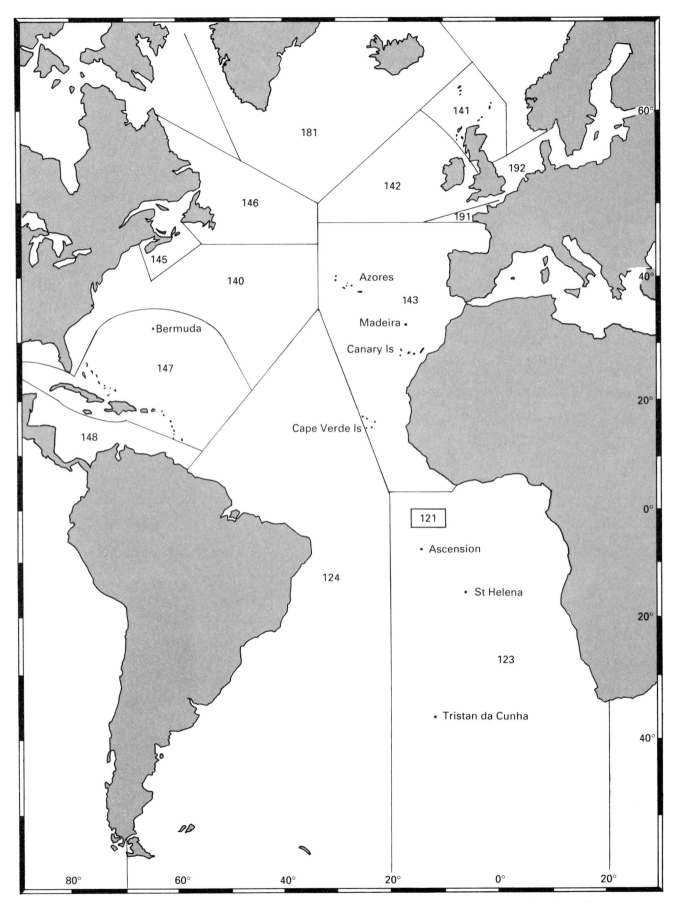

Chart 81 US Defense Mapping Agency *Sailing Directions* for the Atlantic Ocean. Based on US DMA Catalog Vol 10.

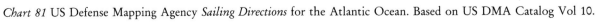

APPENDIX D – Suppliers of Books and Charts

United Kingdom

Brown & Perring Ltd, Redwing House, 36–44 Tabernacle Street, London EC2A 4DT (tel: 071 253 4517; fax: 071 608 0570) (BA, US and Canadian chart agents)

Force 4 Chandlery, 30 Bressingden Place, Buckingham Palace Road, London SW1E 5DB (tel: 071 828 3900/ 3382; fax: 071 828 3383)

Imray Laurie Norie & Wilson Ltd, Wych House, The Broadway, St Ives, Huntingdon, Cambridgeshire PE17 4BT (tel: 0480 62114; fax: 0480 496109)

Kelvin Hughes, Royal Crescent Road, Southampton, Hampshire SO9 1WB (tel: 0703 223772; fax: 0703 330014) (BA, US and Canadian chart agents)

Thomas Foulkes, 9A Sansom Road, Leytonstone, London E11 3HB (tel: 081 539 5084; fax: 081 539 7250)

James Telford & Co Ltd, 5–9 Donegal Quay, Belfast, Northern Ireland BT1 3EF (tel: 0232 326763; fax: 0232 234566) (BA chart agents)

Warsash Nautical Bookshop, 31 Newtown Road, Warsash, Southampton, Hampshire SO3 9FY (tel: 0489 572384; fax: 0489 885756)

USA/Canada

Armchair Sailor Bookstore, Lee's Wharf, Newport, RI 02840 (tel: 800 292 4278; fax: 401 847 1219) (BA, US and Canadian chart agents)

Blue Water Books & Charts, 1481 SE 17th Street, Fort Lauderdale, FL 33316 (tel: 305 763 6533; fax: 305 522 2278) (BA, US and Canadian chart agents)

Boat America, 884 So Pickett Street, Alexandria, VA 22304 (tel: 703 370 4202; fax: 703 461 2852)

Boxells Chandlery, 68 Long Wharf, Boston, MA 02110 (tel: 617 523 5678) (US and Canadian chart agents)

C Plath, 222 Severn Avenue, Annapolis, MD 21403–2569 (tel: 301 263 6700; fax: 301 268 8713) (US distributor for Imray publications)

Cruising Guide Publications, PO Box 13131, Sta 9, Clearwater, FL 34521, USA (tel: 813 796 2469; fax: 813 797 1243)

Fawcetts' Boat Supplies, 110 Compromise Street, Annapolis, MD 21404 (tel: 301 267 8681, 800 456 9151)

International Marine Publishing Co, 21 Elm Street, Camden, ME 04843.

Marine Press of Canada, 224 St Paul Street West, Montreal PQ H2Y 1Z9 (tel: 514 845 8342; fax: 514 845 8368) (BA, US and Canadian chart agents)

Maryland Nautical Sales Inc, 1143 Hull Street, Baltimore, MD 21230 (tel: 301 234 0531; fax: 301 685 5068) (BA, US and Canadian chart agents)

McGill Maritime Services Inc, 369 Place d'Youville, Montreal, PQ, H2Y 2B7 (tel: 514 849 1125; fax: 514 849 5804) (BA, US and Canadian chart agents)

New York Nautical Instrument & Service Corp, 140 West Broadway, New York, NY 10013 (tel: 212 962 4522/4523; fax: 212 406 8420) (BA, US and Canadian chart agents)

Tropic Isle Publishers Inc, PO Box 610935, North Miami, FL 33261–0935, USA

Wescott Cove Publishing Co, PO Box 130, Stamford, CT 6904

West Marine Catalog and Port Supply Chandlers, 500 Westridge Drive, Watsonville, CA 95076 (tel: 408 728 2700, 800 538 0775)

APPENDIX E – European and American Marine VHF Radio Frequencies

(Channels numbered in heavy type are common to both sides of the Atlantic)

	EUROPEAN		CHANNEL	USA		
	Operating frequency (MHz)			Operating frequency (MHz)		
	Receive	Transmit		Receive	Transmit	
(duplex)	160.650	156.050	01	156.050	156.050	(simplex)
(duplex)	160.700	156.100	02	–	–	
(duplex)	160.750	156.150	03	156.150	156.150	(simplex)
(duplex)	160.800	156.200	04	156.200	156.200	(simplex)
(duplex)	160.850	156.250	05	156.250	156.250	(simplex)
(simplex)	156.300	156.300	**06**	156.300	156.300	(simplex)
(duplex)	160.950	156.350	07	156.350	156.350	(simplex)
(simplex)	156.400	156.400	**08**	156.400	156.400	(simplex)
(simplex)	156.450	156.450	**09**	156.450	156.450	(simplex)
(simplex)	156.500	156.500	**10**	156.500	156.500	(simplex)
(simplex)	156.550	156.550	**11**	156.550	156.550	(simplex)
(simplex)	156.600	156.600	**12**	156.600	156.600	(simplex)
(simplex)	156.650	156.650	**13**	156.650	156.650	(simplex)
(simplex)	156.700	156.700	**14**	156.700	156.700	(simplex)
(simplex)	156.750	156.750	**15**	156.750	156.750	(simplex)
(simplex)	**156.800**	**156.800**	**16**	**156.800**	**156.800**	**(simplex)**
(simplex)	156.850	156.850	**17**	156.850	156.850	(simplex)
(duplex)	161.500	156.900	**18**	156.900	156.900	(simplex)
(duplex)	161.550	156.950	**19**	156.950	156.950	(simplex)
(duplex)	161.600	157.000	**20**	161.600	157.000	(duplex)
(duplex)	161.650	157.050	21	157.050	157.050	(simplex)
(duplex)	161.700	157.100	22	157.100	157.100	(simplex)
(duplex)	161.750	157.150	23	157.150	157.150	(simplex)
(duplex)	161.800	157.200	**24**	161.800	157.200	(duplex)
(duplex)	161.850	157.250	**25**	161.850	157.250	(duplex)
(duplex)	161.900	157.300	**26**	161.900	157.300	(duplex)
(duplex)	161.950	157.350	**27**	162.000	157.400	(duplex)
(duplex)	162.000	157.400	**28**	162.000	157.400	(duplex)
(simplex)	157.850	157.850	37	–	–	
(duplex)	160.625	156.025	60	–	–	
(duplex)	160.675	156.075	**61**	160.675	156.075	(duplex)
(duplex)	160.725	156.125	**62**	160.725	156.125	(duplex)
(duplex)	160.775	156.175	**63**	160.775	156.175	(duplex)
(duplex)	160.825	156.225	**64**	160.825	156.225	(duplex)
(duplex)	160.875	156.275	65	156.275	156.275	(simplex)
(duplex)	160.925	156.325	66	156.325	156.325	(simplex)
(simplex)	156.375	156.375	**67**	156.375	156.375	(simplex)
(simplex)	156.425	156.425	**68**	156.425	156.425	(simplex)
(simplex)	156.475	156.475	**69**	156.475	156.475	(simplex)
(simplex)	156.525	156.525	**70**	156.525	156.525	(simplex)
(simplex)	156.575	156.575	**71**	156.575	156.575	(simplex)
(simplex)	156.625	156.625	**72**	156.625	156.625	(simplex)
(simplex)	156.675	156.675	**73**	156.675	156.675	(simplex)
(simplex)	156.725	156.725	**74**	156.725	156.725	(simplex)
	(= European Ch 77)		75	156.875	156.875	(simplex)
	–	–	76	–	–	
(simplex)	156.875	156.875	77	(= USA Channel 75)		
(duplex)	161.525	156.925	78	156.925	156.925	(simplex)
(duplex)	161.575	156.975	79	156.975	156.975	(simplex)

EUROPEAN			CHANNEL	USA		
	Operating frequency (MHz)			Operating frequency (MHz)		
	Receive	Transmit		Receive	Transmit	
(duplex)	161.625	157.025	80	157.025	157.025	(simplex)
(duplex)	161.675	157.075	81	157.075	157.075	(simplex)
(duplex)	161.725	157.125	82	157.125	157.125	(simplex)
(duplex)	161.775	157.175	83	157.175	157.175	(simplex)
(duplex)	161.825	157.225	**84**	161.825	157.225	(duplex)
(duplex)	161.875	157.275	**85**	161.875	157.175	(duplex)
(duplex)	161.925	157.325	**86**	161.925	157.225	(duplex)
(duplex)	161.975	157.375	**87**	161.975	157.275	(duplex)
(duplex)	162.025	157.425	88	157.425	157.425	(simplex)
			WX1	162.550		
			WX2	162.400		
			WX3	162.475		
			WX4	163.275		
			WX5	161.650		
			WX6	161.775		

APPENDIX F – The Beaufort Wind Scale

Beaufort number	Descriptive term	Mean wind speed		Probable mean wave height		Likely sea conditions
		knots	m/sec			
0	Calm	0–1	0–0.2	–	–	Flat glassy calm
1	Light air	1–3	0.3–1.5	0.1 m	4 in	Low glassy ripples
2	Light breeze	4–6	1.6–3.3	0.2 m	8 in	Small waves without crests
3	Gentle breeze	7–10	3.4–5.4	0.6 m	2 ft	Small waves, crests beginning to break
4	Moderate breeze	11–16	5.5–7.9	1 m	3 ft	Longer waves, many with white crests
5	Fresh breeze	17–21	8.0–10.7	2 m	6 ft	Moderate cresting waves, some spray
6	Strong breeze	22–27	10.8–13.8	3 m	10 ft	Large waves with breaking crests
7	Near gale	28–33	13.9–17.1	4 m	13 ft	Large waves with some blown spume
8	Gale	34–40	17.2–20.7	5.5 m	18 ft	Very large waves with foam blow off crests
9	Strong gale	41–47	20.8–24.4	7 m	23 ft	High waves, visibility affected by spray
10	Storm	48–55	24.5–28.4	9 m	30 ft	Very high waves with overhanging crests
11	Violent storm	56–63	28.5–32.6	11.5 m	38 ft	Very high waves, sea white with foam
12	Hurricane	64+	32.7+	14 m+	46 ft+	Giant waves, air full of foam and spray

APPENDIX G – Glossary of British and American Terms

'Two nations divided by a common language' is as true afloat as it is ashore, and particularly where the same term has different meanings on either side of the ocean this can cause considerable confusion. Glossaries of useful words in foreign languages will be found in *Reed's Nautical Almanac* and many cruising guides, but these almost invariably overlook the fact that the starting point itself may be different.

In a few cases one of the following terms may be common to both sides of the Atlantic, but the second used on only one side. Others may be regional. Some have nothing to do with boats or sailing, but are included as they may be of help with the catering or other shopping.

British	American
anchor cable (chain and/or rope)	anchor rode
aubergine	egg plant
autumn	fall
bill (restaurant)	tab or check
biro	ballpoint or Bic
biscuit	cookie
boomed staysail	club staysail
boot top	boot stripe
bottle screw	turnbuckle
broad beans	lima beans
bungey cord	shock cord
cheque	check
chips	french fries
circular saw	skill saw
clinker (construction)	lapstrake (construction)
conical buoy	nun buoy
cornflour	corn starch
courgette	zucchini
cove line	railstripe
cramps	clamps
crisps	chips
crosstrees	spreaders
deckhead	overhead
dodgers	weather cloths
dowel	plug
draught	draft
echo sounder	fathometer/depth sounder
escalator	moving staircase
excess (insurance)	deductible (insurance)
eyelet	grommet
fairlead	chock
fender	fendoff or bumper
foreigner	alien
fortnight	two weeks
fretsaw	coping saw
frying pan	skillet
G-clamp or G-cramp	C-clamp
gas	LPG or propane
grill	broil
gumboots/wellingtons	sea boots

British	American
hatch boards	drop boards
jam	jelly or preserve
jelly	jello
jig saw	sabre saw
jubilee clip	hose clip
kicking strap	boom vang
lee cloth	leeboard
lifejacket	PFD (personal flotation device)
lift (building)	elevator
margarine	oleo
methylated spirits	alcohol (denatured)
mince (beef etc)	ground beef etc
mole wrench	vise grip
nappies	diapers
off licence	liquor store
oilskins	foul weather gear
paracetamol	tylenol
paraffin	kerosene
petrol	gasoline (gas)
polyester	dacron
pontoons	floats
public telephone	pay phone
pumpkin (vegetable)	squash (vegetable)
rachet screwdriver	yankee screwdriver
range	distance
reverse charge call	collect call
rigging screw	turnbuckle
rowlock	oar lock
rubber	eraser
rubbing strake	rubrail
scone	biscuit
shifting spanner	crescent wrench
skin fitting	thru hull
slip	slipway
soya granules	TVP (texturised vegetable protein)
spanner	wrench
split pin/ring	cotter key/pin/ring
spray hood	dodger
squash (orange etc)	cordial
staysail boom	staysail club
stopping	surfacing putty or trowel cement
swage	swedge
Talurite	Nicopress
tap	faucet
term (school or college)	semester
terylene	dacron
torch	flashlight
transit	range
vang	preventer
Very pistol	flare gun
water biscuit	cracker or saltine
yacht	sailboat

American	British	American	British
alcohol (denatured)	methylated spirits	oar lock	rowlock
alien	foreigner	oleo	margarine
anchor rode	anchor cable (chain and/or chain)	overhead	deckhead
		pay phone	public telephone
ballpoint or Bic	biro	PFD (personal flotation device)	lifejacket
biscuit	scone	plug	dowel
boom vang	kicking strap	preventer	vang
boot stripe	boot top	railstripe	cove line
broil	grill	range	transit
bumper	fender	rubrail	rubbing strake
C-clamp	G-cramp	sabre saw	jig saw
check (restaurant)	bill	sailboat	yacht
chips	crisps	sea boots	gumboots/wellingtons
chock	fairlead	semester	term (school or college)
clamps	cramps	shock cord	bungey cord
club staysail	boomed staysail	skill saw	circular saw
collect call	reverse charge call	skillet	frying pan
cookie	biscuit	slip	pontoon or finger berth
coping saw	fretsaw	spreaders	crosstrees
cordial	squash (orange etc)	squash (vegetable)	pumpkin (vegetable)
corn starch	cornflour	staysail club	staysail boom
cotter key/pin/ring	split pin/ring	surfacing putty	stopping
cracker or saltine	water biscuit	swedge	swage
crescent wrench	shifting spanner	tab (restaurant)	bill
custard	baked custard	thru hull	skin fitting
dacron	polyester	trowel cement	stopping
dacron	terylene	turnbuckle	bottle screw or rigging screw
deductible (insurance)	excess (insurance)		
depth sounder	echo sounder	TVP (texturised vegetable protein)	soya granules
diapers	nappies	tylenol	paracetamol
dodger	spray hood	vice grip	mole wrench
draft	draught	weather cloths	dodgers
drop boards	hatch boards	wrench	spanner
egg plant	aubergine	yankee screwdriver	rachet screwdriver
elevator (building)	lift	zucchini	courgette
eraser	rubber		
fall	autumn		
fathometer	echo sounder		
faucet	tap		
fendoff	fender		
flare gun	Very pistol		
flashlight	torch		
floats	pontoons		
foul weather gear	oilskins		
french fries	chips		
gasoline (gas)	petrol		
grommet	eyelet		
ground beef etc	mince (beef etc)		
hose clip	jubilee clip		
jello	jelly		
jelly or preserve	jam		
kerosene	paraffin		
lapstrake	clinker (construction)		
leeboard	lee cloth		
lima beans	broad beans		
liquor store	off licence		
LPG	gas		
Nicopress	Talurite		
nun buoy	conical buoy		

Weights and measures

The following are intended as reminders only – full conversion tables will be found in *Reed's Nautical Almanac* and many other places. Liquid measures are assumed to be of water.

British	American	Metric
(Long) ton = 2240 lb	(Short) ton = 2000 lb	Tonne = 2204 lb
Gallon = 160 fl oz	Gallon = 128 fl oz	
Pint = 20 fl oz	Pint = 16 fl oz	
	Cup = 8 fl oz	

Rope sizes

In the UK rope is measured in millimetres diameter and sold by the metre. It used to be measured in inches circumference and sold by the foot or, in the case of anchor cable, the fathom. In the US it is measured in inches diameter and sold by the foot.

The US Coast Guard publishes numerous leaflets aimed at the owners of yachts and other small vessels. Many, though not all, are concerned with safety and offer general advice rather than details of specific US requirements. Those covering collision avoidance are based primarily on the International Regulations for Preventing Collisions at Sea (though the Coast Guard do publish their own *US Coastguard Navigation Rules, International – Inland*), while other titles include *Visual Distress Signals, Shipshape is Firesafe, Getting Help on the Water* etc. Of particular interest to non-American yachtsmen intending to visit, or pass through, US waters will be:

Federal Requirements for Recreational Boats – details of registration and numbering requirements (not applicable to foreign-owned vessels), law enforcement including 'drink-driving' definitions, required safety equipment (lifejackets and lifebuoys, visual distress signals, fire extinguishers, sound signalling devices, navigation lights, day shapes etc), pollution regulations, and the law regarding the notification of accidents. In theory all safety equipment carried must be 'Coast Guard Approved', but in practice items which conform to BSI or International safety standards are generally accepted.

Coast Guard Aids to Navigation – covers visual, sound and electronic aids (including Loran C). In addition the sheet *Modifications for a New Look in US Aids to Navigation* depicts the standard colours and shapes of buoys and daymarks introduced under the IALA B system since 1983. It is worth noting that not only are the colours reversed on either side of the Atlantic, but characteristic shapes also differ.

A Short Course in Marine Law Enforcement – details of the law covering boardings at sea (including the difference between 'inspection' and 'search') and a brief run-through of the procedure normally followed.

Additionally, the Consumer and Regulatory Affairs Branch of the Coast Guard produce a number of *Consumer Fact Sheets*. Those relevant to transitory yachts include:

7. Coast Guard Boarding Policy
10. US Government Maritime Publications
13. Marine Sanitation Devices on Boats
14. Consumer's Guide to the Coast Guard Boating Safety Standards
18. Disposal of Plastics and other Garbage in waters of the United States

All are available from: The Consumer and Regulatory Affairs Branch, Office of Navigation Safety and Waterway Services, US Coast Guard Headquarters, 2100 Second St SW, Washington, DC 20593–0001, USA.

As with all formal requirements, changes occur from time to time and ignorance of new rulings is no defence in the eyes of the law. It is the responsibility of the individual owner to obtain details of current requirements before entering US waters.

INDEX

Page numbers in bold type refer to illustrations.